PHILOSOPHICAL MYSTICISM IN PLATO, HEGEL, AND THE PRESENT

ALSO AVAILABLE FROM BLOOMSBURY

Plato and Plotinus on Mysticism, Epistemology, and Ethics, David J. Yount
Plato's Trial of Athens, Mark A. Ralkowski
Wittgenstein, Religion and Ethics: New Perspectives from Philosophy and Theology, Mikel Burley
Hegel, Logic and Speculation, ed. by Paolo Diego Bubbio, Alessandro De Cesaris, Maurizio Pagano, Hager Weslati

PHILOSOPHICAL MYSTICISM IN PLATO, HEGEL, AND THE PRESENT

Robert M. Wallace

BLOOMSBURY ACADEMIC
LONDON • NEW YORK • OXFORD • NEW DELHI • SYDNEY

BLOOMSBURY ACADEMIC
Bloomsbury Publishing Plc
50 Bedford Square, London, WC1B 3DP, UK
1385 Broadway, New York, NY 10018, USA
29 Earlsfort Terrace, Dublin 2, Ireland

BLOOMSBURY, BLOOMSBURY ACADEMIC and the Diana logo are trademarks of
Bloomsbury Publishing Plc

First published in Great Britain 2020
This paperback edition published in 2021

Copyright © Robert M. Wallace, 2020

Robert M. Wallace has asserted his right under the Copyright, Designs and Patents Act, 1988, to be identified as Author of this work.

For legal purposes the Acknowledgments on p. viii constitute an extension of this copyright page.

Cover design by Maria Rajka
Cover image: Jerusalem, Plate 1, Frontispiece, William Blake (1757–1827)
© Yale Center for British Art, Paul Mellon Collection

All rights reserved. No part of this publication may be reproduced or transmitted in any form or by any means, electronic or mechanical, including photocopying, recording, or any information storage or retrieval system, without prior permission in writing from the publishers.

Bloomsbury Publishing Plc does not have any control over, or responsibility for, any third-party websites referred to or in this book. All internet addresses given in this book were correct at the time of going to press. The author and publisher regret any inconvenience caused if addresses have changed or sites have ceased to exist, but can accept no responsibility for any such changes.

A catalogue record for this book is available from the British Library.

A catalog record for this book is available from the Library of Congress.

ISBN: HB: 978-1-3500-8286-1
PB: 978-1-3502-6738-1
ePDF: 978-1-3500-8287-8
eBook: 978-1-3500-8288-5

Typeset by Deanta Global Publishing Services, Chennai, India

To find out more about our authors and books visit www.bloomsbury.com and sign up for our newsletters.

This book is dedicated to my wife and muse,
Kathleen Ritger Kouzmanoff.

CONTENTS

Acknowledgments viii
Preface x

Introduction 1

1 "A Worm! A God!" 9

2 "That Which Shows God in Me, Fortifies Me" 29

3 Freedom and Full Reality 67

4 Full Reality Is God 87

5 Plato's Progress 105

6 Plato, Freedom, and Us 135

7 Plato on Reason, Love, and Inspiration 157

8 Plato on "Becoming Like God" 185

9 Ordinary and Extraordinary Experiences of God 205

Appendix: Comparisons Between the Plato/Hegel Argument for a God Within Us, and Several Well-Known Arguments for God 213
Notes 218
Bibliography 251
Index 263

ACKNOWLEDGMENTS

My father introduced me to his favorite writers and philosophers, generously sharing his enthusiasms with the young me. My mother made sure that I had a constant stream of books to explore. Teachers, especially Alan Strain, fed my sense of what might be possible. My slowly growing understanding of Plato owes a great deal to Terence Irwin, Gail Fine, Lloyd Gerson, J. N. Findlay, Rosemary Desjardins, Francisco Gonzales, James Rhodes, H. J. Krämer, G. W. F. Hegel, and Jelaluddin Rumi. In German philosophy, Alan Montefiore, Hans Blumenberg, Karsten Harries, and Allen Wood got me started on my way. In transatlantic correspondence and phone calls, Blumenberg's nurturing spirit was an inspiration to me. I would also like to mention Darrel E. Christensen, who suggested to me some decades ago that "what we really need" is to understand what Hegel and Whitehead have in common—a comment whose wisdom I only came to understand and appreciate much later. In mysticism, I owe a great deal to Kathleen Kouzmanoff, Aldous Huxley (in his *The Perennial Philosophy* [1945]), Jonathan Shear, Jeffrey Kripal, George Herbert, Gerard Manley Hopkins, and Rumi. In proper Platonic fashion, what I owe to Kathy is inseparably intellectual (see her *Lifewheel* [2005]), emotional, and spiritual. I am grateful to anonymous readers who have encouraged and challenged my manuscripts in various ways. Mehmet Tabak gave me very helpful written comments on part of this book. Friends with whom I've profited from discussing these issues include David Duveneck, Graham Andrews, Stephen Theron, Sebastian Job, Ishmael Wallace, Meg Wallace, Tom Bennigson, Barry Goldensohn, Ted Mazza, Ian Johnson, Will Altman, John Bardis, Paul de Angelis, David Brent, Josef Bieniek, Ben Campbell, Robert Stern, Jeff Edwards, Allegra de Laurentiis, Ken Westphal, Willem deVries, Karl Ameriks, Jim Wetzel, John Clark, John Placer, Tushar Irani, John Russell, Michael Wakoff, Giacomo Rinaldi, Marco DeAngelis, Gunter Scholtz, Lenny Moss, Wallace Pinfold, Harrison Fluss, Allen Mathews, Conrad Paul, Jane Paul, Elizabeth Reed, Jay Bregman, John Uebersax, Edward Butler, Thomas Burns, and Samantha Horst. As always, nobody other than me is responsible for what I've failed to learn from them!

I am also grateful to Bertrand Russell, Sir Isaiah Berlin, Charles Taylor, Gregory Vlastos, Martha Nussbaum, and R. C. Zaehner for posing issues forthrightly in their influential writings, to which admirers of Plato and Hegel can benefit by articulating a detailed response. And of course I'm deeply grateful to my protagonists, Plato, Hegel, Emerson, Whitehead, Wittgenstein, Findlay, Murdoch, Sellars, McDowell, Rödl, and the poets.

My greatest personal debts are to my mother, Margaret Marston Wallace, my father, Robert S. Wallace Jr., and my incomparable wife, Kathleen Ritger Kouzmanoff. Thanks also to my children, Ishmael, Vita, Nina, and Meg, all "trailing clouds of glory," for all that they've taught me and the fun that we've shared.

I would also like to thank Liza Thompson at Bloomsbury for her support for this project, and Lucy Russell at Bloomsbury, Leeladevi Ulaganathan at Deanta, and Katharina Munk at Klarso GmbH for their help and their patience.

PREFACE

Philosophical mysticism is the doctrine that we sometimes have direct knowledge of a higher reality or God. Although present-day reference works in philosophy seldom mention philosophical mysticism, Plato, who founded academic philosophy, was widely and uncontroversially known for millennia as (among other things) a "mystic." And versions of philosophical mysticism were still common in the early twentieth century, in Ludwig Wittgenstein, Alfred North Whitehead, and others. But since then, with the rise of logical positivism and other anti-metaphysical doctrines, philosophical mysticism has largely ceased to be taught in philosophy departments. My goal in this book is to revive it as a subject of serious study.

Since it is philosophical, philosophical mysticism doesn't neglect reason; nor is the direct knowledge that is its topic restricted to any small group of people. And the higher reality to which philosophical mysticism draws our attention has implications for numerous perennial problems besides that of God. Within the framework of this higher reality, the issues of science versus religion, fact versus value, rationality versus ethics, intellect versus emotions, mind versus body, and knowers versus the "external world" all become tractable. It turns out that nature, freedom, science, ethics, the arts, and a rational religion-in-the-making constitute an intelligible whole. This is very different from the muddle in which these issues tend to be left by such familiar agnostic doctrines as empiricism, materialism, naturalism, existentialism, and postmodernism.

This is why such major figures in philosophy, religion, and literature as Aristotle, Plotinus, St Augustine, Dante Alighieri, Immanuel Kant, G. W. F. Hegel, William Wordsworth, Ralph Waldo Emerson, Emily Dickinson, Alfred North Whitehead, and Ludwig Wittgenstein have all been strongly attracted to Plato's idea that we can and do know a higher reality. My goal in this book is to show how this attraction and this idea are fully justified and to explore their consequences.

Readers who don't have an extensive knowledge of Western philosophy might like to begin by reading Chapters 1 and 9, which presuppose little specialized knowledge and provide an overview of what the book is about. I have tried to make the book as a whole clear enough to be accessible for any motivated reader.

INTRODUCTION

There if anywhere should a person live his life, beholding that Beauty.
PLATO, *SYMPOSIUM* 211D

The Platonic philosophical theology unifies us with ourselves, with each other, with the world, and with God, by explaining that a higher reality or God is present in this world and in us inasmuch as it inspires our efforts toward inner freedom, love, beauty, truth, and other ideals. These efforts give us a unity, as "ourselves," that we can't have insofar as we're the slaves of our genes, hormones, opinions, self-importance, and so forth. For in contrast to our genes and so forth, which are implanted in us or are reactions to what surrounds us, efforts toward ideals like inner freedom, love, beauty, and truth are more likely to reflect our own choice. So that if anything reflects "us," ourselves, and not just our surroundings, they do.

So through ideals like inner freedom, love, beauty, and truth, something that's "higher," because it's free and fully "us," is in us. Since we often fall short of it and lapse into merely reactive or merely bodily functioning, we can call this higher self-determination, by contrast, "divine." And there's nothing that we know better or more directly than we know this inner choice that we make, to be either automatic and reactive or free and self-determining. So we have every reason to regard the choice as real, and our awareness of it as knowledge. And since "mysticism" is the name for the doctrine that we have direct knowledge of a higher reality or God, and this Platonic train of thought shows how we have such knowledge through awareness of our inner choices, it shows how mysticism in this sense is entirely rational.[1]

Since we often fall short of inner freedom, love, beauty, and truth, they have the "transcendence" that we expect of religion. They are inspiring as well as rational, "above" us as well as "in" us. But what's remarkable is that because this transcendence is rational, it's a feature not only of the higher reality that mysticism and religion celebrate but also of science. In fact, because science is one of the ways in which we choose to pursue truth and thus transcend our genes, hormones, favorite opinions, and self-importance, science is a part or an aspect of the higher reality that mysticism and religion celebrate.

Of course when I say that religion celebrates a transcendence that's rational, I'm not referring to everything that we refer to as religion, but primarily to what Alfred North Whitehead called "religion in the making"—that is, the religion that has been in process of emergence for millennia and is probably not yet in its final form. But as we will see, this religion in the making incorporates everything that seems to be essential to traditional religions, including not only transcendence but also conceptions that are comparable to creation, sin, and salvation. It's probably intimations of the cogency of this religion in the making that have given traditional religions the longevity that they have had.

So rather than inherently conflicting with mysticism and religion, science is a part of the higher reality that mysticism and religion celebrate. Religion and science both transcend by seeking inner freedom and truth. It's just that science, being restricted to what we can know by scientific methods, is narrower. It's only one aspect of the transcendent freedom, love, beauty, and truth, the higher reality, that religion or religion in the making celebrates. This unusual way of understanding the relation between science and religion can free us from a good deal of mental fog and fruitless disputation.

But the relation of science to religion isn't the only familiar issue that the Platonic higher reality transforms. It's probably evident from what I've said that the Platonic higher reality reveals an intimate connection between "fact" and "value." A world in which there was no pursuit of values like love, beauty, and truth, or (as Plato puts it) "the Good," would not be self-determining or fully "itself." If being fully "itself" is the most intensive kind of reality, such a world would lack what's most real. By directing our attention to the role of value in what's most real, Platonism shows the limits of the "disenchanted" and "value-free" account of reality that we associate with scientific objectivity. Important though it is, the reality that science identifies is not the ultimate reality. The reality apart from itself that science in its normal activities identifies is not, in fact, the ultimate reality of which science itself, as a pursuit of truth and thus of self-determination, is an aspect. When science becomes aware of this ultimate reality to which it contributes, and which depends on values such as truth as well as freedom, love, and beauty, it becomes evident that the ultimate "fact" or reality is not actually independent of "value."

Next, there is the issue of our relations to each other. We usually assume that we're external to and separate from each other. But if I am to govern myself fully, and thus be fully "myself," I can't have things affecting me from outside, so I can't be external to others. So to be fully myself, I must go beyond selfishness or mutual "externality," and instead love everyone and treat everyone ethically. We are external to each other in reality as we ordinarily conceive it, but not in the higher reality in which, through freedom, love, beauty, and truth, we are fully ourselves.

From the ordinary point of view, the statement that we're most ourselves when we're not external to others probably seems like a paradox, but to lovers it's simply the truth.

From what I've just said, it's clear that the Platonic view will also bridge the gap that we often experience between intellect and love or intellect and emotions in general. Of course many of our feelings reflect genes, hormones, or experiences of which we may have little memory. But intellect, seeking freedom and wholeness, always asks, Does this feeling make sense, in the context of my other feelings and beliefs? And when the feeling doesn't seem to make sense in this way, intellect tries to help us to clarify the confusion, and thus to rise to feelings, such as those associated with ethics and love, that reflect greater freedom and wholeness. So rather than rejecting the body and its feelings (which would be a recipe for unfreedom), intellect helps it to be more free, self-governing, and real as an aspect of "oneself."

Then there is "mind," in general. Since it's through mind that we achieve freedom, wholeness, and so forth, mind can't be a separate being that interacts with a "body" and with "other minds." Again, such exclusion would prevent the mind from being fully self-governing or free. To be fully self-governing and free, mind must be a higher degree of reality in which bodies cease to function merely as bodies and as separate from others. Mind as the organ of free thought transcends limits.

And this also resolves the modern "problem of knowledge." We wonder how a mind can know a world that is "external" to it. But this problem doesn't arise if in the fullest reality, in which we're fully self-governing and fully ourselves, nothing is separate from and consequently nothing is external to anything else. In that fullest reality, the "things" that we ordinarily think of as separate from us are either equally self-governing and real, in which case we aren't really separate from them or external to them and we know them all "from inside," or they are less self-governing, in which case they are less real and the knowledge that we have of them will be through whatever they contribute to what is self-governing and fully real.

The fundamental notion, in all of this, of a unifying rational activity, and thus a higher degree of freedom and reality "as oneself," which is sometimes achieved by what is otherwise less rational, less unified, less free, and less real as itself, is not as familiar as it may have been in the days of Plato and of Hegel. Most recent philosophy has assumed, by contrast, that reality isn't "more real" or "less real" but is simply a "yes" or "no" issue of existence or nonexistence; and that we are either rational or irrational, free or unfree, but not both. But Plato and his successors make a good case that we experience greater and lesser degrees of freedom and of reality as ourselves when we are more or less integrated, self-determining, or "in charge of our lives." So the notion of a higher degree of freedom and reality which is continuous with lower degrees of freedom and reality, need not be as exotic as it sounds.

The Platonic conceptions certainly contrast with "common sense," which (today at least) leans more toward a reductive materialism or naturalism for which there may not be any freedom or, consequently, any reality that depends on it. But the Platonic conceptions become more plausible when we see how many aspects of our lives they clarify, including our personal functioning, mind, body, love, value, ethics, knowledge, science, and religion. Indeed, the comprehensiveness of the alternative to "common sense" that these conceptions present is one reason to take them seriously. Like powerful proposals in the physical sciences (Galileo, Newton, Einstein), they enable us to see unity in phenomena whose relationship to each other was previously unclear.

In Chapter 1 and in portions of later chapters, I unfold the Platonic view in more detail in my own voice. In the remainder of this Introduction I sum up how the book draws on and explains Plato and his successors, down to the present. To the best of my knowledge, my four chapters on Plato are the only treatment that explains how Plato solves the religion/science, value/fact, ethics/rationality, emotion/intellect, body/mind, and "external world"/knower problems in one swoop, through his conception of rational "ascent" in the *Phaedo*, *Republic*, *Symposium*, *Timaeus*, *Theaetetus*, *Parmenides*, and other dialogues. In doing this, the book presents replies to many of Plato's influential critics, including David Hume, Friedrich Nietzsche, Martin Heidegger, Bertrand Russell, Walter Bröcker, Gregory Vlastos, Richard Rorty, Hans Blumenberg, and Martha Nussbaum. The many modern philosophers who have rejected what they think of as "Platonism" have failed to appreciate Plato's most important discovery, which is the discovery of how we experience a higher reality in ourselves.

Aristotle, who criticizes Plato's way of describing the higher reality, agrees with him about its existence and importance: "The best is . . . to understand what is fine and divine, by being itself either divine or the most divine element in us."[2] Hegel has the same view, maintaining (for example) that "it is not the finite which is the real, but the infinite."[3] Aristotle and Hegel agree with Plato that through a kind of rational "ascent," we experience something that's self-governing and thus higher and essentially divine. In this way, contrary to what's often suggested, Aristotle and Hegel are both entirely serious in what they say about God and the divine, and they both endorse a significant kind of "transcendence." Indeed, and here I depart from the majority of recent commentators on Hegel, the transcendence that Hegel endorses is *more truly transcendent* than competing conceptions. So that describing Hegel as someone who advocates "naturalism" and rejects the "supernatural" is very misleading. What tempts people to call Hegel an advocate of "naturalism" is that he is not a dualist. But what Hegel (like Aristotle and much of Plato) aims to show us is precisely that a notion of rational "ascent" need not entail dualism. It needn't entail dualism if we ourselves engage in and experience transcendence, so that the transcendent and the immanent are united in our experience.

So what Plato, Aristotle, and Hegel have in common, and what (as I will show) Emerson, Whitehead, Wittgenstein, John Niemeyer Findlay, Iris Murdoch, Sebastian Rödl, and others also describe in various ways, is the nexus of a transcendent (higher) freedom, love, and God. Which when it's well understood unites science and religion, fact and value, rational self-government and ethics, intellect and emotion, body and mind, and the "external world" and knowers in the ways that I've indicated.

I give details on how these views are expressed in post-Hegelian writers from Emerson to the present in Chapter 2. There I also discuss the influential recent and contemporary philosophers Wilfrid Sellars and John McDowell, who sympathize with Hegel in certain respects but don't appear to embrace the idea of a higher reality, as such. I give my own account of Hegel in Chapters 2–4 (referring readers to my book on Hegel for further details). Chapter 3 contains a general introduction to Hegel that aims to clear up a number of the issues that people commonly raise about him. And Chapters 5–8 deal with Plato.

I want to say a bit more, here, about the difficult relationship during the last hundred years between philosophy and "mysticism." Alfred North Whitehead and Ludwig Wittgenstein were among the participants in a broad philosophical discussion, which took place in the late nineteenth and early twentieth centuries and also involved Francis Herbert Bradley, William James, Bertrand Russell, and Henri Bergson, and which dealt with what many of the participants called "mysticism." Bradley, Whitehead, and Wittgenstein were all inspired by Plato, either directly or through Hegel or Schopenhauer. But this discussion was broken off during most of the twentieth century because philosophers beginning with Russell weren't able to make sense of Bradley, of Whitehead, or of Wittgenstein's notion of "the mystical." And recent accounts of early twentieth-century philosophy, examining it from the point of view of what followed it, have paid little or no attention to its discussion of mysticism.

My own account explains how Bradley, Whitehead, and Wittgenstein were all trying in various ways to articulate the same notion that's central for Plato and for Hegel, which is the notion of ascent to a more self-governing and thus higher reality. Hegel's central operation of "sublation" or *Aufhebung* ascends to a higher reality, as do Whitehead's "victory of persuasion over force"[4] and Wittgenstein's "ladder," in the *Tractatus*. The goal that Wittgenstein described there as "value," "God," and "the mystical," he described in a Platonic image in his notebooks as "the true world among shadows."[5]

This notion of ascent to the true world was inspired, in all of these thinkers, by the observation that we seem to be able to question what our appetites, our opinions, and our self-importance urge us to do and believe. Questioning them, we seek a higher source of guidance—what Plato refers to as the "Good," Hegel calls the "Idea" or "Spirit," and Whitehead and Wittgenstein call "value" and "God."

They all regard this higher source of guidance not only as more authoritative but also (as Plato and Hegel put it) as more "real" in that it's a self-governing or self-determining whole, and thus real "as itself" and not merely as a product of an endless series of external causes. Wittgenstein conveys this thought in his *Notebooks* (which are in some respects more Platonic, and less unfortunately dualistic, than his *Tractatus*) by comparing the higher reality, as the "good life," to a work of art: "The work of art is the object seen *sub specie aeternitatis*; and the good life is the world seen *sub specie aeternitatis*."[6] The good life is *the world* seen in the way in which we are able to see a mere "object" as (actually) a work of art, governed by its own internal logic rather than by external causes, and thus real, as I say, "as itself." To see the world and life in it in this way is to ascend to a reality that's more real in that it's more self-governing and more "itself" than we often take the world and life to be. It's to ascend to "the true world among shadows."

So this more real reality is what the whole early-twentieth-century group composed of Bradley the "Hegelian," Whitehead the "Platonist," and Wittgenstein who had initially been inspired by Schopenhauer were trying to get into focus. And when we understand this interest that they shared, we can resume the investigation that was abandoned for more than half a century by analytic philosophers including Bertrand Russell, A. J. Ayer, W. V. O. Quine, and their successors, who had no notion of what Bradley, Whitehead, and Wittgenstein had been looking for.

Relatively recent writers who do have an idea of what the early-twentieth-century philosophical "mystics" were after include Michael Polanyi in his *Personal Knowledge* (1958), J. N. Findlay in his *Discipline of the Cave* and *Transcendence of the Cave* (1966–67), Iris Murdoch in her *Metaphysics as a Guide to Morals* (1993), Sebastian Rödl in his *Self-Consciousness* (2007) and other works, and Wolfram Gobsch in his 2012 dissertation, "Bedingungen des Unbedingten."

Findlay and Murdoch both have a strong affinity for Plato, and like Wittgenstein in his *Tractatus*, both of them are unfortunately somewhat prone to a dualism which renders their overall view questionable and incomplete. Findlay contrasts "this world" and "another world or worlds" in a way that unintentionally casts doubt on the unity of human experience and reason.[7] And Murdoch's focus is so exclusively on art, ethics, and religion that she gives no idea how we might relate her very interesting results in those fields to the view of reality that we're likely to find in the natural sciences.

Fortunately Plato in most of his work, and Aristotle, Hegel, Whitehead, Polanyi, Rödl, and Gobsch avoid Findlay's dualism of "this world" and "another world" by understanding what Findlay calls the "other world" as an aspect of this world and of our experience in it. And they avoid Murdoch's implicit dualism of the humanities versus the natural sciences by pointing out how by aiming at truth as such, as opposed to whatever our genes, hormones, self-importance, and so forth, direct us toward, science itself elevates us above "nature" understood as a realm of genes, hormones, self-importance, and so forth. Thus science embodies the same "ascent" toward greater self-government that all Platonists identify in art, ethics, and God. So insofar as it's aware of the nature of its own activity, science can't deny the reality of the Platonic "ascent."

So we see that, so far from being "optional," Platonic ascent and the higher and most real domain of the "mystical" are woven into every aspect of our lives, including science itself. Insofar as we succeed, in science, art, love, ethics, or religion, in being rationally self-governing, we participate in the most real reality, by which we are all irresistibly inspired. Each of these domains has its own internal logic, which when we understand it as such can't be opposed to the others (since that would make it no longer self-governing), but must be a part of the all-subsuming process of rational self-government as such.

As a result of common misunderstandings of Hegel, neither Whitehead nor Polanyi read much of what Hegel wrote, so their broad agreement with him is a result not of direct influence but of the fact that all three of them drew on the broadly Platonic tradition. Findlay wrote a book about Hegel, but he doesn't seem to have understood Hegel's critique of dualism. Whitehead and Polanyi in effect rediscovered a great deal of what Hegel had discovered with the help of Plato and of writers influenced by Plato. And Whitehead and Polanyi themselves have not been as widely read or understood as they deserve to be. The dominant materialism or "naturalism" of our age makes it difficult for people to envision the possibility of a coherent alternative view, such as the Platonic tradition presents. Despite the work of thinkers like Hegel, Whitehead, and Polanyi, many writers still suppose that the only likely alternative to materialism or naturalism is a dualism such as we see in Kant, in Wittgenstein's *Tractatus*, in Findlay, or (implicitly) in Iris Murdoch—which, insofar as it doesn't clarify the relation between its two domains, can't be fully satisfying to the intellect.

Some critics of the currently dominant materialism or naturalism, such as Thomas Nagel (*Mind and Cosmos: Why the Materialist Neo-Darwinian Conception of Nature Is Almost Certainly False* [2012]), nevertheless do indicate sympathy for the alternative that Plato and Hegel outline.[8] And a group of philosophers including John McDowell and Michael Thompson at Pittsburgh, Sebastian Rödl, Andrea Kern, and Wolfram Gobsch at Leipzig, and Irad Kimhi at Chicago have recently been developing a metaphysics and an account of knowledge and action that chime well with what I find in Plato, Hegel, Whitehead, and Polanyi.[9]

These recent writers focus in various ways on the dimension of "ascent," of what's "higher" in reality, which Plato, Hegel, Whitehead, and Polanyi elaborate and on which I focus in this book. They all address the apparent conflict between the third-person, "scientific" account of what we are and the first-person, "humanistic" view which is presupposed by much of our practical thinking. When Plato, Hegel, and their successors point out that science itself is an attempt to rise above merely reactive functioning and to be led instead by truth, so that science's objective, external, third-person gaze is in fact a means to our inner, first-person goal of being self-governing by pursuing truth, they show how science and the humanistic view, external and internal, body and mind, nature and freedom, and "lower" and "higher" are ultimately one. Since the higher pole that is internal, mind, and freedom is self-governing and real as itself, in a way that the lower pole that is external, body, and nature is not, the higher can be seen as subsuming the lower as an aspect of itself.[10] In which case science is an aspect of the humanistic view, the external is an aspect of the internal, and nature is an aspect of boundless, undivided, self-governing freedom.

This view is a version of "idealism" insofar as it makes ideas or thought, by which we are self-governing, essential to full reality. But it differs importantly from George Berkeley's and Immanuel Kant's versions of idealism in that it focuses, precisely, on the difference between what I'm calling full reality or reality "as oneself" and ordinary reality. Rather than being mere "appearance," as Berkeley and Kant say or imply, ordinary reality as Plato says "is and is not" (*Republic* 477a): it is in one respect perfectly real (it "is") while in regard to self-government and reality "as oneself," it "is not." Sticks and stones and remote galaxies certainly *exist* apart from us and our minds. It's only in regard to self-government and the reality "as oneself" that it creates, that sticks, stones, and galaxies have less of something of which animals that are capable of rational self-government have more.

I'll say more about this kind of "idealism" in Chapters 1 and 2. The notion of a higher degree of reality, reality as oneself, changes the entire landscape of philosophical issues. Since the question of whether one is governing oneself and thus is fully oneself underlies all of our issues about "inner" and "outer," mind and body, freedom and nature, emotion and intellect, values and facts, ethics and rationality, and religion and science, it's only by understanding it that we can avoid ongoing confusion about these issues.

This changed philosophical landscape also makes it clear how much our culture in general needs a certain kind of philosophy. For rather than an exploration of abstruse issues that are of interest primarily to specialists, the Plato/Hegel kind of philosophy is a systematic effort to clarify issues—freedom, mind, value, love, ethics, science, religion—with which every one of us is involved in one way or another. I am eager for the clarity and the increased freedom which we will enjoy when the Plato/Hegel philosophical landscape is more widely understood and appreciated.

Chapter 1 gives a second introduction to the book, in my own voice and with little reference to previous writers, and follows that with a more detailed overview of what the book finds in Plato and Hegel, in particular.

1 "A WORM! A GOD!"

Helpless immortal! insect infinite!
A worm! a god!—I tremble at myself,
And in myself am lost.

EDWARD YOUNG, NIGHT THOUGHTS

How could we "know God," whether directly or indirectly? What would that even mean? Are there real values, or does it all boil down to what we're programmed to want? Is there a sense in which we actually are "one" with each other? What do my inner life and my freedom, as I experience them, have to do with my body, my neurons, and the natural world, which I and others can observe?

To explore these questions, I begin by asking another question: Who are we, really? Most of us, I suggest, are in an ongoing identity crisis.[1] A higher reality of inner freedom (which means making up our own minds) and truth and love and beauty is in this world and us, and we experience it directly when we remember it and try to live up to it.[2] This higher reality of inner freedom, truth, love, and beauty inspires us, while lower goals merely attract us. But of course we also have a huge capacity for temporarily forgetting the higher reality, and pursuing lower goals without regard to inner freedom and the rest.

We usually assume that this familiar conflict of goals has nothing to do with who someone is. We suppose that someone is the same person regardless of whether the goals that she pursues are, in anyone's opinion, "higher" or "lower." But a contrasting view is in fact influential in the philosophical tradition beginning with Socrates and Plato. This tradition argues that pursuing inner freedom and truth makes a person more real, more herself, and more of a person, in a way that (say) simply pursuing money or fame does not.

The examined life

Plato suggests that this is why Socrates promoted the "examined life." Someone who examines her life, Plato suggests, by thinking about what's really worth doing and what's really true rather than just doing whatever she initially feels drawn to, is more fully herself.[3] If, in the example that I mentioned, I lost my desire for money or my desire for fame, I myself would presumably still be all there. I would still be the same person. But if, on the other hand, I lost my thinking and was left with nothing but unexamined desires and opinions, I would be, in effect, an automaton rather than a person. So at least part of what makes me a person, and thus makes me fully myself, is my examining or thinking about what's really worth doing and what's really true: my "making up my own mind."

This is why rather than just attracting us, inner freedom or making up our own minds, and truth, love, and beauty (insofar as love and beauty embody inner freedom and truth) *inspire* us. They represent our full presence, our being fully ourselves. This also explains the fact that having to choose between the higher and the lower, between what inspires us and what merely attracts us, is a "crisis" rather than just an ordinary decision. In choosing between the higher and the lower, we decide what kind of being we are going to be.

Higher and lower identities

This notion of a crisis in which we have to choose between higher and lower identities may remind us of traditional religious themes having to do with higher and lower: the sacred and the profane, God and our sinful nature, conversion from the lower and salvation by the higher. It also pervades the writing of philosophers and poets who don't appear to be motivated by (at least) conventional forms of religion. Philosophers from Plato to Rödl explain how through inner freedom, truth, love, and beauty we experience something higher in the world and in ourselves. Poets and creative writers such as Edward Young, Jelaluddin Rumi, Walt Whitman, Rainer Maria Rilke, Virginia Woolf, and Mary Oliver conjure up this same experience.

Much of Asian thought, likewise, speaks of something higher which we can experience in ourselves and in the world, whether it's the "Tao that cannot be named," or "Brahman" that's identical to our soul, or the "Buddha nature" that's in everything but at the same time is truer and thus higher than what it's in. There is more overlap between Asian and Western thought on these issues than we generally realize.[4]

Both Asian teachers and the Plato/Hegel tradition tell us that the central issue is not, as we in the West often suppose, about a separate "supreme being" that a person may or may not "believe in." Rather, the central issue is the nature of the world of which we're a part. Is it, as we tend to assume, essentially "all on one level," or does it have a "vertical" dimension by which some aspects of it really are "higher," through inner freedom, truth, love, and beauty?

The higher as the divine

If some aspects of the world really are higher, one might well think that these are the core of truth in the traditional notions of the sacred, God, conversion, salvation, and worship. In that case, the higher authority of inner freedom, truth, love, and beauty might be the reality that believers in a separate "supreme being" are trying, with only partial success, to get into focus.

We do usually imagine God as a being that's separate from the world. But there may be a surprise in store here, for someone who considers the question carefully. It turns out that a God who's separate from the world can't really transcend (go beyond) the world. This is because a God who's separate from the world would be, as the Jesuit theologian Karl Rahner put it, "a member of the larger household of all reality," which would be composed of these two separate objects, God and the world.[5] But a God who had the same kind of reality as the other members of a larger household wouldn't be truly "higher" than them, or transcendent. However much more "powerful" than the world this "God" might be, it would still be, in an important way, the same kind of thing as the world, and to that extent it wouldn't transcend the world—or deserve to have authority over it.

Transcendence through innerness

How can God transcend the world and deserve to have authority over it, if not by being a separate and very powerful being? The answer that's suggested by Plato and a long line of religious thinkers is that a God who's not a separate being can be distinguished from the world and higher than it by being more "inner" than it, more free, self-governing, loving, and beautiful. God could be the "inside" of the world.[6] Since such a God isn't alongside the world as its equal in a larger household of all reality, such a God can truly go beyond the world (transcend it). Rather than failing to transcend, by being separate and alongside, it transcends by being more inner, free, self-governing, loving, and beautiful.

In which case, it's clear how God has a kind of authority that's entirely distinct from "power" as we usually conceive of it. And it's through this authority, and only through it, that God transcends everything. In our earliest encounters with something radically different and awe-inspiring, we might not have come up with a better word than "power." But sheer physical power, which isn't oriented to any conception of the good, integrates nothing and thus achieves nothing that's "itself," fully real, or (indeed) truly different. By contrast, selfhood, freedom, love, beauty, and rational authority integrate to a maximum degree and thus make it clear how rather than being something merely to fear and placate, God deserves worship (that is, reverence and devotion) as something that's truly *higher* (more authoritative) than us.

We are conditioned to think of the "creator" as distinguished primarily by the sheer "power" that the act of creation implies, while we bow occasionally toward the notion that this power is somehow mysteriously combined with love and other admirable qualities. In doing this we fail to give this creator any authority over its creation beyond the authority of its power to "punish and reward." We forget that a power of that kind deserves no reverence or devotion, being no different in principle from the power of a tyrant.

Whereas the ability to integrate, to be whole through freedom, love, and beauty, gives its possessor a kind of reality, through self-integration, that tyrants don't begin to possess. The possessor of this integration deserves authority over the world that seeks integration and only intermittently achieves it. But it's precisely not "separate" from that world, because what's separate is in a crucial way the same as what it's separate from; it exists "alongside," belongs to the same "household" as the world. Whereas integration, by going "within," truly achieves something that the world, regarded merely as such, as "external" and "side-by-side," does not achieve.

Although conceptions of God as in some way "internal" rather than "separate" don't play much of a role in public discussion today, they have in fact been quite common in Western religious thought. Figures like St Paul (in God "we live and move and have our being"), St Athanasius (God "became man that we might become God"), and St Augustine ("You were more inward [to me] than my most inward part") can be cited in early Christianity. In modern times, Hegel, Alfred North Whitehead, Paul Tillich, and Karl Rahner likewise speak of God in ways that aren't consistent with God's being a separate being.[7] Because they don't identify God with the world but retain a distinction between them, these views are not "pantheistic." Distinct and higher but not separate and not "a being," their God may "create" the world by making it self-determined and fully real, rather than by existing before the world in time and "deciding" to create it.

An objection to this conception

Could it be that since many people do think of God as a separate being, someone who describes God as "distinct but not separate" is really just changing the subject, by not discussing what many people call "God"?

What's important for my purposes is simply that what we're talking about is truly transcendent, deserves to have authority, and is free, loving, beautiful, and accessible to us. The conception of "God" as a separate being, on the other hand, resembles the earlier habits of thinking of God as like a human being or like an animal, in that it makes God resemble something that we're familiar with. These conceptions prevent God from really transcending, really going beyond the ordinary world, and from having the authority that such transcendence would carry with it. So anyone who wants their God to transcend the world and have the authority that goes with that will want to consider the Plato/Hegel God seriously.

Here's a comparison. In recent times we have learned something new about the substance that we call "water," which for a long time we described as a simple "element." Water, it turns out, is actually a composite, made up of atoms of hydrogen and oxygen. Similarly, we may learn something new about the "God" whom many of us habitually describe as a separate being. We may learn that this "God" is actually distinct but not separate from the "lower" beings that make up the world. We wouldn't learn this by empirical investigation, as we did in the case of water, but we would learn it. These stories show how we are able to talk about the same thing, essentially, while our conception of what that thing is, is undergoing change.

Just as we were correct in thinking that water flows, is capable of freezing and boiling, is transparent, and so forth, so we have also been correct in thinking that "God" transcends ordinary beings like us and has great authority as a result of that transcendence. In both cases, we have also been mistaken about significant features of what we're talking about, but that doesn't prevent us from talking, throughout our learning process, of what is essentially the same thing. In this way, it should be possible to compare differing conceptions of "God" without throwing up our hands and saying that we're just not discussing the same subject.

This is my reply to critics of the "philosophers' God" who assert, like Henri Bergson, that "religion . . . regards [God], above all, as a Being who can hold communication with us," so that philosophers like Plato and Aristotle "are speaking to us of something else" (Bergson [1935], p. 241). Bergson doesn't address the question of how God can deserve to have authority over us, nor does he perceive how the Plato/Aristotle/Hegel God is free, loving, beautiful, and deeply involved in our lives at every point.

We have certainly learned in the course of time that our "communication" with this "Being" (to use these terms for a moment) is different from our communication with each other. If it weren't different, the "Being" wouldn't be infinite and wouldn't have the authority that it does. This would likewise be my reply to objections that the Plato/Aristotle/Hegel God doesn't seem like a "person." (I'll say some more about this issue in Chapter 2.) Regarding the notion of God as "an existing thing" (or "a Being," as Bergson puts it), Iris Murdoch says, "No existing thing could be what we have meant by God. Any existing God would be less than God. . . . But what led us to conceive of [God] does exist and is *constantly* experienced and pictured" (Murdoch [1993], p. 508).

I am also impressed, of course, by the fact that central thinkers in Christianity and in other religious traditions have taught a concept of God which does not make God a separate being. For all of these reasons, I propose to use the term "God" for something that transcends by being more inner, free, and loving rather than by being separate. If you prefer to use the word "God" for something else, that's fine. We just need to be clear about what each of us is talking about, at any point in our discussion.

A God whom we can know

Besides being free, loving, the source of all full reality, and truly transcendent because it doesn't fall like us into the category of a separate being, a God who is distinct but not separate is accessible to us; it's a God whom we can know. If this God is distinct from the world by being more "inner" than it, more free, true, loving, and beautiful, but isn't a separate being, then this God's innerness, its freedom, truth, and so forth, can't be separate from ours. So we can know this God by knowing our own inwardness, our own freedom, truth, and so forth. No special faculty, no "*sensus divinitatis*," and no apparatus of "proofs" are required.[8]

That we can know God does not bring God down to "our" ordinary level. For our inwardness or God continue to be higher than much of the world inasmuch as, in our ongoing "identity crisis," our freedom, truth, love, and beauty continue to be higher than much of what we're composed of.

If we can know God as our own freedom, truth, love, beauty, and (in general) inwardness, then what people call "faith" turns out to be our loyalty to this inwardness or this higher reality, in the face of the attractions of lower or more external desires and projects. Which is a loyalty that can be difficult enough to maintain, even though we sometimes experience the higher reality as our own freedom, truth, love, and beauty. For a part of us is often eager to suggest cynically that there is no real freedom, truth, love, or beauty—that our "higher interests" are merely fantasies, because nothing is really "higher." Instincts like fear, anger, and self-protection and ideologies like materialism and naturalism can promote such a view very effectively.

"Nihilism" is one of the common names for this view, whose power most of us have felt.[9] It has also been called the "dark night of the soul," depression, despair, and so forth. Being driven by instinct, these states of mind are very natural. One result that they can have, when we're accustomed to them, is that because a breakthrough of love and freedom is so different from what we're used to thinking that we have inside us, it will often seem to come from "outside" us. The truth is that the freedom and love that are outside us can only affect us because we have the potential for them inside us. But the downward forces that we also have within us can be very persuasive in their denial that there is any such positive potential there (or anywhere at all).[10]

"Mysticism"

The claim that in spite of all of this, we do have freedom and love and thus God and the ultimate reality within us, and that consequently we can know God directly, is the characteristic doctrine of "mysticism." Because this doctrine is often not explained clearly, "mysticism" has acquired additional connotations, such as that the mystical knowledge of God "goes beyond reason," that it's "other-worldly," and that it's experienced only by a select few, on extraordinary occasions.

But I follow common dictionary definitions of the primary sense of "mysticism" as simply "immediate consciousness of (or union with) the transcendent or ultimate reality or God." So I ask readers to set aside other suggestions that may be commonly associated with "mysticism" but are not part of what I mean by the word. In particular, (1) there is no suggestion here that this consciousness or union goes beyond "reason," except insofar as people often define "reason" in dogmatic ways that put unreasonable limits on its method or its realm of application. (2) Nor is there a claim of a peculiar "faculty" that makes this consciousness or union possible. No "*sensus divinitatis.*" (3) Nor is there a suggestion that the mystical consciousness or unity is "ineffable" (though it may certainly be difficult to express).

(4) Nor is there a suggestion that mysticism puts us in touch with "another world"—except in the not particularly controversial sense that it makes us aware of aspects of our everyday world which are in important ways "higher" and which aren't studied by, for example, present-day physics, chemistry, or biology. So "mysticism" as I understand it is not accurately described as "other-worldly." What it makes us conscious of is transcendent or ultimate in the sense that it's *higher*, but not in the sense that it's *separate*. (In keeping with my objection to the notion that God is "separate" from us, I regard the notion of "union with God" as a metaphor for what is actually the discovery of a way in which we have in fact all along *been* God.)

Furthermore, (5) I think it's a mistake to assume, as writers about mysticism generally do, that any person who is conscious of God will *know* that she's conscious of God. If mysticism is immediate consciousness of the transcendent or ultimate reality or God, I suggest that this consciousness is in fact present in our experience of trying to have an open mind, or inner freedom, or love, or forgiveness, or other similar states. In a way that I'll explain in subsequent chapters, true open-mindedness (or inner freedom, and so forth) is the ultimate reality or God, so when we're conscious of our own open-mindedness or our effort to be open-minded, we're conscious of God. But it's easy for a person to be conscious of open-mindedness, inner freedom, love, or forgiveness, and not realize that, as I'm going to argue in this book, these are what the ultimate reality or God is composed of. So in being conscious of them, she's conscious of the ultimate reality or God without knowing that this is what she's conscious of.

We might call such a person a "mystic," even though she doesn't entirely know what she's conscious of. Or we might coin a special term for this intermediate state between unconsciousness of the ultimate reality or God and consciousness of the ultimate reality or God combined with full knowledge about what the consciousness is of. However we choose to designate it, this intermediate state is extremely important, because it means that something that we might call "mysticism" is much more widespread than we generally recognize. Practically everyone experiences open-mindedness, inner freedom, love, or forgiveness, at one time or another. So practically everyone experiences what I will argue is the ultimate reality or God, though most often without knowing that this is what they're experiencing. When we realize this, our attitude toward what we call "mysticism" may change significantly, because an important kind of "mysticism" then turns out to be an almost universal human possession.

Thus, (6) contrary to a widespread assumption, practically all of us are "mystics," in the sense that practically all of us sometimes are immediately conscious of the ultimate reality or God, though often without knowing that this is what we're conscious of. Individuals like Rumi, Whitman, Plato, or Hegel, on the other hand, who know what it is that they're conscious of, and who may be able to evoke this kind of knowledge for others, are "mystics" in a stronger and more familiar sense of the word. Both groups show us something very important, and something that's generally ignored, about human beings. But this very important thing is not the extraordinary "mystical experiences" that we hear so much about. Rather, it's the transcendence that we experience in many much more familiar ways, in everyday life, but which we often don't appreciate as transcendence. I'll say more about this issue throughout the book and especially in Chapter 9.

Plato and Hegel explain the direct knowledge of God in a way that makes it clear that it doesn't have to have any of these other features that are often associated with "mysticism." Part of the purpose of this book is to lay out Plato's and Hegel's explanations so that you can see how mysticism can be perfectly rational and confirmed by your own experience.[11] And, indeed, so that you can see how the knowledge of God, which mysticism shows that we possess, is the fulfillment that's described by traditional religions as salvation or awakening.

I should probably note here that some recent commentators have gone so far as to maintain that Plato himself wasn't actually a "mystic," so that the long tradition of interpreting him as a mystic is based on a mistake. These commentators describe "mysticism" as "other-worldly" (Terence Irwin [1989], p. 114; Peter Adamson [2014], p. 159), and they point out Plato's evident ongoing interest in the ordinary world of nature, politics, and so on. There are also commentators who raise similar objections to describing Hegel as a "mystic." I think these objections are based on a misconception of what mysticism is.[12] The primary meaning of the term is the doctrine that we can have direct knowledge of God or the ultimate reality. But if this God or ultimate reality is "in" the everyday world, as both Plato and Hegel suggest, there's no reason why knowledge of God or the ultimate reality should reduce the mystic's interest in the everyday world—though certainly he or she will see that world in a different light.[13]

A God who, in one way, we are

Let us return, then, to the knowledge of God that mysticism shows that we possess, and the consequent salvation or awakening. We possess this knowledge, salvation, or awakening already, because we already have the freedom, truth, love, and beauty that we dream of—if only in the form of our ideals. Inasmuch as we appreciate what freedom, truth, love, and beauty would be, we possess them, to some degree.[14] So the part of us that has this dream, already is what it dreams of.

And since this inspired part of us is free, which means self-determining, it's fully itself in a way that our other parts, which are determined by what's around them, are not. Indeed, since bounds or limits would involve constraining relations to what's around it, and thus prevent it from being fully self-determined, this "part" must be unbounded, infinite. Through it, then, we are fully ourselves and infinite. Difficult though it is to believe, we are, through this "part" of us, God right now. Bearing in mind, of course, that this "God" that we are is the truly transcendent, free, and loving reality that isn't a separate being from the world.

If the notion that we are (in any respect) "God" sounds grandiose or insane, remember that we are this God only by being loving and fully free, which means precisely not being driven by our separateness from other beings and our self-importance. So Heinrich Heine misunderstood Hegel when he wrote in a much-quoted humorous recollection that "I was young and proud, and it gratified my self-esteem to learn from Hegel that, contrary to what my grandmother thought, it wasn't the Lord in heaven, but I myself here on earth who was God."[15] Pride has to do with one's relations to others, and thus is a feature of a finite and non-self-determining being. So to the extent that Heine was proud, he wasn't God. Whether Heine failed to understand this or, for the sake of his joke, chose not to understand it is hard to determine.

So it's not by accident that when I mention freedom it's always in tandem with love and ethics. People who seek inner freedom sooner or later find out that insisting on our own needs over other people's needs (or on others' needs over our own) prevents us from being fully free, because it means that we're constantly determined by something that isn't us. We're constantly determined, in these cases, by the dividing line between us and the others.

This is why we always exhibit a certain compulsiveness or lack of vision, that is, a lack of freedom, when we're preoccupied with the separation between ourselves and others. For whatever reason, we haven't discovered or we've forgotten what full freedom is like.

So, as I said, the "part" of us that dreams of freedom, truth, love, and beauty, and by appreciating them is them, is God by being fully itself and infinite. I put "part" in scare quotes, here—we are God through this "part" of us—because since it's infinite, this "part" can't really be a mere "part" of anything. It must be the whole.

But you certainly know why I nevertheless want to call it only a "part" of us: because we aren't aware of being God! Ordinarily, we feel like we're anything but God. We feel (at best) limited, imperfect, not fully free, not fully ourselves, and separate from others. So that when Eckhart Tolle asks, "How can you find that which was never lost, the very life that you are? . . . God-realization is the most natural thing there is,"[16] we may be inclined to reply, If it's so natural, why hasn't "God-realization" happened to *us*?

Why we often don't know this

We aren't usually aware of being God because as human beings we're anything but God. Being human carries with it a lot of blindness. But when that blindness is lifted, we discover to our great surprise that we aren't *only* human beings. Insofar as we care about inner freedom, love, and related ideals, we *are* inner freedom, love, and the rest, and thus we're infinite, and we're God. This is the sense in which we really are "one" with each other.

If we are inner freedom and God, and in that sense "one" with each other, why are we, in other respects, so imperfect, so ignorant of who we are, and so "separate"? This is because a truly infinite God can't exclude anything, including what's imperfect, "separate," and ignorant. So there must be imperfect, separate, and ignorant things such as we are in our capacity as human beings, and such as rocks and trees are in their capacity as rocks and trees. True infinity includes every variety of finitude. This is why we must be imperfect, not fully free, not fully ourselves, and largely blind—as well as, through our dreams and ideals, perfect, free, fully ourselves, enlightened, and "one." It's why we must be the ongoing identity crisis—"helpless immortal! insect infinite!"—that we are.

Our ongoing identity crisis between finite and infinite, human and divine, ignorant and knowing is what "humanism" in its various forms overlooks, and what traditional religions through their various mythologies bring to our attention.[17] But within this crisis, clearly our dreams and ideals are the main thing: that we love and admire and sometimes try to emulate the divine freedom, truth, love, and beauty. These are always in us, and however dismal our failures are, however much we fail to realize, our essential divinity outweighs our failures because it's infinite and fully itself—that is, divine.

When we appear not to love, but rather to be hateful or indifferent to our fellow humans, it's because we're preoccupied with the effort to defend merely "our own" individual freedom (as we call it), or the freedom of "the people we care about," against some actual or imagined threat. We haven't yet discovered or we've forgotten that simply opposing "others," even by being indifferent to them, determines us by our relation to these "others" and thus detracts from our self-determination and freedom rather than adding to them.

The discovery that our freedom is and depends on the freedom of everyone, often happens when we experience a major loss, a catastrophe, or a trauma. The experience of being close to death, or to something like it, allows us to see beyond the limits of our "own," individual life—to "die," as the saying goes, "before we die." Our horizon expands beyond what we could previously imagine.

When this happens, we realize that to have inner freedom, we have to love everyone—often by forgiving others, and ourselves as well, for the way we have trampled on our freedom. This is not to say that we will put up no resistance to such trampling by ourselves and others. Rather, it means that such resistance must be offered in ways that are consistent with fundamental love—with being "one."

Hatred and indifference turn out, when we understand them in this way, to be products of an underdeveloped and narrow conception of freedom. They're produced by a conception of freedom that doesn't appreciate either freedom's "inner" aspect or how that aspect requires concern for the freedom of others: how it requires love and ethics.

When we understand this, both intellectually and emotionally, we can see underdeveloped forms or stages of freedom everywhere. However rudimentary they may be, however much pain they may cause to others, they are still forms of freedom, and *in that respect* they're beautiful.

Beauty in everything

When we appreciate the beauty, in all of its imperfection, of these forms or stages of freedom, then our world in which this beauty is everywhere is, in its essence, all beautiful. Everything in it is trying, to the best of its more or less limited ability, to be free and thus divine. As Alfred North Whitehead put it, "Every event on its finer side introduces God into the world."[18] And the finer side is self-determining, fully itself, and fully real as itself, in a way that the event's other, as it were, parasitic side is not.

This is how we can, in William Blake's pregnant words,

> ... see a world in a grain of sand,
> and a heaven in a wild flower,
> hold infinity in the palm of [our] hand
> and eternity in an hour.[19]

When we realize that divine beauty is everywhere because we are, in an important way, what we dream of and because freedom unfolds in stages and, like all of our dreams, we easily forget it, we are reconciled with our ongoing troubles—with our inevitable, ongoing identity crisis. This reconciliation gives us a peace, an "eternity in an hour," that can be found nowhere else.

The Platonic tradition doesn't underestimate the world's injustice and pain. It's clear from the rest of his poetical work that Blake, for example, is anything but a "Pollyanna." But he can still project the vision of reconciliation that we see in this poem. And Plato's writings examine in detail the miseries that we inflict upon ourselves and each other. But in doing so they bring out the beauty, the higher value, which is present in some form in every human effort.

This Platonic reconciliation with our own and the world's imperfection is probably the only real antidote for the moral and religious impatience that drives millenarian and apocalyptic hopes and terrorism. Without dreams of perfect freedom, we might as well be dead. But without compassion for the necessary imperfection of our freedom, we can spread death and destruction in the name of those dreams.[20]

The only solution to this problem is to appreciate as versions of freedom, however rudimentary, the behavior that we and the people around us currently do exhibit. And thus to love ourselves and others as we are at present, and not merely as we "ought to be." Simultaneously to regret our imperfection, and to celebrate the freedom that's present in that imperfection. Because it's only by forgiving imperfection that we can be fully free.[21]

The reconciling peace, the "eternity in an hour" that follows from the love that forgives imperfection, is the enlightenment or salvation that's described by the mystical stream in each of the world's major religions.

Philosophy explains

Few people realize, today, that Western philosophy in Plato and his successors provides a worked-out rational explanation of how we possess this "mystical" peace, enlightenment, and salvation. Though Plato's exploration of these issues in his dialogues is brilliant, it's also complex, tentative, and sometimes gnomic, and so is the work of many of those who have learned from him. Hegel gives the classic modern account of how inner freedom requires forgiveness in the section on "Conscience" of his *Phenomenology of Spirit* (1807) and of how freedom and love are the highest and fullest reality in his *Science of Logic* (1812–14) and *Encyclopedia of the Philosophical Sciences* (1817–). But because of the complexity and exhaustiveness of his account, few interpreters have understood what it's actually about.

Alfred North Whitehead and Ludwig Wittgenstein are the major twentieth-century figures who tried, without drawing on Hegel, to explain the connection between philosophy and what Wittgenstein called "the mystical." But because they didn't articulate their accounts in terms of familiar human experiences such as inner freedom, love, and forgiveness, what they were proposing hasn't been well understood either.

Michael Polanyi, Iris Murdoch, J. N. Findlay, Sebastian Rödl, and Wolfram Gobsch provide the best recent accounts of these matters. I'll discuss most of these writers from Whitehead to Rödl in Chapter 2.[22]

A modern problem: Science

A major reason for our recent difficulties is how impressed we have been, since the nineteenth century, by ideologies that claim to speak with the authority of the natural sciences. There is a vocal party that regularly asserts that only science and technology can really be "rational." In which case, there is no real freedom apart from science and technology, and thus no enlightenment, awakening, or salvation as those are traditionally understood. Such a view shuts the discussion down very quickly.

Philosophical mysticism can respond to these assertions in three ways. First, by pointing out that the claim that only science and technology are really rational can't itself be grounded solely on science and technology, without being circular and merely assuming what it claims to prove. So if someone who makes this claim wants to avoid assuming what he claims to prove, he is already, in effect, engaging in a rational discussion that isn't entirely scientific or technological.

Secondly, philosophical mysticism can point out how inner freedom, love, and beauty in fact strive for and embody something that deserves to be called "reason." Inner freedom is distinguished from mere randomness by its effort to have good reasons for what it does. Love, which celebrates what it loves as admirable, is willing, in the right circumstances, to give reasons why others should admire it too. Beauty, likewise, has its reasons, which taste and critics are aware of and try to articulate.[23]

Though these reasons generally aren't scientific, they all deserve to be called reasons because our processing of them is responsive to information and to open-minded discussion, and thus it reflects a kind of thought (which needn't always be articulated or conscious). If this processing wasn't responsive to information and discussion, it wouldn't be free and its celebration wouldn't be genuine. But we know from our experience that it often is genuine.

I'll explore the role of reason in inner freedom, love, and beauty in Chapters 3 and 5 through 7. Through this role of reason in them, the mysticism that celebrates the reality that's composed of inner freedom, love, and beauty celebrates something that in fact is composed of reason, throughout.

Science as a part of God

But it's not just that science and technology have no monopoly on rationality. The third point that needs to be made, and which I made already in the Introduction, is that insofar as science pursues truth as such, and not merely what might turn out to be "useful," science is itself a form of inner freedom, and thus it's a part of the higher reality of freedom, truth, love, and beauty which philosophical mysticism celebrates.

If the amazing physical powers that the sciences have given us in the course of the last two centuries serve merely to give us what we already unreflectively want, they aren't godlike. For then they leave us in the same inner unfreedom that we were already in; and there's no transcendence in that. Our current great uncertainty about our future on this planet, in view of the cumulative effects of our newly achieved physical powers, testifies to the very un-godlike nature of a great part of what we are.

If, on the other hand, our engagement in science is a pursuit of truth as such, as it seems to be for great scientists like Galileo, Newton, and Einstein, then it takes us beyond our existing wants, opinions, and self-importance, and in this way it liberates us and makes us truly godlike.[24] When we pursue the sciences in this way, they take their place alongside religion, philosophy, ethics, and the arts as taking us beyond our "all too human" qualities. Thus opening up the possibility of something that's more rational, more self-determining, and more "itself," which therefore deserves to be called "a higher reality." Of which all of these cultural and personal efforts, including the sciences, are aspects.

I don't mean to suggest that these "cultural efforts" are incompatible with "nature." As we see in our ongoing "identity crisis," the sciences, religion, philosophy, ethics, and the arts, which go beyond mere mechanistic self-preservation, are nevertheless carried out by creatures who in other respects are very much products of nature. So we can certainly explore how it is that our species and perhaps others have come to be able to pursue truth, self-determining freedom, love, and beauty in various ways for their own sakes, and thus to rise above mechanistic self-preservation as we sometimes do. It's just that we mustn't assume that the ultimate explanation of this going-beyond or rising-above will be in terms of mechanistic self-preservation! For that would defeat the whole effort.

The upshot is that we shouldn't suppose, as we often do, that science shows or assumes that there is no higher reality. Together with religion, philosophy, ethics, and the arts, science is an essential part of the only truly higher and inspiring reality: the reality that's composed of and guided by truth and thought, of various kinds, rather than by genes, hormones, appetites, opinions, self-importance, and so forth.

Science contributes to our understanding of this higher reality, insofar as it elucidates the mechanisms (the genes, hormones, neurons, opinions, self-importance, and so forth) that make the higher reality possible. But as Socrates points out in Plato's *Phaedo* (98d-99c), to show what makes human thought or action possible is not to provide a complete explanation of it. The phenomenon of science itself demonstrates this, insofar as science seeks something that no mechanism as such seeks, namely, truth as such.

When we see how science and religion both contribute to the existence of this higher reality, by rising above the directives of genes, hormones, self-importance, and so forth, then we see that the ongoing controversies between advocates of science and advocates of religion are an unnecessary distraction. What's really needed is a recognition, on each side, that neither of them is the whole story, and that dogmatism on either side prevents it from playing its proper role in the pursuit of truth (and of the freedom, love, and beauty that seek to be guided by truth). By deciding in advance what particular method or belief will lead to truth, dogmatism prevents us from being truly truth-guided or free.

Reconciliation of "object" and "subject," fact and value, and you and me

Besides uniting us with God, in the way that I've been describing, the Plato/Hegel higher unity and higher reality also unites us with ourselves, with nature, and with each other. Insofar as we view ourselves, nature, and each other as "objects," as we do in science and in our instrumental dealings with the world, we are separate from our bodies, nature, and each other. This is true regardless of how often we may call ourselves a "part of nature"; for we are still in fact claiming the rational authority to make this judgment, and that claim to rational authority sets us apart from what the judgment claims to be the case. This is the hidden dualism in philosophical "naturalism." And all of this separateness, from our bodies, from nature, and from each other, may well seem to deprive our world of the beauty and the inherent value that it may have had in our childhood and in earlier epochs of human history.

But when we see that rather than being merely negative, or "disenchanting," as Max Weber put it, this objectification is a part of our positive effort to be fully ourselves by being guided by truth rather than by genes, hormones, self-importance, and the like, then beauty, value, and enchantment return. For now we can see the "objective" world, including our own bodies, as embodying, everywhere, efforts to achieve selfhood and freedom. We human beings, we objects in the natural world, are making these efforts that go beyond bodily mechanisms, self-importance, and the like. And nature as a whole is doing the same thing, through us and (in varying degrees and varying ways) through everything.

And insofar as the "objective" world is pervaded by these efforts that point beyond mere "objectivity," beyond bodily mechanisms, self-importance, and the like, it is thereby as beautiful and valuable as anything could be. "Object" and "subject," the "external world" and the knower, body and mind, fact and value, mechanism and freedom are reconciled—not by reducing either member to the other one, which would be no reconciliation, but by understanding how one is the other going beyond itself. "The good life is *the world* seen *sub specie aeternitatis*."

And by this process, you and I are also reconciled, inasmuch as we aren't merely "objects" to each other or to ourselves, but rather through our shared effort to go beyond the separateness and consequent unfreedom of that "object"-hood, we are a "we." We, as the "good life," are "the world seen *sub specie aeternitatis*."

"Idealism"

Because the single, self-determining, free higher reality that we're talking about is made possible by ideas or thought of some kind, the Plato/Hegel doctrine of the higher reality is often called "idealism." But it's important to note that this kind of "idealism" does not assert, like George Berkeley, that things in general exist by being "ideas" in a human mind or in God's mind. Nor does it assert, like Immanuel Kant, that the objects of knowledge are given some of their key features by the minds that know them. That is, the Plato/Hegel "idealism" differs in principle from the kinds of "idealism" that are usually taken, in recent discussions, as the prototypes of all "idealism."[25]

Berkeley and Kant presuppose (in Berkeley's case, by denying) a contrast between external and internal, object and subject. The "anti-idealist" "realisms" that appear periodically since their time presuppose the same contrast.[26] But Plato and Hegel go beyond this contrast, without denying it, when they show how although "objects" that are independent of "subjects" certainly *exist*, the "subject" as such is more fully real (because it's self-determining) than any mere "object" could be. This notion of a higher degree of reality is what Plato's and Hegel's "idealism" is about.

There is, in fact, good reason to regard the Platonic kind of idealism, rather than Berkeley's or Kant's, as the original prototype of "idealism." It was after all Plato who put "*ideai*" ("Forms," or "Ideas") at the center of the discussion of "reality," two millennia before Berkeley and Kant, and it's likely that their more recent "idealisms" were encouraged, at some level, by inklings of what Plato himself was driving at. Though by not conceiving of a scale of greater and lesser degrees of reality, and instead formulating their "idealisms" in merely contrastive, dualistic ways, they created ongoing confusion that Plato and Hegel avoid.

I discuss the varieties of "idealism" in a bit more detail in Chapter 2. To avoid unnecessary confusion, in most of the book I avoid using the term. But for those who are familiar with the modern debates between versions of "idealism" and versions of "realism," it's very helpful to see how these debates are motivated by a real issue, which however the participants don't fully understand. When we understand how what's self-determining has a higher degree of reality, reality as itself, which is entirely compatible with the reality (in the ordinary sense of "existence") of what's not self-determining, we can understand the modern debates without being drawn into them, in their own terms.

Cultural reconciliation

So the fuller reality that's achieved by subject-hood and self-determination is the core of truth that Plato and other philosophical mystics identify in traditional theism as well as in our experience of ethics, mind, knowledge, science, the arts, and freedom. This core is divine in that it transcends everyday reactive mechanical functioning by being self-determining, free, loving, and beautiful. But this transcendence takes place not through a dualistic contrast, which would itself be reactive and unfree, but rather as a self-transcendence, in which what exists but is not self-determining and in that sense is not fully real sometimes "ascends" to self-determination and thus full reality.

In their collective contribution to this true (because nondualistic) transcendence, nondogmatic science, nondogmatic religion, ethics, the arts, and philosophy are equal partners. For in their various ways they all rise above merely reactive mechanism and help to constitute a reality that deserves to be called "higher."

The resulting differentiated unity of science, religion, ethics, the arts, and philosophy was articulated in Plato's accounts of "ascent" (in the *Republic*, *Symposium*, and so forth), in which science, mathematics, ethics, beauty, and a philosophical religion overlap. We'll explore these accounts in Chapters 5–8. Aristotle articulated a similar unity in his biology, psychology, ethics, politics, poetics, and metaphysical theology, and Hegel articulated another in his account of "Spirit" as rational freedom taking the forms of (among other things) sense perception, intellect, ethics, politics, art, religion, and philosophy.[27]

Emerson wrote that "in the uttermost meaning of the words, thought is devout and devotion is thought," and "it is the office of this age . . . to annul that adulterous divorce which the superstition of many ages has effected between the intellect and holiness," which is to say, between philosophy or science and religion.[28] Robin George Collingwood proposed "to build up the conception of an activity which is at once art, and religion, and science, and the rest."[29] Whitehead wrote that "philosophy . . . attains its chief importance by fusing . . . religion and science into one rational scheme of thought."[30] And Jonathan Lear recently suggested that we consider "the possibility that science and religion might be, not just compatible, but of a piece. . . . Science is, after all, an act of unification, a development of a higher complexity, an act of love."[31]

It can't be said that ideas like these are currently widely understood or shared. My goal is to state as clearly as possible what this tradition of thought has been up to, so as to encourage us to appreciate it and develop it further. How remarkable it would be if the watchwords of the contending sides of our culture—truth, reason, freedom, love, beauty, transcendence, and divinity—all pointed ultimately to the same thing. We could then be less divided, one-sided, or unsure than many of us have been for several centuries now.

An overview of this book

I begin Chapter 2 with a general account of our unifying goal and the single reality or "God within us" that it constitutes, taking passages from Emerson as my point of departure and using an analysis that comes mainly from Hegel. (All of this in ordinary English—no technical jargon!) As I said in the Introduction, in Chapter 2 you will get details about writers from Emerson to Rödl, in Chapters 2–4 you will hear quite a lot about Hegel, and in Chapters 5–8 you will hear even more about Plato.

My interpretation of Emerson as a Platonist may be unfamiliar but it's not unusual in recent scholarship. And though I lay more stress on Whitehead's and Wittgenstein's Platonism than one sometimes sees, my interpretations of them are not so unorthodox as to be incompatible with common interpretations.

My interpretation of Hegel, on the other hand, differs from the nearly universal consensus of recent commentaries in that I take Hegel not to be rejecting the notion of a "transcendent" God but to be giving a more coherent conception of such a God than everyday discourse does. Hegel is providing a conception of a God who is truly transcendent: a "true infinity," as Hegel puts it, which is not rendered finite or (consequently) immanent by being a separate being alongside such other separate beings as ourselves and the world. My book about Hegel (2005) gives a detailed defense of this interpretation of his work.[32] In this book, I discuss only a few of Hegel's key texts in detail, mainly presenting in my own words what I take to be his sound argument for replacing common conceptions of "transcendence" with a more defensible conception.

One result of my way of reading Hegel is that his philosophical theology turns out, in fact, to be in line with much traditional thinking about God, including St Paul (in God we "live and move and have our being") and the many early Christian writers and saints who say that we can in some way "become God."[33] Hegel makes sense of these traditional teachings, which everyday talk about God doesn't try to make sense of.

And this perhaps unexpected continuity between Hegel and Christian teachings has the effect that the common contrast between "modern," supposedly "secular" and non-"transcendent" philosophy and the previous, ancient and Christian epochs needs to be rethought. Major thinkers in all epochs in the West (in recent times, think of Wittgenstein and Whitehead, as well as Hegel) have been drawn to a metaphysics that isn't easily categorized as "secular," while skeptics in all ages have criticized such notions, and there is no reason to expect this dialectic to cease or to be radically transformed, while the makings of these views continue to be present.

So I try to contribute to an understanding of this dialogue across the millennia with my four chapters on Plato. These chapters explore central passages from some of Plato's most important dialogues (especially the *Republic*, *Symposium*, *Phaedrus*, and *Timaeus*) to show how he criticizes empiricism, materialism, and scientism and how he develops an understanding of God or the ultimate reality as freedom, truth, love, and beauty. This is an understanding that differs from everyday talk about God or gods in much the same way that St Paul, the other early Christian writers, and philosophical theists from Hegel to Murdoch differ from it.

Along the way, my discussion of Plato clarifies a series of long-standing issues that people raise in regard to his thought and that commentators haven't fully resolved. First, pointing out that books iv-vii of Plato's *Republic* present what is in fact an illuminating analysis of inner freedom or self-government, I explain how inner freedom together with value or the "Good" enables some things to be, as Plato puts it, "more real" than others. Contrary to a common interpretation which some of his wording encourages, Plato is neither, on the whole, denigrating bodies nor celebrating the soul as something that's inherently separate from its body. Rather, he is drawing attention to the way in which the body goes beyond itself through thinking and soul by being more truth-directed and thus more self-governing than bodies are when they're functioning merely as bodies. (Details on this in Chapters 5–7.) Being more self-governing, what goes beyond bodies in this way is more real as "itself."

Although this notion of a higher degree of reality is fundamental for resolving the major issues that I've been talking about, it hasn't been explained by recent scholarship, but instead it has been treated as though it were some kind of Platonic dogma. I show how it's well justified.

I go on in Chapter 7 to show how Plato shows that reason is essential to eros or love, and thus how and why the lover "must become a lover of all beautiful bodies" and souls, as Diotoma says at *Symposium* 210b. This connection between reason and eros shows how reason and emotion can be allies rather than being, as we often assume, at odds with each other. And this in turn makes possible the rational/emotional ecstasy that Plato describes in some of his most famous and today apparently least understood passages.[34]

Then I show how, although eros must extend to "all beautiful bodies" and souls, it loves individual people, as individuals. How this could be the case has been a vexed question since Gregory Vlastos drew attention to the issue half a century ago, and Martha Nussbaum more recently. It's crucial for seeing how Plato's "ascent" operates within the world, and not merely by escaping it.

Next, in Chapter 8, I reconstruct Plato's justification for his assertion in the *Timaeus* that the divine can't be "jealous" or spiteful, and I show how this doctrine implies that a fully rational/erotic and thus "godlike" person will engage with the world ("go down") and be guided by justice in her dealings with others. This is Plato's answer to the question, "Why be moral?" And finally I show how Plato's mystical theology emerges from and completes this account of human/divine rational/erotic functioning, so that his mysticism is indeed fully rational. This is the synthesis of freedom, love, and God by which so many Western thinkers and poets have been inspired.

Illuminating these texts and issues, the book can serve as an introduction to many of the central themes of the philosophy for which it's appropriate to give Plato credit. It can also serve as an introduction to the broad tradition that has been fed by this philosophy. Aristotle, Plotinus, St Augustine, Dante Alighieri, Immanuel Kant, Hegel, William Wordsworth, Emily Dickinson, Whitehead, Wittgenstein—we can't understand the vertical dimension of reality which all of these authors and many others celebrate, without understanding Plato's notion of "ascent" to a higher reality.[35]

Introducing this tradition, the book introduces the main alternative that Western thought has produced to the doctrines of empiricism, materialism, scientism, existentialism, and postmodernism. These doctrines have attracted much attention during the last couple of centuries, but they don't clarify the central issues that Platonism and the present book address, namely, the relations between religion and science, value and fact, ethics and rationality, emotion and intellect, mind and body, and the knower and the "external world."

2 "THAT WHICH SHOWS GOD IN ME, FORTIFIES ME"

That is always best which gives me to myself. The sublime is excited in me by the great stoical doctrine, Obey thyself. *That which shows God in me, fortifies me.*

EMERSON, "DIVINITY COLLEGE ADDRESS"

We live in division, in parts, in particles. Meantime within man is the soul of the whole; the wise silence; the universal beauty, to which every part and particle is equally related; the eternal One. And this deep power in which we exist, and whose beatitude is all accessible to us, is . . . self-sufficing and perfect in every hour.

EMERSON, "THE OVER-SOUL"

Inner freedom and being oneself

To consider Emerson's teaching in the above quotations, let us begin with his "great stoical doctrine, *Obey thyself*."[1] To follow this doctrine's advice is not as easy as it may sound. Anger, fear, social expectations, self-importance, and self-doubt are among the obstacles that stand in the way of our being fully self-governing and fully ourselves.

Much of the history of literature, philosophy, and psychology is an exploration of these issues. In literature and mythology, the "hero's journey" is her search, so that she can "obey" her true self, for *who she really is*, as opposed to what the external world has made her. Think of Odysseus, Telemachus, Orestes, Oedipus,

Psyche in Apuleius's *Golden Ass*, the Israelites' forty years in the desert, Jesus's testing by Satan, and the Buddha's testing by Mara. Think of Dante's *Divine Comedy*, Shakespeare's Hamlet, George Herbert's self-depiction, Henry Fielding's Tom Jones, Jane Austen's Elizabeth Bennet, James Joyce's Leopold Bloom and Stephen Daedalus, the protagonist of J. R. R. Tolkien's *The Hobbit, or There and Back Again*, and Dorothy in *The Wizard of Oz*.

Psychological analyses of the hero myth have been given by Joseph Campbell (1949) and Erich Neumann (1954 and 1956). Behind Campbell and Neumann stand Sigmund Freud and Carl Gustav Jung, who analyze the goal of obeying one's true self under the headings of the "ego" ("where id was, there ego shall be") and "individuation" and the "Self." In modern philosophy, obeying one's true self is the theme of the "autonomy," "freedom," "self-reliance," or "authenticity" that Kant, Hegel, Emerson, and other modern thinkers hold up as a central ideal. In ancient philosophy, it's the theme of Stoicism (to which Emerson alludes) and of some of Plato's most important dialogues.

When Plato lays out the three "parts of the soul," in *Republic* book iv, he makes it clear that someone who is governed by his appetites or his emotions, rather than by his "rational part," isn't fully in charge of his own life. Rather than operating as "entirely one" (443d), such a person is handing his life over to a mere part of himself. We can apply this analysis to many of the men whom Plato describes in the dialogues, such as Alcibiades who says that "his own soul" objects to the way he "caves in to his desire to please the crowd" (*Symposium* 215e-216b), or Thrasymachus in *Republic* book i, of whom we might wonder whether he has any effective self at all that's distinct from his pride and anger.

Plato goes on to describe in *Republic* books vi and vii how the soul's rational part can function by seeking knowledge of what's truly good, as opposed to what feels good or is said to be good—all of which is likely to have come originally from outside one. So the famous "ascent" from the Cave, which pursues this knowledge of what's truly good, is in fact an aspect of the effort to "obey thyself," as opposed to heteronomy or obeying what is not thyself. In this way, Plato is in fact the first philosopher/psychologist to analyze this issue that continues to be central, after him, in both ancient and modern thought and literature.

And of course this effort to "obey thyself" is identical to the "identity crisis" struggle that I discussed in the previous chapter. Will I be what my ingrained appetites, opinions, and self-importance dictate, or will I be something higher and more "myself" than that?

Being oneself, and God

But Emerson, like Plato and others, suggests that becoming fully oneself is fundamental not only for philosophy and psychology but for true religion as well.

He says in our quotation that when I "obey myself," I'm obeying "*God* in me." Does this make any sense?

According to what's probably the most common way of reading the Bible, God and I are separate beings, so that if I obey God, I'm certainly not obeying myself. If God tells me what to do, and perhaps takes care of me in the manner of a parent, it seems that God can hardly be "in me."

However, I'm inclined to think that Emerson's account of God makes more sense than this God of the conventionally interpreted Bible. And in fact it turns out, as I mentioned in the previous chapter, that many early and recent Christian thinkers seem to have been more in tune with Emerson than with "conventional" thinking on this subject. Saint Paul is said to have endorsed the idea that "in [God] we live and move and have our being," and Saint Athanasius and (to this day) the Roman Catholic Mass speak of the possibility of our "becoming God."[2] So the God that these authorities are talking about doesn't seem to be a simply "separate being," in the usual sense of those words. By focusing on our "having our being in" God and our "becoming" God, Emerson and these evidently quite "orthodox" writers seem to me to have identified the indispensable kernel of truth in the notion of God.

I don't think you'll be surprised when I call an increase in inner freedom an experience that takes us "higher." As Emerson says, "The sublime is excited in [us] by the great stoical doctrine, Obey thyself." The "sublime" is what's higher. When we don't "obey *ourselves*," but instead let ourselves be governed by whatever we've been "wired for" by our past experiences, we lack this higher dimension.

And when we feel the possibility, in our lives, of going "higher" by being more self-governing, we feel what is, in fact, the kernel of truth in the idea of "God." This kernel of truth isn't that something outside us can be higher than us, it's that we ourselves can be higher. "God" is something that we can, to some degree, become. Since the potential for "rising" toward this higher thing, this ideal, is within us, we can say, as Emerson and others do, that this God is "within us"—that, as Rumi says, we "don't need to go outside" in order to find this God.[3]

As I explained in the previous chapter, the idea of "becoming God" isn't a symptom of grandiosity or hubris if the only way to become God is through inner freedom and love, that is, through freedom from self-importance. Self-government, as Plato, Hegel, and Emerson understand it, is anything but self-centered. One "becomes God" only by seeing God in everything.

An innocent response to the idea of "becoming God" might be that if we were created by God, we're inherently lower than God, and that's the end of the matter. The notion of "becoming" one's Creator makes no sense.

But in that case I would have to ask, what makes this God "higher" than what it creates? What gives it authority and makes it worthy of worship—that is, not worthy of mere submission but of reverent love and devotion? To be worthy of worship in that sense, God must transcend us, must belong to a different level of being.

The conventional "God" doesn't transcend

But as I pointed out in the previous chapter, something that's supposed to belong to a different level of being had better not be "separate" from other, "lower" things. It had better not be separate from lower things because something that's separate is *bounded by* what it's separate from and in that way it belongs to the same level of being as what it's separate from.

As Karl Rahner put it in the line that I quoted, a God who is separate from us and from nature would be "a member of the larger household of all reality" which is composed of us and nature and this God.[4] But a God who is another "member" (however powerful) alongside the rest of us, existing in the same way that we do, doesn't transcend us.

To deserve our worship, God must transcend us, must belong to a different level of being from us. But no matter how powerful it may be, a God who is a separate being and thus a "member of a larger household" along with us belongs to the same level of being that we do.

True transcendence

How, then, can anything really transcend something else? The only way for God to really transcend us is for God to be *our own transcendence of ourselves*: the inner freedom, love, and beauty by which we go beyond our merely mechanical reactiveness.

A God that's "within us" in this way doesn't encounter the problem of being a mere "member" alongside what's separate from it. Being everything's full freedom or self-government, it clearly isn't separate from or alongside anything.

But neither is such a God, as you might think at first glance, "immanent in" the world. It isn't immanent because it does *go beyond*—that is, it does *transcend*—the aspects of the world that aren't free. This is the true transcendence that makes worship appropriate.

The true transcendence that I've just outlined was articulated especially clearly by Hegel. I'll lay out Hegel's conception of God, which he derives primarily from the Platonic tradition, in more detail in the next two chapters. Hegel's critique of the conception of God as a separate being has led a large majority of recent commentators to make the mistake of supposing that he rejects "transcendence" in favor of "immanence," and that he thus breaks with the orthodox Christian tradition.[5] But since the God within us, which Hegel calls the "absolute Idea" or "absolute Spirit," transcends us insofar as we're unfree, this God in fact transcends the world. As Hegel puts it, this God goes beyond everything finite. Whereas the "God" who's supposed to be a separate being would not truly transcend (would not truly go beyond, or be "infinite," as Hegel puts it), because being separate it's limited by and thus determined by its relation to the beings that it's separate from. Being limited and determined by its relation to these other beings, such a God can't be fully free and self-governing, and in that way it fails to transcend the world.[6]

So someone who wants God to be truly transcendent, truly "higher than" the world, by being fully self-governing, had better not think of God as a separate being from the world. And as I've pointed out, a central and indisputably orthodox strand of Christian writing (St Paul, St Athanasius, St Augustine, Karl Rahner, Paul Tillich, and numerous others) does more or less explicitly avoid thinking of God as a separate being. It seems that writers who talk about a "transcendent being" as one that's separate from or "outside" the world haven't thought hard enough about what real transcendence would involve.

Loving creator and source of bliss

Furthermore, being separate from nothing, but in everything (as its freedom), the God within us by its very nature *loves* everything, nurturing and emerging as the greatest freedom or self-government of which each thing is capable. This God "fortifies" us, as Emerson puts it.

Indeed, the God that is our freedom does something similar to creating the world. The God that is our freedom is completely free, as the conventional Creator is supposed to be, and it gives the world all the full reality that the world has. Something that governs itself *is* "itself," and is real *as* itself, to a greater degree than something that's simply the product of its surroundings. And one can call what's real as itself more fully real than what's merely the product of its surroundings. In this sense, the God that is our freedom "creates" the world by giving it its fullest reality.

And finally, this God's "beatitude" or blessedness is, as Emerson says, "all accessible to us," and it amounts to what's traditionally called our "salvation." It's accessible to us because this God isn't separate from us, and so far as we are this God, we aren't separate from each other. So through this God we can be united with everything—near, far, past, present, future—that we love. It's "perfect in every hour," as Emerson says, because separateness applies only to finite things, which aren't free in the way that the God within us is.

Is this a "personal" God?

Is the God whom we can "become," or the "God within us," what people call a "*personal* God"? The Plato/Hegel/Emerson God isn't "personal" in the sense of being a separate and thus finite being, whom we might meet in the way that we meet each other. Nor does their God "intervene" in the world from outside it, through "miracles." Being "outside" the world, once again, would make God finite. Nor does their God grant finite "favors" that we might ask for. That, too, would make God finite.

However, the Plato/Hegel/Emerson God is anything but "impersonal" in the sense of disengaged, or unavailable, or indifferent to us. One could say that this God is more personal than we are, inasmuch as it's more free than we often are. And as our own innermost and truest self, the Plato/Hegel/Emerson God is more intimately involved with us than anything else could be; it's always and everywhere available to us, through its freedom and unlimited love; and it gives us, when we turn to it, the greatest conceivable fulfillment, wholeness, salvation, and enlightenment.[7]

In comparison to all of this, face to face meetings and finite favors that we might imagine pale into insignificance. When we have appreciated these things we'll recognize that traditional religions contain a core of truth—that the ultimate reality enables us to be both fully ourselves and united with everything that we care about—which can't reasonably be dismissed as superstition.

While critics of religion need to appreciate this core of truth in religion, believers in God need to make a comparable move from their side. Believers need to understand that in order to really deserve worship and gratitude, by being fully free, our God must be composed of our own inner freedom, our own pursuit of truth, and our own love. Higher than us these certainly are, but in us they must also be, in order to be fully free and genuinely higher. When we understand this, we'll see that rather than potentially being in conflict, the God that we worship and our own freedom, love, and pursuit of truth are the same thing.

Poets and teachers

In the remainder of this chapter, I'd like to survey some of the great poets and teachers who have helped us to understand this higher reality or God within us. Touching briefly on Plato and Hegel, whom I'll discuss in detail in later chapters, I'll go into more detail here on other recent teachers including Emerson, Whitehead, Wittgenstein, J. N. Findlay, Iris Murdoch, Wilfrid Sellars, John McDowell, and Sebastian Rödl.

Book 24 of Homer's *Iliad* tells the remarkable story of Achilles's meeting with Priam, in which the otherwise "wrathful" Achilles discovers sympathy for an old man who makes him think of his own father. Rather than being about Achilles's wrath, as such, is the *Iliad* really about this unique exception to that wrath? Does Homer expect the discerning reader to wonder at this exception, and consider what it might tell us about what even the most "brutal" humans have within them?

In the fourth century BCE, some centuries after Homer, the young Plato was apparently so angry at the people of Athens for condemning to death his beloved teacher, Socrates, that he was tempted to condemn human life, root and branch. I infer Plato's anger from the intemperate language that he sometimes uses about the world, as when he has Socrates say in the *Phaedo* that the true philosopher "despises" food, drink, sex, and bodily ornaments (64d). I'll discuss this aspect of Plato in Chapter 5.

But Plato also found a more forgiving and therefore freer approach to life. This approach centers on the idea of reason as inner freedom and love. God or the true Good, Plato says, is the goal, the pole star of this reason, freedom, and love.[8] Trying to think seriously about what the true Good would be, and to pursue it, makes us whole (we would say, "free") in a way that our appetites and self-importance (*thumos*) can't, because it gives proper attention to the appetites and self-importance without putting them in charge.

This ascent to greater freedom corresponds to what we call "transcendence." Plato describes it in his famous allegory of the man who has spent his life shackled in a cave, studying the shadows on its wall, and is finally able to leave the cave and see physical objects and the sun. The shadows on the cave walls represent our unthinking urges and opinions, while the physical objects and the sun are what we arrive at by thinking about what's truly Good. Plato's constant example of this liberating transcendence is Socrates.

By way of contrast to Socrates, Plato gives vivid descriptions of the unfreedom of other Athenians, such as Euthyphro and Alcibiades. Rather than aiming at the Good, Euthyphro aims at "what the gods want," and Alcibiades aims at personal power and pleasure. But Euthyphro is enslaved to his inflated self-importance as someone who thinks he has special knowledge of the gods, and Alcibiades is enslaved to the mob of voters whom he seeks to be admired by and thus to lead.

Whereas Socrates, as Plato depicts him, doesn't seek to be admired or to experience pride or power or pleasure, but only seeks whatever he thinks is truly good. So he's guided by his own thinking, which is his own if anything is. So we see how pursuing what's truly good enables a person to be guided by himself, and thus free. This is the way, in Emerson's phrase, to "obey thyself."

And because separateness, for humans as much as for God, governs a person by his relations to others and thus prevents him from being fully self-governed, Socrates goes beyond separateness. He treats everyone as he treats himself, that is, he treats everyone with love. This is why he shows no resentment toward the people who have condemned him to death.

By combining inner freedom and love in this way, Socrates inspires Plato to explore in his *Republic*, *Symposium*, *Phaedrus*, and *Timaeus* how inner freedom and love are ultimately inseparable. Much as Homer had explored this connection earlier, in evoking the momentary liberation from self-centeredness which Achilles found in his compassion for Priam.

After the time of Homer and before Plato, Siddhartha Gautama in India had made a similarly dramatic discovery of the inseparability of inner freedom and love. Sitting under the Bo tree, Siddhartha discovered that he was, as he put it later, "a light unto himself." That is, he wasn't merely the product of the environment that had generated his desires and thoughts. In an important way, he went beyond these—not by rejecting them, however, but through compassion. For the Buddha as for Socrates and Plato, love (in the form of compassion and "rightness") flowed from and secured his inner freedom.

Jesus and after

In Palestine some centuries later, when Jesus said that "the last shall be first," and so forth, he criticized conventional values in much the same way that Socrates, Plato, and the Buddha had criticized them. "For what shall it profit a man, if he shall gain the whole world, and lose his own soul?" (Mark 8:36)

The overriding value is inner. This is articulated in Jesus's teachings that we must love our enemies and that the kingdom of God is within us.[9] We must love our enemies because rejection and separateness prevent us from being self-governing. Whereas if we love everyone, we share inner freedom, the "kingdom of God," with everyone.

Throughout this period, people in the Mediterranean basin continued to study Plato's teachings. Plotinus, a student of these teachings who taught at Rome in the third century CE, wrote of the "highest" as "present at many points . . . *within* our nature is such a center," because the Good enables us to be free and ourselves.[10]

There has been a tendency among recent scholars to distinguish Plotinus and his successors from Plato himself, calling the former group "Neoplatonists." (They themselves called themselves simply "Platonists.") In terms of the issues on which I'm focusing in this book, and which I'll explore in Plato's writings in Chapters 5 through 8, the continuity between Plato and later Platonists, including Plotinus, Emerson, Hegel, and Whitehead, stands out.[11]

The North African Christian Saint Augustine followed the Platonists when he wrote in his *Confessions* in the fourth century CE that God was "more inward than his most inward part."[12] That is, God was more inward to everything than everything itself was, and more inward to Augustine, in particular, than Augustine himself was. Thus Augustine combined Plato's and Plotinus's notion that the Good is the key to inwardness or freedom with Jesus's teaching that the kingdom of God is "within us."

Medieval and modern

Christian mystics followed St Augustine and Plotinus in associating God with inwardness, and so did Islamic mystics like Jelaluddin Rumi. In his grief over the disappearance of his teacher and friend Shams of Tabriz, Rumi found the non-separation from God and from others that fills his poems.

Of course most conventional thinking, not understanding that a God who's outside us can't be fully self-governing and free, has always thought of God as outside us and outside the world. When Benedict Spinoza, in the Netherlands in the seventeenth century, proposed that God was "nature" and thus was not a separate, external being, people thought he was suggesting that "everything" was God—the doctrine that's called "pantheism." Because this seemed to imply that God wasn't "higher" than anything, they could hardly accept it, and they roundly condemned Spinoza.

Spinoza's critics and his successors in the eighteenth-century "Enlightenment" in Europe, Voltaire, David Hume, Jean-Jacques Rousseau, and Immanuel Kant, didn't see that a God whom we experience as our own freedom would still be higher than us insofar as we aren't consistently free.[13] Instead they imagined "God" in the common way as a being that's separate from the world, again overlooking the problem that a being that's separate can't be fully self-governing and free.

Kant's attitude to Platonic theology was more complex than Voltaire's, Hume's, or Rousseau's.[14] Kant does regularly speak un-Platonically of God as "a highest being," and he does dismiss "enthusiasm" and "mysticism" as having no rational content. On the other hand, he focuses just like Plato on the role of reason in humans' ascent to self-government; and he speaks systematically and quite Platonically of the divine as the "ideal" (CPuR A567ff.). The problem is that under the influence of his Newtonian conception of the knowledge of nature, Kant gives the divine "ideal" only a "regulative," not a theoretical validity. He "denies knowledge in order to make room for faith" (CPuR Bxxx). This dualistic contrast between knowledge and "faith" generates the futile oscillation, with which we have become so familiar since Kant's time, between "theory" and "practice," "science" and "religion," "intellect" and "feeling," and "fact" and "value."

To avoid these debilitating dualisms, we need to explore the indivisible unity of theory and practice, science and religion, intellect and eros, and fact and value that we see in Plato's and Hegel's conceptions of rational ascent (which I will expound in more detail in the chapters that follow). Rather than being the opposite of knowledge, "faith" is our loyalty to the higher values whose pursuit we know constitutes a higher and truer reality, but to which we nevertheless often fail to be faithful.

Georg Wilhelm Friedrich Hegel

G. W. F. Hegel (1770–1831) grew up in Germany in the late eighteenth century, in the shadow of the Hume/Rousseau/Kant Enlightenment. But Hegel drew on the tradition of Plato, Aristotle, Plotinus, and Spinoza to explain how a God who is in the world can at the same time be higher than it. Hegel showed in detail how through our own liberation and the love that flows from it the world surpasses itself, achieving something that, because it's real "as itself," is both higher and more fully real than the world as such is, and which we can appropriately call "God." Hegel's thorough explanation of this still unfamiliar idea was so complex that it has been almost universally misunderstood, as I'll indicate in the next chapter, where I'll sketch Hegel's life and ideas and try to alleviate some of the major doubts about Hegel that people may have.[15]

But Plato's and Hegel's basic idea keeps surfacing in the work of later writers. In particular, it plays an important role, though without being expressed with full clarity, in a series of nineteenth- and twentieth-century philosophers from Emerson through Wittgenstein and Whitehead to J. N. Findlay and Iris Murdoch who discuss "mysticism" or something like it with great seriousness.

Ralph Waldo Emerson

In Massachusetts, Ralph Waldo Emerson (1803–82) during his most creative years was not aware of Hegel, but he drew on the same Platonic sources that Hegel drew on, to describe a nurturing God within himself. "Within man is the soul of the whole; . . . the eternal One."[16] Like Hegel's "absolute spirit," Emerson's "over-soul" is a title for the fuller reality that's achieved by true freedom and the love that flows from it.

In his most famous essay, entitled "Self-Reliance," Emerson wrote that "Self-existence is the attribute of the Supreme Cause, and it constitutes the measure of good by the degree in which it enters into all lower forms." And "we lie in the lap of immense intelligence, which makes us the receivers of its truth and organs of its activity."[17] Thus, contrary to what many commentators suppose, what Emerson means by "self-reliance" is not reliance on "oneself" in the ordinary sense of the word. Rather, the "self-reliance" that he's recommending seeks to rely on a "self" that's freed from conceptions that originate outside it, so that whatever it generates will reflect its inner, genuine self: its "self-existence" and "truth." So "self-reliance" actually requires a kind of *transcendence*, from mere appetites and opinions to something that's more fully itself than a collection of appetites and opinions can be. In this way, Emerson's views are in line with traditional religion as well as with Plato.

In his essay "The Over-Soul," Emerson writes, "From within or from behind, a light shines through us upon all things, and makes us aware that we are nothing, but the light is all. . . . So there is no bar or wall in the soul where man, the effect, ceases, and God, the cause, begins."[18] The light that shines from behind is a direct borrowing from Plato's Cave allegory; and that it shines also from "within," and "through us," is Plotinus's interpretation of what Plato means by his allegory. If "we are nothing," the "self" on which we're supposed to rely is clearly not "ourselves" in the way that we ordinarily understand that term. Rather, it's the "inner" or "higher" self, to which Plato and Plotinus direct our attention.

Many commentators describe Emerson as a quintessentially "American" writer, or as influenced (as he certainly was) by Hindu thought, or (sometimes) as influenced by a "Neoplatonism" that they suggest is importantly different from Plato's own thought. I invite readers to consider the parallels that I've just pointed out between Emerson's formulations in "Self-Reliance" and "The Over-Soul" and Plato's *Republic*. My detailed discussion of Plato in later chapters should help to confirm that no great divide separates so-called "Neoplatonism," including Emerson, from Plato himself.

Late in his life, after his period of greatest creativity was behind him, Emerson became aware of Hegel's work through English translations and praised it highly.[19]

After Hegel and Emerson

Emerson and Hegel have both had quite a lot of influence. Hegel had a group of admirers in Britain, the "British Idealists" including Edward Caird, Francis Herbert Bradley, and Bernard Bosanquet, who dominated the British philosophical scene in the latter part of the nineteenth century. I'll say something about another self-described admirer of Hegel, Karl Marx, in the next chapter. As for Emerson, he was the biggest single influence on the most influential American poet, Walt Whitman (*Leaves of Grass* [1855]), and Emerson is probably cited more than any other American thinker down to our own day. The "New Age" movement with its enthusiasm for nontraditional "spirituality" views Emerson and Whitman as primary forerunners.

However, both Hegel and Emerson have been more admired than understood. The Harvard philosopher/psychologist William James was the most influential philosophical writer in the United States in the early twentieth century. James as a child had known the elderly Emerson, and he always admired Emerson greatly. But it's clear from James's writings, above all his *The Varieties of Religious Experience* (1902), that James didn't accept and probably didn't understand the Platonic conception of the "self" with which Emerson worked. The notions of a "self-existing Supreme Cause," and that "we are nothing, but the light is all," are not notions that James knew how to take seriously.[20] James was deeply interested in religious experience, and especially in the moral transformation, from self-centeredness to universal compassion, that often accompanies "mystical" experiences. But he had no access to the Plato/Hegel explanation of what these experiences represent and why they have these consequences.

James actually made it clear in a lecture that he gave in Oxford in the year before his death in 1910 that he wished the British Idealists would help him to understand these phenomena. They hadn't provided an explanation that struck him as helpful.[21] It seems to me that the fault for this was not on James's side. Unlike Plato and Hegel, the British Idealists didn't spell out any connection between "mystical" reality and what we experience in our daily lives. They didn't spell out how rational freedom and love, with which we're all familiar, constitute the higher reality. Nor, consequently, did they explain how experience of the higher reality might affect one's daily life.

F. H. Bradley wrote about a mystical "reality" in his *Appearance and Reality* (1893), but based it on abstract arguments against "relations" rather than on the concrete efforts of individuals to be themselves. Bernard Bosanquet (*What Religion Is* [1920], p. 12) relied on Bradley's "You cannot be a whole, unless you join a whole" (F. H. Bradley, *Ethical Studies* [1927/1962], p. 79), and offered no support for this (on the face of it) rather dogmatic claim. Bradley and Bosanquet didn't appreciate Plato's and Hegel's careful exposition of the connection between personal wholeness and larger wholes via the relationship between inner freedom and love (see Chapters 3, 7, and 8). Essentially Bradley and Bosanquet gave no response to Glaucon's challenge on behalf of rational egoism in book ii of Plato's *Republic*. *Assuming* that we will be interested in a kind of transcendence that includes us in a larger whole, they didn't take "commonsense" egoism seriously and consequently they provided no bridge between it and transcendence. So they couldn't provide the explanation of how mystical experiences relate to ordinary life which William James quite properly wished they might provide.

German philosophers after Hegel's death were no more helpful in this regard than the British were. Many of them were busy inventing new ways of thinking about politics (Karl Marx) or psychology (Gustav Fechner). Europeans who were sympathetic to religion, such as Hegel's colleague Friedrich Schleiermacher and the Danish writer Soren Kierkegaard, found Hegel too "intellectual."

The gap

This reflected the widespread failure to grasp how rather than being an optional interest that certain "intellectually inclined" individuals might have, Plato's and Hegel's "ascent" is a pervasive and inescapable feature—we can call it "inner freedom"—of everyday life. However "intellectual" we may or may not be, we all know that our current opinions and desires can mislead us, and we can fail, by blindly following them, to be in charge of our own lives. This knowledge of our own capacity for being misled and for failing to be in charge of our lives fuels our appreciation of whatever glimpses of truth and freedom we may experience in people, in social movements, science, love, the arts, religion, and so forth. Here, however, most recent philosophy fails to see how by making us more free and more "ourselves," our stepping back (if only momentarily) from our current opinions and desires connects us with the maximally free "self-existent" and thus with the divine.

Missing this connection, many creative minds in the generations after Hegel and Emerson, such as the atheist existentialists, Friedrich Nietzsche, Martin Heidegger, and Jean-Paul Sartre, followed pretty much in the path of the eighteenth-century Enlightenment. Positively, the existentialists emphasized our capacity for inner freedom and for being fully ourselves. But failing to see that what's in us in inner freedom is the "self-existent" divine, they put up a wall against the part of experience that we call "religious," and thus limited the freedom that they could actually achieve.[22]

On the other hand, writers who had great sympathy for religion, like Soren Kierkegaard and William James, shared the atheists' inability to connect religion with our everyday experiences of inner freedom in personal decision-making, science, the arts, love, and so forth. Neither side was able to bridge this gap.

Alfred North Whitehead

In the 1920s and 1930s, Alfred North Whitehead went a considerable distance toward bridging this gap, by drawing heavily on Plato. In his *Adventures of Ideas* (1933), Whitehead agrees with Plato's *Timaeus* (48a) that, as Whitehead puts it, "the creation of the world—that is to say, the world of civilized order—is the victory of persuasion over force."[23] In his earlier *Religion in the Making* (1926), Whitehead had given us the golden sentence that God "is the mirror which discloses to every creature its own greatness."[24] This, no doubt, is how "persuasion" triumphs over force.

Whitehead went on:

> The kingdom of heaven is not the isolation of good from evil. It is the overcoming of evil by good.... The power by which God sustains the world is the power of himself as the ideal.... The world lives by its incarnation of God in itself.... [God] is the binding element in the world.... [The world's] adventure is upwards and downwards. Whatever ceases to ascend, fails to preserve itself ... and decays by transmitting its nature to slighter occasions of actuality.[25]

This "victory of persuasion," the role of the "ideal" in "sustaining the world," and the resulting "upwards and downwards" dimension of increasing or diminishing self-governing reality are what all Platonists tell us about the divine Good. Rather than being a self-enclosed separate being, as in "the isolation of good from evil," the Good is everywhere at work in the world by encouraging more integrated wholes ("disclosing to every creature its own greatness"). Evil, then, rather than being a force that's diametrically opposed to the divine goodness, is merely our frequent failure (as a result, no doubt, of deeply rooted preconceptions about what the good for oneself might be) to appreciate this goodness itself and to respond to it.

So the bridge that Platonists and mystics identify between the divine and everyday life is our shared yearning for wholeness or inner freedom: for "upward" motion and the resulting "greatness." Suitably explained, this bridge could have satisfied William James's desire to understand the relation between mystical experiences and moral transformation.

Whitehead's limitations

Judging, however, from the way Whitehead's ideas have been received, more explanation is likely to be needed than he himself provided. Whitehead's broadly Platonic synthesis, like Hegel's, has in fact had only limited influence.[26] I am inclined to think that a major part of the reason for this is that Whitehead and his followers have failed to unfold key parts of the Platonic picture, without which it can't be fully convincing. Whitehead spelled out the ideal of rational self-government only in the most general possible terms, as in "every creature's own greatness," and in particular he didn't address the issues of the apparent rationality of mere appetite-satisfaction and egoism.

Whitehead clearly believes that the archetypal hedonists or egoists (Callicles, Thrasymachus, Alcibiades), whom Plato describes in his *Gorgias*, *Republic*, and *Symposium*, do not achieve their "own greatness." But why is this the case? What is "greatness," and why would we pursue it? What is it that gives appetite-satisfaction and egoism their initial plausibility, and what undermines that plausibility in the final analysis? What is it to be true to "oneself"? Whitehead doesn't pose these questions or give more than hints about how to answer them. Nor, as far as I can see, do his successors in "process philosophy" or "process theology" do this.[27]

But in the absence of an understanding of these issues, we don't really understand the role of reason in the world, or the higher reality that reason, according to Platonism, constitutes. A rational mysticism requires a developed understanding of how appetite and self-importance, on the one hand, and freedom, love, truth, and "greatness," on the other hand, relate to each other. It requires an account of what I've been calling our "identity crisis." Whitehead doesn't give an account of our identity crisis, as such, so his work lacks the power that a full account of our experience would have.

In his *Science and the Modern World* (1925), Whitehead describes how science as "the instinctive faith that there is an Order of Nature" (p. 6) has transformed our relation to the world. The early moderns, Whitehead says, were confident that such an Order would exist because their religion taught the idea of a rational Creator.

But why would such appetitive, selfish, and fearful creatures as we are, ever be at all interested either in an Order of Nature *or* in a rational Creator? What do these things have to do with *us*? Plato's and Hegel's response is that we seek "from having been many things to become entirely one" (*Republic* 443e, adapted). The function of reason, and thus also of the sciences' pursuit of the Order of Nature, is to enable us to be governed by ourselves rather than simply by the appetites, opinions, and self-importance that our history and our environment have instilled in us. Thus the sciences are part of the project of unifying or creating a higher whole, a true self: they are part of the identity crisis and the higher reality that are the themes of religion as well as of Platonism. In this way, a full understanding of what the sciences do for us shows what they have in common with religion. When we take the human identity crisis of appetite and selfishness versus reason and self-unification in its full seriousness, as Platonism does, then the higher phenomena of inner freedom, love, ethics, religion, and science each take their proper place within the picture and cease even to appear to be in competition with one another.[28]

Like Bradley, Whitehead didn't say enough about the content of ordinary human experience, as in (for example) the apparent rationality of mere appetite-satisfaction and egoism, to bring out the crisis and the drama that are involved in the emergence of a fully integrated self from such concerns. This crisis and this drama are the theme of Plato's and of Hegel's work as well as of religion. By expounding them, Plato and Hegel show in what sense we "live and move and have our being" (that is, our true being) in a *higher* reality. It's only within an overt drama of higher versus lower, that either religion or science has a point.

And it's also only in such an overt drama that we can recognize what religion has in common with science, inasmuch as they both seek to rise above mere appetite, opinion, self-importance, and so forth. If we underestimate the drama, the "identity crisis," in which we're all engaged, we can easily lapse into viewing our various activities (religion, science, art, ethics, etc.) as merely disparate "interests," rather than as aspects of an overarching project in which we're always, in various ways, engaged. And then the question of how these various interests relate to each other will tend to be pretty impenetrable.

We take too much for granted

In the twentieth and twenty-first centuries, two things have happened. First, the drama that religion addresses can no longer be assumed as philosophy's unspoken background. Many of us have lost track of the human experiences that are summed up in the notions of temptation, sin, salvation, and so forth. And second, those of us who admire science have come to take it so much for granted that we no longer realize what a surprising phenomenon *it* is. We assume, as we should not, that humans will be interested in truth as such. This drama, too, is lost on us.

The beauty of Whitehead's writings is how wide-eyed and open-minded he is in regard to the great phenomena of human civilization, and above all in regard to both religion and science. He loves them both, on some deep level, and can't imagine rejecting one in favor of the other. But his difficulty is what I just described: that for many of us, in the twentieth century, the deep point of both of these great phenomena has been lost. Whitehead's effort to "fuse . . . religion and science into one rational scheme of thought" hasn't been appreciated or assimilated because we haven't seen the background, the "identity crisis" drama, in relation to which religion and science are indeed partners in a single great project of ascent. Whitehead himself didn't spell out this drama as a crisis, nor have his successors done so. To Whitehead himself, this drama perhaps went without saying. But for many of his contemporaries, and for succeeding generations, it hasn't gone without saying. It needs to be spelled out.

This need became evident immediately among Whitehead's contemporaries in academic philosophy. Bertrand Russell, Whitehead's former collaborator at Cambridge University, and George Edward ("G. E.") Moore, their other leading colleague there, had no instinctive sense either of what religion is about or of what religion and science might have in common. In his essay "The Value of Religion" (1901), Moore saw no reason to go beyond ethical and aesthetic values to any notion of a divine "being" or reality. He had no inkling of how something that's guided by the Good might thereby be more self-governing and thus more real as itself than what's guided merely by its physical environment.

And Russell, in his various writings on Plato and "mysticism," regarded Plato's connecting the Good with reality as amounting to wishful thinking. If Russell read Whitehead's Platonic teaching in the final chapter of *Religion in the Making* (1926), it didn't alter his view of this issue at all.[29] Russell and Moore needed more explicit instruction than Bradley, Bosanquet, or Whitehead gave them regarding the greater reality "as oneself" (what Whitehead called the "greatness") to which the pursuit of the Good, as opposed to appetite, opinion, or self-importance, gives rise.

Russell's failure to grasp Plato's point about how the Good makes possible a fuller reality is particularly sad in view of Russell's recognition in his essay "Mysticism and Logic" that "the possibility of this universal love and joy in all that exists is of supreme importance for the conduct and happiness of life, and gives inestimable value to the mystic emotion."[30] He doesn't try to explain how it can be rational to attach so much importance to an "emotion" when we understand, following his doctrine, that this emotion responds to nothing that we have any good reason to regard as real.

Since Bradley, like Whitehead later on, had provided no account of greater reality "as oneself" or what Whitehead called "every creature's own greatness," it had been reasonable for critics like Moore and Russell to suppose that Bradley's fundamental doctrine was the familiar one that the only reality is minds and the ideas that they contain. This, Moore and Russell not unreasonably supposed, was what the mystical "reality," the hidden truth, that Bradley was driving at, amounted to.[31] Bradley gave them no sense of a vertical dimension of increasing reality. And Whitehead's remarks about "every creature's own greatness" are simply too undeveloped to bring out the process of ascent and increasing reality "as oneself," the crisis and the higher reality, which we need to see and understand in order to understand what Whitehead is really attracted to in religion.

Ludwig Wittgenstein

In view of this failure of Bradley, Bosanquet, and Whitehead to convey what at least Whitehead and probably the others as well were really concerned about, what's surprising is that the topic of mysticism nevertheless did not disappear completely from discussions in Moore's and Russell's Cambridge. Russell's student, Ludwig Wittgenstein in fact gave a kind of mysticism a central role in his influential *Tractatus Logico-Philosophicus* (1921), thus following in the footsteps, despite Moore's and Russell's critique, of Bradley (and of William James). Here was the young genius of the new philosophical movement focusing on precisely the same obscure issue on which the previous generation had focused and on which Moore and Russell, for their part, had pretty much given up as a will-o-the-wisp.

In his book, Wittgenstein proposes a sharp division between what is "inside" space and time and what is "outside" of them (6.4312), asserting that "God does not reveal himself *in* the world" (6.432).[32] On the other hand, "To view the world *sub specie aeterni* is to view it as a whole—as a limited whole. Feeling the world as a limited whole—it is this that is mystical" (6.45). Science deals with questions about the "world," and "we feel that even when all possible scientific questions have been answered, the problems of life remain completely untouched" (6.52). For these problems can't be dealt with, can't even be "expressed," in scientific terms. "Ethics," for example, "cannot be expressed" (6.421). "Propositions can express nothing that is higher" (6.42). "There is indeed the inexpressible. This *shows* itself: it is the mystical" (6.522). But "what we cannot speak about we must pass over in silence" (7). That is, the "mystical," including ethics, all the "problems of life," and everything "higher," is properly a realm of silence.

As Russell pointed out in his Introduction to Wittgenstein's book, Wittgenstein himself had managed to say a good deal about the things that we "cannot speak about." Wittgenstein was aware of this, asserting that the propositions of his book should be "thrown away" like a ladder after one had climbed up them to the realization that they are, properly speaking, "nonsensical" (6.54). What he left us with is the blank duality of what one can "speak about" in a scientific manner versus ethics and everything "higher," with regard to which one should, properly speaking, be silent. That the "mystical" and the "higher" "*shows* itself" is not very consoling, when one is told that one must ultimately "pass [it] over in silence."

Wittgenstein explains his notions of the "mystical" and of its "showing itself" by their opposition to "the world" and its being "expressed," of which he gives an elaborate analysis in the greater part of his book. He uses traditional, redolent words, "value," "ethics," "higher," "mystical," and "God," but he doesn't enter into or explain their content. It would be natural to want to ask, in what sense are this "value," "ethics," "mystical," and "God" truly "*higher*" than the world of "facts"? To make sense of this claim, we would need some dimension along which the two realms can be compared; but Wittgenstein's thesis seems to be that there is no such dimension. One can't speak of the two realms in the same language (since one realm one can't literally "speak of" at all). So there is no "sense" in describing one realm as "higher" than the other.

Wittgenstein's partial Platonism

Wittgenstein's preparatory notebooks for the *Tractatus* do give some suggestive help with this issue. In them, he compared our relation to the world to our relation to a work of art: "The work of art is the object seen *sub specie aeternitatis*; and the good life is the world seen *sub specie aeternitatis*. This is the connection between art and ethics."[33] In order to see the point of ethics, Wittgenstein suggests, we need to see the world as a completed whole, like a work of art. Then he writes,

> As a thing among things, each thing is equally insignificant; as a world, each one is equally significant. If I have been contemplating the stove, and then am told: but now all you know is the stove, my result does indeed seem trivial. For this represents the matter as if I had studied the stove as one among the many things in the world. But if I was contemplating the stove, *it* was my world, and everything else was colorless by contrast with it. . . . For it is equally possible to take the bare present image as the worthless momentary picture in the whole temporal world, or as the true world among shadows.[34]

If I was "contemplating" the stove, "*it* was my world," it was a completed whole, "the true world among shadows." This contrast between the "true world" and "shadows" strongly reminds us of Plato's Cave. We find the "true world," Wittgenstein suggests, the world that has "color" and is no longer "worthless," through what he's calling "contemplating" (*kontemplieren*) the object. In this way a kind of ascent takes place, from "shadows" to the true world of color and value. What's crucial, evidently, is to view the stove as itself, and not merely as "one among the many things in the world": to see it as complete in itself, as we see a work of art. If we could see the world itself in the way that Wittgenstein imagines himself seeing the stove, as itself and not merely "one among the many things," then apparently we would see its value, its "color," and we would have the "good life."

Here Wittgenstein captures one of Plato's basic thoughts, that the thing appreciated as "itself," and not merely as "one among many," is the true thing and the locus of value. So this is a sense in which we could say that one realm is "higher" than the other. One realm or the objects within it are contemplated *as themselves*, and not merely as "one among the many things."

However, under the *Tractatus*'s "silence" doctrine, this whole explanation too would strictly have to be dismissed, because it goes beyond what we can "speak of."[35] What Plato and Hegel do and Wittgenstein does not do is to link the contemplation of "itself"-ness to our experience of *ourselves*, as (potentially) whole and thereby "true" (as in "the true world"). Plato and Hegel agree with Wittgenstein that the higher, "true" realm isn't conceivable from within the lower one, which is "colorless" and without "value." But they point out that we experience the lower realm not by itself, but in its dynamic relationship to the higher one, in what I've called our "identity crisis" between lower and higher conceptions of ourselves. If this identity crisis is our primary experience, then we do have access to a dimension in which the two realms are comparable. It's the dimension of our own potential wholeness, freedom, or being ourselves, as opposed to fragmentariness, heteronomy, and not being ourselves.

In religion this is the dimension of "temptation," in which a person's appetites and self-importance distract the person from his or her higher calling. Plato and Hegel both elaborate on this traditional dramatic pattern: Plato with his account of eros and the unification of the soul and Hegel with his account of "sublation" (*Aufhebung*, "lifting up") as the way Nature becomes Spirit or selfhood. In both cases the traditional drama is explained as the drama of overcoming natural obstacles in order to become fully oneself. Nor is this only a "moral" drama, in the usual sense of the word; for the pursuit of truth is a part of the same drama insofar as we must constantly choose between pursuing truth and protecting our self-importance, by protecting our current opinions. So in both the moral version and the epistemological version of the drama, we choose between lower attractions and the higher aspiration through which we can be fully ourselves, and real as ourselves, and thus contribute the fullest reality to the world.

But in his preoccupation with sheer description of the "world," as such, and with "value" and "God" as counterposed to it, Wittgenstein omits both versions of this traditional inner drama, and with them our contribution to value and God, or full reality. Despite what he wrote in his notebooks about the "true world," he doesn't get into focus the way in which our inner effort and inner drama contribute to that world.[36] And thus he unintentionally encourages the subsequent descent of much English-language philosophy into mere scientism, the doctrine that only the study of objective "facts" is really rational.[37]

Wittgenstein and Schopenhauer

It seems that Wittgenstein's notion of the "mystical" was heavily influenced by Arthur Schopenhauer's notion of it, in his widely read *The World as Will and Representation* (1958, first published 1818). Schopenhauer had been eighteen years younger than Hegel and had competed with him briefly as a university lecturer in Berlin. Schopenhauer's bleak view of the world as a realm of irrational "will" struck several generations of readers as inspiring in its disillusioned "realism," while his mystical side reminded people of Buddhism. And Wittgenstein read Schopenhauer with enthusiasm in his youth.[38]

But Schopenhauer's notion of what we might call the "higher" (mysticism) is neither motivated nor rationally accessible from within the "lower" (what Schopenhauer calls the "will"). Schopenhauer does find glimpses of liberation in the human capacity for compassion and in art, but he doesn't explain how these can be present in the world that by its nature is pervaded by irrational "will." Instead, what Schopenhauer offers is, in effect, a blank, unmediated dualism. There is no intelligible relation between the lower side and the higher side.

And Wittgenstein's model is similar: an interesting dual "metaphysics," but with no mediation between lower and higher through either an account of our "soul" or identity, or a narrative line. One can appreciate Schopenhauer's and Wittgenstein's celebration of "the mystical" without feeling that they respond adequately to our need to understand it. Nor, consequently, do they respond to our need for freedom. Dualisms such as they present deprive us not only of any unifying "sense" but also of real freedom, since freedom without sense winds up being, effectively, arbitrariness.

After Wittgenstein

Unfortunately, philosophers who couldn't see how to appropriate Wittgenstein's dualistic "mystical" did not, in general, go in search of a more intelligible version of mysticism. Not finding clarity on this issue in Bradley or in Whitehead, they abandoned, as Moore and Russell had done before them, the whole notion of a higher reality. And what they were left with was, in general, scientism.

When Alfred Jules Ayer asserted in his *Language, Truth, and Logic* (1946, first published 1936) that "statements of value . . . are simply expressions of emotion which can be neither true nor false," he assumed that he was merely restating (among other things) Wittgenstein's doctrine in the *Tractatus* that ethics "cannot be expressed" in a logical form.[39] Ayer gave no attention to Wittgenstein's allusions to what "shows itself," nor to what Wittgenstein might have meant by his gnomic remarks about "value," "God," and "the mystical."[40] Though it can be said in Ayer's defense that Ayer had even less text from which to understand Wittgenstein's early thinking than we have, because Wittgenstein's preparatory notebooks for the *Tractatus* weren't published until years after Ayer wrote his book. And of course it's true that science is an amazing human accomplishment.

Contrary to Wittgenstein's notion in his notebooks of the "good life" as "the true world," Ayer dismissed all questions of value as mere "emotion." Since they weren't capable of being discussed rationally, he felt no need to say or do anything constructive about them. This was effectively nihilism. Given the difficulty of articulating in a useful way Wittgenstein's notion of what "shows itself," it's hard to blame Ayer for drawing this conclusion—if he wasn't prepared to look further than Wittgenstein and Russell for help.

Due, then, to the unsolved problems that Bradley, Whitehead, and Wittgenstein had left behind them, an anti-Platonist scientism resembling Ayer's had a hegemony over English-speaking philosophy in the mid-twentieth century, in writers like Rudolf Carnap, who moved from Vienna to the United States, and Willard Van Orman Quine at Harvard. Today, following Quine, what amounts to the same view presents itself in the guise of "naturalism," which is just as dogmatic as Ayer's scientism in its a priori exclusion of the idea of higher degrees of reality or a higher standard than "nature." On the other hand, the whole history of English-language "meta-ethics" during the latter half of the twentieth century, in writers such as Richard Hare, Philippa Foot, David Gauthier, Allan Gibbard, John McDowell, Christine Korsgaard, and Thomas Scanlon, is a protracted effort to find a way of thinking about value which would escape the ethical nihilism to which a fascination with science had led the previous generation.

One natural though extreme response to this situation was to hold science itself responsible for it, as Martin Heidegger did when he described science as a part of the modern "demonic" "enfeeblement" of spirit.[41] The major streams of twentieth-century philosophy, the scientistic and the anti-scientist, were so to speak hypnotized by science, either worshipping it or demonizing it. And Wittgenstein's dichotomy of what can be "expressed" and what "shows itself" didn't show a way out of this hypnosis, insofar as it didn't make the relationship between the two intelligible.

None of these thinkers noted how by pursuing truth rather than appetite-satisfaction or self-importance or the confirming of preexisting opinions, the activity of science itself surpassed "nature" in an important way and thus helped to constitute a higher, "supernatural" reality. So that science falls into place among the several ways, including ethics, love, the arts, and religion, in which humans intermittently surpass "nature" and thus participate in a higher reality.

A comprehensive view of these forms of ascent, such as Plato and Hegel adumbrate, gives us a freedom that the dominant twentieth- and twenty-first-century views can't give us because they all involve unresolved and apparently arbitrary boundaries, such as the boundary between science and the "humanities" or between what can be expressed and what "shows itself."

Fortunately, a number of recent writers have tried to be more integrative than the pro- and anti-science schools of thought. Among them, I will discuss John Niemeyer Findlay (1903–87), Iris Murdoch (1919–99), Wilfrid Sellars (1912–89), John McDowell (1942–), and Sebastian Rödl (1967–). For lack of space I am going to have to omit, with regret, a discussion of the work of Michael Polanyi (1891–1976), in his *Personal Knowledge* (1958) and other works, which presented a basically Platonic ontology, epistemology, and theology, deeply grounded in twentieth-century science and very creative in its categorial structure.

J. N. Findlay's "Transcendence of the Cave"

Having written separate books on Plato, Kant, and Hegel, plus two volumes of Gifford Lectures, *The Discipline of the Cave* (1966) and *The Transcendence of the Cave* (1967), in which he developed his own version of philosophical mysticism, John Niemeyer Findlay should, it seems, have made the present book unnecessary. I treasure large parts of, especially, *The Transcendence of the Cave*. But I have problems with Findlay's work.

I'll begin with the historical issue. Regarding Plato and Hegel, both of whom he greatly admires, Plato is Findlay's exemplar of philosophical "transcendence," as in "the transcendence of the cave," while he takes Hegel, by contrast, to be an advocate of a "radically immanent teleology."[42] It hasn't occurred to Findlay that one could understand Hegel as justifiably criticizing conventional conceptions of "transcendence" and advocating an alternative "true transcendence" which would parallel Hegel's well-known "true infinity." So that Hegel like Aristotle would be a great "Platonist," in an important sense of the term, who agrees with Plato about the centrality of "ascent" (i.e., transcendence) and with a great deal of Plato's work about the integral role of the body within that process of ascent.

In his *Hegel: A Re-Examination* (1958), Findlay's interpretation of Hegel's doctrine of true infinity is that

> true Infinity is ... simply finitude associated with *free variability*. A mathematical or logical formula is "infinite" in the Hegelian sense since it admits of an indefinite number of valid substitutions. I, the subject, am likewise infinite, since I can, without prejudice to my identity, *imagine myself* in anyone and everyone's shoes. (p. 164; emphases altered)

What is missing from this interpretation is the notion of freedom as self-determination. Hegel's critique of the finite, the critique that makes the finite give way to the infinite, is that the finite isn't really itself (isn't "*an sich*") because it is made what it is by its relationships to innumerable other finite things. And likewise his critique of the "spurious infinite" (*schlechte Unendlichkeit*) that is defined as not being the finite is that the spurious infinite equally fails to be self-determining, because it's defined and determined by this relationship of not being the finite. So the whole point of true infinity is that it *achieves* self-determination, by including the finite within itself by being the finite's going beyond itself. As Hegel says, "Infinity *is* only as a self-transcending of the finite."[43] None of this is captured by notions of "free variability" or "imagining oneself" in other people's shoes.

What we need to realize is that Hegel's critique of the finite and of the spurious infinite is also, in effect, a critique of ordinary conceptions of *transcendence*, such as Findlay relies on when he asserts, in *The Transcendence of the Cave*, that he will go beyond Hegel's "cave." Such an assertion, which defines the outcome by its contrast to what it supposedly goes beyond, produces what is consequently merely another finitude, limited by that contrast, and thus (in effect) another segment of what is really just a single world, a single collection of finite things. There is no real transcendence here.

In fact, however, it turns out that despite Findlay's programmatic statements, including the title of his Chapter 6, "Other-worldly Geography," we learn within that chapter that his "other world is . . . not so much another world as *another half of one world*, which two halves only make full rounded sense when seen in their mutual relevance and interconnection" (p. 121; emphasis added). In which case, Findlay would not be flouting the principle of true infinity as he appears to with his talk of "other-worldly geography."

Thus I think that contrary to his programmatic claims, Findlay's *Transcendence of the Cave* can serve to illustrate and elaborate on what is, in fact, essentially the same picture that Hegel presents. It is unfortunate that Findlay distracts us from this relationship with his contrast between what he calls Platonic "other-worldly geography" and Hegelian "immanent teleology."

Underlying these historical and conceptual issues, the fundamental problem with *Transcendence of the Cave* is that like Bradley, Whitehead, and Wittgenstein, Findlay doesn't focus on self-determining freedom or explain its role in connecting our everyday experience with higher levels of reality. The absence of this lived connection between lower and higher gives Findlay's overall presentation a flavor of detached intellectualism, which is only partially ameliorated by the charmingly Wordsworthian poetical remarks in his final chapter. This may be part of the reason why, as also happened with Bradley, Whitehead, and Wittgenstein, Findlay's philosophical mysticism has not found a wide audience and has not, as far as I can tell, been further developed by the generation of philosophers that came after him.

Iris Murdoch

Iris Murdoch's *Metaphysics as a Guide to Morals* (1993) contains the following highly suggestive passage:

> The work of art unifies our sensibility . . . while removing our petty egoistic anxiety. The art object is an analogy of the person-object, we intuit our best selves in its mirror.. . . . Art with which we are familiar stays with us as an intimation that love has power and the world makes sense. [And] we see in God in a magnified form the analogy between work of art and person. (p. 81)

By focusing on the "art object" and the analogous "person-object," Murdoch echoes Wittgenstein's analogy in his *Notebooks* between the work of art and the good life ("The work of art is the object seen *sub specie aeternitatis*; and the good life is the world seen *sub specie aeternitatis*"). In both the art object and the ("best-self") person-object one might say there is a wholeness that we miss when we view the object, as Wittgenstein said, merely as "one among the many things in the world."

With her suggestion that the art work's unifying of our sensibility removes "our petty egoistic anxiety," Murdoch conjures up the "identity crisis" drama that is fundamental for Platonism. Will we achieve wholeness, or will we remain mere collections of appetites, opinions, and self-importance? For the wholeness that is egoism's opposite, Murdoch uses the same image that Whitehead used: the mirror in which we see "our best selves" (in Whitehead, our "greatness"). For Murdoch as for Wittgenstein and Whitehead, God is the most comprehensive instance ("in a magnified form") of this unifying wholeness that we see initially in art and in the person.

And finally Murdoch elaborates art's role and, by implication, the roles of person and God as well, with her description of art as "an intimation that love has power and the world makes sense." She is suggesting that we should understand our unification or wholeness, and our ascent toward them, as a function of love. What love is, what kind of power it has, and how the world can make sense—this is indeed a great part of what the Platonic tradition aims to show us. Like Plato and Hegel, Murdoch unifies art, life, and God through their shared theme of unification through love.[44]

This unification is why she can say later on that "no existing thing could be what we have meant by God. Any existing God would be less than God" (p. 508). For, as Hegel and Plato explain, every existing thing is bounded and constrained by other existing things, and thus can't be entirely itself, entirely unified. "But," Murdoch goes on, "what led us to conceive of [God] does exist and is *constantly* experienced and pictured," in, I presume, our experience (which points beyond the limits of mere existing things) of unification and wholeness in ourselves and in art. If we think of God not as an existing thing among others but as a unification ("*sub specie aeternitatis*," as Wittgenstein puts it) that goes beyond everything that exists among other things, we perhaps glimpse what God-talk has really wanted to be about.

Unfortunately, Murdoch doesn't address fundamental questions that the Plato/Hegel tradition addresses in detail, in particular, the issue of the relation between art/persons/God and the physical sciences, and the issue of the relation between rationality and morality. (If egoism is "petty," why do so many theorists regard it as a fully rational policy?) So what Murdoch gives us is only a brilliant *portion* of Platonism.

Wilfrid Sellars's "incipient *Meditations Hegeliennes*"

Now I turn to two recent thinkers who are aware of having a significant affinity to Hegel, though neither of them endorses a "higher" reality or mysticism, as such. Wilfrid Sellars and John McDowell resemble Hegel in that they each make a systematic effort to (as Sellars puts it) "fuse into one vision" the scientific and the humanistic points of view.[45]

Sellars sought to unite the descriptive and explanatory resources of science with the "language of community and individual intentions," which "provide[s] the ambience of principles and standards (above all, those which make meaningful discourse and rationality itself possible) within which we live our own individual lives."[46] Thus Sellars recognized that science itself, as a rational endeavor, presupposes an "ambience of principles and standards" which may or may not be recognized by particular sciences as being objectively present in what they study, but which will be recognized by self-aware scientists as the preconditions of the rational inquiry that they aim to engage in. Here Sellars departs in an important way from conventional "naturalism," and of course I applaud his doing so. He is acknowledging that not all truth can necessarily be grasped by the methods of the natural sciences.

However, it's not clear how successful Sellars is in "fusing" the space of reasons, or normativity, with the space of natural laws. That self-aware scientists must acknowledge the authority of something other than natural laws doesn't settle the question of what "community and individual intentions" in particular they should acknowledge. Most fundamentally, one might ask, why should communities or individuals embrace anything like science, at all? Why should we think of ourselves as rational beings? There is after all a tradition from Epicurus through David Hume which asserts that reason is and ought to be the slave of the passions—that is, that knowledge and truth, as such, are distractions from the real business of human life. If this tradition is correct, then Sellars's "space of reasons" is a mere distraction. Sellars assumes throughout his work that we are interested in knowledge, truth, and science, and not merely in satisfying whatever desires we may have. But insofar as he doesn't show why this is or ought to be the case, he doesn't fully "fuse" the human realm, including the pursuit of truth and science, with the world as the sciences describe and explain it. For he hasn't demonstrated why the human realm needs to include the pursuit of truth and science.

A second problem is, in fact, acknowledged by Sellars at the end of his *Science and Metaphysics* (1968), where he says that although he thinks he has shown that thinking of oneself as a rational being entails accepting epistemic oughts that are binding on all rational beings, he can't show that a rational being is obliged to concern herself about the general (not merely epistemic) welfare of all rational beings (pp. 225–6). That is, he can't show that a rational being needs to be moral.

With regard to both of these problems, Plato and Hegel are more thorough. Regarding the question of why we should think of ourselves as rational beings, Plato and Hegel describe the role of the pursuit of truth in our becoming self-governing and thus fully ourselves, rather than being mere puppets of our heritage and environment. Kant, too, picks up this theme in a major way, with his notion of rational "autonomy." Sellars, however, in his extensive discussion of Kant, doesn't focus on autonomy. Like the many other twentieth-century thinkers who take science too much for granted, Sellars doesn't articulate the drama of "higher" versus "lower" goals and satisfactions. Lacking this grounding in common experience, his effort to overcome the dualism of the sciences versus the humanities can't be fully successful.

As for the issue of why a rational being should regard itself as part of a moral community, Plato and Hegel again focus on the way in which rational functioning is self-government. Insofar as one seeks to be self-governing, one must not be governed by the boundary between oneself and others, because this would entail being governed by something (namely, the boundary) that's other than oneself. Hence, nothing that's fully self-governing can make a primary issue, as the paradigmatic nonmoral agent does, of the boundary between itself and others. Rather, the "I" that fully governs itself must become a boundless "we."

This transition to a kind of "infinity," which Hegel spells out in his *Science of Logic* and his *Encyclopedia* and Plato adumbrates in his *Republic, Symposium, Theaetetus*, and *Timaeus* cannot be made if one assumes, as Sellars does, that persons are simply finite beings. One result of this assumption, as Plato and Hegel point out, is that neither you nor I can be fully self-governing. And a second result is that neither you nor I, so conceived, are rationally required to concern ourselves about the welfare of others.

So when Sellars referred to his essay on "Empiricism and the Philosophy of Mind" as his "incipient *Meditations Hegeliennes*,"[47] he was neither alluding to the essential feature of Hegel's thought which is his notion of rational self-government and his resulting critique of and transcendence of the finite, nor, of course, drawing on Plato's parallel thoughts (which I'll discuss in Chapters 7 and 8). And consequently both the general importance of Sellars's "space of reasons," and its ethical content, remain unclear. But without clarity on these issues, we haven't "fused" the world as it's understood by the sciences with some of the most important features of our individual and communal functioning.

John McDowell's "Partial Enchantment"

Like Hegel and Sellars, John McDowell in his *Mind and World* (1994) wants to overcome the modern dualism in which "reason is separated from our animal nature" (p. 108), and we consequently have trouble understanding how they can relate to each other and interact. This problem of interaction takes two forms. First, it's difficult to understand how the products of reason, its concepts, can *apply to* nonrational nature. Coming, as they do, from a different source, there seems to be no guarantee that they will have anything to do with the nature that we hope they will illuminate. "The more we play up the connection between reason and freedom, the more we risk losing our grip on how exercises of concepts can constitute warranted judgments about the world. What we wanted to conceive as exercises of concepts threaten to degenerate into moves in a self-contained game" (p. 5).[48]

And second, reason's separation from our animal nature threatens us with a "disenchantment" (as Max Weber called it) which would empty nature of "meaning" (pp. 70–71). The world, viewed as nature, would be understood simply as a realm of natural laws, and not of reasons.

McDowell's response to the first (epistemological) form of the problem, how our concepts apply to a world that has a different source from theirs, is to suggest that since we're always viewing the world *through* our concepts, we can't view the relation between our concepts and nature from the "sideways-on" perspective that the supposed problem presupposes (pp. 34–36). The problem arises for us only in a realm of abstraction that has nothing to do with our actual lives.

As for the second (metaphysical) form of the problem, McDowell's way of preserving meaning in the world is to "keep nature as it were partially enchanted" (p. 85) by insisting on the reality of a "second nature" such as Aristotle suggested with his notion of ethical habituation, in *Nicomachean Ethics* book ii. The ethical habituation that Aristotle describes is, McDowell suggests, "a particular case of a general phenomenon: initiation into conceptual capacities . . . having one's eyes opened to reasons at large" (p. 84). "Such initiation," McDowell says,

> is a normal part of what it is for a human being to come to maturity, and that is why, although the structure of the space of reasons is alien to the layout of nature conceived as the realm of law, it does not take on the remoteness from the human that rampant platonism envisages. (p. 84)

(By "rampant platonism," I imagine McDowell is referring to the antagonistic dualism that people often find in Plato's *Phaedo*, which I'll discuss in Chapter 5.)

McDowell says that his picture of humans being initiated, through habituation, into conceptual capacities, "gives human reason enough of a foothold in the realm of law to satisfy any proper respect for modern natural science" (p. 84). That is, McDowell's picture shows how a creature that's based in the realm of natural law nevertheless rises (as I would say) above it, when it learns to respond to (ethical and other) reasons. This proposal seems to address both forms of the issue of reason's separation from our animal nature. It addresses the issue of "disenchantment" by giving us a world of reasons, and not just of natural laws; and it addresses the issue of how our rational concepts apply to the world of natural laws, by giving reason a "foothold" in that realm.

However, regarding his explanation of the "general phenomenon" of "initiation into conceptual capacities," McDowell like Sellars doesn't ask why we should regard such initiation as desirable. Why should we be guided by what McDowell regards as "normal human maturity"? Why are "concepts" preferable to merely reactive modes of functioning? If we say that concepts promise access to truth, we'll then have to explain why access to truth is desirable. It isn't helpful to say that we've simply been habituated to the rational kind of functioning, when David Hume and others regularly tell us that reason is and ought to be the slave of the passions.

I imagine McDowell might respond to these Humean doubts with the same quietism that was his response to the first form of the problem of reason versus our animal nature. We have in fact been initiated into conceptual capacities, we see the world through them, and that's, for us, the end of the matter.

But I have to ask, in response to McDowell's solution to both of these problems, doesn't it forcibly foreclose a natural inquiry? Naturalism has, in fact, been an ongoing preoccupation of inquirers since the atomists and sophists of ancient Greece. And it seems that we're quite familiar, not only in theoretical speculations but in everyday life, with the kinds of questions that naturalism tries, in its limited way, to explore. As when we face the question whether to satisfy a bodily desire or to curb it; or whether to maintain our opinion stoutly against criticism, or to try looking at the issue from our opponent's point of view as well as our own. These are familiar, everyday, practical questions. Not asking why initiation into conceptual capacities is desirable, McDowell doesn't identify or address the permanent "identity crisis" in which we're constantly having to decide whether, in fact, to be guided by reason or by our animal nature.

And it seems that our experience of this identity crisis should also be the key to grasping the relation between reason and our animal nature. There is nothing that we know better than this relation, with which most of us struggle, to one degree or another, every day. We know our animal nature by its contrast to reason, and we know reason by its contrast to our animal nature. This contrast is, as Hegel says, "concrete." Its extremes, when abstracted from the experience, are, in comparison, abstract.⁴⁹ The extremes, codified in naturalism and in "rampant Platonism," are what Kant, Sellars, and McDowell are struggling with. The solution, Plato and Hegel propose, is to focus not on the extremes as separate from each other but on our concrete experience of having to choose between them. Seen in that context, the relation between the extremes couldn't be clearer. It's only the abstractions that result from one-sided responses to the relation that land us in apparently insoluble problems.

McDowell and Hegel's "I am not in an *other*"

McDowell draws attention on p. 44 of *Mind and World* to the fact that Hegel addresses the issue of reason's relation to our animal nature with his assertion in the "Self-Consciousness" chapter of the *Phenomenology of Spirit* that "in thinking . . . I am not in an *other*" (§197; SuW 3:156). In his article "The Apperceptive I and the Empirical Self: Towards a Heterodox Reading of 'Lordship and Bondage' in Hegel's *Phenomenology*" (2003), McDowell aims to show in some detail how Hegel's "Self-Consciousness" chapter resolves the issue of reason's relation to our animal nature. And McDowell does show how, contrary to first appearances, the famous "Lordship and Bondage" section of the chapter can be understood as contributing to this project.⁵⁰ But McDowell omits what I take to be a crucial part of Hegel's argument, a part that in fact makes the argument more illuminating than what McDowell finds in it.

I show in my Hegel book (Wallace [2005], Chapters 3–6) that Hegel's account of reason's relation to our animal nature is that reason (as "infinity," the "Concept," or "Spirit") is *the self-transcending of* our animal nature (as the "finite," "Substance," or "Nature"). The sentence that McDowell quotes from the *Phenomenology of Spirit* ("In thinking . . . I am not in an *other*") in fact sums up what results from the "infinity" that Hegel had arrived at in the previous chapter (§§160-163; TWA 3:131-133). What Hegel calls "self-consciousness," the topic of the new chapter, is introduced in §163 (TWA 3:133) of the previous chapter as summing up that "infinity."

To be more specific about this "infinity," it's helpful to turn to Hegel's *Science of Logic*, in which he describes infinity more perspicuously than he does in the *Phenomenology*, where his account is shrouded in metaphor. In the *Science of Logic*, Hegel describes infinity as the finite's transcending or "sublating" itself:

> Infinity *is* only as a self-transcending [*Hinausgehen über sich*] of the finite. . . . The finite is not sublated [*aufgehoben*] by the infinite as by a power existing outside it; on the contrary, its infinity consists in sublating its own self.⁵¹

I have repeatedly mentioned the reason for this position that Hegel takes, which is that an "infinity" or "transcendence" which was "a power existing outside" the finite or the immanent, would fail to be infinite or to transcend, since it would be bounded by the finite and thus it would itself be finite, like what it aims to transcend. It would be what Hegel calls a "spurious infinity" (*schlechte Unendlichkeit*), something that was supposed to be infinite but failed.

Now in the sentence that McDowell quotes from the *Phenomenology*, Hegel assumes that the "thinking" to which he refers is infinite, and truly (not "spuriously") so. (Just as, later on in Hegel's system, the Concept's "subjectivity" is truly infinite in relation to Substance's finitude, and Spirit is truly infinite in relation to Nature.) And thus the reason why, as Hegel says, this "thinking" isn't "in" something that's "other" than itself is that a true infinity, as he says in the *Logic*, "*is* only as a *self-transcending* of the finite," and in that sense it's "in," rather than being "other than," what it transcends and thinks about. Thus the "reason" that McDowell refers to, and which Hegel refers to in the quoted sentence (*Phenomenology of Spirit*, §197) as "thinking," "*is*" (in Hegel's words in the *Logic*) "only as a self-transcending of" what McDowell calls our "animal nature." They are not fundamentally separate phenomena or realms: the infinite, reason, and thinking are, as we might say, "in" the finite and "in" "our animal nature," inasmuch as they are the self-transcending of the finite and of our animal nature.

Here Hegel is making the point that I've been making here: that what links our experience of our animal nature to our experience of rational norms is our experience of choosing between the two, and often of trying to rise above the one to the other. Rational norms are "in" our animal nature insofar as they are the effort of the animals that we are, to go beyond being merely animals.

So this is Hegel's solution, which he elaborates in the third part of his *Logic* as the "Concept" (*Begriff*) and in his *Encyclopedia* as "Spirit" (*Geist*), to the modern dualism, which McDowell is addressing, of reason versus our animal nature. Hegel's solution applies to both the epistemological and the metaphysical forms of the issue. On the epistemological side, it explains that our rational concepts apply to the physical world because we belong, both prior to and after our self-transcendence, to the physical world. What happens here is *Aufhebung*, "sublation," "lifting up," rather than rejection. And on the metaphysical side Hegel explains that thanks to that *Aufhebung*, that self-transcendence, our world is an ("enchanted") world of reasons, and not merely of natural laws.

Hegel's chapter in the *Phenomenology* on "Self-consciousness," of which McDowell brings out important features, is an earlier elaboration of this same solution, which Hegel thinks he has already arrived at in principle in the previous chapter of the *Phenomenology* with his conception of infinity.

McDowell and Hegel: The upshot

Now the main thing that I want to say about the relationship between Hegel and McDowell that's emerging from this bit of textual commentary, is that McDowell is hampered in his agenda by his not following Hegel more closely. McDowell is hampered by the fact that he doesn't bring out, as Hegel does, the way in which a self that deserves the name because it's self-determining emerges through the "identity crisis" that we often experience between the higher activities of reason and the lower satisfactions of our "animal nature." As was the case with Whitehead, Wittgenstein, Murdoch, and Sellars, McDowell too leaves the drama of reason versus appetites and mere opinions so unspoken that his readers may well never in fact think of it as a drama. But it's our experience of this drama that gives us the means to solve McDowell's problem of the relation between reason and our animal nature. For this experience shows us precisely how reason is at work *in* the being that we might otherwise be inclined to identify simply in terms of its animal nature. This is what Hegel shows us with his conception, which McDowell overlooks, of true infinity as the finite's transcending itself.[52]

Self-determination is, in fact, a frequent topic of McDowell's later *Having the World in View* (2009), as is appropriate for a book that deals extensively with German Idealism. But McDowell doesn't mention how this self-determination brings something into being that's more *itself* than what's not self-determining. In his response to Robert Pippin's reading of Hegel, McDowell asserts that "we should not be frightened away from holding that initiation into the right sort of communal practice makes a *metaphysical* difference. . . . Responsiveness to reasons . . . marks out a fully-fledged human individual as no longer a merely biological particular, but a being of a metaphysically new kind" (p. 172). But I don't find in McDowell any spelled-out account of how this metaphysically new kind of being relates to the other, merely biological kind of being. That the former has a "foothold" in the latter is only a hint. How is it that the world contains two fundamentally different kinds of being? How is it that what looks in many respects like many "nonrational" animals is in fact a metaphysically new kind of being? How did it become a "normal" part of this being's "coming to maturity" that it is initiated into a space of reasons? Why, in fact, does reason arise and distinguish itself from "animal nature"?

Plato and Hegel answer these questions by locating the two kinds of being within the single process of the emergence of the one from the other. We experience this process constantly in our efforts to be self-determining, which we understand as aiming at the goal of our being a real self. The ultimate explanation, then, is that what is more real, by being self-determining, must supersede what is less real. Though our understanding of what it would take for us to be truly real is often limited, none of us wants to be anything less than that.

Why should we regard what is self-determining as more real than what is not self-determining? What is self-determining is real as itself, or *an sich* as Hegel puts it in the *Science of Logic*, rather than "for others" (*Seinfüranderes*); and what is real as itself clearly has a kind of reality that other beings don't have. Hegel dubs this reality simply "reality" [*Realität*] (in contrast to "being," "being-for-others," and so forth). His thought, which he lays out at length in the first two chapters of the *Science of Logic*, is simply that what is fully "itself" *is* in a way that what is partly through others is not. Which, I suggest, we can all confirm through the experience that we have of being more fully ourselves at some times than at others. We know what it's like to be real "as ourselves," and not merely as a product of our environment, and given the choice, we prefer the former. We want to really be ourselves. (Though in various kinds of despair, we certainly can sometimes feel that we have no choice about the matter.)

Hegel's philosophical system elaborates everywhere on this notion of becoming fully real or real as oneself. His themes of "sublation" (*Aufhebung*, literally, "lifting up"), "reality," "infinity," "freedom," the "Idea," "Spirit," "God," and "elevation to God" (*Erhebung zu Gott*) all refer in their various ways to this same nisus or process. His fundamental conclusion in this regard is that "it is not the finite which is the real [*das Reale*], but the infinite" (HSL p. 149; GW 21:136; SuW 5:164). The finite isn't "real" because it's determined in part by its relation, through its limit, to something that's other than it, namely, to other finite things. Infinity, on the other hand, has no "other," and consequently can't lose "reality" to an other. "Freedom," the "Idea," "Spirit," and "God" (whether as "absolute Idea" or as "absolute Spirit") each represents a successful ascent to this kind of infinity or "reality."[53]

If we don't bring out this theme of ascent in Hegel, we don't bring out the most obvious way in which he speaks to everyday human experience and to historical human culture as we see it in religion, ethics, psychology, and literature. Nor do we bring out his proposal that what connects reason and our animal nature, which is to say, infinity and finitude or "Spirit" and "Nature," is precisely our ongoing, everyday experience of choosing between them and trying (sometimes) to rise above one of them, to the other.

It connects them because, as I've said, this rising above, this sublation or ascent, in Hegel, is always a *self*-transcendence, a preservation as well as a cancellation, a true infinity, which is why it can be the familiar experience ("trying to rise above") that it is. This is how Hegel avoids the philosophical "abstractions" that create an apparent metaphysical and epistemological problem (as opposed to a familiar moral challenge) about the relation between reason and our animal nature. The fuller, because self-determining reality that is the rational self is "in" the less real, because not self-determining "animal nature" because it is the latter's self-transcendence. This is Hegel's solution to the metaphysical problem. And as for the epistemological problem, since the rational self's concepts are ways in which the material "animals" that we are transcend our mere (non-spontaneous and finite) materiality and constitute something that's spontaneous and infinite, they are ways in which these material animals function "in" the material world, and thus they must apply to non-spontaneous and finite materiality, if only by identifying the way in which that materiality transcends itself.

Thus the notion of ascent to infinity, and the associated notions of the Concept and Spirit, as Hegel elaborates them, are crucially important for the issues that McDowell is addressing. Indeed, the Platonic tradition which Hegel is following here, and which McDowell and others don't draw on as much as Hegel does, has resources that are indispensable for addressing these issues.

Sebastian Rödl on "self-consciousness" and nature

In a series of recent books, Sebastian Rödl has presented what is, to the best of my knowledge, the most articulate and coherent recent account of the higher reality of "self-consciousness," and thus of what Plato, Aristotle, Kant, and Hegel are all driving at. Rödl shows in convincing detail how fundamental concepts shared by (especially) Aristotle and Hegel resolve central present-day debates that are often conducted without reference to these concepts. I will pick out a few especially significant pieces of Rödl's evolving oeuvre.

Rödl's second book in English, *Categories of the Temporal: An Inquiry into the Forms of the Finite Intellect* ("CT," 2012), offers an improved version of Kant's alternative to empiricism.[54] Rödl's thesis, according to the dust jacket, is that "the temporal and the sensible, and the atemporal and the intelligible, are aspects of one reality and cannot be understood independently of one another." He demonstrates this by showing how empiricism, which accepts only the temporal as real, makes the temporal unintelligible (CT pp. 12–15), whereas the (atemporal) "categories of" the temporal—substance, state, movement form, substance form, subject form—constitute, together with the temporal and the sensible, an intelligible totality. This is similar to Hegel's "true infinity" (and to Hegel's *Encyclopedia* as a whole, which gets its structure from true infinity), in which the merely finite or temporal is, as such, unreal, but it can "transcend itself" through the infinite (the atemporal categories of Hegel's *Logic*) and thus constitute something real.

Species of Rödl's general "substance form" are "phusis" (nature) and "psyche" (life, soul) (CT p. 11), of which reason and knowledge are an actualization ("energeia") (CT p. 207). We learn about reason and knowledge in Rödl's *Self-Consciousness* ("SC," 2007) and *Self-Consciousness and Objectivity: An Introduction to Absolute Idealism* ("SCO," 2018), which deal with the "power of knowledge" or of "judgment." "The science of man, of which the theory of knowledge forms a part, is not an empirical science. It is pursued not by observing men and drawing inferences from these data but by articulating what we know of man *by being men*"

(SC p.164, emphasis added). That is, it proceeds, like Plato's *Phaedo* (98b-99c) and like Kant, from first-person experience, the "I think."

Rödl begins by arguing that an "I think" needs to be guided by a normative order, and not merely by occurrent desires, because desires come and go, while an "I" unifies temporal stages in extended intentional projects. So an "I" must be guided not by occurrent desires but by what Rödl calls "infinite ends," such as health (SC p. 38). Unlike occurrent desires, infinite ends aren't indexed to the individual at a particular point in time. An imperative, which expresses an infinite end, "brings its object under a normative order, representing it as bound to, yet liable to fall from, this order" (SC p. 66). This is the fundamental Platonic vertical axis on which I harp in this book: we are "bound to, yet liable to fall from" higher ideals or norms, constantly faced with the choice of whether or not to be guided by them.

"Action," then, is a temporally integrated process that is in fact guided by a normative (higher) order of infinite ends. Regarding such action, Rödl comments that

> it has been held that, since its essential normativity cannot be accommodated within the natural sciences, we might be forced to throw the concept of action and with it action concepts on the trash heap of outdated theories. [But . . .] Renouncing action concepts is a form of self-annihilation: logical self-annihilation. It annihilates the power to think and say "I." (SC p. 63)

To which one might add that insofar as we aim to make up our own minds about what to do and believe, the notion of the "self" and the "I" is not one that we can do without.[55]

As to the relation between action and other sorts of events in the world, Rödl writes,

> An action concept . . . signifies the principle of temporal unity of its instances. . . . Even if one could apprehend all the phases of someone's making breakfast without employing action concepts, one would not thereby apprehend her *making breakfast.*. . . It is impossible to isolate what happens when someone is acting intentionally from the mind of the acting subject. (SC pp. 51–55; emphasis added)

This last sentence is the fundamental thesis of Plato/Hegel "idealism," first stated in Plato's *Phaedo* (98b-99c) or perhaps in Parmenides's fragment 3 (*to gar auto noein estin te kai einai* ["for the same thing can be thought as can be"]). Much of reality can't be identified as such without reference to what is going on in the minds of acting subjects; and the reality that has this character is (as I put it) "higher" in that, as Rödl says, we are "bound to, yet liable to fall from" the rational order through which this reality says "I."

Parallel to this account of action and action explanation, Rödl presents an account of belief and belief explanation:

> Belief, or theoretical thought, is a reality that includes its subject's knowledge of it, which knowledge therefore is unmediated first-person knowledge. For, beliefs essentially figure in belief explanations, and it defines this form of explanation that, if a belief can be explained in this way, its subject is in a position thus to explain it. Her knowledge that and why she believes what she does, which she expresses in giving the explanation, is not a separate existence from what it represents. (SC p. 100)

That is, as the action of making breakfast depends upon the maker's intention to make breakfast, the existence of a belief depends upon the believer's knowledge of it. The intention and the making are not separate realities, nor are the belief and the believer's knowledge of it. Because these are not separate realities, the maker and the believer have direct knowledge of their making and belief, respectively.

But as Rödl goes on to show, this reality of action and belief of which we have direct knowledge is also a "material" reality, inasmuch as we predicate of ourselves changes of state and movements, and these require "a principle of temporal unity of [their] object," which will be a material substance concept such as "man" (SC p. 130). So Rödl's "idealism" doesn't reject the notion of material substance. As he says, "Our account of 'I' yields a metaphysics that is as idealist as it is materialist" (SC p. 15). The only thing that Rödl's account rejects is the empiricist notion that the only source of knowledge is passive receptivity. Rather, we have first-person knowledge of our actions and beliefs, and thus of the reality that they constitute, from their non-receptive, rational "spontaneity."

But while Rödl's view combines rational spontaneity and material substances, it's not (in this respect, at least) a dualism. Since we material substances possess this spontaneity, and first-person knowledge of it, it's clear that spontaneity and first-person knowledge are not a domain that's separate from the material world, but rather something like what Hegel calls the finite's or nature's (the material world's) transcending itself[56]—transcending, in that their action constitutes something that knows itself, and thus has a self, in a way that finite things and nature as such do not.

Rödl's Hegelian "Self-Constitution" and Hegel's "Absolute Idea"

In a recent essay entitled "The Science of Logic as the Self-Constitution of the Power of Knowledge" (2017), Rödl draws a detailed parallel between his account of knowers as rationally spontaneous material substances and Hegel's derivation, in the *Science of Logic*, of teleology, life, and knowledge from mechanism. What Rödl unfolds here, following Hegel, subsumes and thus illuminates Rödl's accounts in SC of action as causation, of material substance's spontaneity, and of the power of knowledge. The process that Hegel and Rödl present is "self-constituting" because it is the emergence of an integrated self from, and through, previously disparate multiplicities. Which indeed is what we saw earlier in true infinity, in which the infinite surpasses the finite's unreality or lack of selfhood through the finite's going beyond its finitude into *self*-determination. The sequence from mechanical causation to the power of knowledge, which Hegel unfolds and which Rödl partly unfolds, is an elaborate true infinity.

I say that Rödl *partly* unfolds this sequence because Rödl's version, in this paper and his other publications up to the present, lacks one important feature that makes Hegel's version, unlike Rödl's, an actual infinity. This is a problem that I haven't posed for any of the preceding more or less Hegelian thinkers, because none of them come close enough to Hegel's full accomplishment to make it appropriate to raise this issue.

In Hegel's exposition, knowledge (or "cognition": *Erkennen*) is divided into theoretical and practical, the Idea of the True and the Idea of the Good, and these are integrated as the Absolute Idea; whereas in Rödl's version, the unfolding stops at knowledge as such. And Hegel's division and integration of theoretical and practical is not at all accidental, because it's anticipated by and completes the prior development of the entire *Logic* from Being to the Subject. One can see in that development how subjectivity and knowledge necessarily have theoretical and practical, "fact," and "value" aspects. This is the case because when subjectivity first emerges in the *Logic*'s Doctrine of Being ("only the beginning of the Subject," as Hegel puts it [HSL p. 115; GW 21:103; SuW 5:123]), it is in connection with the issue of how being can be determinate, whether "in itself" (*an sich*) or only through its relation to others (*Sein-für-anderes*). There is no distinction here between fact and value, knowledge and action; the whole issue is how something can be "itself" at all. But the attentive reader will realize that being "oneself" is already implicitly the issue of self-determination and inner freedom,[57] which is what Hegel means by "Subject" and what he finally unfolds explicitly in the *Logic*'s culminating "Subjective Logic."

Because a Subject is incomplete without an Object, the Subjective Logic takes the forms successively of Subjectivity and Objectivity. And then the issues of theoretical cognition (the Subject's knowledge of Objects) and practical cognition (the Subject's influence on Objects), or "fact" and "value," are already implicitly present. Hegel develops Objectivity first (and this is where Rödl's narrative begins) as Mechanism, which however fails to render anything "itself." But to be fully real, an Object must be fully itself. This, as Rödl points out, is why Hegel proceeds from Mechanism to Teleology. Teleology then fails in a similar way, and gives way to Life, as another candidate for "itself"-ness; and Life similarly has to give way to

Cognition (*Erkennen*, which Rödl represents as "knowledge"). Rödl's treatment of this sequence is valuable. But as I say, he does not go on, as Hegel does, to divide Cognition into the "Idea of the True" and the "Idea of the Good." Hegel carries out this division in order to reflect the issues of Subject versus Object, theory versus practice, and fact versus value, which as we just saw (but Rödl does not note) are inherent in Subject-hood as such.

And then, as I said, Hegel finally integrates the Idea of the True and the Idea of the Good as the "Absolute Idea," as he must do in order for Cognition to enable Being to be fully "itself." If, as occurs in Kant and in Wittgenstein's *Tractatus*, the true and the good, theory and practice, and fact and value were left facing each other, with their relationship to each other unclear, we wouldn't have achieved anything that's fully clarified or (therefore) anything that's fully itself. But Hegel's point is that when we understand that the agenda of the entire exercise, that is, of his *Logic* as a whole, has been to find a version of Being that is in fact fully itself, by being fully self-determining, then we can see these aspects, the pursuit of the true and the pursuit of the good, as both serving that goal. This is because, as I've explained, pursuing ideals like truth and goodness makes us, ourselves, self-determining, and fully ourselves, as a puppet of externally induced opinions and appetites cannot be; and if we are thus self-determining, reality in general is self-determining, through us.

And when in this way we see the pursuit of the true and the pursuit of the good as both serving the goal of self-determination (in opposite directions, as it were), then their relationship to each other is indeed fully clear, and we do have before us a true infinity, a fully self-determining whole. Inasmuch as it's fully self-determining and thus fully "itself," this whole deserves the title of "reality" more than anything else does. Neither Subject nor Object (if the two are understood as opposed to each other) and neither fact nor value alone is self-determining or real in this sense.

In contrast to what I've just described in Hegel's *Logic*, Rödl's work does not yet integrate theory and practice, fact and value, in any explicit fashion, and thus it doesn't present a fully self-determining whole, a "reality" in Hegel's sense. Instead, Rödl's work leaves us with a residual unclarified dualism of theory versus practice, fact versus value. Nevertheless, through his accounts of the unfolding of selfhood from mechanical causation through knowledge, and thus of rational spontaneity as something that's accomplished by the material substances that we call human beings, Rödl does integrate the "humanistic" and the "scientific" conceptions of reality more systematically than Wittgenstein, Murdoch, Sellars, or McDowell have been able to.

And the poets

While philosophers try to clarify various aspects of the nexus of rational self-government, love, ethics, science, the arts, reality, and God, literary artists conjure up the nexus itself with images. Walt Whitman, Emily Dickinson, Gerard Manley Hopkins, Rainer Maria Rilke, Virginia Woolf, W. B. Yeats, T. S. Eliot, Mary Oliver, and others celebrate the incomparable experience of something free and transcendent in themselves and in the world:

> In the faces of men and women I see God, and in my own face in the glass. . . .
> I ascend from the moon.. . . . I ascend from the night,
> And perceive of the ghastly glimmer the sunbeams reflected,
> And debouch to the steady and central from the offspring great or small. . . .
> There is that in me . . . . I do not know what it is. . . .
> Do you see O my brothers and sisters?
> It is not chaos or death. . . . It is form and union and plan. . . . it is eternal life.. . . it is happiness.
>
> **(WALT WHITMAN)**[58]

3 FREEDOM AND FULL REALITY

The reason why the world lacks unity, and lies broken and in heaps, is, because man is disunited with himself.

                        RALPH WALDO EMERSON, *NATURE*, CHAPTER VIII

What does "God" have to do with "freedom"?

The idea that knowledge of God can be based on our experience of freedom and love may sound a bit strange. Much of what we hear about "God" connects God not with freedom but with an external authority that tells us what we should believe and do.

For example, the "militant" spirituality of Muslim and Christian fundamentalists shows little interest in listening to its opponents' thoughts or arguments. So it suggests that far from supporting the idea of "God," really free inquiry would probably undermine it. The long history of religious dogmatism and intolerance only seems to confirm that "God" and free inquiry don't mix well. Orthodox Christianity has consigned its opponents not only to hellfire but also sometimes to earthly fire. The emperor Constantine, the prophet Muhammad's wars, the medieval Crusades, and the seventeenth century's wars of religion in Europe all allied religion to political domination. Nowadays, religious pressure causes the effective exclusion of the serious teaching of modern biology from many public and private schools in the United States.

This history obviously also makes one wonder what the idea of "God" really has to do with *love*. The dogmatic programs that I'm referring to clearly aren't motivated by love of human beings in general. Prominent promoters of these programs often seem to be more interested in power than in love. These promoters often associate adherents of other views with "Evil," a force that's absolutely opposed to the "Good" that they believe themselves to represent.

What in the idea of "God" encourages "Crusades" and "holy wars"? Why do people who take themselves to be "believers in God" slaughter people whom they regard as "unbelievers"? Could it be, as many "humanists" suspect, that the best defense against such behavior would be simply to reject the idea of God altogether, and thus rid ourselves of one of the main issues that puts us at each other's throats?

In this connection, one can't help noting that each of the major monotheistic religions starts out from the assumption that certain actions or beliefs can simply be *prescribed*. They are "dogma," the church's "teaching" and the prescribed contents of "faith" or right living, "orthodoxy" which we're expected just to accept if we want to be on the right side of God. It's easy to imagine that when people are raised in a tradition whose basic commitments are put beyond question, they might be more inclined to dismiss other traditions' beliefs outright, and to adopt the "militant" stance according to which only they have access to the truth.[1]

Would a "God"-oriented human being even be responsible for her actions?

If these problems weren't difficult enough, thinking about dogmatism can also provoke a more general question. If "God" is a supreme authority that, in the last resort, tells us what to believe and what to do, doesn't this "God" override our ordinary human freedom of thought and action? If God really overrides our freedom in this way, how can we be fully responsible for our actions? If the ultimate standard by which our actions will be judged is simply imposed on us by an external authority, shouldn't that authority, rather than we, be responsible for our actions? These are some of the most important objections that modern atheism raises against theology.

If someone replies that God *made us* free and responsible, one has to ask, how can one agent who has great power and makes all the rules "make" another agent who has by comparison miniscule power truly "responsible"? As Immanuel Kant said in a lecture in the 1770s, "But if I assume: it [the soul] is a being derived from another, then it appears to be quite probable that it is also determined by this cause in all its thoughts and actions."[2]

But if God didn't override our freedom in these ways, would God even "make a difference"?

So the problem is, How can there be a real God, a God who "makes a difference," who doesn't effectively eliminate human freedom and responsibility?

Why "God" at all?

In response to these problems, I propose to show that successful human life can't rely simply on humans as such, with whatever desires and attitudes they happen to have. Successful human life requires us to go beyond these things, beyond "nature," to something that can appropriately be called "God." But when we understand this God, we'll see why these issues about the compatibility of God with human responsibility don't actually arise.

As I've said, I find the argument for these conclusions mainly in Plato and in Hegel. Plato presents it in highly suggestive fragments, in his *Republic* and other writings. Emerson's remarks about God or the "Over-Soul," published in the 1840s, are based on these suggestions of Plato's together with Plotinus's and other writers' elaborations on them. Hegel brings Plato's suggestions (in many cases mediated through intervening thinkers including Aristotle, Spinoza, and Kant) together into a single systematic presentation, in his *Science of Logic* (1812–14) and his *Encyclopedia of the Philosophical Sciences* (1817–30). Emerson didn't have access to Hegel's works until his own period of greatest creativity was past. When he did read some Hegel in English translation, his response was enthusiastic. As for Whitehead, Wittgenstein, Michael Polanyi, and Iris Murdoch, they construct versions of Platonic thinking which, as a result of intervening misunderstandings of Hegel, do not have the benefit of his work.

G. W. F. Hegel

The first thing I need to say about Hegel is that whatever you may think you know about him probably has very little to do with what I value in him. His name carries many negative or unhelpful associations for people. But I feel that justice requires me to give Hegel credit for what he has taught me, both about God and freedom themselves and about how to understand Plato, Emerson, and (indeed) Whitehead, Wittgenstein, Murdoch, and many other thinkers.

If you just want to know what I think I've learned from Plato and Hegel, you can skip ahead several sections. But if you'd like a brief introduction to Hegel, the controversial historical figure, here it is.

Like many members of his generation, Hegel was inspired by Immanuel Kant, in the generation before him. Kant's central idea is that we humans are capable of a kind of rational self-government, in what we believe and in what we do, that distinguishes us from what is merely mechanical. Hegel embraced this idea wholeheartedly, but he wanted to do a better job than Kant had done of explaining how our rational self-government relates to nature and what is merely mechanical, how ethics relates to science, and how ethics and science relate to religion.[3] (Which are of course the same issues that I explored in post-Hegelian thinkers in the previous chapter.) Hegel lectured regularly on the philosophy of religion, and all of his lectures and his books use religious language freely, if not always in the most conventional ways.

In his lectures, Hegel gave special attention to philosophy's history and to the history of political, social, and intellectual freedom. More than any of his predecessors, he made an explicit effort to appropriate and make sense of the entire tradition of Western philosophical thought, up to his time.

Unfortunately, the feature of Hegel's philosophy that is best known to many readers is his unusual pattern of thought which commentators often call his "dialectical method." This is a feature of Hegel's philosophy that the self-proclaimed atheist, Karl Marx, regarded as valuable and claimed to have applied in his own political philosophy. As a student, Marx attended university lectures given by followers of Hegel in Berlin. Years later, in a famous Afterword to his *Das Kapital* (1873), Marx wrote that because Hegel was an "idealist," his dialectic was standing "on its head." So, Marx says, Marx turned it "right side up again," so as to "discover the rational kernel within the mystical shell."[4] Because of these claims that Marx made, many readers suppose that there is an important continuity between Hegel and Marx. This leads many people who sympathize with Marxism to have qualified sympathy for Hegel, and it has led many people who reject Marxism to reject Hegel as well.

Beyond what I have said, there is very little agreement about the best way to describe Hegel's thinking or his relation to later thinkers including Marx. Trying to explain what Hegel's "dialectic" is, encyclopedia articles quickly get bogged down in issues of terminology and give their readers very little idea of what the real point of the exercise is supposed to be.

In the social and political realm, in addition to Marx, fascist thinkers such as Giovanni Gentile in Italy and Ivan Ilyin in Russia claimed to be influenced by Hegel. And between the Marxist and fascist extremes, broadly "social liberal" writers such as Bernard Bosanquet in England drew on Hegel. So the social and political implications of Hegel's thought have been and continue to be controversial.

In the realm of metaphysics and religion, likewise, there is little agreement about what it is that Hegel thinks he emerges with from his extensive study of Western thought. Followers of Marx, and other atheists or humanists, often praise Hegel for his apparently critical attitude toward traditional religion. Other scholars take seriously Hegel's repeated statements that he is a Lutheran Christian and his use of apparently theological or mystical terminology, such as "Spirit" (*Geist*). Here is a golden statement from his *Science of Logic*:

> The universal is therefore *free* power; . . . it could also be called *free love* and *boundless blessedness*, for it bears itself towards what is different from it as towards its own self.[5]

There is no dogma here: no appeal to the authority of a sacred book or prophet. But why does Hegel use such redolent words as "love" and "blessedness" (*Seligkeit*), if not to signal a fundamental sympathy for the theological discourse in which such words are at home?

Hegel does indeed criticize conventional religion. What he criticizes is the conventional conception of God as outside us, which (he points out) makes God limited, by being separate from the world and from us, and thus bounded by and partially determined by his relation to the world and us. As I have pointed out, Hegel didn't invent the idea of the "God within us." It is suggested by well-known passages in scripture and canonical early Christian writings, and it is influential in Christian, Muslim, Jewish, and Neoplatonic mysticism and in Vedanta. So Hegel is not an essentially atheistic thinker, as is often suggested, unless canonical Christianity and Christian, Muslim, Jewish, and Neoplatonic mysticism and Vedanta are also atheistic. Which would come as quite a surprise to the people who embrace them.

Writers for whom religion is not a major concern have trouble imagining how it could be a major concern for Hegel. When Robert Pippin refers to Hegel's use of theological language as "metaphorical" (Pippin [2018], p. 278 n. 9), he doesn't specify what a contrasting, literal use of theological language would entail. It's not obvious, to me at least, that the metaphysical language that Pippin quotes from Hegel (that "the exposition of the pure concept" is "the absolute divine concept itself," and "the logical course of God's self-determination as being") is incompatible with the theology of, for example, St Athanasius or St Augustine. And when Pippin refers in Blaise Pascal's phrase to Hegel's God as a "God of the philosophers" (Pippin [2018], p. 134 n. 72) and implies that such a God can't also be the God of religion, he assumes what he needs to demonstrate.

Hegel versus Feuerbach's "anthropotheism"

To further clarify Hegel's relation to religion it is useful to contrast him with an influential early critic of Hegel who had initially been a follower: Ludwig Feuerbach. Feuerbach advocated a doctrine of "anthropotheism," according to which humans as such literally are God. In *The Essence of Christianity* (1841), Feuerbach maintained that "man was already *in* God, was already *God himself*, before God became man" (as Jesus).[6] Feuerbach explained the apparent difference between God and man by his notion of God as a *projection* of what is actually entirely human: "Is not the love of God to man ... the love of man to himself *made an object* ...?"[7]

In 1842, Feuerbach identified religion and God with "emotion, feeling, heart, and love," explicitly contrasting this view with what he took to be Hegel's preoccupation with the intellect. "The *heart*," Feuerbach wrote, "denies the *difference* between God and man, but [traditional and Hegelian] theology affirms it."[8] "The Hegelian philosophy is the last refuge and the last rational mainstay of theology."[9] And Feuerbach went on in his Preface to the second edition of *The Essence of Christianity* (1843) to assert that "I base my thoughts on *materials* that are given to us only through the activity of the senses.... In the field of theoretical philosophy, I subscribe—in direct contrast to the philosophy of Hegel, which holds exactly the opposite view—to *realism* or materialism in the mentioned sense."[10]

Feuerbach was right: Hegel does agree with traditional theology in seeing a difference between God and man. Feuerbach didn't note that there needs to be a difference between God and man, if God is to deserve authority, awe, and worship. Humans merely as such, no matter how much "heart" we may have, don't deserve authority, awe, or worship. What deserves those things is something that's in some important respect higher than humans as such—and likewise higher than the inputs of the senses, as such. In his hurry to replace the "old" philosophy with his "new" philosophy, Feuerbach neglected the entire point of the Plato/Hegel tradition, that what's rational has an authority that humans and the deliverances of their senses, as such, do not have.

Feuerbach wanted to close the gap between God and humans which results from the conventional conception of God as a separate being from humans. He may have had an inkling that, as Hegel points out, this gap makes God finite. But Feuerbach didn't notice that Plato and Hegel, together with many early Christian writers, had already closed the gap by rejecting the conventional conception of God—but without making God finite by eliminating all difference between the merely human, which is certainly finite, and the divine. This is the point of Hegel's notion of God as a "true infinity," in which the finite truly goes beyond itself but without being a being that's separate from the finite; and it's the point of Plato's conception of the divine as within us, as intellect, as well as beyond us. Plato and Hegel preserve the point of religion, that there is something that's genuinely higher than humans merely as such, without projecting what's higher as a separate being.

Despite Feuerbach's early enthusiasm (prior to the texts that I've quoted) for Hegel, Feuerbach unfortunately wasn't able to comprehend what Plato and Hegel were proposing. His failure to grasp this is manifest in the dualistic, either-or contrast that he frequently draws, in his later, anti-Hegelian writings, between his own "materialism" and Kant's and Hegel's "spiritualism." Because he can't conceive of a nondualistic way of expressing the claims that are made in what he calls "spiritualism," he rejects it and opts for its supposed opposite, "materialism" and "nature."[11] I explained Plato's and Hegel's nondualistic notions of "transcendence" and "spirit" in the previous chapter, and I'll explore them further in this and subsequent chapters.

Feuerbach's final mistake is his suggestion that Hegel focuses on the intellect as opposed to the heart. Like Plato, Hegel thinks that heart and intellect are intimately connected, especially at higher levels of human (or, as we might also call it, "superhuman") functioning. And it's this distinction between lower and higher levels of functioning, which Plato and Hegel insist on, that preserves a difference between humans, merely as such, and God.

Hegel versus Marx

Finally we can consider Karl Marx's claim to have put Hegel's "dialectic" "right side up again." Hegel's *Science of Logic*, which lays the foundation of his philosophical system and explains his "dialectic," is so difficult to read that few commentators discuss it in detail. Marx himself never wrote about it in any detail, and it seems to me that if he read it, he failed to understand its central argument. For, as I have shown in three long chapters of my book on Hegel, his *Science of Logic* makes it clear that his "dialectic" can't be separated from his philosophical theology.

Beginning with the *Science of Logic*, Hegel's entire system unfolds the consequences of the fact that some beings seek to be guided by something that's higher than their animal urges and socially ingrained thoughts. His dialectic is a way of articulating those consequences.[12] If "the ideal" were merely, as Marx says, "the material world reflected by the human mind,"[13] then Hegel's dialectic would have no function, because there would be no higher authority and no higher reality than the material world. Since Hegel's dialectic is tied up with his "idealism" in this way, Marx's claim to have preserved the "rational kernel" of Hegel's dialectic while putting it "right side up again" with his own atheistic materialism, can't be true.

Also, when Marx contrasts the "rational kernel" of Hegel's thinking with its "mystical shell," he assumes that reason and mysticism are necessarily in conflict with one another. But Plato and his followers including Hegel think they have good reasons to disagree with Marx about this. Of course they understand "mysticism" not as praising unreason or mystery as such but rather as describing how we know God directly, through our experience of freedom and love. It's the doctrine of the "God within us," which Plato and Hegel claim is fully rational, regardless of the fact that it doesn't coincide with conventional "common sense."[14]

So apart from the concern that Hegel shares with Marx about the unfortunate side effects of modern industrial capitalism, Hegel's thinking is very different from Marx's. Despite Marx's manifest humanitarian passion, Marx implements his reduction of the "ideal" to the "material world" by giving no more systematic attention to ethics than to theology. In fact, he sometimes describes morality as mere "bourgeois ideology." As a result, people who claim to be Marx's followers and who are morally ruthless have been able to cite his own texts in support of ignoring moral considerations. The historical consequences of this attitude of Marx's, in places like twentieth-century Russia and China, show how disastrous it can be to live without an acknowledged and self-critical "idealism."

There is a recurring pattern of more or less millenarian impatience that thinks it can dispense with moral quibbles regarding the process by which the imminent golden age will be brought about.[15] A similar pattern seems to be operative in people's willingness to submit without question to the supposed authority of guru figures, or of fascist leaders. The new world that is being born or the "greatness" that needs to be regained are thought to be so incommensurable with the existing world that the transition to them can only be "by any means necessary." It's easy to see how a dualism in which white is nowhere to be found in the present black or is only to be found in a miraculously segregated, perhaps "divinely sanctioned" individual or group, can easily lead to totalitarianism or terrorism.

Hegel opposes this pattern by insisting that if the "new world" or the regained "greatness" are supposed to embody freedom, they cannot be diametrically opposed to the existing world, because whatever is opposed to something else is not self-determining and thus is not free. So anyone who is looking for full freedom must look for it in the existing world as well as in the future and in the past.

Hegel, history, and the "Idea"

Because Hegel looks for freedom everywhere, his interest in history is very different from Marx's interest in history (as well as from fascist notions of past and potential "greatness"). Marx claims to have identified laws of development in history which enable him to predict the advent of true freedom in the future. Hegel makes no such claim. History, for Hegel, is not the unfolding of truth. Rather, it's only *to the extent that* history exhibits rational progress (in, for example, the Christian doctrine that all humans are made in the image of God, or in the legal abolition of slavery) that it qualifies as an aspect of Spirit. Apart from its doing that, history is just as full of random accidents as nature is.

This is the light in which we must see Hegel's well-known descriptions of history as progressing from East to West, from Asian theocracies to Greek "beautiful freedom," Roman submission to universal law, and Muslim/Christian "spirituality and spiritual reconciliation."[16] Hegel likes to tell stories like this one, in which major historical phenomena appear to form a necessary progression. "World history has an absolute East," he says, because it has "a definite eastern extremity, i.e. Asia."[17] But the supposed "absolute" that he refers to here is actually a throw-away: it reflects no systematic development, and thus it has nothing in common with his development of the "Absolute Idea" in the *Science of Logic* or of "Absolute Spirit" in the *Encyclopedia*. These latter developments, which compose Hegel's systematic thought, aren't stories. They don't trace a sequence of events in time or across the face of the globe. And they have a necessity that stories of events in time or across the face of the globe can't have and that Hegel doesn't impute to such stories in the way that he imputes necessity to his systematic writings.

Because Hegel's treatments of history don't describe a necessary pattern of temporal development, they say nothing about what we can or should expect to happen in any particular stretch of time. As a result, future-oriented thinkers are disappointed by Hegel. They should realize that the reason for his almost complete silence about the future is that his philosophy, as distinct from his occasional storytelling, deals with a timeless reason, to which temporal development is irrelevant. This makes it particularly inappropriate for future-oriented thinkers to claim that they are redeploying or reformulating key features of Hegel's thinking, such as his "dialectic." His dialectic has nothing to do with temporal development or prediction.

This also makes it quite inappropriate to cite historical disasters like the Holocaust as somehow invalidating Hegel's thinking. Hegel said nothing about inevitable processes in time, so what happens in any given time period is irrelevant to his analysis. The progress that Hegel describes is necessary and significant only insofar as it reflects the necessity of the Idea, which is beyond time and guarantees nothing within time.

When Hegel famously writes that "philosophy teaches us that . . . God's will must always prevail in the end, and that world history is nothing but the plan of providence," and that philosophy "transfigures reality with all its apparent injustices and reconciles it with the rational [or] the divine Idea,"[18] we have to ask what this "in the end" and this "Idea" are. Hegel's full explanation of the "Idea" is in his *Science of Logic*, and there it is clear that the "Idea" as such is timeless. Time and space enter in only as aspects of nature, which is subsequent to the *Logic*. And the consummation of "Spirit," and thus of human experience, is not found in the state or in history, but in Absolute Spirit, which is composed of the arts, religion, and philosophy, and in which Nature and Spirit return to the Idea (*Encyclopedia* §574) and thus go beyond time and space. So the "in the end" and the "reconciliation" that Hegel speaks of are not to be found in history as such, the sequence of events in time.[19]

Karl Löwith described Hegel's philosophy of history as a "secularization of the Christian faith . . . degrading sacred history to the level of secular history and exalting the latter to the level of the first" (Löwith [1949], pp. 57 and 59). And he added that "Hegel displaces the Christian expectation of the end of the world of time into the course of the world process, and the absolute of faith into the rational realm of history" (Löwith [1967], p. 33). Löwith neglected both Hegel's *Logic*, with its evidently orthodox conception of God or the Idea as timeless, and the way in which Hegel's *Encyclopedia* account of Spirit relates time, space, and history back to the timeless Idea. So that history is in fact a part not of "Absolute Spirit" but merely of "objective Spirit," all of which is prior to art, religion, philosophy, and the reality (God or the Idea, again) that they constitute, which is ultimately timeless and thus hardly "secular."

As for Löwith's contrast of reason versus "the absolute of faith," my discussion (inspired by Plato and Hegel) of faith in Chapter 1 has shown how faith can play a central role in our experience without being dualistically contrasted with "reason." Löwith's dualistic contrasts of sacred versus secular and faith versus reason eliminate the freedom, and the truly higher reality composed of it, which are Hegel's central concern.

In his *Hegel Handbuch* (2003), Walter Jaeschke regrets that Hegel "touches on the connection between Spirit and history, but neglects to work this connection out systematically in the form that his philosophy makes possible and suggests: Everything spiritual must be thought as historical" (p. 352; my translation). Jaeschke regrets that while Hegel discusses the histories of art, religion, and philosophy, individually, he doesn't focus on the history of Absolute Spirit, as such (same page). But Jaeschke fails to consider how by returning to the Idea, Absolute Spirit goes beyond time, and thus also beyond history. It must do so in order to be "absolute," that is, fully free. So Hegel has a good reason *not* to hold that "everything spiritual must be thought as historical."

"World history" exhibits a "providence," as Hegel says it does, only insofar as world history shows us phenomena whose significance goes beyond time. So when one understands what Hegel means by the "Idea," one can reject his claim that world history exhibits the Idea's providence only if one is prepared to reject the idea that world history at some times and places realizes a significant degree of freedom.

As for the religious significance of this "providence," all humans benefit from it insofar as what is fully real in each of us is incorporated in it, and thus it takes us beyond spatial and temporal divisions and beyond finitude in general. This is the process that Hegel details, primarily, under the heading of Absolute Spirit, and not in his discussions of history.

Hegel's proclivity for telling dramatic stories, as in the "absolute East" (and so forth) of world history, has misled many readers. But the main reason they have been misled is that in his discussions of world history he always has his metaphysical theology in mind, but he spells that theology out elsewhere, in the *Science of Logic* and in "Absolute Spirit" in the *Encyclopedia*, where few people read or understand it.

Besides excluding Marxist notions of predictable future liberation, Hegel likewise excludes fascist notions of retrieving past "greatness." Just as there is no "golden age" in the future, so too there is no "golden age" in the past. If we are to be free, we must examine every phenomenon, every age, and both our outer and our inner lives, for traces both of freedom and of its absence. And full freedom, as in Absolute Spirit, always points beyond the finitude of time.[20]

Hegel's "naturalism"? (Terry Pinkard)

In line with the twentieth-century tendency to reject "metaphysics" in favor of doctrines that seem to be more in keeping with the natural sciences, efforts have been made since the 1970s to present Hegel as "non-metaphysical," and more recently as advocating "naturalism."[21] Terry Pinkard sums up what he calls "Hegel's naturalism" in the following way: "We are self-conscious, self-interpreting animals, natural creatures whose 'nonnaturalness' is not a metaphysical difference (as that, say, between spiritual and physical 'stuff') or the exercise of a special form of causality."[22] For Pinkard, "naturalism" is apparently equivalent to the denial of any non-physical stuff or "special form of causality."

Everything then depends on what one means by denying what's "non-physical" or "special." Does this mean denying that there can be such a thing as a choice to pursue an ideal such as goodness or truth, and a higher kind of reality that is the result of such a choice? If this is what is meant, then, in the absence of further argument, the position seems to be dogmatic.

If, on the other hand, the rejection of what's "non-physical" or "special" is not to be understood as denying such choices or anything distinctive that results from them, then this rejection appears to exclude only outright dualism: two parallel types of "stuff" or of causation. It wouldn't exclude the sort of (prima facie) "supernatural" reality that Hegel lays out when he makes it clear that although what he calls "spirit" isn't *separate from* what he calls "nature," it's nevertheless certainly in some sense *higher and more real than* that. For example, when he tells us that "for us, Spirit has for its presupposition, Nature, of which it is the truth, and for that reason its absolute prius. In this truth, Nature has vanished." And "the absolute is Spirit; this is the highest definition of the absolute" (*Encyclopedia of the Philosophical Sciences* §381 and §384R). Nature has "vanished" and Spirit is "the highest definition of the absolute" because Nature, as such, is sublated in Spirit; Spirit, in contrast to Nature, is infinite; and "it is not the finite which is the real, but the infinite" (HSL p. 149; GW 21:136; SuW 5:164).

The point of Hegel's doctrines of sublation/*Aufhebung*, of the "infinite," and of "Spirit," is precisely that some aspects of the world are higher and more real than others in the sense that they're more self-determining and therefore more themselves (as I like to put it) and more "real" (as Hegel himself puts it) and more authoritative ("absolute")—even though, in accordance with the principles of sublation and true infinity, these aspects of the world don't exist separately from its less self-determining aspects. Pinkard overlooks all of these features of Hegel's definitive expositions of the relation between Nature and Spirit, and between the finite and the infinite. Pinkard is quite right that Hegel rejects any dualism of different kinds of "stuff" or inexplicably "special forms of causality." But it doesn't follow from this that nothing is "higher than" (nothing is "super-") anything else. "Higher," in a nondualistic way, is precisely what the infinite and Spirit, according to the above texts, are.

Aristotle says at *Metaphysics* 100a32-35 that "there is someone who is even above the student of nature, [namely, he] who studies universal and primary substance." And he says in the *Nicomachean Ethics* (X.7, 1177a14-15) that "the best is ... to understand what is fine and divine, by being itself either divine or the most divine element in us." The "above" and the "divine" here make it clear that Aristotle is not a programmatic "naturalist," in the sense of rejecting higher realities. And, as we can see from the passages that I quoted, neither is Hegel.

Hegel and Plato

Having, as I hope, put some of these often discussed issues about Hegel to rest, let's turn now to his relation to Plato. In a quotable passage in the penultimate paragraph of his *Lectures on the History of Philosophy*, Hegel said that "we can now be Platonists no longer." He likewise said or implied that we can no longer be "Spinozists" or "Kantians" either, but this doesn't make Spinoza or Kant minor figures in Hegel's formation. Likewise for Plato. If one contrasts Plato and Hegel with such flatly anti-Platonic writers as Gorgias, Sextus Empiricus, Epicurus, Lucretius, Thomas Hobbes, David Hume, and their successors in modern relativism, skepticism, materialism, empiricism, logical positivism, and deconstruction, one will see how much Plato and Hegel have in common. Gorgias and Hume and the others all reject the vertical dimension of reality, the divine "higher reality," which Plato immortalized in his Forms (or "Ideas") and his ascent from the Cave, and which Hegel preserves in his conceptions of sublation or "lifting up" (*Aufhebung*), infinity, freedom, Spirit, "the Idea" (precisely), and "elevation to God" (*Erhebung zu Gott*).

Rather than being committed to any particular prior conception of the higher reality or the divine, what Plato and Hegel are committed to and try to clarify is the vertical dimension, the dimension of something "higher," as such. Lloyd Gerson specifies the content of what he calls "Ur-Platonism" as "antimaterialism, antimechanism, antirelativism, and antiskepticism."[23] What these all have in common is the notion of an "ascent" to a truth or reality that's more true or more real than one's starting point; that is, they have in common what I call a "vertical dimension." We see all of this in Hegel's *Science of Logic* and *Encyclopedia of the Philosophical Sciences* just as much as we see it in Plato and Plotinus.

Robert Pippin argues that concepts, for Hegel, "are supposed to be moments in the process of thought's attempt to determine its own possibility," rather than being "apprehended realities, eidetic things." So an assimilation of Hegel to Plato "would leave unaccounted for all [Hegel's] references to subjectivity, the active universal, deeds, and that brought about."[24] But what's most important about Plato's Forms is not their apparent "thing"-hood, but the role that they play in the soul's achievement of unity, which is the primary locus of "ascent." The Forms make the soul's ascent to unity possible by giving it a source of guidance that has more authority than the pushes and pulls of appetites and prior opinions. (I take the Sun, Line, and Cave similes in *Republic* books vi and vii as filling out what's required for the unity that's described in book iv, 443d.) By uniting the soul in this way, the Forms make subjectivity or a real "self" possible, against materialism, mechanism, relativism, and skepticism. Which is precisely what Hegel, too, is seeking to do with his notions of subjectivity, the active universal, and so forth. I'll explain this way of reading Plato in some detail Chapters 5 and 6. Through it, Plato is more "modern" than we generally recognize, and we can see how Hegel and the modern focus on the "subject" or the "self" continue Plato's line of inquiry rather than starting a new one.

What does differentiate Hegel from Plato is that in the name of the dimension of "ascent," Plato unlike Hegel sometimes seems to encourage us simply to reject the body and the physical world. However, Plato is by no means consistent in this rejection. In fact, the greater part of his work (in particular, his *Republic*, *Symposium*, and *Timaeus*) can be read as explaining how the physical world itself goes beyond its mere physicality. I'll explain this aspect of Plato in Chapters 5–8.

Transcendence, freedom, and being maximally real

So now we can return to Plato's and Hegel's arguments for God, which examine the "vertical dimension" and its consequences. There is no reliance here on what's called "revelation" nor on the evidence of miracles, the authority of tradition, or the apparent "design" in nature. Instead, Plato and Hegel offer a careful examination of what human life is like.[25] Their examination points to a familiar and essentially uncontroversial experience: the experience of open-minded inquiry, of questioning one's initial opinions or desires or emotions, and looking for a better basis for one's beliefs and actions. Plato and Hegel suggest that our engaging in these activities constitutes a commitment to a kind of transcendence, a kind of "going beyond" the views and feelings that constitute our initial world. Not only do we go beyond particular opinions, desires, or emotions in this process of questioning, we go beyond them to something that's both "higher," because it's more authoritative, and in an important sense *infinite*. The new opinions, desires, and emotions that we come up with are always open to further questioning and revision, through the same process, in a way that's in principle unlimited. This is the literal meaning of "infinite."

Both in "going beyond" our initial world, and in entering something that's "infinite," this process parallels the traditional notion of the "transcendence" by which God "goes beyond" the world. And even the atheist who denies the existence of any God uses the sort of process that Plato and Hegel describe, when she encourages other people to go beyond their initial opinions (blind faith in God), toward opinions that will be better justified (that there is no God). So it's very hard to see how either "believers" or "non-believers" could ever do without the kind of transcendence that Plato and Hegel are describing.

But what, one might ask, does this "infinite" process described by Plato and Hegel have to do with the "infinite" reality that's traditionally called God? To answer this question, Hegel suggests that we look at the notion of "reality" itself. What is a "reality"?—he asks; in particular, what would be the *most* "real" thing that we can think of?

To this question, Hegel has a surprising and important answer. Consider ourselves, he says. How "real" are *we*? And the first point he makes in response to this question is that the desires and emotions that we initially feel and the opinions that we initially lean toward have probably been produced, in us, by our social environment or our biological heredity. Which means they've been produced by something that's not ourselves. In this way, we're pretty much the products of things that aren't ourselves. So *as ourselves*, as distinct from the effects of our environment and our heredity, we aren't particularly real at all.

What, however, if we question our initial feelings and opinions, as we sometimes seem to do, and thus set ourselves off from the people, the heredity, and so forth, that have caused us to have these feelings and opinions? This questioning might enable us to be guided by *ourselves*, as opposed to those other things. Being guided by ourselves, we could *be* ourselves, and thus be *real* (*as* ourselves), to a greater degree than something that's merely the puppet of its initial feelings and opinions, and through them of things that aren't itself. This being guided by ourselves, rather than by what our environment or our heredity have produced in us, is presumably a major part of what we think of as our "freedom."

This process of questioning and the resulting self-guidance makes something more real *as itself* than something that's merely a product of other things around it. This isn't to say that things that are produced by other things are illusions. But being less self-sufficient than something that's real as itself, what they are is less "their own." And thus as themselves, they're less real than something that's more self-sufficient.

How can something be more "real" than a rock? Plato/Hegel "idealism"

How can something be more "real" or more "self-sufficient" than a rock? A rock is real enough to cause real pain, for sure, but it isn't real enough to make itself what it is. Instead, to a large extent, far from being self-sufficient, it is what it is because of its environment and history. Questioners and inquirers, on the other hand, seem to be able to separate themselves off from what they question, such as their initial feelings and opinions. By doing this they can make themselves what they are, and thus be more real, as themselves, than a rock is. In fact, it seems that by bringing the possibility of something's being fully "itself" into the world, questioners or inquirers make it possible for the world as a whole to have a kind of reality that it would otherwise lack.

This is the insight that leads Hegel to call himself and Plato "idealists." As I've mentioned, there are two other well-known varieties of "idealism" in modern philosophy, neither of which is based (or at least, directly based) on this Plato/Hegel insight. The Irish philosopher George Berkeley, in the eighteenth century, argued that material objects were ultimately composed of "ideas" in human minds or in the mind of God. Many people suppose that this famous doctrine is what philosophical "idealism," in general, boils down to.[26] This is what G. E. Moore supposed, in his famous "Refutation of Idealism" paper in 1902. Since most of us are inclined to think that the best explanation of the large measure of agreement between your ideas of the world and my ideas of the world is that there is a world that's separate from those ideas, few people have been willing to abandon the idea of such a separate world.[27]

A second version of "idealism" is the "transcendental idealism" of Immanuel Kant. (The "Transcendentalism" of Emerson and his New England friends took its name from Kant's terminology.) Kant maintained that the mind in some sense "imposes" certain key features on all the reality that it knows.[28] Kant's idealism faces the difficult problem of explaining why we should regard features that the mind imposes on its experience as features of *reality*.

Fortunately, neither Plato nor Hegel endorses either Berkeley's doctrine that everything is ideas or minds or Kant's doctrine that minds impose key features on reality. So that Moore's "Refutation of Idealism" was irrelevant to Plato's and Hegel's versions of "idealism."

Unlike Berkeley's or Kant's versions of "idealism," Plato's and Hegel's version says that thought makes it possible for some things, such as humans, to be more fully real than rocks, by being more self-determining, and thus real as themselves. So the most real things, according to Plato and Hegel, are things that embody thought and freedom (and love, as we'll see later). Rather than containing everything else that exists, or imposing features on it, minds create what's most self-determining and consequently most real as itself, and thus they lend to the world as a whole whatever *full* reality (reality as itself) it possesses.

This Plato/Hegel "idealism" of self-determination certainly isn't identical with what we call "common sense," but it doesn't directly contradict common sense, as Berkeley's and Kant's doctrines do. Instead, you might say, it "adds to" common sense. It's the result of common sense's "going beyond itself," by giving closer attention than it generally gives to some of its basic concerns, such as freedom and reality.[29]

For purposes of interpreting Plato and Hegel, it's crucial to see that reality, for them, can't be "in the minds of" finite beings like ourselves, because such beings, insofar as they are finite, can't themselves be fully real. It's only through the "kinship" that Plato thinks souls have with the original reality (*Meno* 81d) that they can know any true reality, and Hegel (for whom only the infinite is real, HSL p. 149, GW 21:136; SuW 5:164) holds essentially the same view.

Is this view "anthropocentric"?

Seen in the light of the Plato/Hegel "idealism," Berkeley's and Kant's "idealisms" look like unsuccessful attempts to articulate an important truth. The truth is that by functioning in the world, minds enable the world to have a fuller reality than it can have without them. They enable it to be more self-determining. Berkeley and Kant fail to make this clear, when they make nature's sheer existence, or its possession of some of its key features, depend upon the presence of minds. Failing to articulate the important truth that Plato and Hegel articulate, Berkeley and Kant invite the charge of anthropocentrism: that they give an unjustifiable centrality, in the universe, to humans as such.

In 1910, George Santayana described philosophy since Socrates as "egotistical" and "anthropocentric."[30] Santayana was evidently seeing the Socratic tradition as epitomized in Berkeley's or Kant's type of idealism. He didn't envisage the possibility that Plato and Hegel put forward: that it's not the "universe" of which freedom is the center. Rather, it's something that the universe *accomplishes*, in the form of self-determining freedom.

Rather than making humans the center of the universe, Plato and Hegel make human freedom (as well as the freedom of any other species that has comparable capacities) the center of the highest thing, the fullest reality, that the universe accomplishes.[31] A proper modesty, on our part, needn't prevent us from drawing the manifestly significant distinction between the kind of self-determination that trees and rocks achieve and the kind that humans can apparently achieve. We blame humans who injure us, in a way that we don't blame trees and rocks that injure us. Humans can govern themselves in a way that trees and rocks can't. Since we make this distinction, we should recognize as well that beings that (to some extent) govern themselves have greater reality, as *themselves*, than beings that don't. Recognizing this, we can appropriately describe such beings as contributing to something that goes beyond the reality of trees and rocks, as such.

Nor should we think that "being oneself" is just an "interest" that certain species or certain individuals happen to have. This interest seems to have clear implications for the kind of reality that those species or individuals can achieve. Those that succeed, sometimes, in being themselves are (to that extent) more real, *as* themselves. Those that don't succeed in being themselves, are real only through their relations to other things.[32]

When Friedrich Nietzsche lamented, "Hasn't precisely the self-belittlement of man, his *will* to self-belittlement been marching relentlessly forward since Copernicus?" he wasn't regretting that humans can no longer think of themselves as the center of the universe.[33] Nietzsche had no nostalgia for a geocentric universe. Rather, he was thinking that humans shouldn't *belittle* themselves, and that to the extent that humans do so, something that's beyond humans may be needed. Something that won't belittle itself, but instead will have proper respect for its own power or accomplishment.

Nietzsche didn't agree with the specifics of Plato's or Hegel's way of conceiving human accomplishment, but he did agree with them in thinking of humans as being capable of participating in something of great importance. And this importance had nothing to do with our being located at the cosmos's physical center, or with our giving it its sheer existence or basic features.

What does this freedom look like in practice? Spiritual groundedness versus charisma

What does inner freedom or becoming one's true self look like in practice? Think of the more spiritually gifted people we've encountered. I don't mean "gurus," though I imagine some of them would qualify, but just the people among us who really "have something." Maybe they've "been through a lot," and emerged with a wisdom that sets them apart from the ordinary run of people; or maybe they seem to have been "born with" a spiritual gift that does that.

Don't such people give us a sense of "solidity," of embodying something that's more reliable and lasting than most of us manage to embody? They're probably fluid and adaptable, in many respects, but beneath that adaptability, there's a bedrock or a still point, which doesn't need to adapt, because it's (in effect) eternal. This is the "reality" that I'm talking about: the thing that's really *itself*. Its presence gives the world as a whole, in spite of all of its fragility and change, an eternity that it would otherwise lack.

Note that the quality that I'm describing isn't the same as "charisma," such as many show business people and religious and political leaders have. Charisma sets people apart, just as spiritual groundedness does. And spiritual groundedness generally gives a person one kind of charisma. But unlike spiritual groundedness, charisma doesn't need to be associated with any significant degree of self-understanding.

To have what I'm calling spiritual groundedness, by being truly herself, a person needs to have become free of her "baggage." She needs to be free of any obsessions, compulsions, and fears she may have acquired in her early years, which would otherwise keep her under the power of what's other than herself. Any politician, preacher, or movie star who has to be "on," in public, because he depends upon an audience's adulation to make him feel okay with himself, clearly is not free in this way.

Freedom, and love and compassion

Picturing these spiritually grounded people is likely to bring to mind another feature that these people all seem to possess in addition to freedom. This feature seems to be separate, in principle, from true freedom, but they're not ultimately separable. It's universal love or compassion. People who have become free from the power of what's other than themselves have the opportunity to care for others in a way the rest of us don't. We fail to care for other things and people because we're preoccupied with our own needs and desires—that is, with ourselves. The free person, not being preoccupied by her personal desires, can relate to what's really going on with other people. This gives the other people the sense that they're deeply understood by the free person, in a way that they wouldn't be understood by someone who is (as we say) self-involved.

And free people not only have this opportunity to truly understand others, they seem automatically to take it. As Rumi says, "Why would you refuse to give this joy to anyone?"[34] Suppose you're in a posture of separating yourself off from something, such as other people's needs or their freedom. If only by paying a kind of attention to your own needs that you don't pay to the needs of others. Then you're dominated by your relationship to—your closure toward—the other people, and you're not free.[35] Much freer to be the "ocean" that Rumi refers to in his poem.

No doubt each of us has a "separate life" to live, as far as our biological existence is concerned. And it's certainly an appropriate division of labor that each of us should take particular care, most of the time, of our own biological needs. But when my life can contribute to yours, and yours to mine, the biological dividing lines cease to have the importance that they have when we're each preoccupied primarily or exclusively with our personal needs and wants.

So at least in close-to-ideal cases, it seems that the questioning or inquiring that constitutes freedom necessarily carries with it a developed capacity for love or compassion. We all know people who seem to be much more developed in questioning than in love or compassion, or in love or compassion than in questioning. This is because the capacity for questioning is a more intellectual capacity, and the capacity for love or compassion is a more emotional one, and intellectual and emotional development don't always go hand in hand. But in close-to-ideal cases they have to go hand in hand, because excluding other people from our concern reduces our personal freedom. So people who really have their eye on (inner as well as outer) freedom always show a developed concern for other people as well.

Are this freedom and "full reality" really possible?

Whatever you think about love and compassion, you may well wonder whether it's realistic to suppose that freedom of the kind that I'm describing can actually exist in the physical world. Can humans really separate themselves from their environment and become self-determining, and thus more "real," as themselves? Shouldn't we assume on the contrary that every thought, like every other event in the world, is caused by previous events in the world, many of which took place outside the person? Wouldn't this imply that the person's thinking can never be fully "self-determining"?

These are important questions. But we have commonsense evidence of our ability to separate ourselves from our environment. This is our everyday experience of trying to arrive at conceptions of reality and plans of action that are better justified than our initial opinions and desires. We do this every day, for example, in the very discussion we've having right now, about whether freedom is real. We're trying to figure out what conception of reality is most justified. Likewise when we wonder which would really be the best career or the best life partner for us.

In these discussions and wonderings, we're trying to go beyond our initial opinions and find something that will be better justified. But if we succeed in doing this, it seems clear that we'll become more self-guided and therefore more "ourselves" than we were before. Rather than being guided by whatever first comes to mind, which could come from anywhere, we'll be guided by our own thinking, which is "us" if anything is.

In this way, all of our serious thoughts presuppose that we can be more self-guided. They presuppose that we can be guided by what's justified, as opposed to what we instinctively, initially, think or desire. Consequently, if we are to take seriously an analysis of the relation between causation and freedom or self-guidance, that analysis will have to explain, rather than undermine, this experience of making ourselves more self-guided. For if the analysis undermined this experience, it would undermine itself.

Note that in saying that we can be more self-guided, I'm not claiming that there will be no external causes for what we do. I'm not taking any position about the relation between causation and freedom, or about what's "external" and what's "internal." I suspect that causation, like freedom, is a topic that we don't yet understand very well.[36] The one thing that I'm certain of is that I need to take seriously my own interest in figuring out what's most justified. That, and not the "absence of external causes," as such, is what's essential to "self-guidance."

I conclude, then, that our everyday experience strongly supports the idea that we are sometimes more self-guided than we are at other times. This is all that my notion of inner freedom and self-guidance supposes.[37]

The idea of self-guidance as "separating ourselves from our environment" may suggest an unattractive picture of mutually impenetrable, hermetically sealed boxes. But if we influence each other through love, which values and promotes the freedom of the other person, and by sharing thought, which does the same, we can have any amount of mutual "influence" without reducing each other's freedom at all. A person who is self-guided doesn't ignore the world and the people around her. She evaluates whatever they tell her in the light of her own thinking about what's true and what's good, and when she concludes that what they tell her is probably itself true or good, she embraces it. What "separates" her from her environment is simply the fact that she evaluates everything in the light of her own thinking.

4 FULL REALITY IS GOD

From within or from behind, a light shines through us upon all things, and makes us aware that we are nothing, but the light is all. . . . What we commonly call man, . . . him we do not respect, but the soul, whose organ he is, would he but let it appear through his action, would make our knees bend. . . . So [there is] no bar or wall in the soul where man, the effect, ceases, and God, the cause, begins.

EMERSON, "THE OVER-SOUL"

From being oneself to God

So what does this "transcendence," self-guidance, and being real as oneself have to do with God? "God" or "the divine" is the traditional name for something that's more real than the everyday world and that lends some of its own reality to that world, by, as the Bible says, "creating" it. But the questioner that Plato and Hegel describe, who goes beyond everyday "reality" and thereby gives it a fuller reality than it would have by itself, seems to do something exactly parallel to what "God" traditionally does. The questioner makes the world (more) real, more self-sufficient and self-determining.

So Plato and Hegel both suggest that this questioner is the key to the rational core of religion.[1] The activity of questioning creates the vertical dimension, in which X "is higher than" Y, that religion has always been about. By virtue of its questioning, X is superior to Y, more authoritative and more self-determining or more fully real than Y. X "transcends" Y.

Religion, Plato and Hegel say, doesn't need to be about the sheer "power" of a heavenly "father," who lays down the law and protects or punishes his "children"— nor does it need to be about the sheer "powers" of a pantheon of gods. These are natural primitive images for what religion is about. But if we take these images literally, they make God merely a very powerful part of the world, the same kind of thing that the world itself is, rather than something that's truly higher than the world because it has an inherent authority that the world does not have.

So what the most rationally defensible religion is about, Plato and Hegel suggest, is the authority that anyone may achieve, to the extent that they go beyond their instinctive urges and achieve freedom and love. The germ of truth in the idea of God as "father" is that many fathers and mothers do in fact go beyond mere instinct, in this way, and thus do achieve some real authority. Being about this real authority, religion is also about the way this authority's presence in the world changes the world, by making it more self-determining, and in that sense, more real.

It's probably a more familiar idea that *love* transforms the world, than that questioning one's initial desires and opinions transforms the world. We're familiar with the idea that a strong emotion, like love, can change everything for us. And we're also familiar with the suggestion that God is love, and that the presence of this love in the world changes everything.

What I've been offering in this account of Plato's and Hegel's conception of questioning, and the way *it* "changes everything," is in fact only the other side of the coin of the way love, or God as love, changes everything. A person who seeks freedom can't afford to cut herself off from the world, because to be cut off from something is to be defined by one's relationship to that thing. So questioning and freedom aren't cut off, but instead they're loving and compassionate.

As I said earlier, this is true in the ideal case, and not necessarily in intermediate cases like you and me. But God, obviously, is the ideal case. Thus God is the sum of all the best functioning, both in the sense of questioning and in the sense of love, that there is.

What religion expresses is the thought that this "going beyond" initial urges, and the freedom and love that result from this "going beyond," transform everything. That, in fact, they make everything more real, more self-sufficient, more "itself," than it is when it's merely finite, material, and natural. We can understand all the major religious notions, including "creation," "law-giving," "transcendence," "eternity," "heaven," "liberation," "enlightenment," "salvation," and "worship" as being about this greater reality, self-sufficiency, "itself"-ness, and love. And we can understand in the same way "sin," "divine punishment," and "damnation," which are our state of being (self-) exiled from the greater reality of freedom and from the love that goes with it.

Isn't "God" supposed to be a separate being?

As I've pointed out in previous chapters, monotheists generally agree that God is infinite, unbounded. Only something that's infinite can be completely self-determining, completely free, and everyone agrees that the one God should be as free as possible. But if God is a separate being, God can't be unbounded or infinite, because a God who is "separate" clearly is bounded by the other beings that this God is "separate from." So a separate God clearly is not unbounded, not infinite, and not completely free.

So to make God infinite and free, Platonists think of God not as a separate being but as the interiority, the capacity for becoming more "itself," of the world of ordinary beings. God is "within us," as Plotinus puts it.[2] As Hegel puts it, God is ordinary beings' transcending what they ordinarily are, by achieving freedom (self-determination) and love. Hegel calls this a *"true* infinity" because, since it's not "separate from" anything else, it's not prevented, by being bounded by what it's separate from, from being infinite.

Plato and Hegel recognize that it's difficult to talk about this truly infinite God, so that for many purposes a kind of storytelling is legitimate in which we speak "as though" God were a separate being (or separate beings). But these stories must always be taken as stories. The literal truth will be that the truly infinite God is composed of the transcendence by which finite beings like ourselves sometimes go beyond our instinctive urges and opinions and become, to a significant degree, self-determining and thus infinite.

This doctrine doesn't say that God is humans

Of course I have to explain immediately that this doctrine that God is composed of our going beyond our instinctive urges doesn't imply that God just is human beings. It doesn't imply this because insofar as we humans are guided simply by our initial urges and opinions, we clearly are not God, because we aren't self-determining. Rather, it's what we do and what anything else in the universe does that *goes beyond* initial urges and opinions, that "is God," by bringing a fuller (because self-determining) reality into the world.

Both Plato and Hegel suggest that the freedom and love that go beyond initial urges and opinions, also go beyond what's merely "human," and that this makes them, in effect, divine. God is what humans, and anything else in the universe that has capacities similar to ours, become when we go beyond our initial urges and opinions by means of rational questioning and self-determination. For in this way we become something that's no longer merely human: something higher and something more fully *real* (because real as ourselves) than we are when we're mere puppets of our environments, which gave us our urges and opinions.

I discussed Ludwig Feuerbach's convoluted "anthropotheism," for which God apparently is human beings, in the previous chapter.

But the doctrine does connect humans to God, in an important way

Though Plato's and Hegel's God is not humans, as such, their God is intimately connected to humans. Inspired by the Platonists, St Augustine wrote that God "is more inward [to me] than I am myself." And Jelaluddin Rumi, "When you look for God, God is in the look of your eyes, in the thought of looking,"[3] because a genuine search for God takes you beyond your initial, natural urges and opinions, and into something that's no longer merely human, but higher. In that sense, your search for God is God's own looking and God's own thought.

This connection between God and our search for God is what the mystical traditions are pointing to when they tell us that God is "within us," and therefore is "in" the world—that, as Rumi says, "there's no need to go outside." What's truly within us, Rumi is saying, is truly beyond our normal desires and opinions and has the authority that comes from the full reality of self-determination. So when they say that God is "nearer to us than ourselves," Augustine and Rumi aren't giving us just a provocative paradox; they're pointing to the crucial fact that we can always go deeper, further "within," than our present conception of who we are.

Talk about God, Plato and Hegel tell us, is ultimately based on the experience of going "within," which is also the experience of going "higher than" our normal, everyday desires and opinions, in search of desires and opinions that have more authority because they're more truly our own. This is an experience that every one of us has, insofar as we question our initial desires and opinions, and ask ourselves what we should really be guided by. "God" is our image or name for the possibility that we might find a satisfying answer to that question.

It seems clear that we can't do without some such idea, without abandoning a fundamental human function: asking ourselves what we should really be guided by. And what's striking, when we see the connection between "God" and this human function, is how intimately "God" and humans then are interconnected. They're not identical, but they're manifestly inseparable. "There's no need to go outside," to get from one to the other.

It seems, then, that if we abandon "God"-talk we may be in danger of abandoning a fundamental human function, which is our search, beyond our normal, everyday desires and opinions, for desires and opinions that would be more truly our own. "Nearer to us than ourselves," as we normally conceive of ourselves. Being more truly our own, this goal of ours constitutes a higher reality than our everyday desires and opinions, and thus we can appropriately call it "God."

But when we've finally seen why we can't abandon this fundamental human function, and "God" in it, we also see how mistaken are some of the consequences that people have drawn from conventional "God"-talk. In particular, the idea that we don't have to think about what we should do or believe, but just be "told by

God" what to do or believe. This idea is mistaken because Plato and Hegel (and Rumi) have shown us that what the idea of "God" itself is really about is our going beyond our initial feelings and opinions, precisely by thinking.

But we shouldn't interpret this lesson in a way that turns it, in its turn, into a mere dogma. For example, we shouldn't suppose that "prayer," then, is an inappropriate way to relate to God. For much traditional "prayer" might in fact qualify very well as "thinking," if it involves emptying one's mind of extraneous matters and trying to be open to new, clarifying insights, coming from somewhere "higher" than one's everyday thoughts.

So now we can see why God and free inquiry are inseparable. Free inquiry makes possible the genuine self-determination that is God. And when we understand how free inquiry does this, we understand that if free inquiry exists, God exists.

Free inquiry, as doubt, is part of God

If free inquiry is part of what constitutes God, so that "you don't need to go outside" to find God, then doubting the existence of God is pretty futile. For that very doubt is part of God. The most real thing, the *ens realissimum*, achieves its reality *by* doubting every initial opinion, since this doubting enables it to be *self-determining*, and thus real in a way that things that can't engage in doubt can't be. So doubting the existence of God is just a necessary part of the universal doubt and resulting self-determination that constitutes God.

More precisely, this universal doubt *helps* to constitute God. For an equally essential part of God is universal love. Since intellect and the emotions are partially independent of each other, transcendence can't be understood solely in terms of intellect (inquiry) *or* solely in terms of the emotions (love). It has to be understood in terms of both of them, acting together.

But in the ideal case, as I've explained, intellectual transcendence and emotional transcendence must go together. So in the ideal case the love of truth, or thought, will go beyond egoism to universal love. And since God, clearly, is the ideal case, the universal doubt or inquiry that is one aspect of God will necessarily be accompanied by God's other aspect, which is universal love.

But what's true in the "ideal case" will also be true in the portion or aspect of actual life that *embodies* the ideal. So if rational doubt, the pursuit of truth, is truly present, then we can infer that something truly self-determining is present, which (as such) is more real than anything else that we're acquainted with. And if we consider only the truly self-determining aspect of what's going on, this aspect must also embody universal love.

But if the discussion that we're having *now* doesn't really pursue truth and attempt to be rational, then this discussion is pointless and we might as well drop it. So if we suppose that our present discussion *isn't* pointless, we should hope or suppose that something that's truly truth-pursuing and rational, and thus truly self-determining, is present in it.

But nothing can be more real than what's truly self-determining. So we should hope or suppose that the most real thing, the *ens realissimum*, is present, at least to some degree, in our discussion. And to the extent that this most real thing is present, universal love is also present.

So from the plausible premise that rational doubt or the pursuit of truth is truly present in our current discussion, we seem to have demonstrated the presence in our discussion of something that's more real than anything else and that embodies universal love. What else could we call this thing but "God"?

Well, of course we could decide to reserve the word, "God," for a very powerful external and finite reality such as God often seems to be in the Hebrew scriptures. Then we could call the truly infinite God within us something else, such as "the philosophers' God," or "the Absolute," or whatever.

I myself think that traditional religion *meant* to talk about something that's truly infinite, even though it was often unclear about how to do so. So it seems appropriate to me to call the truly infinite God, simply "God."

So that if I doubt, God exists

Thus, revising Rene Descartes's famous formula, in his *Meditations* (1641), that "I think, therefore I am," which he also expressed as "I doubt, therefore I am," we can say that "I doubt, therefore God exists."

Descartes's original formulation has problems. It's reasonable to wonder whether he was justified in inferring *his own* existence from his thinking or his doubting, since such an inference would have to justify him in asserting the existence of something that was himself as distinct from other things. When he's aware that thinking is going on, how does he know that *he* rather than you or I is doing this thinking? How does he know anything about the distinction between himself and others, and how to apply it, in this case?

But there is less reason to doubt the inference from "I doubt" to "Something is present that's potentially self-determining, and not self-centered, but loving, and thus divine." For such a divinity, as I've been suggesting, needn't be distinct from other things in the questionable way in which Descartes himself apparently has to be, for his own inference to be valid.

As Rumi says, God in a sense is "nearer to you than yourself." For God is more "inner" to you than your identity as a particular person or thing, among other persons or things. It's because of God's being "within" us, as our doubt, self-determination, and love, that we can know that God exists. And it's because the doubt, self-determination, and love that are within us in this way, *go beyond* us, and beyond the finite world in general, by having an authority that finite beings as such can't have, that it's appropriate for us to call them "God."[4]

And we are free and responsible

Having outlined Plato's and Hegel's conception of God, we can return to the question of whether there could be a real God who wouldn't need to override human freedom of thought and action and human responsibility. Plato's and Hegel's God can't override human freedom, because this God *is* human freedom. (With the emphasis on the "*freedom*," as I've explained, rather than on the "human," which by itself certainly isn't God.)

Fundamentalists and dogmatists are right to insist on our need for something that goes beyond our merely human ideas and feelings and standards of conduct. But they're wrong to think that the only place where we can find such a higher standard is in "commands" that are imposed on us and which have nothing to do with our own free thought and insight. Rather, the higher standard must be found by the kind of thinking that goes beyond initial opinions and feelings, in an effort to arrive at something that's better justified than they are.

We've all had the experience of revising our initial opinions and our initial feelings as a result of thought, so we all know that in some way, it's possible to go beyond them. And it's this going beyond, Plato and Hegel suggest, that underlies the idea of a "higher standard." Fundamentalists and dogmatists are right to insist on the need for such a standard, but wrong to think of it as resulting from the sheer commands of a God whom we must obey, but whom we can't hope to understand or freely embrace.

The fundamentalists and dogmatists and the atheists who suspect that a real "God" would deprive us of our freedom all miss the key point. That point is that we can have a higher standard that's not alien to us, and consequently doesn't threaten our freedom, if we understand both the higher standard *and* our freedom as being created by the process of revising our initial opinions and desires through thought.

Our freedom results from this process because questioning and revising our initial opinions and desires allows us to be guided less by things that are external to us, and more by ourselves, than we are initially. If our freedom and our true self is our ability to go beyond our initial desires and opinions, then the result of that going beyond isn't alien to us. We *are* this going beyond, insofar as we're free, and truly ourselves. The only aspect of us to which this God is alien, and which she or he "overrides," is our "merely human" aspect. We can welcome even our merely human aspect into the fold, when and if it questions and goes beyond itself and thus achieves freedom and full reality. And as "God," we have infinite loving patience.

Once we've established that our own freedom is compatible with, and indeed helps to constitute, the higher reality that we call "God," it's clear that this God no longer threatens our responsibility for our actions. If we're free, we're responsible. This, no doubt, is why Kant wrote in his *Opus postumum* that "the commanding subject is God," but "this commanding being is not outside man as a substance different from man" (Akad. 21:21).[5] To solve his long-standing problem of how divine creation and human freedom could be compatible, Kant was apparently reaching for the Plato/Hegel conception of a transcendent God that is not "a separate being."

Finally, we have the familiar issue of how we can be responsible for our actions if God was able, from eternity, to foresee them and prevent them if God wished to do so. The story about God that I've been telling makes it clear that God isn't an "independent agent," set over against our actions and able to "interfere" with them in the way that we suppose when we formulate this issue. God is the highest reality, more real than we (as mere human beings) are, but God's reality nevertheless has a kind of dependence upon the lower realities that we are. If we weren't free to make a mess of things, through actions that we'll regret later, we wouldn't be able truly to go beyond ourselves through freedom and love, and in that case there would be no God or ultimate reality.

In this way, the seemingly interminable dispute between "orthodox" and "Pelagian" thinking, in Christianity, is revealed as misconceived and unnecessary. Those who emphasize God's agency and those who emphasize human freedom are in fact emphasizing the same thing. The reason why, as orthodoxy correctly insists, we often feel powerless to save ourselves is not that we need to be saved by some "other being," but that inner freedom (and the love that goes with it) often seem to be out of our reach. Our own freedom and love often emerge only in response to the freedom and love of other people. Orthodox thinking is right to insist on this human experience of needing the "grace" of something "other." One could interpret the doctrine of original sin as a poetic way of expressing this reality, which does call for a certain kind of "surrender," a turning to something "other" for what we ourselves most need.

However, Pelagians are nevertheless right to insist that taken as a totality, freedom and love are self-sufficient. There is no parcel of freedom and love to which we have to turn that's essentially separate from us humans and our world. For if there were such a separate parcel, it wouldn't be fully free and therefore it wouldn't be able to give us what we need. In order to be fully free, God and God's love must be in the world. This is the fundamental adequacy of the "human" will that Pelagians correctly emphasize.

But it doesn't mean that we humans, as such, are (together with the world) the only reality. Without freedom and love, we aren't fully ourselves and thus we aren't fully real. As orthodox thinking insists, there is in fact a higher and fuller reality (of freedom and love). What orthodoxy often overlooks, however, is how this higher and fuller reality must be in "this" world, the world that we experience every day, by being our potential or actual freedom and love. Insofar as Pelagianism makes this latter point, it too is indispensable. Thus God's being in the world, as the world's own freedom and love, dissolves the antinomy of orthodoxy versus Pelagianism. When each of them is properly interpreted, it's compatible with the other.

An unconventional conception of God

What I've been saying raises a natural question. How can I call this highest reality "God," if he, she, or it is "inseparable from" or "has a kind of dependence on" the lower realities that we are? Isn't God supposed to be completely "independent" of everything else?

Here I need to remind you that a God who's defined as *not* being other things and *not* depending on them, is in fact made dependent by that relationship. "The God who *is not* all these other things" depends on the others in the most intimate possible way, through its very definition. Such a God is defined not by itself but by its relationship to these other things, and thus is radically dependent and limited.

Whereas a God who includes other things, but includes them by being their going beyond themselves, doesn't depend upon them and isn't limited by them, precisely inasmuch as it goes beyond them. So that, paradoxically but truly, the way to be fully independent is to *include* (in this way), rather than to exclude, what's "other" than oneself.

Does the God that I've been describing, who doesn't "intervene" in events in the world from "outside" it, nevertheless "make a difference"? The greatest difference one could imagine, because this God makes the world fully real, self-determining, and itself, in a way that nature by itself, without going beyond itself, couldn't do. And in a way that the conventional God, who's defined as "*not* being" all other things, can't do either, because this definition prevents the conventional God from being self-determining, so the conventional God has no full reality to lend to anything else. The conventional "God" is simply another being, alongside the beings that make up "nature," and just as limited by its relations to those beings as they are by their relations to each other. Regardless of how much power it may have over other beings, if it's in the same category as they are, as a countable, additional "being," it's limited by its relationship to them and isn't fully self-determining.

This is Hegel's critique of the conventional conception of God. What I've been laying out in the preceding pages is his alternative to that conventional conception. Since Hegel's God is the way in which nature or the world goes beyond itself, through our questioning, his God isn't limited by what it goes beyond, and thus his God really is supernatural, beyond nature.

Not the conventional "creator"

Hegel's God doesn't, indeed, correspond to the conventional conception of the "Creator." Richard Dawkins spells that conception out in what he calls "the God hypothesis," that "there exists a superhuman, supernatural intelligence which deliberately designed and created the universe and everything in it, including us."[6] The hypothesis that Dawkins describes is certainly familiar, but that doesn't mean that it makes sense. An intelligence that deliberately designed and created the universe would not be truly *supernatural*, because its separate existence over against the universe that it created would make it limited, finite. Nature, presumably, includes all finite beings. So rather than really going beyond nature, this very powerful intelligence would be an additional, rather unusual being that we should add to our list of the beings that a comprehensive survey of nature would have to include. It's only by trying to describe a God that isn't (in fact) just another finite being, like the beings that she or he "creates," that we can hope to arrive at something that's truly infinite and thus truly supernatural, beyond nature.

A thinking believer who becomes aware of this fact about what's truly infinite and truly supernatural will want to revise the conventional notions of "God" and the "Creator" so that what they describe will be truly infinite and truly beyond nature. Plato and Hegel show us how to do this. If we think of God as including the world of finite things, by being that world's surpassing of its finite-ness, through freedom, then this God isn't limited by the world, but is truly infinite.

The Plato/Hegel "God within us" that gives the world its only full reality, its reality as itself, without being opposed to the world as yet another "being," is the truth that underlies the conventional, anthropomorphic idea of a separate "creator" God, which Richard Dawkins describes. Unlike the God that Dawkins describes, the Plato/Hegel God is truly supernatural. And unlike the God that Dawkins describes, the Plato/Hegel God is directly known by us, since it's our own freedom.

Thus Dawkins is mistaken in assuming that his conventional "God hypothesis" is representative of the best thinking about God, so that by discrediting it he can show that "God," as such, is a "delusion." Like the best thinking in many other fields, the best thinking about God isn't necessarily the best-known or the most conventional thinking.

Nor, as I've mentioned in previous chapters, is conventional thinking necessarily the same as "orthodox" religious doctrine. For the notion of our "becoming God," and thus of God's not being simply a separate being from us, appears very early in the history of Christianity and is preserved in such repositories of orthodoxy as the Roman Catholic Catechism and Mass.

Why this isn't "pantheism"

In his widely read book, *Mere Christianity*, C. S. Lewis described Hegel's conception of God as "pantheist" and said that people who believe in pantheism "don't take the difference between good and bad very seriously."[7]

According to the dictionary, "pantheism" is "a doctrine that equates God with the forces and laws of the universe." And it's true that a God who was identical with the forces and laws of the universe wouldn't seem to exhibit or embody much concern about the difference between good and bad. But Hegel in fact identifies God with the universe's going *beyond itself* toward something that's more rational and (in that way) more self-determining; and a God that was identical with the universe's forces and laws clearly wouldn't do that. So Hegel can't be a pantheist.

Lewis seems to assume that God must either be a being that's separate from the world or be identical with the world. Lewis doesn't realize that a being that's separate from the world would, to that extent, be limited, and thus not self-determining, and not truly supernatural. He also, consequently, doesn't see how Hegel's God succeeds in being self-determining, and truly supernatural, by being the world's going beyond itself.

Only nature can be truly supernatural, by going beyond itself, by seeking what's rational. This is because something that's opposed to nature, in the way that "God" as conventionally conceived is opposed to nature, is thereby limited and might as well be counted as a part of nature. This paradoxical but necessary fact is what Hegel's "dialectic," in his *Science of Logic*, is all about. It's about how we can get guidance from something that's *truly* "higher" than ourselves, and higher than nature, rather than just being another being (however powerful) alongside us and nature.

Hegel certainly can't fairly be accused of not taking the difference between good and bad seriously, since his conception of God is built around precisely the process of our going beyond our initial, limited desires and opinions, in pursuit of what's higher and more rational. Which indeed appears under its traditional name, as the "Good," toward the end of Hegel's *Science of Logic*.[8]

Probably Lewis didn't realize how central the difference between the rational (and the "good") and the merely instinctive is in Hegel's thinking, because the British Idealists, who advocated Hegel's importance in the generation before Lewis, didn't get this aspect of Hegel's thinking into focus. So Lewis is, unfortunately, in good company here. I focus on Lewis's brief discussion only because it's widely read.

How it differs from "life force" or "quantum" theology

Lewis mentions another alternative to his own conventional Christian theology: the doctrine of "creative evolution," propounded by the French philosopher Henri

Bergson, or the notion of a "life force," popularized by the Irish/British dramatist, George Bernard Shaw. Lewis accuses these doctrines, as he accuses Hegel's, of involving "no morals," and therefore of offering "all of the thrills of religion and none of the cost."[9]

Looking for comparable conceptions in our own time, we might think of the "quantum" theology of Fritjof Capra, Fred Alan Wolf, Deepak Chopra, and the popular film, *What the "Bleep" Do We Know?* They all suggest that quantum indeterminacy, and the role of the "observer" in resolving it, demonstrate the reality of something like God, or the soul, or the Tao.[10] Certainly modern physics is weird, and some professional physicists do draw connections between the widely accepted weird physical theories and broader metaphysical views. But Plato and Hegel, like Lewis, would object that the recent advocates of "quantum" theology don't explain what's "higher," or good, or deserving of worship, in the God or soul or Tao that they think quantum physics points to.

For their part, Plato and Hegel explain that what's good about God and the soul is that they seek to be guided by what's good, and thus to be free, instead of responding in a merely automatic way to their environment. This feature of God and the soul is what makes it useful to talk about God and the soul, rather than just talking about quanta and atoms and the human brain.

Classical Chinese Taoism seems to resemble Plato and Hegel, on this point, when it contrasts "heaven" and "earth," where "heaven" seems to be that which is "above," or good, and earth seems to be the finite and imperfect. Taoism may not be "dualistic" in the way that the "quantum" theologians often object to, but it does assume that there's a significant distinction between heaven and earth:

> People model themselves on the earth.
> The earth models itself on Heaven.
> Heaven models itself on the Way.
> The Way models itself on what is self-so.[11]

Since quantum physics tells us nothing about seeking to be guided by something "higher," it fails to illuminate this key feature of God or the soul or the Tao. So whatever quantum physics may or may not "prove," it looks as though we still need the sort of philosophical theology that I'm presenting in this book, in order to understand what God or the soul or the Tao is really about.

Lewis is right to criticize some of the recent popular theologies for apparently leaving out the moral dimension. But he's mistaken in thinking that Hegel's theology leaves it out.

How it differs from "deism"

Another recognized alternative to the conventional conception of God is "deism." According to this view, again according to a dictionary definition, there is an all-powerful Creator who designed the world, in the beginning, and brought it into being complete with the laws of nature that govern it, but took no interest in it after that, leaving it to run on its own. Some eighteenth-century intellectuals saw deism as a way to separate God from the domain of science, without doing away with God altogether.

It's clear that Hegel and the Platonic tradition, as I've presented them, aren't "deist," in this sense, because they describe God as intimately involved with the world, at all times and places. It's true that they don't describe God as "intervening" in the world through "miracles." They agree with deism in that respect. But unlike deism's God, Plato's and Hegel's God, as our innermost "self," is intimately connected with everything, especially with humans, and completely "available" whenever we turn to it. In this way, Plato's and Hegel's God stands much closer to traditional conceptions of God than deism does.

How it fulfills Martin Heidegger's requirements

In a much-quoted passage, Martin Heidegger stated without argument that "one can neither pray nor sacrifice to this [god of philosophy]. Before the *causa sui*, man can neither fall to his knees in awe nor can he play music and dance before this god" (*Identity and Difference* [2002], p. 72). But we do in fact pray and sacrifice to the Plato/Hegel God, inasmuch as we seek its guidance and the resulting peace of mind, and we give up our selfish and self-important schemes. And quantities of awe and music and dance are in fact addressed to this God, both outside institutionalized religion and within it. For whenever we celebrate the infinite power and authority of inner freedom, love, forgiveness, or beauty, we celebrate this God. The "insect" (Edward Young) that we can feel ourselves to be, in comparison to this power, can and does fall to its knees in awe.

Heidegger was understandably impressed by the apparently unspiritual character of modern science and technology and by the apparent decline, in modern times, of traditional forms of worship and religious doctrine—the decline that Nietzsche heralded with his pronouncement that "God is dead." These are undoubtedly among the major reasons for Heidegger's failure to see how deeply and ubiquitously we are involved, in modern times as much as in other times, with the Plato/Hegel God, and it with us.

Are we really in a "secular age"?

It seems to me that a major part of what's going on in the world of "religion" and "spirituality," in our time, is a sorting out of the issue of what is genuinely transcendent. Much conventional religion seems to be stuck in the habit of conceiving of God as a separate being, despite the fact that when it's carefully examined, such a being would be finite and thus wouldn't really transcend the world at all. Plus, it's hard to know how we would know anything about such a being, which is defined as being both separate from us and inaccessible to our physical senses. In response to these difficulties, more or less clearly understood, many people have ceased to believe in such a being and ceased to support wholeheartedly the institutions that appear to preach such a being. Thus we have the apparent "secularization" of major parts of (at least) European and North American societies.

But at the same time, people's desire to identify and relate to something that's truly transcendent seems to be as strong as it has ever been. This could hardly not be the case if, as I've been suggesting, transcendence is an inherent (though often unrecognized) feature of human thought, freedom, and love, as such. One of the current manifestations of this perennial interest in transcendence is the proliferation, in the West, of nontraditional religious or spiritual organizations and movements, including Buddhism, Vedanta, Taoism, shamanism, Wicca, mysticism, "New Age" and Jungian ideas, Romantic poetry and nature writing, and so forth.[12]

For those of us who wonder what's really going on here, it's very helpful to know that an important part of the Western spiritual tradition was never, in fact, committed to the problematic notion of God as a separate being. Plato, Plotinus, St Paul, St Athanasius, St Augustine, Meister Eckhart, Rumi, Hegel, Emerson, Whitman, Whitehead, Tillich, Rahner, and many other poets and thinkers in all phases of the Western tradition have thought, instead, of something like the "God within us" that I've been outlining here. The notion of God as a separate being has, of course, been highly visible in public discourse, but if it's less widely accepted today, that's no reason to think that transcendence as such is losing importance for people. For the nontraditional movements that I mentioned all embrace transcendence in some form (though not always, of course, by that name).

Equally important is the seldom-recognized fact that science itself constitutes a form of transcendence, inasmuch as a person who seeks knowledge seeks, in doing so, to rise above the sort of existence in which she would be governed merely by her preexisting appetites and opinions. Thus the age of science is an age that seeks, as much as any other age does, to transcend. Of course this raises the important question of how different forms of "transcendence" relate to one another. But at least it makes it clear that the modern period is as much involved in transcendence, in general, as any other age has been.

So we don't have to picture what's happening in the West as a relentless process of "secularization," by which "transcendence" is gradually or rapidly being replaced by "immanence." Transcendence has been a feature of every phase of Western thought and experience, and it's just as manifest in the current period as it has ever been. What's different is simply that some of its more familiar and institutionalized advocates appear to be losing influence, partly (I suspect) because the separate being that they seem to identify with transcendence is rationally inaccessible and can't truly transcend.[13]

Regarding our supposedly "secular age," Charles Taylor's influential book, *A Secular Age* (2007), seems to me to be excessively preoccupied with the fortunes of Christian "belief" (as Taylor calls it), as distinct from transcendence in general, as, for example, Plato explains it. A decline in "belief" need not entail a reduced interest in transcendence as such. Taylor seems insufficiently aware of the critique of the conception of God as a "separate being," which is also a critique of much conventional Christian "belief" and which was already implicit in Plato, St Paul, St Augustine, and Meister Eckhart and is explicit in Hegel. Overlooking this Platonic critique of conventional "belief" and overlooking the alternative conception of transcendence that Plato and Hegel develop, Taylor grants more credibility than I would grant to the claims of what he calls "immanent humanism" to function without any appeal to transcendence.[14]

If "humanism" and philosophy engage in transcendence, are they still "secular"?

"Humanism" certainly refuses to rely on a God who's conceived as a being that's separate from the world, but it seldom says anything about the alternative conception of transcendence that's developed in the Platonic tradition. And any serious attempt, such as "humanism" certainly is, to be guided by truth rather than by mere opinion and appetite, is itself necessarily engaged, whether it realizes this or not, in a kind of transcendence. So transcendence is a built-in feature of the humanism and science that many people take to be opposing transcendence.

We should view references to "secular philosophy" or "secular ethics" with skepticism for similar reasons.[15] If philosophy, as a pursuit of truth, necessarily involves an important kind of transcendence, is it (in fact) fully "secular"? Were Plato's or Aristotle's philosophy or Aristotle's ethics "secular"?

I don't think these questions can have clear answers. This is because the term, "secular", has a clear application only in our particular historical circumstances, in the aftermath of the dominance of institutional Christianity in our societies. Societies in which church institutions lose power can be called more "secular," but this implies nothing in particular regarding the prevalence or significance of transcendence in general, in those societies. The change that has taken place is primarily sociological, having to do with particular institutions, rather than metaphysical.

When we understand this development correctly, we're also in a better position to understand the relationship between "Western" thought and non-"Western" including Asian thought. For we're able to see forms of transcendence in doctrines that don't match up with "theism" as it's conventionally conceived of.

How mysticism is "perennial"

One doctrine that contrasts with the notion of "secularism" is the idea of a "perennial philosophy," which was popularized by various authors including Aldous Huxley in his classic anthology with commentary, *The Perennial Philosophy* (1944). I should explain how the Plato/Hegel philosophical approach to mysticism and God relates to Huxley's "perennial philosophy." Plato and Hegel certainly agree with Huxley that there is a transcendent truth that's permanent, regardless of the comings and goings of particular religious organizations and cultural formations, each of which reflects only a partial grasp of that truth. So that if one could actually function without transcendence, as secular humanism often claims to do, one would deprive oneself of this fundamental truth.

To Huxley's thesis, R. C. Zaehner, Steven Katz, and other scholars have objected that since mystical experiences take different forms reflecting particular cultural traditions and individual psychology, there is no justification for treating them all as reflecting one uniform transcendent reality. Other writers, in turn, have responded to Zaehner and Katz.[16]

Seen in the light of the Plato/Hegel approach, it's not surprising that what we call "mystical experiences" take different forms. The specific form that they take is likely to reflect the individual's cultural and personal background. But the truth that underlies these extraordinary "mystical" experiences is not to be found in these experiences taken by themselves and regarded as extraordinary, but rather in the everyday experiences of inner freedom, love, forgiveness, and so forth, and in the reality that they constitute.[17]

"Mystical experiences" often sum up and comment on this reality, but they do so in different ways. There is no reason to expect inner freedom as such, love as such, or the reality that they constitute to vary from culture to culture and individual to individual in the way that mystical experiences appear to vary. Though no doubt different cultures and individuals will have different terms with which to describe them, different theories about them, and likewise different ways of experiencing them, inner freedom, love, and the transcendent reality that they constitute are simply themselves.

Mysticism is "perennial" not in that all mystical experiences are necessarily the same, but in that the reality that underlies them is the same, as we learn from analyzing everyday human experience and its implications. I'll say more in Chapters 8 and 9 about how the study of "mystical" knowledge (i.e., direct knowledge of the divine) should be distinguished from the study of extraordinary "mystical experiences," as such.

"Monistic" mysticism versus "theistic" mysticism

Finally, the Plato/Hegel approach offers a novel perspective on a more specific version of the "perennialism" issue. This is the contrast between "monistic" experiences, in which one discovers the unity of everything, and "theistic" experiences, which emphasize an "encounter" between the human mystic and an independent entity, which is understood to be God. Monistic experiences include those described by Advaita ("nondual") Vedanta and certain medieval Christian mystics such as the Beghards and perhaps Meister Eckhart, while theistic experiences include those described by Dvaita ("dual") Vedanta, Jan van Ruysbroeck, St Teresa of Avila, and St John of the Cross. This contrast between unity and theistic duality appears to create a major difficulty for the perennialists' suggestion that all mystical experience ultimately reveals a single, "perennial" reality.[18]

As with the diversity of numerous kinds of mystical experience, the notion that this particular diversity, of monism versus theism, is irreducible is also undermined by the Plato/Hegel approach. For here too, Plato and Hegel suggest that the ultimate issue is not some irreducible "experience," whether monistic, theistic, or other, but rather whether there is a structure of human experience in general which constitutes an ultimate reality.

If there is such a structure, it could inform various kinds of "experience" in various ways, including the "monistic" way and the "theistic" way. "Monistic" experiences apparently reflect the fact, which Plato and Hegel establish, that the divine can't be a "separate being" from the world (because that would make it finite and thus non-divine). "Theistic" experiences, on the other hand, reflect the fact, which Plato and Hegel also illuminate, that the divine does in fact often impinge upon us *as though* it were a separate being. It does this because our ordinary conception of ourselves as finite "beings" often causes us to experience the irruption of infinite freedom and love as coming from a source that's external to ourselves, and which we therefore very naturally *imagine as* a separate being. In each case, the experience reflects a very real aspect of the ultimate reality, but since they're actually only aspects of it, there is no need to regard them as competing with each other to represent the true divine reality.

That we "imagine" in a certain way what we seem to be encountering need not imply that we are aware of conjuring up and thus consciously controlling an image. The "imagining" that comes from sources of which we're not fully conscious, such as an encounter with the deep structure of our relation to reality, can have the character instead of what we call a "vision" or a dream. When suitably interpreted, as Freud and Jung have shown, a dream can embody a remarkable amount of truth. A waking "vision," such as mystics and religious prophets sometimes have, can embody truth in a similar way—always subject to interpretation and criticism by conscious thought, as I'll discuss in Chapter 6. And this interpretation and criticism will inevitably bring in such independently ascertained facts as the theological implications, which Plato and Hegel show us, of human experience in general.

5 PLATO'S PROGRESS

Fleeing is not a liberation from what is . . . fled from; the one that excludes still remains connected to what it excludes.

G. W. F. HEGEL, *SCIENCE OF LOGIC*

Nobody is satisfied to acquire things that are merely believed to be good . . . but everyone wants the things that really are good and disdains mere belief here.

PLATO, *REPUBLIC* 505D

Alienating "dualisms" and Plato

I've been suggesting all along that the broadly Platonic tradition can help us to integrate ourselves and be fully free, without "fleeing" from the world and consequently, as Hegel says, "remaining connected" to it and unfree. But this claim about the Platonic tradition might seem rather questionable. Plato is often described as the originator of a "dualism" of soul versus body, in which the body would be the "enemy" of the soul, and precisely something to "flee" from. How can the same philosopher who seems to be centrally responsible, through at least some of his writings, for the highly oppositional tradition of soul/body dualism, offer us the help that we need in order to avoid what Hegel calls "fleeing [that] is not a liberation"?

Plato can do this because from the beginning he undermined his own apparent dualism, seeking to capture what's true in it without making himself divided and unfree. In this way, he anticipated the West's long debates between the dualisms of the Gnostics, Martin Luther, Descartes, Kant, Schopenhauer, and the early Wittgenstein, on the one hand, and the more "monistic" but spiritual syntheses of Plotinus, Erasmus, Spinoza, Hegel, and Whitehead, on the other.

Plato is contested territory

As with Hegel, many people who are aware of Plato have strong opinions about him. We correctly associate Plato with ideas that are regarded as religious, like the soul, transcendence, and the like. So people who have had bad experiences with institutions that call themselves religious may be inclined to take a jaundiced view of Plato. We also correctly associate Plato with "reason," of which some people are very suspicious because reason in the form of modern science and technology seems to have disenchanted our world and left us with little room for love, beauty, and the like. When Plato criticizes the arts as promoting irrationality, this seems to confirm that he has taken the wrong side on this great issue.

Political battles also come into play, because Plato, in this respect resembling some modern people who present themselves as religious, had major doubts about democracy. And so we project our modern political struggles onto Plato and onto writers who find value in his work.

In the next several chapters, I'll try to show that Plato in fact embraces all "sides," religion and art and reason and also democracy and criticism of democracy, in a way that's both intelligible and deeply helpful. Beyond that, I'll show how the "rational religion" that Plato outlines is as inspiring as any religion could be, by virtue of the relationship that Plato uncovers between reason and love. And how the nondualistic transcendence on which this religion is based can explain, also, how reason requires justice, how mind relates to body, and how value relates to "fact."

Plato's progress

Let's begin, then, with the issue of "dualism"—of Plato's apparent belief that there is an inherent and inevitable antagonism between "soul" and "body."

Plato was apparently responding, over the course of his life's work, to two initial traumas. He may never have fully worked through them, but he did deal with them in increasingly adequate ways. The first trauma was the reign of terror conducted against the Athenian democrats in 404–403 BCE, when Plato was twenty-three years old, by an aristocratic clique, the "Thirty Tyrants," who were led by Plato's uncle, Critias. The second trauma, five years later in 399 BCE, was Athens's judicial execution of Plato's hero, Socrates, for allegedly "corrupting the youth" of Athens and not worshipping Athens's gods.

Conflict between the "aristocrats" of inherited wealth and the ordinary craftspeople and merchants who formed a majority in Athens's decision-making assembly was a chronic feature of Athenian life in the fifth century. It was driven to a high pitch by the long war between Athens and Sparta which was carried on largely by the "democratic" party, initially under the leadership of Pericles. When Sparta defeated Athens, in 404, Sparta installed the Athenian aristocrats in power in the city, and the aristocrats seized the opportunity to settle old scores, brutally. After the "Thirty" fell from power, in 403, the resurgent democrats wisely enacted an amnesty, so as to avoid an ongoing battle of tit for tat between the parties. But strong feelings undoubtedly persisted for a long time thereafter.

Socrates himself wasn't rich, and he believed in a government of laws and justice, as opposed to tyranny. So he disapproved (and Plato clearly shared his disapproval) of the actions of the "Thirty" and refused, at considerable personal risk, to cooperate with them.

Despite Socrates's resistance to the "Thirty," there may have been a connection between what happened when they were in power and the jury's conviction of Socrates, five years later. Many of the jurors may have mistakenly thought of Socrates as a supporter of the "Thirty," and harbored negative feelings toward him for that reason. This is because Socrates's circle of associates over the years included quite a few members, such as Plato himself, of the aristocratic families from which the "Thirty" drew their members.[1] In view of this circumstance that is likely to have contributed to Socrates's being convicted, it's quite possible that Plato may have felt some indirect responsibility, through his family, for Socrates's death.

What's certain is that Socrates's death was a watershed event for Plato. "Socrates" is the main protagonist, always presented in a very positive light, in the written dialogues to which Plato devoted many years of work. From them we derive most of our knowledge of the actual Socrates and of the philosophy that Plato developed in response to Socrates's teaching and various other influences.

In the *Republic*, the character called "Socrates" suggests that ordinary people would be likely to want to kill a person who had found more truth than they had found, and who tried to share it with them (517a). This is one of many indications in the dialogues that Plato was preoccupied, in all of his thinking about politics and ethics, with the issue of Socrates's death, and how a society might be created in which such tragic events wouldn't occur. It may be easier for us to understand the quite undemocratic nature of the political institutions that Plato seems to recommend, if we remember that the Athenian democracy had executed Plato's teacher and hero.

In addition to Plato's thinking about politics, one could easily interpret some of his best-known ideas about the human "soul," itself, and its relation to the "body," as at least partly a response to his extended trauma. If the soul is separate from the body and survives it, then Socrates's soul can be with the immortals, regardless of what the ignorant Athenians did to his body. In this way, the "dualistic" Plato could have been Plato's first, very natural reaction to his trauma.

But other aspects of Plato's thinking could reflect a realization that his dualism might not actually give him as much freedom as it seemed to—that "fleeing" might not, in fact, make him free. These other aspects of Plato's thinking are subtle and aren't flagged as dramatically as the initial dualism was. So writers who are all clearly influenced by Plato can nevertheless wind up disagreeing with each other in major ways on these central issues.

Dualism recurs in the Gnostics, in aspects of Plotinus and Rumi, in Martin Luther, in Rene Descartes, in Kant's Critiques, in Schopenhauer, and in Wittgenstein's *Tractatus*. A nondualistic but still broadly Platonic view appears in Aristotle, in other aspects of Plotinus and Rumi, in Meister Eckhart, Erasmus, Spinoza, Hegel, Whitehead, Polanyi, and Rödl.

While Plato gave us what seems to be a powerful statement of dualism, in the early part of his *Phaedo*, he also set in motion these nondualistic trains of thought. He did this first of all through his thinking about reality, the Forms, God, and the world, which was never really as bluntly dualistic as it sometimes sounds. He did it also through his systematic study of the intermediate realm, between "body" and rational "soul," which we call "emotion." Plato examines pride, anger, and especially love and shows us how they all combine bodily aspects and important "rational" aspects.

Let's begin with a brief look at his apparent dualism.

Plato the apparent dualist

Plato's *Phaedo* concludes with the scene in which Socrates, in prison, says farewell to his friends and drinks the poison hemlock to which the Athenian court has condemned him, because he (allegedly) corrupted the youth of Athens and didn't worship Athens's gods. Plato describes Socrates as spending the day of his execution in a lengthy discussion, with his friends, of the possible immortality of the individual human soul. The connection of this topic with Socrates's impending death is clear to everyone. And Socrates in fact asserts, in the dialogue, that he's convinced that souls are immortal, and offers several elaborate arguments in support of this idea.

In terms of its sheer historical influence, the most important of these arguments is probably the first major one, in which Socrates appeals to the existence of what he calls "Forms." These are (for example) "the Just," "the Beautiful," "the Good," "Bigness," "Health," "Strength"—that is, they are what just, beautiful, good, big, healthy, or strong things "essentially" are (65d). These underlying essences can't be observed directly in particular things in the world, since those things are only *imperfectly* just, beautiful, big, and so forth. So Socrates suggests that our souls must have become acquainted with these essences when our souls existed apart from the body, before our present lives (76c). And thus we can know that our souls can and sometimes do exist apart from our bodies.

In connection with this argument, Socrates asserts that philosophers, who understand these facts, "despise" food, drink, sex, bodily ornaments, and everything that has to do with the body (64e). They do their best to "flee" from the body (65d), by purifying the soul of bodily concerns (69c), so as to consort as much as possible with the bodiless truth that is the Forms. This is the famous Platonic "asceticism" (or "rampant Platonism," as John McDowell calls it), which Friedrich Nietzsche influentially diagnosed as "an expression of hatred for a world that makes one suffer," adding that "the *ressentiment* of metaphysicians is here creative."[2]

It's easy to suppose that if Plato himself endorsed this version of immortality, which he conjures up in quite a few places, it must have given him some consolation for, in particular, the loss of Socrates himself. Socrates's soul survives, in the company of the immortals.

However that may be, this passage in the *Phaedo* has indeed been one of the great documents of body-rejecting ascetic dualism, inspiring to many people, and to many others questionable, or itself needing to be rejected. To me its apparent message is definitely questionable. It seems clear to me that (as Hegel says) "fleeing" from something doesn't make you free of it. Instead, fleeing chains you to the thing from which you flee: it ensures that your functioning will be deeply imprinted by that thing, and by your relationship to it. To be imprinted in this way may be better than being uncritically mixed up with the thing, but it's hardly full freedom, since it's not *self*-determination.

Many of Plato's modern critics, such as David Hume, Friedrich Nietzsche, and Bertrand Russell, focus their objections on the soul/body antagonism that we seem to see in the *Phaedo*.[3] I myself sympathized with their objections for a long time, for the reason that I just mentioned. Antagonism toward the body seemed not to be fully free.

Plato the nondual rationalist

But in viewing Plato in this way, the critics and I were overlooking the radical explanation that Plato begins to articulate in the *Phaedo* and fills in in more detail in the *Republic* and later dialogues. In "fleeing" the body, Plato says, we're fleeing something that isn't fully real! If we understand the diminished reality that Plato imputes to the body, we'll see that "flight from" the body is a manner of speaking, which is better put, in many other contexts in the dialogues, as the pursuit of what is fully real.[4] In which case, the one who pursues would not be imprinted by the body and entangled with it in the way that we critics have suspected Plato of being.

I still suspect that Plato's talk of "fleeing" and "despising" probably betrays an emotional unfreedom that may have been an important part of his initial response to the double trauma that I described. I doubt very much that Plato's extended study of the emotions was motivated solely by "disinterested" curiosity. He had had major emotional experiences, including the traumas that I mentioned, and his analytical thinking about inner freedom, pride, and love must have helped him to work through these experiences.

But what impresses me now is how early in that process he seems to begin to get beyond the antagonism that his habitual language still suggests. In the passage in the *Phaedo* that has set off warning bells for many readers, Plato's central concern is not, in fact, with the negative influence of the body, but rather with the positive affinity between the soul and the (non-bodily) Forms. In the passage at 65c-d that describes the soul as "disdaining" and "fleeing" the body, Socrates's main concern is with how the soul can gain access to "truth" or "reality." Suggesting that the body's senses deceive the soul and confuse it, he proposes that the soul that is successful in the search for truth seeks to be "by itself" (65d), and thus to track down realities "pure and by themselves" (66a).

Here we might think especially of the search for mathematical truths. Mathematics was one of Plato's major interests, and some of his friends were brilliant mathematicians. In the dialogue called the *Meno*, Plato's Socrates has a discussion with an untutored slave boy from whom he elicits unexpected understanding of how one could find a square whose area is double that of a previously given square. (Answer: construct the square on the diagonal of the initial square.) Socrates suggests that this understanding derives not primarily from the slave boy's observation of the particular squares that Socrates draws in the dust, but rather from the birth of insight, in him, into the reasons why all squares must obey this general rule.

Through our familiarity with abstract reasoning in mathematics, we're accustomed to the idea that (at least) certain kinds of knowledge are based not on inspecting what we touch or see, as such, but rather on abstract reasoning. No number of measurements of particular squares can prove that the diagonal of an initial square will always yield a square with double its area. Only arguments from (possibly) self-evident axioms can do that. This experience of learning through mathematical proof is one of the main sources of Plato's notion that the soul can indeed usefully be "by itself" and find realities that don't depend upon sense perception.

So Plato's primary concern in the passage in the *Phaedo*, with its famous "despising" and "fleeing" of the body, is not with the body as such but rather with a kind of functioning, in the "soul," which seems to be most successful when it ignores the body. A functioning, as he puts it, of the soul "by itself." The notorious language of "despising," and so forth, is a secondary feature of a train of thought that's primarily concerned with something quite different, namely, with the abstractness that characterizes certain very fruitful kinds of inquiry, and from which the body's senses can be a source of distraction.[5]

Platonism and "embodied human experience"

At this point I can imagine someone saying,

> But human beings aren't theorems in mathematics! Surely if we leave behind sight, touch, hearing, and smell, and the emotions that go with them, we'll leave behind concrete human life and wind up with empty abstractions. To call mathematics and Forms "more real" than the human experience of embodiment is impossibly paradoxical. My bodily experience is my paradigm of what's real. I can't imagine how someone could seriously propose that something else is more real than it.

Plato's most effective single response to this kind of objection is contained in a passage in book vi of the *Republic* whose full importance isn't often recognized. The passage culminates in the statement that I quoted in the epigraph of this chapter: "Nobody is satisfied to acquire things that are merely believed to be good . . . but everyone wants the things that really *are* good and disdains mere belief here" (505d).

To explain how this dictum speaks to the issue of "reality" and bodily experience, I need to outline its context, which is a discussion that begins in Plato's account of the three "parts of the soul," in book iv.[6] There, Socrates describes how we make up our minds about what to do. We experience "appetites," such as thirst, that urge courses of action, such as drinking. But sometimes we also experience the thought that we should resist the appetite, and not do what it urges. For example, that we shouldn't drink what's in front of us, because it will harm us in some way. This familiar experience, Socrates says, shows that the soul has at least two different parts: the appetites, on the one hand, and the "reasoning" part, on the other. The conflict that we experience is the evidence that these are different parts.

Socrates goes on to identify a third part of the soul, as well: the part that gets angry when someone mistreats us or when we mistreat ourselves. In Socrates's striking example, a man named Leontius feels a desire to look at some recently executed corpses, but is also angry at himself for giving in to this ignoble desire. This shows, Socrates says, that besides the appetites and the reasoning part, our souls also have a "spirited" part (*thumos*, in Greek), which gets indignant at actions that it regards as incompatible with the person's dignity. The spirited part is obviously different from the appetites, which inspire these actions, but it's also different from the reasoning part, because sometimes we feel anger at things that our reasoning part eventually says are okay. The spirited part claims to speak on behalf of reason, as opposed to appetites like Leontius's desire to look at the corpses; but because the spirited part is emotional and hasty, it doesn't always accurately reflect what reason will eventually conclude.

What I want to examine now is the conflict between appetite and the rational part. What Plato has Socrates say about it may not seem very controversial. So it's important to remember that influential thinkers have in fact suggested that when reason appears to be coming into conflict with an appetite, all that's really happening is that *one appetite is coming into conflict with another*. Our appetite for a drink is coming into conflict, say, with our appetite for other satisfactions that we won't be able to enjoy if the drink that's in front of us turns out to be poisonous and we don't live long enough to satisfy the other appetites. This is the view of Epicurus, in ancient Greece, of Thomas Hobbes and David Hume, in seventeenth- and eighteenth-century Britain, and of perhaps all twentieth-century materialists, naturalists, empiricists, and positivists.

If what we call "reasoning" were really just weighing one appetite against others and figuring out which appetite or group of appetites is the strongest, then the inner conflict that Plato describes would simply be a competition among the parts of the appetitive part, to see which one is stronger. It wouldn't be a negotiation between the appetitive part and something outside it. Then our situation would be one in which, as David Hume put it, "reason is, and ought only to be the slave of the passions, and can never pretend to any other office than to serve and obey them," by figuring out how to get what our appetites want.[7]

We need to examine this view carefully, because it's extremely influential in our own time, especially among social scientists. When the Harvard psychologist, B. F. Skinner compared human behavior to rat behavior, he assumed that neither the rats nor the humans go beyond the kind of competition among appetites, to see which appetite is the strongest, that Epicurus and Hume take to be going on in us.[8] The "cognitive scientists" who have recently criticized Skinner's "behaviorism" for its excessive skepticism about the existence of "inner" mental mechanisms, don't seem to differ importantly from Skinner, Epicurus, and Hume about the role of reason in our practical decision-making. And when economists and political scientists describe us as acting to satisfy our "preferences," they employ a similar conception of human decision-making.

In none of these models does "reason" get any role other than figuring out which appetite or preference is stronger, and how to satisfy the stronger one, or a mixture of the two which reflects their relative strengths. Something like this is widely thought to be the only "scientific" view of human decision-making, and people who see the matter in this way are likely to regard "idealists" or "rationalists," who disagree with this sort of view, as unscientific wishful thinkers. But in the passage that I quoted from *Republic* book vi, Plato aims to show that however widespread this "naturalist" or "empiricist" view may be, it nevertheless is mistaken.

Questioning and what's really good

In the case of just and beautiful things, many people are content with what are believed to be so, even if they aren't really so. [But] nobody is satisfied to acquire things that are merely believed to be *good* ... everyone wants the things that really *are* good and disdains mere belief here. (*Republic* 505d)

Here Socrates is saying that regarding the things, experiences, relationships, and so forth, that we get for ourselves, we want to be sure that they really are good, rather than just being what we, or other people, *think* is good. We don't want to live in a "fool's paradise," thinking that we're experiencing what's really good, when in fact it isn't really good.

Even if we could be sure that we would remain in this fool's paradise for our entire lives, and never find out that we had been mistaken, we hate the thought that that might be the case—that what we take to be really good might not really be good. If that were the case, we feel, our lives would have been wasted, whether or not we ever found out that they were wasted. We can joke about how *other* people are "blissfully ignorant," but I have yet to meet a person who says that she would choose to have less information about what's really good, if by doing so she could be sure of getting lots of what she *currently thinks* is good. The notion of choice, itself, seems to be oriented toward finding out (if possible) what's really good, rather than just being guided by one's current desires or one's current opinions about what's good.

As applied to Skinner's view of human motivation, and other naturalist or empiricist views, what Socrates's response says is that since we want what's *really* good, what we feel drawn to right now isn't the final word regarding what we really want. Because if we came to the conclusion that what we feel drawn to right now wasn't really good, we would stop wanting it, or at least stop wanting it wholeheartedly, and start wanting what we had concluded was really good.

That is, we humans are able to *question* our wants and our appetites and resist them or revise them or work around them when we conclude that they are ill-informed or mistaken. No doubt some of our wants, such as for things that we're addicted to, will be difficult to resist. But nobody doubts that we can sometimes do things that will at least reduce the likelihood that we'll act on wants that we've concluded were mistaken.

This ability to question what we feel drawn to right now, and to draw practical consequences from this questioning, is not something that naturalist or empiricist views take adequately into account. Their advocates try to describe the experience of questioning as just another case of conflict between wants and appetites. When I question whether the drink that's in front of me will be good for me, they say, what I'm really doing is asking whether I have other wants that will be frustrated if I drink the drink, such as wanting to see the sun rise tomorrow, or whatever it might be. But Plato's response is that I can question any and *all* of my wants, including my wanting to see the sun rise tomorrow, by asking whether it will really be *good* for me to satisfy these wants.

We may well wonder how we could answer questions like these. If we question all of our wants at once, what standard will be left, by reference to which we can answer all of these innumerable questions? Is this project of unlimited questioning, a project that we can actually afford to embark upon? As B. F. Skinner complained, "The disputing of values... is interminable."[9] But regardless of how difficult it may be to implement it in practice, Plato's initial point seems like a strong one. We need to raise these questions because we want to wind up with what's really good, and not just what we currently feel drawn to as a result of what we ate for breakfast this morning, or what our parents told us is good, or what evolution has wired us to want.

Contradictions in naturalism

The naturalist or empiricist view seems to say: Shut up and *do* what your breakfast or your parents or your evolutionary history has wired you to do! But if I'm a serious person and I'm deciding (for example) how to spend my life, I'm not going to find the naturalist's or empiricist's advice very attractive. I want a life that's *really* good for me, not just a life that I'm wired to live. As long as there is hope of finding out what's really good, that's what I'm going to want to do.[10]

Rats, I suppose, can't ask questions like these, and thus can't get into the kind of quandary of which the history of philosophy and religion is certainly full. But as long as it seems that I can ask this kind of question, it seems that I ought to, because if I don't ask it, I'm only half alive.

In fact, if the naturalist or empiricist actually said that I should stop trying to ask this kind of question, and just be satisfied with what I'm wired to do, they wouldn't just be telling me what I'm wired to do. For if I were just plain wired to do it, they wouldn't have to urge me to do it. Rather, in telling me to stop asking questions they would be telling me what I really ought to do or what it would be best for me to do, and thus conceding by their actions that these are important things to think about and discuss.

When a naturalist or empiricist becomes involved in public controversy about matters of value, she should be embarrassed, since according to her theory that reason "is and ought to be the slave of the passions," there is no rational way to settle such a controversy. But in fact, the issue with naturalism isn't just about what we should really *do* but also about what we should really *believe*. If reason "ought to be the slave of the passions," this will apply just as much to belief as to anything else, and we will no longer be able to say that we ought to believe what has been tested by science, as opposed to whatever just pops into our heads. A thoroughgoing naturalist can't tell us that we "ought" to proceed differently in the case of science than we do in the case of life-planning and ethics. It will all depend upon what our "passions" happen to be.

In this way it's hard to see how one can consistently take Hume's naturalistic line that reason ought to be the slave of the passions, while maintaining, as most self-described naturalists do, that we rationally ought to give authority in our lives to science rather than superstition. Plato's analysis of the soul speaks to this practical contradiction in naturalism. Plato concludes from what we've observed about our attitudes toward science and toward what's really good, that regardless of what we may say, we don't really believe that reason ought to be the slave of the passions. Rather, the "reasoning part" of the soul has an independent role to play, which is to question everything that we're currently inclined to want and to believe, so as to get behind it, to what's really good and what's really true.

How exactly such "reasoning" will operate remains to be seen. My point is simply that Plato seems to have given us a good reason to take the "reasoning part" seriously, as something with its own distinctive role to play, rather than as a mere slave of the passions.

Questioning and the existence of Forms

In fact, we might take this account of the soul's investment in seeking what's really good and really true as one of Plato's major reasons for taking seriously his notion of Forms that have a reality that can't be reduced to what we can experience with our five senses. In mathematics, we persist in thinking that the diagonal of a given square will yield a square with twice the area in every case, and not just in the squares that we have measured or will measure. And in conducting our lives, Plato suggests in *Republic* 505d, we persist in thinking that what's really good need not be reducible to what we will ever want, or believe is good. In both cases, we want what's really true, rather than just what seems on the basis of our present or future sense experience or beliefs to be true.

That we want this is one of Plato's strongest arguments for his proposition that there is in fact a truth, the Forms, that isn't reducible to sense experience. Perhaps it could be the case that this "want" is chimerical, that what we want doesn't in fact exist. But Plato is pointing out that a major part of our mental activity *presupposes* that this truth that we want does exist, in the case of our life conduct just as much as in the case of mathematics.

The Forms as "more real"

Plato repeatedly tells us that the Forms are "more real" than what we experience with our senses.[11] We can see now what he might mean by this. The Forms are the truth, about mathematical objects, about what's good, and about other objects as well. What we experience with our senses may be responsive to this truth, or it may not. To the extent that it's responsive to this truth, it's really real, and to the extent that it isn't responsive, it isn't really real, though in both cases it equally *exists*.

By calling what we experience with our senses less real than the Forms, Plato is not saying that what we experience with our senses is simply illusion. The "reality" that the Forms have more of is not simply their not being illusions. If that's not what their extra reality is, what is it? The easiest place to see how one could suppose that something that isn't an illusion, is nevertheless less real than something else, is in our experience of ourselves.

In *Republic* book iv, Plato's examination of the different "parts of the soul" leads him to the conclusion that only the rational part can integrate the soul into one, and thus make it truly "just." Here is his description of the effect of a person's being governed by his rational part, and therefore "just":

> Justice . . . is concerned with what is truly himself and his own. . . . [The person who is just] binds together [his] parts . . . and from having been many things he becomes entirely one, moderate, and harmonious. Only then does he act. (443d-e)

Our interest here (I'll discuss the "justice" issue later) is that by "binding together his parts" and "becoming entirely one," this person is "*truly himself.*" That is, as I put it in earlier chapters, a person who is governed by his rational part is real not merely as a collection of various ingredients or "parts," but *as himself*. A person who acts purely out of appetite, without any examination of whether that appetite is for something that will actually be "good," is enacting his appetite, rather than anything that can appropriately be called "himself." Likewise for a person who acts purely out of anger, without examining whether the anger is justified by what's genuinely good. Whereas a person who thinks about these issues before acting "becomes entirely one" and acts, therefore, in a way that expresses something that can appropriately be called "himself."

In this way, rational self-governance brings into being an additional kind of reality, which we might describe as *more fully* real than what was there before, because it integrates those parts in a way that the parts themselves are not integrated. A person who acts "as one," is more real *as himself* than a person who merely enacts some part or parts of himself. He is present and functioning as himself, rather than just as a collection of ingredients or inputs.

We all from time to time experience periods of distraction, absence of mind, or depression, in which we aren't fully present as ourselves. Considering these periods from a vantage point at which we are fully present and functioning as ourselves, we can see what Plato means by saying that some non-illusory things are more real than other non-illusory things. There are times when we ourselves are more real as ourselves than we are at other times.

Indeed, we can see nature as a whole as illustrating this issue of how fully integrated and "real as itself" a being can be. Plants are more integrated than rocks, in that they're able to process nutrients and reproduce themselves, and thus they're less at the mercy of their environment. So we could say that plants are more effectively focused on being themselves than rocks are, and in that sense they're more real as themselves. Rocks may be less vulnerable than plants are, but what's the use of invulnerability if what's invulnerable isn't *you*?

Animals, in turn, are more integrated than plants are, in that animals' senses allow them to learn about their environment and navigate through it in ways that plants can't. So animals are still more effectively focused on being themselves than plants are, and thus more real as themselves.

Humans, in turn, can be more effectively focused on being themselves than many animals are, insofar as humans can determine for themselves what's good, rather than having this be determined for them by their genetic heritage and their environment. Nutrition and reproduction, motility and sensation, and a thinking pursuit of the Good each bring into being a more intensive reality as oneself than is present without them.[12]

Now, what all of this has to do with the Forms and their supposedly greater reality than our sense experience is that it's by virtue of its pursuit of knowledge of what's really good, that the rational part of the soul distinguishes itself from the soul's appetites and anger and so forth. The Form of the Good is the embodiment of what's really good. So pursuing knowledge of the Form of the Good is what enables the rational part of the soul to govern us, and thus makes us fully present, fully real, as ourselves. In this way, the Form of the Good is a precondition of our being fully real, as ourselves.

But presumably something that's a precondition of our being fully real must be at least as real as we are when we are fully real. It's at least as real as we are, because we can't deny its reality without denying our own functioning as creatures who are guided by it or are trying to be guided by it.[13] And since it's at least as real as we are, it's more (fully) real than the material things that aren't guided by it and thus aren't real as themselves.

This, then, is how Plato can seriously propose that something is more real than the human embodiment that we think of as paradigmatically real. Human embodiment is certainly real in the sense that it's not (on the whole) illusory. But it's not real in the sense of being fully itself, or making itself what it is. It depends upon many other things to make it what it is. Whereas what is "itself" and is "by itself," as Socrates puts it at *Phaedo* 65d, does not depend upon other things to make it what it is. It's real as itself, self-determining, self-contained. It's not surprising that Plato took this, rather than the mere absence of illusion, as his paradigm of full reality, and described it in the *Republic* as a human being's highest accomplishment.[14]

Contra Vlastos and Bröcker

Gregory Vlastos discussed Plato's "degrees of reality" view in two papers, "Metaphysical Paradox" and "Degrees of Reality," reprinted in Vlastos (1973 and 1981). In the first paper, he says that "in vision of Form, Plato discovers . . . his own personal bridge from [time as a state of bondage] to [time under the aspect of eternity, regeneration] via [eternity, the blessedness of release]." (I combine two sentences of which Vlastos confusingly indexes one to the other.) "How natural then for [Plato] to say that the eternal things, the Forms, are the 'really real' ones. In seeing [the Forms,] a creature of time touches eternity." Vlastos calls the resulting *"restructuring of what there is on the scaffolding of what is more and less real . . .* one of Plato's greatest achievements, perhaps his greatest," but adds that Plato should have acknowledged that it was "a personal vision for which demonstrative certainty cannot be claimed" (pp. 55–56; emphasis added).

I would suggest that the way the *Republic* connects the vision of Forms with inner freedom and unity makes Plato's view much less of an optional "personal vision" than Vlastos takes it to be. For inner freedom and unity are sought, in one way or another, by all of us, and thus insofar as the vision of Forms is a precondition of inner freedom and unity, we all seek the vision of Forms as well.[15] If inner freedom and unity aren't optional, then the vision of Forms isn't optional either.

So when Walter Bröcker wrote in his critique of Plato and Hegel that Plato's introduction of degrees of reality was "an act of compensation" for the "removal of gods from the world of the senses by the thinking of the 'natural philosophers'" who preceded him ([1959], p. 425; my translation), Bröcker overlooked an important alternative explanation. Namely, that Plato was identifying a vertical dimension in the human experience of reality which had given the traditional gods their plausibility in the first place, and which the natural philosophers hadn't gotten into focus. Plato and Hegel do indeed have a good reason "to grant what is thinkable a higher rank than what is perceivable" (Bröcker, p. 424), which is that more than perception, thinking enables the thinker to be herself, and (in that sense) more real than what doesn't think. So that thinking gives the world as a whole a higher degree of reality as itself than it would otherwise possess.

Reality as a vertical dimension

In modern times most of us have become accustomed to understanding "reality" simply as a uniform, horizontal plane, as (so to speak) a standard minimum endowment. This is in contrast to Plato and those who follow him who see reality as having an essential vertical dimension, a hierarchy of gradations, whereby some things are more successful in being themselves and in that sense they're more fully real than others.[16] This view of reality is more plausible when we see how it corresponds to an understanding of ourselves which recognizes how we can and often do fail to be fully in charge of our lives, fail to "be ourselves," and fail (in that sense) to be real, as ourselves.

When we consider how various kinds of living beings achieve lesser and greater degrees of self-government and (thus) lesser and greater degrees of reality "as themselves," we can begin to see that "reality" isn't merely a standard minimum endowment. Rather, it exhibits a hierarchy of lesser and greater degrees of what we might call "realization."[17]

This fundamental recognition is expressed in various ways in the world's religions and systems of metaphysics. Once one appreciates the experience that underlies and motivates this way of seeing the world, one can hardly dismiss it as mere anthropocentric illusion. For it doesn't focus merely on human beings. It's entirely ready to acknowledge that other living things may exhibit the same self-government as humans, and perhaps forms of self-government that we humans can barely imagine. And it traces a hierarchy of self-government in "lower" forms of life with which we still have a great deal in common.

To say, as enthusiasts of Darwinian biology sometimes do, that humans are "merely" the tools of (say) their genes in an endless struggle for survival is to ignore the hierarchy of degrees of self-government that life has achieved. Which is a hierarchy that is exhibited by the very pursuit of truth in whose name the Darwinist speaks. For rather than viewing his way of understanding life as something that merely increases the survival chances of his genes, the Darwinist clearly views it and expects us to be interested in it as something that may be objectively true.

We want to be guided by reality, in our lives, whether or not that guidance increases the survival chances of our genes. Being guided by reality means not being guided merely by our desires or illusions, which are, in general, things that we're "subjected to" by forces that we don't understand or control. Whereas the thinking by means of which we determine what's truly real is something that we seem to be able, to a significant degree, to understand and control. If it's true that we have such control, then our thinking expresses not just what we're subjected to but us. And thus our success in tracking what's truly real expresses us.

It's possible, in some sense, that we don't have any real control over our thinking. That would be the scenario of the extremest skepticism. But it's not a scenario that we can usefully discuss, because the conduct of such a discussion, like the conduct of any serious attempt to determine what's true, presupposes that we do have control over our thinking. We can't assert that our current discussion or thinking isn't under our control, without bringing it, effectively, to a grinding halt.

But controlling our own thinking, rather than letting it be a mere response to external inputs, is a form of self-government. Science is a prime example of disciplined, self-controlled thinking, and therefore of self-government. So we must assume that science's pursuit of objective truth is itself an instance of the ascent to a higher degree of self-government, and thus to a higher degree of reality as oneself, to which Plato and his followers are drawing our attention. Science, as I've said, is itself a project of transcendence.

And so is any other form of disciplined thinking, such as thinking about what's really Good. It's unfortunate that few present-day accounts of Platonism bring out the way in which Platonism's "vertical" hierarchy of increasing reality corresponds to our personal pursuit of greater self-government and thus of greater reality as ourselves. Drawing on his very plausible point that we want what's really good, in our lives, rather than merely whatever we currently feel or think is good, Plato's account of our greater self-government makes it clear why he attaches such great significance to the Forms, and the Form of the Good in particular. These are not only key ingredients in our understanding of the world and ourselves through mathematics, science, and value-inquiry, they are also key ingredients, thereby, in our effort to be fully real, as ourselves.

Two interpreters of Plato's metaphysics from whom I have learned a great deal, J. N. Findlay and Lloyd Gerson, exhibit the common weakness that they don't make it clear why an uncommitted bystander should take seriously Plato's claim that the Forms are more real than our human embodiment. Findlay suggests that one's attitude on this subject may be a matter of temperament or social contingency.[18] Gerson too refers to temperament, saying that "someone who unreservedly recognizes himself as ideally a thinker is probably the only plausible candidate for the sort of self-transformation Plato recommends. . . . The rarity of the true philosophical temperament, as Plato understands that, is hardly in doubt."[19]

Whereas it seems to me that Plato provides considerations, in his account of the soul's self-government, that will speak to any thoughtful person. I've just shown how something like Plato's account of the soul's self-government seems to be presupposed by any serious discussion about what's objectively true about the world. It may be true that people who are "unreservedly" committed to this goal at any given time are rare, but it seems to me that most people experience its attraction quite frequently, and in that sense we are all candidates for the self-transformation that Plato recommends.

No need for *ressentiment*

So, as I suggested earlier, the vertical dimension that Plato sees in reality needn't reflect any negative feelings about the body or the physical world as such. It simply reflects the insight that a person who is guided by her five senses and her felt desires and opinions rather than being guided by thought is guided by external inputs of one kind or another rather than by herself, and thus fails to be fully herself and fully real, as herself.

I quoted above Nietzsche's famous remark from *The Will to Power* about the metaphysicians' *ressentiment*. Bertrand Russell, quoting George Santayana, made a similar accusation against "the great philosophers who were mystics": that they were "'malicious' in regard to the world of science and common sense."[20] In *The Fragility of Goodness*, Martha Nussbaum also endorsed Nietzsche's "deep and no doubt correct insight into a part of the appeal of Plato's arguments," the insight that the Platonic "ascent" is motivated by *ressentiment*.[21] In her later *Upheavals of Thought*, Nussbaum similarly insisted that Plato's "ascent strategy" in the *Symposium* is "a therapeutic program undertaken for reasons of health, because the strains of ordinary *eros* are too costly."[22]

In opposition to all of these allegations, I suggest that our wanting "the things that really are good" (*Republic* 505d), and thus to function fully as ourselves, is a sufficient explanation of the ascent in both dialogues, the *Republic* and the *Symposium*. (I'll discuss the *Symposium*'s account of eros in Chapter 7.) These "masters of suspicion," Nietzsche, Santayana, Russell, and Nussbaum, who seek to liberate us from the illusions of idealism, have in fact obscured what idealism is about.

The general issue of the contribution that thought and "ideas" can make to what we succeed in being, and thus to what the world as a whole succeeds in being, has unfortunately been the subject of widespread confusion since at least the nineteenth century. That what we succeed in being might contribute something to what the world as a whole succeeds in being, is no longer a familiar thought. Probably because intellect has come to be associated almost exclusively with science and technology, our understanding of its role in our life as a whole has been reduced to a stock of stereotypical and unrealistic images. We have, for example, the "rational man" who has no emotions, the "intellectual" who is preoccupied with ideas at the expense of actually living life, the "romantic" who has no interest in reason, and the "existentialist" who pursues projects that come out of the blue.

Recent instances of this "existentialist" theme are Bernard Williams's hypostatizing of what he calls "ground projects" in Williams (1986), and Richard Rorty's proposal to "substitute Freedom for Truth as the goal of thinking and of social progress" in Rorty (1989) (p. xiii). Earlier instances are to be found in Kierkegaard, Heidegger, and Andre Gide. These writers are all centrally concerned with the goal of "being oneself" or being free, but none of them seem to appreciate what Plato, Plotinus, Kant, and Hegel have to say on this subject. According to them, thought that seeks truth and thus is less at the mercy of external influences than other human functions are is consequently more free and more truly one's "own" and thus is the primary route to being truly oneself and free. That is, the pursuit of Truth is the primary route to real Freedom.

Plato isn't looking for people who have no emotions, or who are preoccupied with what we call "ideas," and he's certainly not looking for people who have no interest in reason or whose projects come out of the blue. Following Socrates's principle that the unexamined life is not worth living (*Apology of Socrates* 38a), Plato is looking for people whose dominant concerns don't obviously stem from some unexamined external influence. So that their lives may express in an important way themselves, their own processing, as distinct from their antecedents and environment.

"*Obey thyself*," as Emerson says. The vertical ascent is the dimension of oneself, of one's own processing. It may not be easy to define precisely what this processing consists in. But everyone knows in practice the difference between simply acting on an appetite, an emotion, or a bright idea, or considering it with an uncommitted, open mind, so that one's eventual decision is "all things considered." This difference is what Platonism is about, and it's what makes us fully real, as ourselves.

By focusing on what's needed in order for us to be fully real, as ourselves, Platonism shows us something crucial about reality in general which is ignored by accounts of reality which address only what's "out there," separate from the observing self. The crucial thing that such accounts ignore is the way in which an observing, thinking, and evaluating self enables a reality to govern itself and thus (as we say) to "be itself," rather than just being the effect of its antecedents and environment. The self's attention to itself, in Platonism, is not mere "navel-gazing," as "practical" thinking might suspect. It brings to light a dimension of the physical universe, namely, its ability to achieve true self-government, which we can easily overlook when we're engaged in our necessary efforts to understand and control what's "out there," separate from ourselves.

The way in which the "self" or subject contributes to the physical universe's achievement of reality "as itself" is the aspect of Platonism that's spelled out most explicitly by German Idealism, and especially by Hegel in his study of how, as he puts it, "substance is essentially subject."[23] Students of Platonism who appreciate the German Idealists may pick up important aspects of Plato that others might miss.

When Eric Perl, for example, asserts as a fundamental principle for Plato that "the intellect by nature demands to see goodness in its object in order to understand, to make sense of it," I imagine that many admirers of natural science would probably dismiss this statement as simple dogmatism.[24] Whereas when Plato himself states (in *Phaedo* 99c, which Perl quotes here) that those who give merely mechanical accounts of nature "think that, truly, the good and the right do not bind and hold anything together," Plato alludes to the phenomenon that he explores in detail in *Republic* books iv-vii: that an interest in the Good can "bind something together" in the clear sense that it enables that thing to be guided by its own thinking and not merely by external inputs.[25] Having thus identified a higher degree of reality, reality as itself, Plato like Aristotle and Hegel can then quite reasonably understand other forms of life as approximating in varying degrees to this higher degree of reality.

How knowledge in the strongest sense is knowledge of self

Taking the reality that's real "as itself" as the paradigm of full reality, Plato takes our knowledge of this kind of reality as the paradigm, also, of knowledge. The Forms, especially the Form of the Good but also the subordinate Forms, which enable things to be real as themselves by having a definite identity ("Square," "Tree," "Human Being," and so forth), are therefore the proper objects of knowledge. Particular sense experiences convey knowledge only insofar as they have to do with a Form or Forms, and (to that extent) with a self-determining, self-governing reality.

During the first half of the twentieth century, an empiricist position was influential in Anglophone philosophy (Bertrand Russell, A. J. Ayer) according to which knowledge is constructed out of "sense-data," which are how the world affects us through our five senses. Criticism of this notion by philosophers including W. V. O. Quine and Wilfrid Sellars eventually made it clear that excitations of sense organs, as such, contain no knowledge, because no quantity of sense organ excitations, as such, would be sufficient to say something about the world.[26] As Sebastian Rödl points out,

> When I say "This is an apple" and only see the front of the apple, then what I say goes beyond what I see. It includes the back, which I do not see. Therefore it is possible that I walk around the ostensible apple and discover that there is no apple. Now, no sum of perceptions can exclude that later perceptions will show that despite appearances there is no apple. Like a general judgment, the judgment "There is an apple" goes beyond everything that we will ever have perceived. . . . If what is sensibly given in itself falls under the category of substance . . . then empirical knowledge always already contains general knowledge, which therefore is not inferred inductively from the former. (Rödl [2012], pp. 12–13)

The category of "substance" (*ousia*, "being") can't be based on sense perception alone. Like "Square," "Tree," "Human Being," and "Apple," the concept of a "Substance" can't be reduced to any number of actual or possible sense perceptions. This is the same point that I made above about mathematics: There is something at work here that can't be reduced to sensations. This is one important consideration that led Plato to his notion of "Forms."

But in placing the Form of the Good above all other Forms (*Republic* 509b), Plato had an additional consideration in mind, namely, that humans, apples, and other substances can be more or less successful in being the substances that they are. For we humans, at any rate, pursue the Good more at some times than we do at other times. Insofar as we do this, we're more "ourselves" and more human, by fulfilling human capacities, at some times than at others. There is thus a scale of degrees of reality, degrees of embodiment of the relevant Form, at least in ourselves. And in this way we can see that the Forms play a guiding role in a world that follows them to some degree, and to some degree fails to follow them.

Plus, as before, we can interpret the hierarchy of life, from plant to human, as fulfilling in lesser and greater degrees the Form of the Good and thus the Form (as it were) of self-determination, of being fully oneself. Of course from a mechanistic point of view, such an interpretation of life would be highly suspicious. But when one has seen the Good's relevance, in the human case, to self-determination and thus to being real as oneself, nothing is more natural than to extend this thought to life as a whole. (I'll say more about this "teleological" view of reality in Chapter 8.)

Our acquaintance with cases in which we seem to lack interest in the Good and with cases in which the world seems to lack interest in the Good are then something less than full "knowledge," since their object isn't what's fully real. Full knowledge is only of what's fully real, by being real as itself.

Of course, the issue isn't about how the word "knowledge" should be used. The issue is about what we should recognize as most real, and about our access to that. When we recognize a vertical dimension and a "higher," more fully "real" world within the familiar world, words like "reality" and "knowledge" take on a stronger meaning than they have in the "flat" world that we moderns normally think we inhabit. And since our experience of ourselves is a primary instance of this higher reality, our ability to know it is assured. We know it, as I've said, "from inside."[27]

Hans Blumenberg's critique of Plato's conception of knowledge

The account of Plato's conception of knowledge that I've been outlining enables us to reply to Hans Blumenberg's skeptical suggestion that Plato's conception imposes an "excessive demand" on us.[28] We can reply that what Plato "demands" is simply what follows from our interest in being in charge of our own lives, so that it's difficult to imagine a self-conscious life that doesn't seek to meet Plato's demand in some way. The fundamental question isn't, as Blumenberg suggests, the question whether humans are constitutionally "poor" or, alternatively, "rich"[29] through access to definitive "evidentness."[30] Our actual "riches," this much is evident to us, are in our capacity to be in charge of our lives by *seeking* what's true and what's truly good. This is the crucial Platonic claim, which underlies and motivates "Ur-Platonism's" rejection of doctrines such as materialism, mechanism, relativism, and skepticism, which make it difficult to see how we could be in charge of our lives.[31]

Blumenberg's extensive discussion in his *Höhlenausgänge* (1996), Part II, of Plato's image of the exit from the cave doesn't mention Plato's premise, articulated in *Republic* book iv, that "everyone wants the things that really *are* good and disdains mere belief here" (505e). Which is clearly the motive for ascent from the shadow world to the higher realities. Nor does Blumenberg refer to Plato's theme of the unification of the soul (443e), and how ascent, through this unification, enables the soul to be self-governing rather than governed by what's other than itself. Blumenberg understands Plato's "parts of the soul" only in terms of hierarchy (*Höhlenausgänge* [1996], p. 123), and not in terms of the soul's potential for unity and, thus, self-government.

Failing to notice these Platonic connections (that we want what really is good, and that by pursuing it we can be self-governing and whole), Blumenberg comes to the drastic conclusion that Plato recognized that he would have to use force to motivate anyone to leave the shadow world (pp. 87–89, 751). Blumenberg doesn't consider the possibility that Plato's references to force and compulsion (515c) are not meant to imply that we have no motive to leave the cave, but rather that the motive that we do have has to overcome our powerful habitual attachment to appetites, opinions, and self-importance, which are represented by the shadows on the wall of the cave. I'll say more about this struggle later in this chapter and in the next chapter. It's the "identity crisis" that I've been talking about all along, and which Blumenberg like many post-Hegel philosophers does not get into focus.

Blumenberg also does not consider the possible relevance of Plato's images of "birth in beauty" (*Symposium* 206c-e) and of Socrates as midwife (*Theaetetus* 150b), which together with the principle that "everyone wants the things that really are good" suggest ways in which departure from the shadow world might be more internally motivated than it appears in *Republic* vii. I'll discuss these other images in Chapters 7 and 8. A more comprehensive account of Plato's texts can help us to avoid being misled by peculiarities of his presentation in the *Republic*.

Blumenberg's drastic conclusion, resulting from his neglect of Plato's principle and of texts outside the *Republic*, limits what he can accomplish in what is otherwise a uniquely wide-ranging and perceptive account of "exits from the cave" in Western philosophy and culture.

This knowledge subsumes body within soul

By showing us how the soul that unifies itself by seeking truth and the truly good is more fully itself and (in that sense) more fully real than what's governed merely by its relations to its antecedents and environment, Plato shows us how bodily mechanisms can't claim to be the fullest reality. He spells this out in the passage in the *Phaedo* about how the truly good "binds and holds" things together. There Socrates objects to Anaxagoras's apparent materialism, in which he

> made no use of Mind, nor gave it any responsibility for the management of things, but mentioned as causes air and ether and water and many other strange things. That seemed to me much like [saying] that the reason that I am sitting here is because my body consists of bones and sinews, [and neglecting] to mention the true causes, that, after the Athenians decided it was better to condemn me, for this reason it seemed best to me to sit here and more right to remain and to endure whatever penalty they ordered. . . . Imagine not being able to distinguish the real cause from that without which the cause would not be able to act as a cause. . . . [They] do not believe that the truly good and "binding" binds and holds them together. (98b–99c)

Plato's point is that when we see how the pursuit of the Good unifies Socrates as a self-governing agent, we can no longer see air and ether and bones and sinews as the determining realities here. (The same thought would apply, in our day, to hormones, neurons, neurotransmitters, and so forth.) Rather, these material mechanisms are subsumed in a higher unity that's more real insofar as it's more self-governing.

In this way, the doctrine of a dimension of lesser and greater degrees of reality shows us how to escape the perennial debates between materialism and mind/body dualism, both of which fail to see how a more self-governing whole both includes and surpasses material mechanisms. Tying the philosophy of mind together with the philosophy of will and freedom, Plato's doctrine of degrees of reality points to a single underlying issue that generates most of our ongoing confusion in these areas.

This notion of the self-governing higher degree of reality, which is adumbrated here in the *Phaedo* and elaborated in *Republic* books iv–vi, puts in a different light both the *Phaedo*'s earlier remarks about "despising" bodily pleasures and adornments and Plato's various quasi-mythical stories about the soul's non-bodily itinerary (*Phaedo* 107–114; *Republic* 514–517, 614–621). We have good reason to think of the soul as more real than the body, insofar as it's more self-governing and thus more real as itself. And as a result it can be appropriate to think of the soul as making "journeys" that the body, as such, can't make—journeys, in particular, toward greater self-understanding and corresponding self-government: as in the "hero's journey" and the "soul's journey to God." But these should not be understood as taking place in a space that resembles the one in which bodily journeys take place. They are allegories—"stories," as Plato says. The "distance" that is covered in these stories, and their other features, represent inner processes of learning and thus becoming more real. Through his account of the "higher" dimension of self-government, Plato opens up what we've subsequently come to describe as the "inner" world of thought, self-discovery, and the divine.

Higher degree of reality is a simpler solution than Heidegger's

In his *Introduction to Metaphysics* (1953/1961), Martin Heidegger tells us that it was common in his day to contrast Platonic "idealism" with Aristotelian "realism," and to describe Parmenides's Fragment 5 (sic) (*to gar auto noein estin te kai einai* ["for the same thing can be thought as can be"]) as having the result, also thought to be operative in German Idealism, that "everything becomes subjective. Nothing is in itself" (p. 115).[32] Heidegger himself thought he saw an early instance of this kind of "subjectivity" in Plato's notion of the true as *idea*, Form or "idea" (pp. 150–53), so that Plato was already putting us on the "idealism"/"realism" seesaw by which modern philosophy has been plagued. And Heidegger consequently tried at some length to show how we could avoid that seesaw by developing a more "authentic" understanding (p. 116) of Parmenides's principle than Plato possessed.

However, Heidegger didn't notice how the ascent to "ideas," in Plato, enables the "subject" to be self-governing and thus real as itself, so that Platonic "idealism" precisely does not render everything "subjective" in contrast to "objective," but rather shows how the subject can surpass that contrast by achieving a kind of reality (namely, self-government and the resulting reality "as itself") that "objects," taken merely as such, can't possess. It's not difficult to interpret Parmenides's principle as suggesting something like this, if by "*einai*" in it we understand the full reality of what is real as itself.

Proceeding in this way, Plato (and Hegel too, following Plato) surpassed the contrast of "subject" with "object" in which, as Heidegger correctly observed, much modern philosophy is chronically entangled. And they did so without having to replace or radically reinterpret much of the vocabulary of Greek and modern philosophy, as Heidegger thought he needed to do.

And this reality, knowledge, and subject/object unity depend upon value

Besides going beyond the familiar subject/object and "idealism"/"realism" seesaw, Plato's doctrine of a higher degree of reality unifies another major dualism. By showing the role of the pursuit of what's truly good in bringing about the fuller reality of self-government, Plato shows that value, the Good, is an integral aspect of reality itself. The soul that seeks what's truly good, and not just whatever it's presently drawn to, is thereby able to govern itself rather than being a product merely of whatever produced its current urges and opinions. And what governs itself appears to be real in the strongest sense, by being real as itself. But in that case, value (what's truly good) plays an integral part in making what's real in the strongest sense, *real*. The pursuit of the Good gives full reality to what has full reality. Which means that "fact" and "value," or the "is" (as it's often put) and the "ought," aren't independent of each other. What's most real, what most "is," depends upon its pursuit of value, or the "ought," to be what it is. And likewise value, or the "ought," will be found in what most "is."[33]

This may be the single most important way in which Platonism challenges the conception of reality that dominates most of our present-day thinking. We assume that if anything can tell us about what's "real," it's the natural sciences, and that our experiences of value-clarification, freedom, love, and ecstasy, on the other hand, tell us nothing about what's real, but at most about what we "feel" or "value." But Plato and his followers including Hegel show how what's real as itself, and thus arguably more fully real than anything else, becomes so only through its pursuit of what's really good. So value, what's really good, plays an indispensable role in the genesis of what's most real. Insofar, then, as the natural sciences ignore the question of what's really good, they can't be the final arbiters of what's real. They give us only a part of the answer to that central question.

This is, once again, the issue of whether reality is merely "horizontal," a feature that things either have or don't, or also has a "vertical" dimension, whereby some things are more real than others. Modern thinking in general assumes that reality is something that things either have or don't. Platonism, on the other hand, argues that we need to recognize a "vertical" dimension, a way in which some things are more real than others, though the others do have a degree of reality (they "are and are not"). And the things that are more real achieve this through their pursuit of what's truly good, as opposed to whatever they may be naturally programmed to pursue. So that the fullest reality, the vertical dimension, depends entirely upon value.

And, at the same time, value depends entirely on the fullest reality. Not on what we currently want nor on what we "would" want under "ideal conditions" (whatever those might be), nor on what we receive through some special "faculty," but on what gives us the most reality. So that everything that we learn about our own functioning in relation to the world contributes to our understanding of value in ourselves and the world, and vice versa. This value is transcendent insofar as our fullest reality transcends our lower aspects, and it's immanent insofar as our fullest reality is what we contribute to the world.

This dual Platonic thesis is intimately tied up with our daily experience, in which we move, through the absence or presence of inner freedom, from being less fully ourselves to being more so, and vice versa. This is how Platonism is an account of what human experience shows us about reality, and not merely an account of entities ("Forms") that, if they're thought of as "separate," could be remote (as Blumenberg and others allege) from our experience.

Without the Platonic insight into the role of inner freedom and value in constituting our own fullest reality and the world's fullest reality, we have no satisfactory way of understanding ethics or the mind/body relationship, and we're stuck in incessant battles between "horizontal" materialism or naturalism and rationally unsatisfactory versions of transcendence. Hopefully the interest, which is so widespread today, in experiencing inner freedom and transcendence will eventually lead people back to the tradition from Plato to Hegel which explains what inner freedom and transcendence *are*, and how they're fully rational.

Then, in conducting our lives together, we'll be able to draw simultaneously on all of our relevant kinds of experience, religious, ethical, scientific, and (indeed) aesthetic, because we'll see how the essence of each is compatible with that of the others. And we'll have the full benefit of the Platonic tradition, which is always available to us but to which for long periods we often manage to be rather deaf.

So this reality is what true learning and true education will be about

Closely tied up with the question of what's real and how we can know it is the question of the nature and methods of education and what priorities individuals and societies should have for it. Plato makes it clear that true learning—namely, learning that's about the fullest reality, and contributes to it—is not an acquisition of information about external states of affairs. Since it's learning about what makes oneself fully functional and real in oneself, it's primarily "subjective" and internal— though useful things can be said about it from a more external perspective, as Plato tries to do.

Plato says in *Republic* vii that the essential first step to gaining this knowledge involves "turning the whole soul" (518c) from everyday concerns to a concern with the true good. This "turning" may be the first description, in Western literature, of what has subsequently (though often in a narrower, exclusively "religious" sense) been described as the experience of "conversion." Seen as part of Plato's big picture in *Republic* iv-vii, this turning takes us from a "horizontal" world in which all realities are equal—equally shadows on the wall of the cave—to a vertically organized world in which some realities are more self-governing, more themselves, and in that sense more real than others. In this way, it creates (one might say) the "self" itself, as something that's more internal and more fully itself than the "dependently co-arising" shadows.

Plato seems rather ambivalent about the prospects for bringing about this turning and this self. On the one hand, he speaks pretty drastically in *Republic* vii of "compelling" a person (515c) (the phrase that Blumenberg emphasizes) and of "hammering" on the soul "from childhood," so as to "free it from the bonds of kinship with becoming, which have been fastened to it by feasting, greed, and other pleasures" (519a). On the other hand, he has Socrates describe himself in the *Theaetetus* as a "midwife" (150b) and in the *Symposium* as one who promotes what Diotima calls "birth in beauty" (206c-e). These more organic processes of emergence, in which the teacher only assists, are consistent with the thought that what is essentially internal wouldn't, in any case, be something that can be brought about from outside. Plato's apparent progress from the external images of compelling and hammering to the more internal images of birth and midwifery is completed by Plotinus who places the emphasis entirely "within" when he describes God as being within us (*Enneads* V.I.11).[34]

This latter view of the most important kind of education, which sees it as coming from inside and receiving only assistance from outside, has been developed by modern writers such as Jean-Jacques Rousseau and John Dewey and fits well with the thought of the German Idealists. To say that the most important kind of knowledge—in the strict sense, the only true knowledge, inasmuch as it relates to the only full reality—is internal and can't be "put into" a person is not to say, obviously, that the curricular content that we ordinarily call "knowledge" is insignificant. Nor is it to say that a society can't support and encourage the pursuit of the most important, internal kind of knowledge. We are fortunate that our culture does contain traditions, particularly centered around psychology, literature, education, and religion, that have a considerable awareness of this most important kind of knowledge. I suspect that most of these traditions have been influenced, directly or indirectly, by Plato.[35]

The vertical dimension in human personalities

To see how concerned Plato was with issues of education as liberation, it's useful to look at some of the numerous "case studies" (as we might call them) or portraits that Plato presents in his dialogues. They make it very clear that he must have developed his account of the "parts of the soul" in part through close observation of individual human personalities.

Euthyphro, in the dialogue that bears his name, claims to be, and is proud to be, an expert on the gods. But he isn't able to explain what makes one action godly and another ungodly. Blithely confident that it's perfectly godly to take his father to court, as he is doing, for letting a servant die—no false "family piety" for Euthyphro—his primary motive seems to be self-congratulation, and we're bound to wonder how he got to be this way. Plato's picture of Euthyphro suggests that a person who is preoccupied with what he takes to be his own outstanding virtues, and is bothered by none of the doubts that ordinary people might feel, is governed by a need that he doesn't understand. A comic figure in his one-sidedness, Euthyphro is, in effect, a puppet of this unexamined force of self-importance that's at work in him. He shows us how there is nothing highfalutin' about Socrates's prescription of self-examination; it is a precondition of everyday human wholeness. A person who can't effectively examine his own motives is at the mercy of what he can't examine, and thus can't be fully in charge of his life.

A second example: Thrasymachus, in *Republic* book i, is proud of what he takes to be his independent thinking, exhibited in his convictions that justice is power and tyrants are admirable. But when he tries to defend these ideas, it becomes clear that they aren't the result of much real thought. Falling back on ridicule, he makes it clear that his convictions reflect emotional investments—probably a need to feel important—more than cognitive investments. Thrasymachus apparently lacks a sense of his own power and seeks to bolster himself by braggadocio, bluster, and aggressiveness. This lack of a sense of his own power, a lack of which he clearly has no understanding, motivates the main lines of his behavior. So one can hardly say that his behavior expresses himself, except in the sense that it shows how little effective "self" he possesses. Like Euthyphro, he is at the mercy of motives that he doesn't understand and can't control.

But Plato's prize example of inner disunity is always Alcibiades, the handsome, brilliant, and charismatic young leader who says in the *Symposium* that Socrates makes him ashamed of his way of living, but he can't help living that way.

> I have heard Pericles and many other great orators, and I have admired their speeches. But . . . they never upset me so deeply that my very own soul started protesting that my life—*my* life!—was no better than the most miserable slave's. And yet that is exactly how [Socrates] makes me feel all the time. . . . Socrates is the only man in the world who has made me feel shame. . . . Yet, the moment I leave his side, I go back to my old ways: I cave in to my desire to please the crowd. (215e-216b)

Alcibiades's "desire to please the crowd" overrules his "very own soul": this most gifted young man of his generation fails to enact what he himself takes to be good, and allows himself to be governed by what isn't him. His actions are governed by a desire that he doesn't understand well enough to be able to choose whether or not to follow it. So his "own soul" is present only in his shame, and not in his actions. Like Euthyphro and Thrasymachus, Alcibiades himself isn't really in charge of his life.

The *Symposium*'s narrator describes Socrates as maintaining, during the wee hours of the morning at the end of the party, that authors should be able to write both comedy and tragedy (223d). We might think that in his depiction of Alcibiades, Plato meets this standard very well. In the *Symposium* itself, Alcibiades is a charismatic reveler, a poetic storyteller, and a charmingly candid self-deprecator. Like Robin Williams, in our day, he has his audience in the palm of his hand. But as Plato's readers all knew, the historical Alcibiades had come to a bad end and had taken the flower of Athenian youth with him, when the city's military expedition to Syracuse, which Alcibiades had promoted, turned out to be a military disaster. Alcibiades was also suspected of having desecrated religious mysteries, during a late-night drinking spree, in a way that might have been thought to endanger Athens. These facts must have been in the foreground for Plato, as he wrote the *Symposium*, and for his readers. One has to suppose that if Alcibiades had had a better grasp of his own character and life, things would have turned out differently for him and for Athens also, in significant respects. So the light-hearted comedy that Plato shares with us in the *Symposium* opens, outside its frame, into an archetypal tragedy.

Euthyphro, Thrasymachus, and Alcibiades all exhibit the more or less dramatic consequences of the all too familiar, all too human failure to be in charge of one's own life. In the case of Alcibiades, this failure is all the more poignant because of the great gifts that Alcibiades clearly possessed. What "helpless immortals" these are, indeed!

Does anyone in the dialogues have a successful life, one that expresses his true self rather than expressing external forces that he doesn't understand or control? Evidently, Socrates does. Socrates exhibits no self-congratulation, no anger, shame, or desire to please anyone. Instead, his life expresses his own processing, and the people around him who aren't blinded by anger at having their ignorance revealed by his examination are fascinated by this highly unusual phenomenon. In Socrates, we see what the pursuit of the Good, of the vertical dimension in which we become fully ourselves, can achieve.

Plato was clearly aware of the painful irony that Socrates, who exemplifies self-realization in this exceptional way, was unable to help his beloved Alcibiades to get beyond his "desire to please the crowd" and get in charge of his own life. And the same is the case with many of Socrates's other interlocutors. They dramatize the difficult fact that the impetus for self-realization has to come from within. But this doesn't lead Plato to despair, since in Diotima's speech (in the *Symposium*) and elsewhere he continues to hold up for us the possibility that when such an impetus is present, friends can be deeply helpful.

It seems likely that Plato's apparent confidence that friends *can* be helpful in this way, even though he gives us no extended case study of how this has happened in a particular person, is due at least in part to his own personal experience of interaction with Socrates. No doubt because of modesty on Plato's part, we don't know any details of what that interaction was like. But the fact that it apparently led Plato to make such an extended study of the process by which personal freedom can come about gives us some idea of how important that experience must have been for Plato himself.

From the care that Plato gives to describing Alcibiades and his other "case studies," it's clear that he is interested in freedom in all of its aspects. There is no such thing for him as "mere psychology," as opposed to philosophy. Nor is there "mere literature," though his studies of the personalities that I've mentioned seem to me to amount to one of the first and greatest novels in Western literature. The next chapter will examine in more detail what Plato shows us about freedom, and it will also say something about his well-known ambivalence about political freedom and democracy.

6 PLATO, FREEDOM, AND US

Therefore I print; nor vain my types shall be:
Heaven, Earth, & Hell, henceforth shall live in harmony.
WILLIAM BLAKE, *JERUSALEM*

Plato's way of understanding the world as a hierarchy of increasing degrees of reality "as oneself," opens up all sorts of possibilities for us. It enables us to think of ourselves as having a "vertical" dimension, by which we're involved with "higher things," without becoming entangled in the sort of alienating relationships of rejection (e.g., of "Heaven" versus "Hell"!) that such a vertical dimension at first seems to suggest. It also allows us to think of ourselves as having an "inner self," which is more truly us than our "outer" thoughts, desires, and actions. And this vertical dimension, or this interiority, can also be crucial for our relationships with each other, as we know from literature, psychology, and personal experience.

Let's explore these new dimensions in a bit more detail.

How the "ascent" takes place

Plato knows that the idea of "going beyond," by which the "reasoning" part of the soul leads us "higher" in the knowledge of the good, is still pretty abstract for us. He needs to give us a more concrete idea of what such an ascent would involve.

He does this in book vi of the *Republic* by having Socrates sketch two theories of what's really good. One is the theory that pleasure is the good, and the other is the theory that knowledge is the good. Socrates produces objections to both of these theories that appear to drive both of them from the field. *Pleasure* can't be the sole good, because everyone agrees that some pleasures are bad (505c). (Presumably Socrates has in mind, for example, the pleasure that Leontius expects to get from looking at the corpses.) If some pleasures are bad, then evidently something else is involved in determining whether X is good, besides whether X is "pleasant" or not.

But *knowledge* can't be the good, Socrates says, because when they're asked which knowledge in particular they have in mind, the advocates of this theory say that it's the knowledge of what's good. And that, of course, means that the question of what *is* good still remains to be answered (505b-c).

So Socrates drops both of these theories and begins to discuss more abstractly how a person can hope to have knowledge of this sort of thing at all. He talks about the "Form" of the good. Then he mentions mathematics as a discipline that seems to find knowledge of abstract things like squares and numbers, which go beyond any particular sensation that we might have (510e), just as the good, apparently, goes beyond particular sensations like pleasure. Squares and numbers go beyond any particular sensation because they apply to innumerable particular experiences, both actual experiences and possible ones. Our knowledge of these abstract topics in mathematics is always one of Plato's favorite examples of how knowledge apparently goes beyond any number of particular sense experiences. It has a kind of generality that seems to require some additional basis besides sensations as such. Hence his suggestions in the *Meno* and *Phaedo* that the soul has an affinity with the Forms which goes beyond our present lifetimes.

What does this talk about Forms and about mathematics have to do with the question of what's really *good*? I think we need to remember the two theories that Socrates started with: that pleasure is the good and that knowledge is the good. I doubt that he expects us simply to forget about these suggestions, once he has shown that neither of them is adequate, by itself. When he's talking about knowledge of squares and numbers, in mathematics, he tells us that the diagrams that mathematicians draw, and the other things that they see in the world around them, are like reflections in water. They're "images" of the real square or the real "odd," of which the mathematicians are seeking knowledge. You can't base knowledge of squares as such on one diagram, by itself. But the diagram does have some relationship to the real square: it's a "reflection," a rough approximation to the real thing. The same idea is at work, of course, in the cave story with its shadows on the walls of the cave. They don't tell you everything about what's casting the shadow, but they do tell you *something* about it, once you realize that they aren't the real thing, themselves.

Similarly, I suggest, neither the theory that the good is pleasure nor the theory that it is knowledge tells us *everything* about the good itself. Two incompatible theories obviously can't provide the final story about the good itself. But probably they do each tell us something about what the good itself is. Maybe the good is something that often includes pleasure, and that in important cases also includes knowledge. And when we understand exactly what it is, we'll see why it has these particular features, among others.

For creatures, like us, that can experience pleasure, the experience of what's really good is probably bound to carry pleasure with it. And for creatures that are capable of connecting with reality in the way that we call "knowing," it seems likely that having that sort of connection with reality is a key feature of what's good for them. This explains why we're likely to come up with theories like the two that Socrates has mentioned, when we're asked what's really good. For us, at least, there are intimate connections between the phenomena of pleasure and knowledge, on the one hand, and the good, on the other.

This suggests that Plato wants us to think that the pursuit of knowledge of important subjects, such as mathematics and the "good," inevitably starts with rough approximations, which are familiar to us in one way or another from our everyday experience. Then it refines those approximations, by comparing them to each other and trying to figure out which aspects of each of the competing approximations are dispensable, and which are indispensable and thus are aspects of the good itself. Or of the square itself, or whatever it may be that we're seeking to know. We figure out how to reconcile the approximations with one another, in a coherent way. As we do this, we get further and further away from the approximations themselves, and closer and closer to an adequate conception of the good, the square, or whatever it may be.

This process of moving away from approximations and toward real knowledge is what Plato dramatizes as the ascent from the cave into the sunlight.[1] If you think about it as a description of increasing maturity, for example, I think you'll agree that this is not an unrealistic description of what we really go through. Over time, we get increasing intuitive understanding of what human life is really about. In the case of the "good," probably not much of this process is very conscious or explicit, for most of us. And yet we know which of our friends and relatives have made more progress on it, and which have made less, at different times in their lives and in different areas of their lives.

This may not be an explicitly "intellectual" process, like mathematics, but that doesn't prevent it from being a very real process of learning. It's a process of acquiring important knowledge, which manifests itself in the innumerable decisions that the person makes in the course of a day, a year, or a lifetime, even though she may never spell much of it out in words.

So if this is the right way to understand it, the cave allegory is meant to show how it's reasonable for us to think that we can get improved understanding of difficult subjects. In particular, of the nature of the good, of what's really worthwhile. It's meant to show that these subjects aren't just "matters of opinion," or of mere "feeling," where any suggestion or feeling is as good as any other suggestion or feeling. On the contrary, we can in fact make progress on these subjects, by considering all of our initial "approximations" in an open-minded and thoughtful way.

When we acquire knowledge of what's really good, we may be able to get for ourselves what Socrates has plausibly suggested we all want: what's really good, rather than merely what's believed to be good. But we also achieve something else that's equally or even more important. By pursuing this kind of knowledge, we activate the reasoning part of our soul. We activate the part that's distinguished from the appetites and from the "spirited" part by the fact that it systematically pursues not merely knowledge of how to satisfy the desires that we feel but knowledge of what's really good. And by activating this part we activate a part of our soul that's capable of having legitimate authority over the other parts, and thus we make it possible for our soul, which has been "many things," to "become one" (as Socrates puts it at *Republic* 443d).

And we might well think that this "becoming one" is a necessary aspect of full human freedom. For if my actions merely reflect certain parts of me, rather than me as "one," it looks as though rather than being free and responsible for these actions, I'm not even fully *present*, as "myself," in what's going on.

The ascent from the cave as an allegory of freedom

In one obvious way, the cave allegory reads like an allegory of freedom. The cave people are "fixed in the same place, with their necks and legs fettered, able to see only in front of them" (514a), so that the only thing they can see is the shadows on the wall of the cave, in front of them. They have no opportunity to engage in anything like the process of learning that I've said the cave allegory is about.

But when Plato goes on to describe the one person who does have the opportunity to engage in a process of learning as being "freed and suddenly *compelled* to stand up" (515c), we might wonder what this learning has to do with freedom. And Plato describes him as *resisting* each of the new things that he's forced to look at, and only very gradually becoming accustomed to these higher realities.

As I mentioned in the previous chapter, Hans Blumenberg (for one) takes at face value these remarks about the cave person's resisting and being compelled, as evidence that Plato thinks that there is no motive sufficient to lead a person to leave the cave behind of their own free will. I suggest, less drastically, that what's happening here is that Plato is dramatizing the great difference between our familiar, everyday existence, amid our familiar (though mutually incompatible) "approximations," and the kind of existence that we'll have if we try to go beyond those approximations. All of our *instincts*, Plato suggests, *attach us to* those approximations, regardless of the fact that they're incompatible with one another. The only way to move toward a more adequate, less approximate understanding is to begin by freeing ourselves from these instinctive attachments, and this freeing will initially be horribly disorienting and uncomfortable.

Plato's description of the process of ascent is meant to dramatize this disorientation and discomfort. It's also meant to serve as an explanation of the violent treatment that Socrates received from his fellow citizens, when he invited them to leave their instinctive attachments behind them. Socrates says toward the end of the allegory: "As for anyone who tried to free them and lead them upward, if they could somehow get their hands on him, wouldn't they kill him?" (517a).

These features of Plato's dramatization certainly make the ascent from the cave seem like a very unlikely event, and they could make us wonder why anyone would ever actually want to leave the cave. But we can see why people would want to, if we remember the context from book iv and book vi that I outlined in the previous chapter. Our motive for leaving the cave is to *be ourselves*, to "become entirely one," and, for that purpose, to be guided by what's really good, rather than by mere belief.

If we focus on this motivation, then we'll see that Plato's overall intention in the cave allegory isn't to describe how one of the cave dwellers is mysteriously yanked out of his accustomed surroundings and then equally mysteriously reinserted into those surroundings. Rather, Plato wants to describe how making progress toward being ourselves is likely to be disorienting and uncomfortable. But he also wants us to see that this project reflects a deep *need*, which in modern parlance we might describe as the need for "authenticity" or "self-determination" or "freedom."

To see how Plato's argument up to this point revolves around that need, is to see that Plato has a lot more in common than he's generally thought to have in common with *modern* philosophy. By which I mean modern thinking about human life and action, as exemplified by such thinkers as John Locke ("*freedom* from absolute, arbitrary power"), Thomas Jefferson ("life, *liberty*, and the pursuit of happiness"), John Stuart Mill (*On Liberty*), and Jean-Paul Sartre ("man is condemned to be free"). As well as Jean-Jacques Rousseau, Mary Wollstonecraft, Immanuel Kant, Virginia Woolf, W. E. B. Dubois, and many others. For all of these writers, personal freedom in one sense or another is the single most central issue of all. If the cave allegory is, in fact, centrally relevant to the issue of what freedom *is*, then Plato's *Republic* can speak to modern readers just as directly as these modern thinkers do. Rather than speaking to us across a gulf of cultural difference or "fundamentally different interests."

There is in fact quite an influential scholarly trend that says that the Greeks were concerned about "virtue" or the "good" or "natural law," while leading modern thinkers like Kant and John Stuart Mill (in his *On Liberty*) are more concerned about individual freedom or autonomy. But to contrast a concern about the Good with the modern concern about autonomy is to miss Plato's point. Plato is concerned about the Good because he's concerned about our autonomy, our being "one" and whole and self-governing, and the pursuit of the Good *is* autonomy, is being one and whole and self-governing. So his central concern is essentially the same as that of "moderns" including Kant, Hegel, and Mill.

Writers who suggest that ancient and modern ethics are fundamentally different include Leo Strauss, *Natural Right and History* (1953); G. E. M. Anscombe, "Modern Moral Philosophy" (1958); Alasdair MacIntyre, *After Virtue* (1981/2007); Charles Taylor, *Sources of the Self: The Making of the Modern Identity* (1989); J. B. Schneewind, *The Invention of Autonomy: A History of Modern Moral Philosophy* (1997); and John Christman, "Autonomy in Moral and Political Philosophy" (Stanford Encyclopedia of Philosophy, online, 2009), which calls autonomy "very much a modern development."

Most of these authors suggest that while leading modern thinkers are concerned about autonomy, the ancients were concerned about "virtue," the Good, "order," or "natural law." None of them connect the Good to autonomy or having a self in the way that I see Plato connecting them in *Republic* iv-vii. These scholars often have in mind Aristotle as the most important Greek ethical or political theorist, but Aristotle's "virtue ethics" is actually about autonomy in the same way that Plato's ethical thinking is. The "*ergon*" or "function" argument (*Nicomachean Ethics* i.7, 1097b-1098a), in which Aristotle draws attention to the centrality of reason in human functioning, is where rational self-government or autonomy presents itself in Aristotle. Desires and emotions are subordinated to reason through the doctrine of the "mean," so that "virtue" is the implementation of reason.[2]

A good corrective to our tendency to see the Greeks as concerned with different issues from those that concern modern thinkers is to consider the relativism, nihilism, and egoism that were taught in fourth-century BCE Athens by men like Protagoras, Gorgias, and Thrasymachus. And then consider how much the question of a rational response to relativism, nihilism, and egoism dominates our own agenda today, just as it dominated Plato's and Aristotle's agendas in ancient Athens.

How Plato connects rational freedom or autonomy to ethical treatment of others, I'll explain in the next two chapters. (Please note that it should not be assumed that a thinker who emphasizes rational freedom or autonomy will regard free or autonomous people as only externally related to other people.)

Plato, a philosopher of *freedom*?

By now, though, readers who know something about Plato's *political* ideas in the *Republic* may have some pressing questions. How could the philosopher who wants each social class to mind its own business, while the community is ruled by the smallest class of all (the "philosopher-kings"), be described as a philosopher of *freedom*? And while literature including Homer's poetry and the Greek tragedies is censored so that children won't grow up with the wrong ideas? Not to mention the fact that Plato raises no objection to the institution of slavery.

Here we undeniably have a major paradox on our hands. Plato makes it clear, in the *Republic*, that he has no great love for democracy. After all, it was the Athenian democracy that put his teacher, Socrates, to death. Consequently, Plato is more inclined to trust the opinions of the "wise," than the opinions of the "many." And it's obvious to him, as it presumably is to us as well, that in any community the wise will be a small minority. So the political parts of the *Republic* aim to describe a set of institutions that would maximize the chances that people who are actually wise would be in charge of the community, regardless of whether this maximizes the freedom of the citizens in general.

Indeed, Plato's Socrates speaks of the soldiers and the business and craftspeople of the city as each fulfilling their natures completely within these roles, and having (apparently) no significant capacity for participating in public affairs, as well. Socrates even suggests that the ideal city's founders could encourage the remainder of the population to stay in their places by telling them a "noble lie" (414b) according to which they're made of a different "metal" from the ruling group. This is just the crowning denial of the rational capacities of most of the population.

On the other hand, when Plato is writing about the education that occurs through being led out of the cave, he makes Socrates flatly assert that "the power to learn is in *everyone's* soul" (518c; emphasis added). Which is a doctrine that seems, in fact, to follow necessarily from what he said in book iv about the parts of the "the soul." Not about the parts of the "philosopher's" soul but about the parts of "the" soul, as such. If every soul contains a "reasoning" part, then every soul, apparently, has the capacity to learn about the good. And if it has that capacity, it's not clear why it shouldn't participate, in some fashion, in governing its community in accordance with what it learns.

It seems clear that Plato has fundamentally conflicting thoughts about social order. Probably especially because of the trauma that he experienced when he lost his hero, Socrates, to the death penalty imposed by the Athenian people, Plato has a deep distrust of "the people." But he has also seen the learning that all sorts of people experienced from associating with Socrates, and this leads him to think of "everyone's soul" as having the power to learn.

This latter side of Plato is the one that appeals to most of us, but I think that we should be able to understand his emotional reluctance, as a result of his trauma, to rely entirely on "education." He was evidently working in two incompatible directions at once, as he wrote the *Republic*, and people who have experienced the deeply confusing long-term effects of trauma can probably understand how he could contradict himself in this way. Plato's willingness to recommend a fundamental falsehood, a "noble lie," may reflect his desire to avoid the repetition of his early traumas. While his tentative willingness to respect others, as well as his own body, and to seek to educate them toward willing cooperation, corresponds to the liberating effects of love and forgiveness.

In *Republic* book v, Plato has Socrates contrast "lovers of opinion" with "lovers of wisdom and knowledge" (479–80), and from book ii to book ix he repeatedly has

Socrates say that people differ by "nature," with different parts of the soul "ruling" in different classes of people, "philosophic, victory-loving, and profit-loving" (581c). It's noteworthy, however, that Socrates often describes these differences as differences of degree, rather than of kind. "Each of us differs *somewhat* in nature from the others"; "one learned it *easily*, the other *with difficulty*" (370a and 455b; emphasis added). So the doctrine of differing "natures" may not flatly contradict the doctrine that "the power to learn is in everyone's soul" (518c).

The sharp contrast between "lovers of opinion" and "lovers of knowledge," on the other hand, is hard to square with the statement that "everyone wants the things that really *are* good, and disdains mere belief here" (505d). If that were so, then presumably everyone would love the knowledge that would ensure that they get the things that really are good. I suppose we are meant to understand that those who *appear* to love "opinion," in fact love the mistaken opinions that they take to be knowledge. Plato certainly is fairly pessimistic about the chances of such people coming to recognize their mistakes, in practice, but his analysis of the tripartite soul in *Republic* iv would lose its whole point if the rational part weren't the properly governing part, and if humans weren't in general on some level aware of this. We all want knowledge and not merely opinion, because we all want what's truly good and not just whatever we currently think is good.

It is certainly the case that Plato's *Republic* and his *Laws* present political and cultural institutions that are meant to guide citizens who don't have knowledge of what's truly good and who could benefit (to some degree) from the guidance of those who might have such knowledge. Plato is very concerned to provide for the "non-ideal" circumstances in which this is the case. But it doesn't follow from this that his account of "the" soul's capacity for self-government (its "power to learn") through its relation to the Good is not meant to apply to every one of us. Thus when Carlos Fraenkel says that in modern times a "new . . . paradigm" gained influence, which had been anticipated by Socrates but not by Plato, according to which "all human beings are *equally* able to rationally rule themselves," I would say that this "new paradigm" played a fundamental role throughout Plato's work as well, though he certainly did hedge it, as Fraenkel describes.[3]

Maybe it's not such a paradox, after all, that the greatest philosopher of freedom, as I would describe Plato, may have had a harder time fully embracing freedom than many of us armchair types think we have. Real inner freedom may not be as easy to come by as we like to suppose.

I should emphasize that my hypotheses about the psychological background of Plato's political suggestions in the *Republic* are simply hypotheses. We have little or no reliable information about Plato's personal life. The authenticity of the "letters" that are ascribed to him and included in his "complete works" is disputed. We do know, however, that Plato always presents tyranny in a very unfavorable light, and (obviously) that he greatly admired Socrates. So my suggestion that Plato experienced both the reign of the Thirty and the death of Socrates as traumatic seems pretty plausible. And his willingness even to fantasize about a "noble lie," which is to be addressed to people whose souls he himself describes as capable of learning the truth, certainly calls for some sort of explanation.

The distinctiveness of Plato's theory of freedom

So the place where we find Plato analyzing and advocating freedom is not in his discussions of politics, as such, but in his discussions of the internal functioning of individuals. Unlike his thoughts in the *Republic* about ideal political institutions, his analysis and advocacy of individual freedom, with its account of what's involved in "becoming one" and leading a life that's really one's own, is just as plausible and relevant today as it was when he wrote it.

What is the upshot of Plato's analysis of what we might call "inner freedom," which he himself calls "becoming one," in the *Republic*? It's that freedom or becoming one isn't merely a matter of not being coerced or interfered with by other people. My freedom isn't just the "negative" fact that other people aren't interfering in my life. Because whether or not other people are interfering in my life, the question can still be asked, Do my actions reflect me, as "one," or do they merely reflect parts of me, such as particular appetites, or passions like anger or shame or contempt? If they merely reflect parts of me, they aren't fully *my own*, in the way that the actions that reflect my unified "soul" are my own. That kind of scattered, non-"united" action seems just as unfree, in its way, as an action that's forced upon me by the interference of other people. In both cases the action doesn't fully reflect me but instead reflects things that aren't fully myself, whether they're parts of me or actually other people.

So this is why Plato's conception of freedom or "becoming one" gives a central role to the reasoning part of the soul. It's not because Plato wants to abolish other features of human life, such as appetite and emotion, but because only reason can unify a person in such a way that she can own her actions and have them reflect herself. So only reason allows her to be fully herself and (in modern parlance) be free: fully responsible for her actions.

Parenthetically, it may sound as though Plato is saying that a person is responsible for her actions only when her soul is functioning perfectly, but Plato's approach doesn't require that. What it requires is that the person has developed the *ability* to think matters through and act "as one," even if she didn't choose to act that way in a particular case. Her choice not to act this way, not to think when she knew that thought was called for, makes her responsible in the same way that actual thought would make her responsible. Much of our functioning is, in practice, habitual, but thought is still relevant insofar as we know that we're ultimately responsible for our habits, as well as for our fully calculated actions. If those habits are dangerous, we ought to take steps to eliminate them or prevent them from governing our important actions.

A familiar theory of freedom or being responsible for one's actions which differs from Plato's theory, says that freedom is the simple *absence of external causes* that explain one's actions. (The external causes that are supposed to be absent would, of course, include interfering or coercive actions by other people.) This simple view, which is often called "voluntarism," was advocated by the eighteenth-century Scottish philosopher Thomas Reid, to some extent also by Immanuel Kant, and apparently by twentieth-century existentialists like Jean-Paul Sartre.

But the voluntarist theory has problems. No one doubts that if other people coerce you, this makes you less free and less responsible for your actions. But many people doubt that it's possible for a human action to be affected by no external causes whatever, as this theory seems to require in cases where a person is responsible for an action. For presumably (we imagine) the ideas and feelings that influence your action were themselves caused by experiences that you had or by inherited instincts or patterns of behavior, which ultimately came from outside you.

Some of the philosophers who have these doubts about the voluntarist theory are attracted to a third theory of freedom or responsibility, according to which a person is free or responsible for her actions when her actions reflect her *character*. They think this is true, regardless of what causes may have brought that character about. If this is simply you, it doesn't matter what caused it. You are responsible for the actions that flow from you. This is the view of empiricists such as Thomas Hobbes and David Hume.

In response to this empiricist theory, a critic could point out that sometimes people have strong objections to well-established aspects of their own character. Would a person still be fully responsible for actions that reflect aspects of his character which he wishes he could get rid of, and has tried (perhaps unsuccessfully) to get rid of? It doesn't seem fair to hold a person fully responsible for something that he has tried to get rid of.

Neither the voluntarist theory nor the empiricist theory provides for "unifying" a person in the way that Plato's account does, with its focus on the role of reason. While the voluntarist theory of responsibility would apparently exonerate a person of responsibility for actions that flowed from aspects of his character that weren't spontaneous but were caused by (say) his early environment, Plato's theory would not. For, Plato would point out, a person who has had a difficult early environment may be able to recognize, to some degree, the resulting flaws in his character, and to work to limit or reduce their effects on his actions. This is the kind of thing that reason can do, and which we clearly take into account in evaluating a person's degree of responsibility. By describing actions for which we're responsible as somehow purely *spontaneous*, voluntarism directs our attention away from the practical issue of what a person can do to make herself more fully responsible, more free, more "united." Whereas Plato's theory, with its focus on the interaction of reason and appetites and emotions, directs our attention precisely toward practical issues like these.

As for the empiricist theory, with its focus on the person's concrete character, it doesn't make voluntarism's mistake of directing attention toward an abstract spontaneity. What the empiricist theory, on its side, overlooks is the whole issue of the person's knowledge of and attitude toward his character. As we know from modern psychotherapy, it is possible to make significant changes in aspects of one's character that were produced by difficult early experiences, but this can be an arduous process and getting it started at all may seem to depend upon unusually favorable circumstances. Even simply being aware of one's character as something over which one might have some control, isn't something that can be taken for granted. Since all of this is the case, it hardly seems fair to hold a person *fully* responsible for actions that reflect character flaws that he hasn't been able to or perhaps hasn't even tried to root out. But given that there were things that he (in some sense) *could* have done to not be the kind of person that he is, it doesn't seem that we should exonerate him entirely, either. It's a very complicated issue.

This whole complex issue is one that Plato's theory, with its focus on the dynamic relations between reason and emotion, consciousness and character, encourages us to explore. The empiricist theory on the other hand, which simply says, "These character traits are *you*," hardly seems to do justice to these issues. The case is similar with the voluntarist theory, which ignores the issue of how conscious you are and how much control you have over your character.

Neither the voluntarist nor the empiricist theory seems to do as good a job as Plato does of explaining how and why we view *persons*, and not just *parts* of persons (their character traits, or their supposed spontaneity), as responsible for their actions.[4] Nor do they explain as well what's absent when we think that a person isn't responsible for her actions. If a person "wasn't able to tell the difference between right and wrong," as we say, and therefore wasn't fully responsible for her action, Plato would say that this was because the reasoning part of her soul was absent or out of commission for some reason. (Say, the person was in the grip of psychotic delusions.) And if, on the other hand, we think that the person *was* responsible for her action, one key reason for this must be that her reasoning part was *present* and able to function.

The libertarian and empiricist theories have no ready explanation of the basis for this common judgment ("She wasn't able to tell the difference between right and wrong") that we make when we say that a person wasn't responsible for her action. In that respect as well, Plato's theory of the soul seems much the most practical of these three leading theories of freedom or responsibility. Which is another good reason for rejecting the common stereotype according to which Platonism is unworldly or impractical.

An important weakness of modern "existentialism," as well, is that it fails to focus on the role of thinking about what's really good, in making a person free and responsible. What the existentialists do usefully focus on is our need to have the courage to face the real facts of our situation. But they don't clarify how a fully free person would function once she has faced those facts. Consequently, they often leave us with the impression that there's something ultimately arbitrary, in "free choice" or in what a person who manages to be "authentic," or truly "herself," really "is" and does. Whereas, when we understand Plato's explanation of the role of the "reasoning part" in unifying the soul and thus making it fully real, we see why arbitrariness couldn't unify the soul, or even make a person fully responsible for what she does.

In the twentieth and early twenty-first centuries, relatively few prominent writers seem to have grasped Plato's point, and the consequent role of "reason" in freedom.[5] Because Plato's account speaks so directly to the issue of what it is to be a functioning human being, I think it deserves to be much better known than it is.

Modern controversies about the Plato/Hegel theory

Hegel has been the most prominent modern advocate of Plato's view of freedom and responsibility, as opposed to those of the voluntarists (Reid, Kant, Sartre) and the empiricists (Hobbes and Hume). During the twentieth century, the disagreement between the Plato/Hegel view of freedom and voluntarist or empiricist views unfortunately became tangled up with contemporary political issues in a way that caused a lot of confusion.

Many philosophers were naturally horrified by the human rights disasters of fascism and communism that befell much of Europe and Asia in the twentieth century. Some of them came to the conclusion that the philosophers who were influential in Germany in the nineteenth century, including Plato and Hegel, might have been partly to blame for these developments. For one thing, Karl Marx asserted that he owed a good deal to Hegel's philosophy. And despite Marx's evident humanitarian passion, he certainly bears a lot of responsibility for the dictatorship and disregard for human rights that we saw in the Soviet Union and in communist China. In his passionate advocacy of the empowerment of the downtrodden, Marx ignored issues about ethics, democratic processes, and individual freedom, thus giving a semblance of legitimacy to the way the Soviet and Chinese dictators likewise ignored those issues. And as for fascism, the most murderous fascists, the Nazis, emerged in Hegel's homeland.

Karl Popper connected Plato and Hegel with twentieth-century totalitarianism in his *The Open Society and Its Enemies* (1945), and Isaiah Berlin made a similar suggestion in his influential essay, "Two Concepts of Liberty" (1958). In that essay, Berlin distinguished between "negative" and "positive" conceptions of liberty. My "negative" liberty is the fact that no one else interferes with my actions. Hobbes and Hume focus on this absence of interference, together with the requirement that my action reflects my character. Plato and Hegel, on the other hand, have a "positive" conception of liberty, in that they think that in order to be fully free, I must have a certain relationship to "reason." Berlin suggested that "positive" conceptions of liberty threaten free social relations by making it possible to criticize individuals and perhaps to interfere with their actions in order to promote the "reason" that they're supposedly neglecting.[6]

Unfortunately, Berlin didn't address the issue of whether a person could be described as "free" if, for example, she was in the grip of schizophrenic delusions. Or if she was a "wanton" who simply did whatever came into her head at the time, without being able to subject it to any thought whatever. So he didn't see that Plato's and Hegel's conceptions of "freedom" address a very practical issue. It's so practical that it's constantly being addressed, for example, in criminal courts, where judges and juries have to decide whether defendants were fully responsible for their actions because they "understood the difference between right and wrong." (Or as Plato and Hegel would put it, whether they were capable of *thinking* about what to do, rather than simply responding to impulses.) Failing to appreciate this concretely practical relevance of Plato's and Hegel's thinking about freedom, Berlin apparently concluded that Plato's well-known opposition to democracy must have been grounded in his theory of freedom as involving reason.

I've acknowledged that advocates of political liberty have good grounds for suspecting Plato of not respecting it. But we shouldn't let this fact discredit all of Plato's ideas for us. Plato's theory of the inner freedom of the philosopher, of which he actually tells us that all souls are capable, has nothing to do with his rather "controlling" theory of social order. Instead, as I've pointed out, it points in a very different direction.

Plato's and Hegel's conceptions of inner freedom do indeed raise the possibility that aspects of a person's freedom of action can legitimately be interfered with if the community concludes that she isn't able to apply "reason" to govern her own actions. But it's very unlikely that Isaiah Berlin would actually have disagreed with this view, if it were applied (for example) to a person whose schizophrenic delusions were causing her to try to commit suicide, or some other drastic action.

Obviously, the community's interference with people's actions needs to be very carefully limited, so that it doesn't wind up interfering with behavior that's merely unconventional, as opposed to disastrously irrational. But it seems clear that careful thought about these issues will be aided, rather than undermined, by figuring out how much "reason" a person must be capable of in order for us to say that we ought to respect her decision (say) to refuse medical treatment, or to end her life in other ways. Certainly Hobbes's and Hume's classical empiricist conception of responsibility offers little or no help in these difficult cases. Neither does Reid's and Sartre's voluntarism. Of the theorists I've mentioned, Plato and Hegel are the only ones whose theories of freedom actually speak to this issue in a direct and useful way.

As for Hegel's supposed influence on Marx and, through him, on Soviet totalitarianism, it's notable that whatever Marx may have learned from Hegel, he didn't learn to pay careful attention to ethics, nor did he learn to think carefully about freedom. Marx didn't refer to these aspects of Hegel's philosophy, nor did Marx give any attention, himself, to developing a satisfactory conception of ethics or of freedom. And as for the Nazis, they were extremely suspicious of Hegel, precisely because of the explicit centrality of freedom in all of his thinking.[7]

An additional misfortune of the twentieth century was the way Plato's and Hegel's conceptions of inner freedom and responsibility were blamed for these political developments in which the main actors showed no concern for inner freedom or responsibility. A more sympathetic and nuanced understanding of Plato and of Hegel is still struggling to emerge from this rather dark age.

Condemning, forgiving, and understanding

When we achieve such an understanding, it will aid us in understanding not only Plato and Hegel but ourselves. Plato shows us, in book iv of the *Republic*, how his rationalist conception of freedom can unify a person "vertically," by bringing her appetites and her rational part into harmony with each other. In this way, it can (potentially) overcome a great deal of the "alienation" that often takes place within individuals. When a person's rational part understands the way his emotional habits emerged from his early experiences, it can work gradually and intelligently to change those habits, rather than responding to them (say) with denial and ineffective repression. Likewise for our bodily appetites, we can sympathize with them without being simply dominated by them. We don't need to be at war with ourselves, our soul versus our body, as the dualistic approach that's suggested by some of Plato's language in the *Phaedo* suggests. Fortunately for us, Plato's systematic thinking in *Republic* iv avoids the antagonistic dualism that his habitual language (especially in parts of the *Phaedo*) helped to catapult into our collective consciousness.

Plato's conception of freedom can also help us to overcome much of the alienation that occurs not within but *between* individuals. We need to hold each other responsible for our actions if we're to have a society that's based on mutual respect rather than on sheer force. If we are responsible for our actions, we are capable (in principle) of thinking about them and responding to rational discussion about how we ought to act. So responsibility is central for a society that hopes to be guided by reasoning and not just by coercion. But if we hope to be fully free and unalienated, by being defined or determined by ourselves rather than by our inevitable conflicts with each other, we also need to be able to forgive each other.

Bear in mind that forgiving an action doesn't mean tolerating it or even allowing it. We often need, in this life, to struggle (in various ways) with other people's thoughts and actions. People often won't respond immediately, if at all, to what seem to us to be good reasons for acting in various ways. What forgiveness accomplishes, in these situations, is that it prevents these people from becoming simply our "enemies." It keeps us in touch with what we have in common with them. And thus it protects us against the demonizing of "the enemy," to which demagogues regularly resort in order to enlist our support for their rule and their policies.

Plato's conception of freedom makes it possible for us to forgive each other because it shows us how to understand evil as a corrupted understanding of what's good, rather than (say) as a love of something that's the opposite of the good. Following Plato's conception, we can understand a person like Adolf Hitler, for example, as, first, having been convinced, probably by experiences in his early childhood, that personal power is a good thing and, second, having failed to get beyond those convictions in order to discover how other things are also good which place limits on the goodness of personal power, as such.

Hitler's theory of the "good" is certainly very primitive, but we can still recognize it as a theory *of the* "*good*," rather than a decision (say) to adopt evil, as such, as his guide. So that, rather than being merely "sick," or in the grip of an unintelligible "force of evil," Hitler is, in a certain way, perfectly intelligible. We can understand and identify with his desire to have what he perceives as "good," even while we regret the emotional and intellectual distortion of his perception, utterly condemn the actions to which his perception led him, and do our best to prevent those actions from being carried out.

Why do people sometimes "choose evil"? Because they see it in some way as good! Not "morally" good, in a conventional sense, of course, but not merely a "luxury" good for themselves, either, but an indispensable good for their existence and self-respect, and thus a good that they think the world owes them. If they didn't see their choice of what we call "evil" as good in this way, it wouldn't be intelligible as a *choice*. It would just be a random flip of a coin, for the outcome of which no one is responsible.

If we see Hitler's actions not as random but as seeking the good, while disastrously failing to find it, it becomes possible to forgive his actions. Excruciatingly difficult, no doubt, but possible. Whereas it would probably not be possible to forgive his actions if we viewed him as merely "sick," as purely "evil," or as literally "inhuman." If we were to put him in any of those categories, we wouldn't be able to understand him as making real choices, and consequently wouldn't be able either to blame him for those choices or to forgive him for them either.

If we can't *blame* Hitler, we'll be in a very difficult position with many human actions that cause havoc and destruction. Don't we object to them, and don't we seek to give reasons why they're unacceptable? But if we blame Hitler and we combat him but we can't *forgive* him, perhaps because we think of him as sheer "evil" or as simply "insane," we're still not in a good position, since then our world contains people who seem to be our sheer "enemies," not reachable even in principle by any kind of reasoned appeal. Our lives are then, in principle, a constant state of war, and we can never be fully free.

In a review of Ralph Wedgwood (2007), Alan Millar asks,

> Why should we suppose that intention *constitutively* aims at choiceworthy action . . .? The view that it does echoes the classical view [that is, Plato's view—RMW] that action constitutively aims at the good. While such a view is still quite widely held, it is doubtful that it is psychologically realistic. . . . People all too easily form and carry out intentions that are weak-willed or perverse, *knowingly* acting for reasons that even by their own lights have nothing to do with what is worthy of choice on any natural understanding of what that would amount to. A father who kills his children to spite their mother need not conceal from himself that nothing good can come of it, only satisfaction of an urge to teach the mother a bitter lesson. (*Mind* 119 [January 2010], p. 265)

I think there is greater "psychological realism" in understanding such a father as seeking the indispensable "good" of (as I imagine) vindicating his own highly threatened ego, his efficacy in the world, against what he feels is a threat of obliteration. This renders his action intelligible in a way that describing it as "perverse," tempting though such descriptions undoubtedly often are, simply fails to do. "Weakness of will" must also be understandable in similar ways. Otherwise, we make vast ranges of human behavior essentially unintelligible. Of course the intelligibility that results from the view that I recommend renders human "intellectual" functioning a lifelong and seldom fully conscious process, which is only partially captured by what an individual can articulate (as "his own lights") at any particular point in time. But this too seems realistic.

Plato and our "dark side"

Plato and the Platonic tradition have often been suspected of being foolishly "idealistic," in the sense of underestimating the evil in human beings and the "tragic" side of human experience. Plato's contemporary, the great Greek historian Thucydides, described Athens's policies toward its "allied" cities as ruthless and motivated by brute calculations of self-interest. Writing during the English Civil War of the 1600s, Thomas Hobbes argued that the only way for humans to avoid destroying one another through mutual predation is to set up a dictatorial power over society which will terrify us all into submission. And in the nineteenth century, Friedrich Nietzsche suggested that the Platonic "ascent" and the Christian interest in a "world to come" were both motivated by a desire to get a phantom "revenge" for pain suffered in the material world. Thus all three of these "masters of suspicion" suggest that appeals to justice and virtue, and discussions about them, are likely to overlook less admirable and more self-centered human motives, or even to contain disguised forms of them.

I mentioned that Plato's own family contained people who acted in ways that might seem to confirm these writers' suspicions about human nature. Plato's uncle, Critias, was the leader of the "Thirty Tyrants" who took ruthless actions against their democratic opponents during their short-lived tyranny over Athens in 404–403 BCE. Plato presents Critias as a bewildered victim of Socrates's questioning in the *Charmides*, which is set in 432 BCE, several years before Plato's birth. The only hint, in this dialogue, of the ugliness that was to come is when Charmides, who is Critias's nephew and was himself later one of the "Thirty," joking seriously tells Socrates that Socrates has no choice but to serve as Charmides's teacher (176c). We know from Plato's *Apology of Socrates* that the "Thirty" in fact did try, unsuccessfully, to use the threat of death to force Socrates to become an accomplice in their misdeeds. Thus, without publicly "washing his family's dirty linen," Plato hints at the moral agony that he must have experienced when his relatives resorted to overt coercion against the people of Athens and against Plato's hero and teacher, Socrates.

In other dialogues, Plato describes individuals who at the time of the dialogue's action are clearly on, or close to, the "dark side." Callicles, in Plato's *Gorgias*, maintains that those who praise self-control and justice do so merely because they're too weak to take what they want from others (492a). And Thrasymachus, in the first book of the *Republic*, carries Callicles's thought further by praising tyrants for achieving happiness and bliss (344c). Thrasymachus's aggressive manner frightens people, and when Socrates's questioning makes Thrasymachus uncomfortable, Thrasymachus resorts to insults: "Tell me, Socrates, do you still have a wet nurse?" (343a) Thrasymachus's notion of discussion is modeled on wrestling: "Now practice your harm-doing and false witnessing on that if you can—I ask no concessions from you—but you won't be able to" (341b). His goal is to win, and his failure to do so puts him into an angry and sarcastic huff. Plato sticks to the dramatic context, offering us no hypotheses about Thrasymachus's childhood environment, but we can see in Thrasymachus the habits of the schoolyard bully who has a weakness that he's ashamed of, and goes on the offensive so as to hide it.

You might say that Thrasymachus shows us what the "spirited part" that Socrates analyzes in *Republic* book iv can turn into when the rational part doesn't understand or control it. It is self-importance carried to the *n*th degree. But I would add that the rational part's failure, in these cases, isn't accidental or unintelligible. Rather, Thrasymachus's rational part has developed only to the point of identifying success (the good) with "winning." Its ability to think about other dimensions of the good has been stunted, probably because the issue of winning has been given such salience by its traumatic early experience that no attention is left over for these other dimensions.

So Plato certainly doesn't underestimate the power of the damaged ego to create havoc in the world. What he does do is to help us neither to "run screaming" from this phenomenon nor to build ourselves up by distancing ourselves from it, by (for example) interpreting it as sheer "evil," or as a symptom of "illness," outside the moral realm, or as "monstrosity" or "brutality": being mis-born or less than human. On the contrary, Plato clearly thinks of the power-admirer's psychology as all too human, and perfectly intelligible. By presenting it in this way, he helps us to preserve the possibility of full freedom, in which we can identify with everything in our world as an attempt at freedom, rather than simply rejecting big pieces of our world, and thus denying ourselves full freedom.

"To call the wolf my brother"

Carl Gustav Jung wrote that "modern man's" problem is "to learn how he is to reconcile himself with his own nature—how he is to love the enemy in his own heart and call the wolf his brother." Here Jung put his finger on an issue that Plato was already addressing two millennia earlier, with his theory of the "Good" and the potential unity of the three parts of the soul. Because the attitude of judgment or condemnation which is the first step in rational functioning makes us disunited or "alienated," and thus while making us free also limits our freedom, the act of identifying what deserves to be condemned fails to make us fully free. We must also be able to love what we condemn—the "wolf," the enemy, whether outside us or within us. And invite it into the fold.

To invite the damaged ego into the fold, we must understand what its goal is, and how its conception of its goal may have been warped by its (probably early) experience. To understand this, in ourselves, we must be much more loving and patient with ourselves than we probably usually are. We aren't likely to achieve this love and patience unless we understand that the ego is a project of *thought* about what's good, rather than a mere random drive toward "good" or "evil," "human" satisfactions or "bestial" ones. Understanding the ego as a project of thought about what's good, we may be able, over time and with patience, to unravel its early, now habitual thoughts, correct them, and reknit them.

No doubt our success in this endeavor will always be limited. But knowing that it's achievable in principle, we won't despair of human nature and condemn it as irredeemable, thus condemning our world and ourselves as irredeemable. Knowing that this reknitting can, in principle, be done, because the ego is a project of thought, we have accomplished, in principle, the reconciliation that Jung speaks of.

This is, obviously, a profoundly reassuring development. Having the tendency to skepticism that we properly have, the only thing that can make such a development possible for us is the careful, unsentimental examination of human experience that Plato and his successors carry out. Among whom we can count many twentieth-century psychotherapists, although, like Jung, they may not know a great deal about Plato himself. Thanks to the long tradition of broadly Platonic "soul"-work, whether it's called philosophy or literature or religion or psychotherapy, we know that "Pollyanna" sentimentality is not the only alternative to the courageous cynicism of the "masters of suspicion," such as Thucydides, Hobbes, and Nietzsche.

"God-given madness" (*Phaedrus*)

It's clear that the kind of "reconciliation" that we're talking about here is not a "merely intellectual" event. It involves physical and emotional depths with which the intellect, often, has little contact. The rarity of this sort of contact provides some justification for the skepticism that the masters of suspicion encourage, regarding the intellect's powers.

But such contact does occur. Not all mental processes are conscious, and not all unconscious processes are "irrational." I think Plato could accept Jung's discovery of the constructive role of the unconscious, as a "friendly amendment" to his theory of the role of thought in human life. This is another case in which conscious thought can find and appreciate the friendly cooperation of other "parts of the soul."

In fact, the same friendly amendment that Jung proposes was already, in effect, proposed by Plato himself, when he wrote in various places about the positive contribution to human life that's made by certain apparently irrational phenomena. According to Plato, Socrates himself frequently experienced what he called a "divine sign," a sense that he shouldn't do something that he otherwise would have done. Socrates always obeyed this "sign," with what appear to be good results (*Apology* 31d). Socrates also experienced protracted periods of apparent trance, in which no one knew what Socrates was doing.[8] Plato's most explicit theoretical account of phenomena like these is in his *Phaedrus*, where Socrates lists four different kinds of divine inspiration, producing "madness" (*mania*) in humans, which in every case is beneficial. These are the inspired ravings of Apollo's prophetesses at Delphi and Dodona, Dionysian rites and purifications, songs and poetry that are inspired by the Muses, and the divinely inspired state of love (244–45).

It's noteworthy that Plato here seems to suggest a much more open-minded view both of poetry and of love than he had in the *Republic*.[9] Perhaps he was becoming more aware than he had been initially of some of the liberal implications of the *Republic*'s account of the Good and the soul.

In any case, it seems reasonable to think of the wisdom that we sometimes find in our dreams, as belonging alongside the poetry, purification, prophecy, and love that Plato lists here as "God-given." Like the other kinds of "madness" that Socrates lists, these dreams seem to be manifestations of a process of something like thought, which however we aren't conscious of engaging in as thought. This unconscious thought gives us what our conscious mind can sometimes recognize as inspired commentary.

By these observations, Plato obviously doesn't intend to praise "madness" in general. He's careful to specify that the kinds of madness that he's talking about are the "god-given" ones, thus suggesting that other kinds of madness probably don't have the beneficial effects that these have. People who have first-hand experience of both the "god-given" and the other kinds of madness will probably be inclined to agree with Plato about this.

Here again, Plato isn't "starry-eyed" but eminently realistic. As for Jung, so also for Plato, the great achievement is when the "rational part" of the soul is able to appreciate and to work with the other parts, including the "madness" that conveys to us the results of thought processes that we're not conscious of engaging in.

A less fearful rationality

Plato's investigation of the role of thought arrives at less pessimistic results than the "masters of suspicion" arrive at. This isn't because Plato averts his eyes from our "dark side" or from our unconscious functioning, but because he examines them with more care than the masters of suspicion do. Plato doesn't assume the worst: for example, that we seek only our own power, survival, and self-centered satisfactions. Or that our unconscious functioning is simply a domain of repressed desires. Instead, he notices that we actually seek "the things that really *are* good" (*Republic* 505d), whatever those may turn out to be, and he describes how this often conscious search interacts with less conscious kinds of searching for the same thing.

Just as the "rational part" has to judge the validity of the spirited part's strong feelings, so it also has to judge the messages that it receives from unconscious thought processes. Something has to decide which unconscious thought processes are the "god-given" ones and which ones aren't. We might think, for example, of the famous story in the book of Genesis in which we're told that "God" instructs Abraham to prepare to sacrifice his son, Isaac. Is Abraham justified in believing that this is, in fact, the voice of God, rather than of some less authoritative part of the universe? The only plausible candidate for the job of making these decisions is Abraham's rational part.

The story of Abraham and Isaac was Soren Kierkegaard's prize exhibit in his critical response to what he took to be Hegel's narrow-minded adherence to "reason."

Kierkegaard felt that in his rationalism, Hegel had betrayed religion's inherent commitment to something that goes beyond mere human comprehension.[10] In response, I would suggest that Plato and Hegel both acknowledge that there are modes of thought or reason at work in the world with which our conscious mind has only limited contact.[11] And that it is highly appropriate for us to acknowledge and to seek to learn from these "unconscious" modes of thought or reason, as Jung and others have taught us to do, through the study of dreams and synchronicities.

But Plato and Hegel both point out that it's not appropriate to embrace everything that comes from unconscious sources. Our "rational part" needs to be at work, distinguishing as best it can the "madness" that's probably "God-given" from the madness that's *not* God-given. This is the aspect of the relation between religion and reason that Kierkegaard seems to neglect, in his discussion of the story of Abraham and Isaac and his critique of Hegel's supposedly un-"religious" rationalism. For if true religion required us to embrace everything that comes to us with a voice of authority from unconscious sources, then true religion would not be merely paradoxical, as Kierkegaard describes it, but literally insane. To say in response that religion requires us only to embrace what comes *from God* is to invite precisely the question, How do you distinguish what comes from God from what comes from other sources?

Plato's formulation in the *Phaedrus* about "God-given madness," which suggests that not all madness is "God-given," points to this issue of how we should distinguish what's God-given from what's not; and Plato addresses this issue in his *Euthyphro* and *Timaeus* (71e–72b). It's hardly likely that Plato meant his talk of God-given madness to open the gates indiscriminately to every claim to divine inspiration.

A major reason why people are attracted to Kierkegaard's notion of faith as "absurd," and to similar doctrines about religion, is that they have the quite justified impression that modern culture in the name of what it calls "reason" has to a large extent leveled off the vertical dimension of the sacred, the higher reality. But when we see with Plato's or Hegel's help that such levelling-off is not, in fact, ultimately rational, we can see that the defense of a higher reality doesn't need to embrace anything that's opposed to rationality.

Freedom and divinity

It's no wonder, then, that Plato's conceptions of the Good and the soul have influenced many serious thinkers, in the West, about human functioning and human society. And they have also influenced many serious thinkers about the relation between humans and God. The "vertical" dimension of ascent toward knowledge of the Good and consequently toward greater unity, freedom, and reality as oneself is a very suggestive way to conceptualize the relation between finite, imperfect beings like ourselves, and whatever is divine. Plato consequently alludes to the possibility that a "philosopher," who makes an ascent like the one from the Cave, would "become like God" (*Theaetetus* 176b).

Apart from the question of how much "like God" a human could become, the vertical dimension that Plato has projected provides the main alternative to conceptions of God as distinguished from the world mainly by God's great "power." Rather than thinking of God in terms of "power" as such, the Platonic tradition thinks of God as distinguished specifically by the power to bring about what I call "reality as oneself." Since "power" as such seems to be a completely worldly or "natural" characteristic, the Platonic conception of God as achieving reality as oneself has the advantage of presenting a God who seems truly to go beyond the world or nature.

Plus, when this going beyond is understood on the analogy of the way persons go beyond their appetites and emotions, in the unification of the three-part "soul," it gives us a conception of God not as in futile opposition to the world but as truly and completely self-governed. That is, it gives us the kind of conception of God that Hegel spelled out later, as we discussed in Chapter 4, and which Plato adumbrated in a complex set of dialogues which we'll discuss in the next two chapters.

Limits of the *Republic*

I have suggested that because it makes forgiveness possible, the search for what's really good can be the theme not only of unity within oneself but also of a unity between oneself and other people. But what I've said in this chapter about unity between oneself and other people has been my extrapolation of implications that I find in the *Republic*, but which aren't spelled out in it.

The *Republic* itself doesn't explain very clearly how the search for what's really good unites people with each other. It really only opens the question up, with its strange combination of radical equality and radical inequality: every soul is capable of seeking the good, but only a few souls will do this reliably, and the others must be lied to. In its political sections, the *Republic* exhibits what seems to be a rather "controlling" response, on Plato's part, to his multiple traumas.

In his *Symposium*, on the other hand, which we'll consider in the next chapter, Plato constructs a different model around the notion of "giving birth" in others. This idea is intimately connected to the *Republic*'s theme of education and to Plato's well-known comparison of Socrates to a midwife (*Theaetetus* 149a-b). According to the *Symposium*'s model, souls can and must relate, on a basis both of fundamental equality and of truth-telling, with a number of others which has no obvious limit. This model also lends itself very much to a philosophical theology that understands the divine in terms of inner freedom and reality as oneself. I'll take up Plato's account of love and "giving birth" in the next chapter, and his explicit theology in Chapter 8.

7 PLATO ON REASON, LOVE, AND INSPIRATION

Beauty is truth, truth beauty...
JOHN KEATS, ODE ON A GRECIAN URN

ché 'l bene, in quanto ben, come s'intende, così accende amore, e tanto maggio quanto più di bontate in sé comprende.
(For good, when understood as such, enkindles love, and more so the more goodness it contains.)
DANTE, *DIVINE COMEDY, PARADISO* XXVI, 28

In this chapter and the next one I aim to do something that may well seem impossible. I aim to reveal philosophy's heart: to show how philosophy is inseparable from love.

The academic philosophy that many of us have been exposed to seems to have everything to do with the head, and little or nothing to do with the heart. Courses introducing philosophy's main topics seldom touch on love. The "philosophy of love and sex," which has nevertheless come into existence in the last few decades, is a small subspecialty among twenty or thirty subspecialties of Anglo-American philosophy. Of the "great" modern philosophers, only Hegel gives systematic attention to love.[1] In the nearly two centuries since Hegel, academic philosophy has been preoccupied with the sciences, and secondarily with ethics and politics and perhaps with the arts or religion. Love, which appears to be peripheral to all of these, has not been a priority.[2]

This is no doubt part of what the German sociologist Max Weber called the "disenchantment of the world," which we have undergone in the age of science. We perceive love as, at most, a personal experience, not as a fundamental reality. So we let literature and psychology deal with it. Shakespeare's comedies and Jane

Austen's novels speak to us across the centuries because they remind us how the experience of love can transform us and our world. But we think of such transformations as merely "subjective," having nothing to do with reality, as such. Dante's *Divine Comedy* constructed an entire worldview, a cosmos, around the author's experience of love. But no contemporary writer, it seems, could do that. Probably, we suppose, only a Christian believer could do it.

Well, as a matter of fact, a Greek philosopher did it, before Christianity was dreamed of. Love plays such a central role in Plato's thought that he is sometimes described, in a not too misleading formula, as simply a philosopher of love. And I'm convinced that Plato was onto something here, which our recent philosophy and culture have neglected to our great loss. Christianity, Dante, and the Romantic poets were right to feel that love is a reality that is at least as deep as the reality that the physical sciences reveal. Hegel was right to seek to vindicate this reality as an aspect of philosophy or systematic knowledge. And Plato's much earlier treatment of this reality, in his *Lysis*, *Phaedrus*, and *Symposium*, penetrates as deeply into it as any other writing that we have.

Reason, love, and inspiration

Since Plato is also correctly known as an arch-advocate of "reason," we might well wonder how the same writer can make central two things that seem to have as little to do with each other as reason and love. Shouldn't he rather have to choose between them, as the eighteenth-century Enlightenment, for example, is reputed to have chosen reason, and the Romantics, by contrast, chose love?

I don't know of any commentator who has made fully clear how reason and love relate to each other in Plato.[3] My own proposal will be that Plato's development of the idea of love, in Diotima's speech in the *Symposium*, shows that love depends upon the deep kind of "reason" that he analyzed in the *Phaedo* and the *Republic*. So one of love's essential ingredients is, in fact, the kind of reason that we have been examining in the last two chapters. And it turns out, as we'll see in the next chapter, that the kind of reason that we have been examining likewise requires and turns into love.

This intimate connection between reason and love is also essential to the mystical theology that Plato suggests through Diotima's speech, and of which we get glimpses in other dialogues as well. For what emerges is that freedom, love, immortality, and divinity are all based, as Plato presents them, on the deep conception of reason and its role in human life that he expounds, especially, in the *Phaedo* and the *Republic*. This deep conception of reason shows how we are less separate from each other, and less separate from God, than we usually assume we are. We are necessarily linked with each other and with God, through reason/love.

Plato is aware that many people, when they hear of the role that he assigns to reason in human life, will suspect that such a philosophy would take all of the inspiration out of life. They'll imagine that its conception of religion, if any, must be bleakly "rationalistic." Friedrich Schleiermacher and Soren Kierkegaard reacted to Hegel's conception of religion in this way. That's not *religion*, they said, that's *philosophy*. They overlooked the central role of love and ecstasy in Hegel's thinking, and how it recapitulated the role of love and ecstasy in Plato. Similarly Friedrich Nietzsche, ignoring the inspiration and ecstasy that Plato evokes in his *Symposium* and *Phaedrus*, described Socrates and Plato as uninspired, constrained, "Appollonian" rationalists in contrast to inspired, unconstrained, "Dionysian" irrationality.[4]

Probably one of Plato's major goals in writing the *Symposium*, in particular, was to head off the kind of misunderstanding of "reason" that Schleiermacher, Kierkegaard, and Nietzsche exhibit. Plato aims to do this by showing how one of our most inspiring experiences, the experience of sexual or romantic love, itself implicitly involves something very much like the deep kind of reason that he has been exploring in the *Republic*. And by showing, in the same stroke, how the equally inspiring experience of mysticism involves that same deep kind of reason.

With regard to Plato's conception of love in the *Symposium*, E. R. Dodds wrote that Plato "never, as it seems to me, fully integrated this line of thought with the rest of his philosophy; had he done so, the notion of the intellect as a self-sufficient entity independent of the body might have been imperiled, and Plato was not going to risk that."[5] I discussed the issue of the intellect's "independence of the body" in Chapter 5, and in this chapter I will show how closely Plato integrates his conception of love with his conception of the intellect's rational "ascent."

If Plato shows, as I'm suggesting, that love, God, mysticism, and reason are inseparable, then the many Jews, Christians, and Muslims who have used ideas that originated in Plato as aids in their efforts toward developing a systematic interpretation of their own sacred teachings were not mistaken in doing so. What could be more inspiring than a demonstration that we don't need to be drawn in opposite directions by our reasoning and our love, because (on the contrary) true reason necessarily leads to true love?

The setting of the *Symposium*

The *Symposium* presents itself as a report of a series of improvised speeches given at a drinking party (Greek *sym-posion*="drinking together"). Agathon, a young Athenian aristocrat and poet whose play has just won the prize at one of the festivals of Dionysus, is the host. The festivals of Dionysus were the events at which the great Athenian tragedies and comedies were performed. Agathon was a real person and a real playwright, but his plays aren't among the ones that have survived the intervening millennia for us to read.

Dionysus, whose festival is being celebrated, is also known as "Bacchus." He isn't one of the traditional Olympian gods. According to tradition, Dionysus's worship had a "barbarian," non-Greek origin, and prominent male Greeks tried in vain to resist it, when it first came to Greece. Dionysus interacted closely with his human followers, especially women, through rites that are often described as "orgiastic." They are described in Euripides's play, the "Bacchae." According to one version of Dionysus's story, he was torn to pieces as an infant and eaten by the Titans, but his heart was saved and he was reborn, so that he's known as the "twice-born." In this way he anticipates the Christian theme of divine death and resurrection. Dionysus's worshippers reenacted his self-abandonment, dancing over the mountains under the influence of wine and music, and sometimes tearing to pieces animals or unlucky shepherds whom they might encounter. It may be that Plato sets the Symposium during a festival of Dionysus so as to suggest that like eros, even the worship of this wild god ultimately relies in an important way on reason.

Love in Athens

Another circumstance that sets Plato's dialogues about love apart from most modern writing on the subject is that love is understood here almost entirely as a relationship between man and man. Women in classical Athens were excluded from most education and public life, so that they seemed not to be capable of equal partnership with men in anything, including love. Plato himself famously made the suggestion, in book v of the *Republic*, that women could play an equal role in public life and serve as "philosopher-kings," but he expected most of his male contemporaries to view this suggestion as plainly ridiculous—which (as we see, for example, in Aristotle) they did.

As a result of this social setup, marriage in Athens was understood, as it has been in many societies, primarily as a social, political, and child-producing alliance, rather than a matter of romance. So romantic love was discovered primarily outside marriage, and usually (as it was by another famous Greek writer, Sappho) in homosexual relationships. Athens had a recognized form of man-boy love, *paederastia*, to which allusions are made throughout the *Symposium*. And although most men apparently settled down and married women at some point, their homosexual romantic relationships sometimes extended outside the marriage throughout their lives.[6]

So if we want to apply Plato's account of love to heterosexual relationships as well, or to relationships that take the form of marriage, we'll need to take it somewhat outside its original context. Which, however, turns out not to be particularly difficult, since the issues and patterns that Plato identifies are of quite a universal character.

Eros

So the topic of the series of speeches that make up the *Symposium* is eros. The atmosphere appears to be one of convivial banter, as one would expect at a drinking party. But as James Rhodes points out in his illuminating account of the dialogue, the other speakers have all been, in one way or another, at odds with Socrates in other dialogues.[7] Phaedrus, Pausanias, Erixymachus, and Agathon were all introduced in Plato's *Protagoras* as students of the prominent sophists, Hippias and Prodicus. Pausanias and Agathon have since become students of the sophist Gorgias, whom Socrates cross-examines in the dialogue that bears Gorgias's name. The sophists were itinerant teachers of social skills, basically how to influence other people and get what you want. Protagoras was famous for his thesis that "man is the measure of all things," drawing no distinction between higher and lower aspects of "man," and Gorgias went further, maintaining that there is no truth, but only opinions.

Socrates, by contrast, maintains that we want knowledge of what's really good (and thus what's really "higher"), which can't depend merely on our prior desires or opinions. Since the *Symposium* features less Socratic cross-examination than the *Protagoras* and *Gorgias* do, it doesn't foreground Plato's dispute with the sophists in the way that those dialogues do. But that dispute is undoubtedly an issue just beneath the surface of this dialogue as well.

As for the other two participants besides Socrates, Aristophanes, in his comedy, the "Clouds," had presented Socrates in a very unflattering light. Socrates in his *Apology* says that the play probably contributed to the charges against which he is defending himself at his trial and for which, as everyone knows, he was condemned to death. And Plato regularly presents Alcibiades, the gifted and charismatic young political and military leader, as not responding well to Socrates's efforts to inspire his interest in wisdom. So all six of the other participants in the *Symposium* have affiliations or habits that are (at the very least) problematic, from Socrates's point of view.

The first three speakers talk about ways in which erotic relationships can encourage behavior that's commonly regarded as good. Phaedrus and Pausanias talk about how lovers encourage each other to do admirable acts of self-sacrifice on behalf of their city. Eryximachus, who is a doctor, describes the "orderly kind of love" as a principle of physiological harmony, and of musical and cosmic harmony as well.

All three of these speakers explicitly or implicitly contrast a good kind of love, such as the "orderly kind," with a bad kind of love, tracing love's good effects to the good kind of love, of course, rather than to the bad kind. They leave good and bad unanalyzed, and they don't address what makes both kinds of love "love," so their rather banal observations don't illuminate love as such.

My "other half"

The subsequent speakers are Aristophanes; then Agathon, who is the host of the party; then Socrates; and finally Alcibiades, who arrives late and drunk.

Aristophanes, in his speech, offers a myth of the origin of love which has a lot of intuitive plausibility. Humans, he says, originally were spherical, with four legs, two faces, and other double organs. So when Zeus became irritated with them for having the ambition of mounting to heaven and attacking the gods, his solution was to weaken them by splitting them in half, down the middle. The result of this surgery is not only that humans now walk on two legs but also that each half of the former sphere yearns for its lost other half.

> And so, when a person meets the half that is his very own . . . then something wonderful happens: the two are struck from their senses by love, by a sense of belonging to one another, and by desire, and they don't want to be separated from one another, not even for a moment. These are the people who finish out their lives together and still cannot say what it is that they want from one another. No one would think it is the intimacy of sex—that mere sex is the reason each lover takes so great and deep a joy in being with the other. (192b-c)

"The people who finish out their lives together and still cannot say what it is that they want from one another"—this is indeed the mystery of being "in love," that it's hard to explain its depth and intensity, in comparison to our other relationships. We're likely to feel that Aristophanes's entertaining myth of the lost "other half" may be as good an explanation of this familiar mystery as we're likely to get. Certainly Plato makes it seem quite appealing.

But he himself is not satisfied with it. This becomes clear in the final planned speech of the evening, Socrates's speech. Most of Socrates's speech is composed of his report of what he says he was taught, early in his life, by a priestess from Mantinea, whose name was Diotima.[8] Socrates says that Diotima told him that

> there is a certain story, according to which lovers are those people who seek their other halves. But according to *my* story, a lover does not seek the half or the whole unless, my friend, it turns out to be *good* as well. I say this because people are even willing to cut off their own arms and legs if they are diseased. I don't think an individual takes joy in what belongs to him personally unless by "belonging to me" he means "good." . . . That's because what everyone loves is really nothing other than the good. (205e; emphasis added)

These comments remind us of Plato's equally pivotal argument in the *Republic* (505d) that people ultimately want for themselves what's *good*, and not just whatever they're viscerally attracted to at the moment. Diotima is saying, in effect:

Suppose that you discover that your mate, whom you think of as your "other half," is actually (unbeknownst to you) a conscienceless mass murderer. Then your attachment to her, your feeling that she's your "other half," is likely to be undermined, in a big way.

So evidently your feeling that your mate "belongs to you," as your other half, depends, at least to some extent, on your seeing him or her as *good*. If your arm or leg becomes diseased and can't be saved, or if you come to regard cunning not as good but as bad, you'll let go of the arm or the leg or the cunning mate whom you previously admired, without feeling that you've lost "part of yourself."

Why don't we have this experience often, of discovering that what we thought was our "other half" is really not "part of us" at all? With most people who fall in love, probably part of what causes them to fall in love is precisely the perception that the person they're falling in love with is, in fact, good. Meaning not only that the person has pretty good habits but also that he's actually interested, himself, in learning more about what's *really* good, so that when his partner makes some progress on this subject, he's glad to share in that learning process. This is why we don't often find one partner leaving the other behind, in terms of learning about goodness, and having to conclude that the other person wasn't really "part of them," after all. If their love for each other includes a love for the other's interest in learning about what's good, then it will tend to be the case that they'll share what they learn, rather than one leaving the other behind.

Does Plato speak to the "intellectually inclined" or to everyone?

There is an evident connection between Diotima's discussion of what makes another person my "other half," and the agenda that I suggested that Plato has, of showing that *eros* and "inspiration" aren't ultimately irrational. Clearly, by introducing the theme of "goodness," Plato is creating a connection with "reason": with figuring out what is not merely desired but also truly good. This makes it natural to wonder whether Plato at this point might have simply abandoned the topic of the usual kind of *eros*, which is simple sexual desire. Has he just changed the subject, so that he's now addressing only would-be "philosophers," as we might call the people who care about goodness, and not people who are attracted by Dionysian enthusiasm?

The answer, I believe, is that Plato supposes that the Dionysian enthusiast will in fact want to claim that her life is a good one—indeed, the best one. She may not want to invest her time in defending that claim, but she certainly relies on it. So it's not only "intellectuals" who are interested in the question of what's really good.

Thus I disagree with Frisbee Sheffield's suggestion that only those who are "intellectually inclined" can be expected to be concerned with the question of what's really good.[9] Our interpretation of what Plato means to say here will determine whether we think his account of love is relevant to human experience in general, or only to the experience of the relatively small group of humans who are "intellectually inclined." And this will determine whether we think Plato really has anything to say to his fellow symposiasts, the sophists, who seem only superficially "intellectually inclined," and would probably admit (if they were candid) that they are consciously much more interested in power and fame than in intellect as such.

My view is that in keeping with Socrates's statements that the unexamined life is not worth living (*Apology of Socrates* 38a) and that "everyone wants the things that really *are* good, and disdains mere belief here" (*Republic* vi, 505d), we should assume that Plato's basic view is that knowledge of what really is good is a universal human need. Though the ability to pursue such knowledge in a systematic and explicit way is no doubt much less widespread. The sophists need knowledge of what's really good as much as anyone needs it, in that they certainly want to believe that the lives that they envisage for themselves are in fact the best lives for human beings.

Eros as "reproduction"

To make his case about the nature of *eros* more concrete, Plato now has Diotima turn to a more detailed discussion of familiar features of love. Diotima proposes to Socrates that love is not just wanting what's good but wanting to have it "forever" (206a). The way we mortals can do this, Diotima says, is through "reproduction," which is "everlasting and immortal as far as is possible for something mortal" (206e–207a). We are "pregnant . . . both in body and in soul" (206c), and we seek either through bodily procreation or by educating another person to "give birth in beauty" (206b) to something that's like ourselves.

We do this, Diotima says, even within the limits of our own individual body, since our "manners, customs, opinions, desires, pleasures, pains and fears" are always passing away and needing to be replaced. We seek to replace them, she says, with manners, customs, and so forth that are like the ones that we have now (207e–208b). And beyond the life of our own body, some of us seek to have physical offspring, and others, who are "pregnant in soul," try to inspire in younger people manners, customs, and so forth that are like our own. Poets, such as Homer and Hesiod, and lawgivers, such as Lycurgus and Solon, are particularly successful at doing this, and famous for it. Their soul-children, Diotima says, are in fact "more immortal" (209c) than the children of those who are merely pregnant in body.

The most important question that's raised by this rich passage is this: If we want to reproduce ourselves, as Diotima says, why should we particularly want to reproduce our *souls*, our "manners, customs, opinions," and so forth, by educating other people, rather than just reproducing our *bodies*, by having physical offspring? Why are soul-children "more immortal" than ordinary offspring?

Why are soul-children "more immortal"?

Diotima mentions that "shrines" have been set up to honor people like Homer, Hesiod, Lycurgus, and Solon, the great Greek poets and lawgivers, who "beget virtue" in others, but not for people who simply have physical offspring (210a). But she doesn't explain why a person shouldn't be satisfied with the "immortality, remembrance and happiness" that nevertheless do appear to go with ordinary physical procreation (208e).

The Greek appetite for "immortal *fame*," which seems to be part of her answer, in its turn raises the same issue. Why do people often attach greater importance to "fame" than they attach to having biological descendants?

It's not too difficult to explain why we should want to reproduce our souls in particular, as Diotima says the poets and lawgivers do, if we remember Plato's account, in *Republic* book iv, of what it takes to make a person "one." Plato argued there that it's only when the appetites, the "spirited" part, and the rational part of a person's soul are harmonized under the leadership of the rational part, that "from having been many things he becomes entirely one," and can act as such (443d). This was because only the rational part had the ability to understand each of the other parts in such a way that it could harmonize all three of them.

What this has to do with reproducing our souls, in the form of our manners, customs, opinions, and virtues, is that these "soul" features are features that can reflect the functioning of the rational part, in particular. They reflect the functioning of the rational part insofar as a person may *decide* to act and think in certain ways, and such decisions can reflect thinking, rather than just the feelings provoked by appetites and the "spirited" part.

This is important because insofar as these decisions do reflect thinking, they are capable of reflecting the person himself, as "entirely one," rather than just some part of him, as the functioning of the appetites or the spirited part alone would do. Decisions made by the rational part reflect the person himself because the rational part is the part that's capable of harmonizing the three parts of the soul into one person. Consequently, it's possible for "soul" features like manners, customs, opinions, and virtues to reflect the person himself, as a whole, in a way that merely physical features, like height, shape, and so forth, don't. Physical features, presumably, are more likely to be determined by the person's biological heritage, and thus by at most one part of him.

There's no *guarantee*, of course, that "soul" features like manners, customs, opinions, and virtues will reflect the person's thinking and thus reflect the person himself. They could reflect mainly the effects on him of people around him, his childhood environment, and that sort of thing. But they *can* reflect his thinking and thus himself, whereas physical features, in general, probably can't.

And this, I suggest, is probably why Plato's Diotima thinks that a thoughtful person won't be satisfied with the "immortality, remembrance and happiness" that appear to go with ordinary physical procreation. For that sort of remembrance won't, in general, reflect the person himself, who's being "reproduced." Of course, biological offspring can reflect the procreator himself if they're educated by him, but this simply shows that education is what really counts here, rather than procreation as such.

This probably also explains why Diotima thinks that soul-children are "more immortal" than ordinary offspring. Presumably this is another way of saying that soul-children (and their soul-children, and so on) are likely to reflect the parent himself, in a way that biological children don't necessarily do. So that someone who seeks to reproduce himself or herself will do best to educate, and not merely to procreate.

This would also be Diotima's explanation of the fact that many people prefer having fame to having biological descendants. For fame presumably reflects one's choices in life, and thus one's thinking and one's "self," in a way that biological reproduction, as such, does not.

My interpretation of Diotima's preference for "soul-children" as being due to the fact that soul-children reflect the "parent's" *thinking* and thus her *self* in a way that physical children don't has an important consequence. It means that interpreters who take the *Symposium* to advocate the simple rejection of individuality, in favor of a supposedly mystical "earlier state of unity," are mistaken. Rather than rejecting individuality, the *Symposium* preserves it and goes beyond it.[10] This feature of Plato's account is of major importance for anyone who's interested in getting clear about love and mystical reality. For it shows how a loving unity with all of reality need not involve ceasing to think for oneself.

Before exploring these questions further, we need to bring out a further parallel to the *Republic*. Remembering Diotima's earlier emphasis on the role of the good, in particular, in love, we might want to ask another question about her discussion of "reproduction." Does a person really want to reproduce *all* of her (physical and social) features, in her future self and in other people, or does she only want to reproduce those that she regards as *admirable or good*?

"Me" or my good qualities?

To ask this question is practically to answer it. I surely don't want my future self or my child or my protégé to have the same birthmarks and the same amount of irrational anger that I possess. What I want them to inherit from me is those of my features that I regard as *desirable*. If they inherit those, as a result of my efforts, I'll feel that they've reproduced *me* in the only way that I care about being reproduced.

So not only is the reproduction of "soul"-qualities more important than the reproduction of physical qualities. Among "soul"-qualities, the ones whose reproduction is truly important to me will be the ones that seem to me to be desirable or good. The reason they're most important is, again, precisely that what seems to me to be desirable or good is what I myself have chosen and tried to acquire, or will choose and try to acquire. Thus these qualities are the ones that most of all will reflect *me*. That's why the qualities that I regard as desirable are also the ones that, if I contribute to their embodiment in another person, will reproduce me in that other person.

Diotima doesn't explicitly raise this question of whether a person wants to reproduce all of his physical and social features, or only those that he regards as admirable or good. But she seems to realize that it follows naturally from her earlier emphasis on the role of the good. This is evident from the fact that the final part of her talk describes *eros* as itself addressing precisely the issue of what is truly desirable.

> First [a lover] should love one body . . . then he should realize that the beauty of one body is brother to the beauty of any other. . . . The beauty of all bodies is one and the same. When he grasps this, he must become a lover of all beautiful bodies. . . . After this he must think that the beauty of people's souls is more valuable than the beauty of their bodies. . . . [After this] our lover will be forced to gaze at the beauty of activities and laws, and to see that all this is akin to itself. . . . After customs he must move on to various kinds of knowledge . . . [so that] the lover is turned to the great sea of beauty, and gazing upon this, he gives birth to many gloriously beautiful ideas and theories . . . [until finally] he comes to know just what it is to be beautiful. (210a–211d)

This ascent, which Diotima compares to "rising stairs" (211c), is bound to remind us of the ascent of the Cave-dweller, in the *Republic*, to knowledge of the Good.[11] As in the *Republic*, Plato doesn't spell out just what it is that drives the climber from one step to the next higher one. Why "must" he think that the beauty of people's souls is more valuable than the beauty of their bodies? Why "must" he move from activities and laws to various kinds of knowledge, ideas, and theories?

The simplest explanation of these steps is that the climber is seeking knowledge, as Plato says at the end of the passage, of "just what it is to be beautiful," or, as we might also put it, of *just what it is that he loves* in the original beautiful body. In the first step, he realizes that "the beauty of all bodies is one and the same"—that what he loves in his first love isn't unique but is a quality that it shares with other beautiful bodies. In the second step, souls, which we know through their "activities and laws" and their "ideas and theories," exhibit beauty more clearly than bodies do, because qualities of the soul are likely to have been chosen precisely *because of* their beauty.[12] And "knowledge, ideas and theories" are even more likely to have been chosen in this way than activities and laws, since activities and laws may be merely conventional.

Why "all beautiful bodies" and not just one?

Before we get to any of these higher stages of the "ascent," though, we might wonder whether the "lover" must really "become a lover of *all* beautiful bodies"? Isn't "love" proverbially *exclusive* and *blind* to the virtues of other individuals than the one with whom one is "in love"? Has Plato replaced the experience of *eros*, as ordinary people know it, with the very unusual experience of (so to speak) a "born philosopher," who for some peculiar reason is in love with universals, rather than with particular human beings?[13]

The answer to this natural question is contained in the context of the ascent, in the discussion of "reproduction" and its pursuit of the next best thing to immortality, to which Diotima has given so much attention. There is every reason to think that Diotima is deepening the account that she has given in the first part of her exposition, rather than turning away to something that renders the first part irrelevant.

And the way she's deepening it is by answering our last question, about the role of the good in reproduction. She explains that a person who seeks to reproduce "herself" will determine what her true self is by determining what she really thinks is "beautiful." She won't want to reproduce her merely accidental qualities like her taste in ice cream or her excessive anger at politicians, because she doesn't really think those are beautiful, and consequently she doesn't think of them as really "herself." Nor will she want to reproduce her bodily features as much as she'll want to reproduce her activities and ideas and so forth, because her activities and ideas will represent *her* more than her body can represent her.[14]

This whole attitude to "reproduction" presupposes that a person can, in fact, distinguish between parts of herself that are relatively accidental and external and parts of herself that do indeed reflect her own thought. It presupposes that there *is* such a thing as thought about what's really "beautiful" or desirable. So this is what Diotima now seeks to demonstrate, with her story about the "ascent" to knowledge of the beautiful.

What I'm suggesting, then, is that eros certainly can address itself to particular human beings. But nevertheless, Plato is suggesting, eros isn't totally "blind" but wants to think of what it's attracted to as genuinely beautiful (or "fine") and wants therefore to have an idea of what genuine beauty (or "fineness") *is*. And I'm suggesting that this dimension of eros particularly emerges when the lover is wondering what sort of *influence* to exercise on the beloved individual. It emerges when the lover is wondering which of the beloved's qualities to encourage—because the lover really does love those qualities, in the beloved and in herself—and which of the beloved's qualities to try to help the beloved to rise above. That is, it emerges in the context of what Diotima calls "giving birth" or "reproduction."

How to *influence* the beloved?

Why does this issue arise at all, of how to "influence" the beloved? It's certainly not an obvious part of the usual narratives of romantic love, say, in "Tristan and Isolde" or "Romeo and Juliet" or *Wuthering Heights*. Does Plato's interest in the issue of how one should influence one's beloved show that he's really just a "schoolmaster," rather than someone who actually knows something about the inspired experience of eros?

Plato's answer to these questions is, first, that because the lover wants to possess what's truly good, the lover must have some conception of what it is that's good (or in this case, "beautiful"). Plus, since love "wants to possess the good *for ever*" (206a), the lover will encourage his beloved to continue to embody and to develop this quality that's truly good. Love may be proverbially blind, but it's also proverbially *possessive*. It wants not to be a transient episode, but to have its object forever. But to understand what it is to have something forever, we must have some idea of what that something *is*. But if a lover has such an idea, then his *eros* is not blind! It has an "intellectual" dimension.

Where else does love poetry come from, if not from the desire to express what it is that fascinates the lover, in his or her beloved? It's famously difficult, as Aristophanes says, to articulate "what it is that they want from one another" (192c). But we seek to do it nevertheless, and the beloved feels more loved, not less, when her lover is able to articulate some of what it is that he finds fascinating in her. And what he praises, he obviously *encourages*, and "reproduces," to the extent that he possesses it himself.

Thus, I submit, Plato's discovery of an "intellectual" dimension in *eros* isn't just a schoolmaster's projection. It's an articulation of something that we're all familiar with, on one level or another. If you have no *idea* whatever of what it is that fascinates you, and what you want to praise (and thus encourage), then it's open to question whether you're really in love.

Eros's intellectual dimension is illustrated by the famous final section of the *Symposium*, in which the drunken Alcibiades crashes the party and, in his speech, confesses his love for Socrates. Alcibiades doesn't just say that he's fascinated by this particular person. He also says a great deal about *what it is* that fascinates him in Socrates, namely, his good humor, his stoicism in the face of hardship, his great mental fertility and passion for the truth, his inner life, and his ability to make Alcibiades himself ashamed of his own moral and intellectual flightiness.

Here Alcibiades shows us both the intellectual dimension of his own love and the unfortunate failure of that intellectual dimension to bring him to *emulate* his beloved, by giving birth to deeds that would be in keeping with virtues like Socrates's. The readers of the *Symposium*, which was written years after the time that it depicts, were all very aware that Alcibiades had in the meantime turned out to be a traitor to Athens, who joined its enemies when his schemes for glory as an

Athenian leader didn't pan out. He had also been accused of desecrating Athenian religious statues and the Eleusinian mysteries.[15]

All of these were actions that no one could possibly imagine Socrates himself engaging in. So that evidently Alcibiades's admiration for Socrates's virtues had failed to triumph over Alcibiades's love of his own bodily beauty and fame. Apparently Alcibiades had some sort of hidden issue which made his personal beauty and charisma more important to him than such things were to Socrates. He wasn't able to focus fully on the virtues because of the continual distraction that this concern for his beauty and fame represented for him. So that despite his admiration for Socrates's virtues, Alcibiades failed, ultimately, to make the crucial step in Diotima's "ladder" from love of particular instances of "beauty" or virtue to love of *all* of their instances[16]—which would have caused him to try to cultivate virtues (inner beauty) like Socrates's in himself.

So we see that the presence of an intellectual dimension in eros doesn't guarantee that the person who experiences eros will in fact make the "ascent," up that dimension, that Plato describes. But that dimension is, nevertheless, always implicitly present in eros as we experience it, because to love something is to praise it, and thus to regard it as truly good; and we all know that only the intellect is in a position fully to address the question of what *is* truly good.

So Diotima's depiction of the "ascent" of eros to the knowledge of the beautiful or the good is in no way imposed upon the official topic of the *Symposium*. It's an articulation of the goal of loving something that we have a reason to love, because it's truly beautiful or good. And this goal is apparently an integral part of eros as such, because it's only in this way that we possess *the good* and continue to possess it.[17]

Reason inherent in inspiration: Value

And this brings us back to the agenda that I suggested we would find in the *Symposium*: to show that reason is an inherent feature of some of the highest states of inspiration that we experience, namely, those of love. It seems that by bringing out the "intellectual dimension" of love which he reveals through Diotima's discussion of "reproduction" and "ascent," Plato has indeed followed through on this agenda.

He hasn't shown, of course, that we fall in love as a result of cold calculation. That would eliminate love's "inspiration" aspect. What he has shown is that when we're inspired or intoxicated by a relationship, it's not because we've been hit by a purely random arrow from Cupid's bow. Rather, it's because we sense a kinship with the other person, which has something to do with a conception of value.

In the most primitive cases, it may be a conception of the value simply of physical beauty. But insofar as it's a *conception*, a specification of what is beautiful or fine, it can't identify that value solely by reference to its one possessor, but must acknowledge that it can in principle be exhibited by many. As a conception, it implicitly opens the general question of what value (fineness) in a person really is. What is the real content of the "kinship" between the lover and the beloved—of the conception of value that one or both of them instantiates, and that they both recognize as valid? That question is the fundamentally "intellectual" issue that, it now seems, is inherent in love, as such.

The only way eros can be kept separate from conceptions of value, and (thus) from the intellect, is if it's reduced to what we might call sheer mindless "lust." We do often speak of sex as a "blind force of nature." A virtue of Sigmund Freud's writing about sex is that he recognized that sex can be (as he called it) "sublimated" into higher cultural forms such as romantic love and the arts and the sciences.[18] The role of admiration and praise in erotic relationships, to which Plato draws our attention, helps us to understand how this "sublimation" occurs. After all, we can get "sexual release" without involving another person at all. So it seems that our interest in sex that involves us with another person is directed at something more than the mere satisfaction of an appetite (as in "sheer mindless lust"). That something more is (presumably) a specific kind of relationship, responding to and "giving birth" to specific positive qualities in another human being. We love to "give birth" to what we admire. The celebration and creativity that are characteristic of the arts and the sciences seem to be additional, analogous processes of appreciating, responding, and "giving birth." That's the sense in which they are "sublimated" forms of "sex."

It's probably evident from what I've been saying that "sex" or eros, for Plato, is not simply a matter of penetration, ejaculation, or orgasm. Instead he speaks of pregnancy, giving birth, and reproduction, and thus (as I've been putting it) of relationships of appreciating, responding, and encouraging. In the *Republic*, Plato describes the philosopher as having "intercourse" with what really is and "begetting understanding and truth," thus "truly living" and only after all of this being "relieved from the pains of giving birth" (490b). The mixture of normally male and normally female roles, in all of this, is striking. As eros rises above mere biology, it appears to become androgynous. In any case, it's productive, and oriented toward appreciation and truth. Plato is drawing on a broad sense of eros, which will probably speak to people who've had some experience of life, and not only of masturbation and "hooking up." It evidently spoke to Freud, who wrote that "what psychoanalysis calls sexuality . . . had far more resemblance to the all-inclusive and all-embracing love of Plato's *Symposium*."[19]

Unfortunately, Freud (no doubt reflecting the philosophical climate of his time) didn't see how Plato's "all-embracing love" depends upon intellect, as the faculty that does the evaluation that's reflected in love's characteristic appreciation, encouragement, and "giving birth." So Freud didn't give a role to intellect or intellectual ascent in his models of psychic functioning nor have most of his successors in psychological theory done this.

Freud's failure to understand the role of intellect in love as explained by Diotima's speech was probably especially a result of the influence on him and his contemporaries of Arthur Schopenhauer's entirely biological account of love, in which Schopenhauer depicts lovers as duped by the needs of their species for reproduction.[20] Here Schopenhauer ignores the two topics to which Diotima gives particular attention, namely, the (non-biological) reproduction of virtues, or "soul-reproduction," and the intellectual ascent by which we seek to clarify what the "virtues" really are.

In general, while Schopenhauer appropriated terminology from Plato and from Kant, he ignored the context that gave that terminology its significance, as in Plato's account of rational self-government in *Republic* books iv-vii and the *Symposium*, and Kant's account of the same topic in his *Groundwork of the Metaphysics of Morals*. But Schopenhauer's confident writing and his apparently disillusioning and thus liberating pessimism, including his brutally "candid" account of love, made his work very influential in Germany for a long time.

Biology is indeed liberating insofar as it shows us what we have in common with other species. For full freedom necessarily seeks truth. Biology only ceases to be liberating when this commonality is over-generalized in a reductionist or dualistic manner and prevents us from seeing the vertical dimension, the "sublimation," that Plato and his successors identify in the natural and spiritual world. Laboring under Schopenhauer's influence, Nietzsche and Freud did not regain access to Plato's or Kant's (or Hegel's) central concerns, their pursuit of wholeness or freedom through rational ascent. Though Freud was evidently drawn to Plato's account of love, he remained vague about its actual content because he had no access to Plato's notions of rational self-government and intellectual ascent, and of eros as admiration and encouragement and thus as involving intellect.

If Plato is right in viewing intellectual ascent as a crucial feature of our experience of love, then our omission of it leaves a major gap in our understanding of human functioning. Much of the responsibility for this omission, in the course of the last two centuries, belongs to anti-"intellectual" Romantics like Schopenhauer and Nietzsche, who have followed Plato's Aristophanes in viewing inspiration as the antithesis of intellect. It's unfortunately not surprising that Freud and the rest of us have been so impressed by this simple and powerful antithesis that we regularly overlook the equally simple feature of erotic inspiration that Plato and Hegel are trying to bring to our attention. Namely, that we are inspired not by just anything but by what we perceive as in some way "good," admirable, and *therefore* inspiring.[21]

We need to resist our natural tendency to "ideologize," to embrace a theory that speaks to one powerful feeling that we have (in this case, to intoxication or inspiration) while ignoring other features of our experience (in this case, the role of intellect in inspiration). A valuable byproduct of paying closer attention to these other features will be that we'll have much more access not just to Plato but to the whole tradition of Platonic thought and poetry up through the seventeenth century. From Plotinus through Rumi, Dante, Nicolas Cusanus, Marsilio Ficino, George Herbert, G. W. Leibniz, and the Cambridge Platonists, the members of this tradition all presuppose that love, inspiration, and reason are inseparable in the way that Plato points out, and which our own "scientifically" anti-intellectual age finds so counterintuitive.

Reason/value in love stories

But if Plato is right about the role of intellect within our most inspired states, why do such great love stories as "Tristan and Isolde," "Romeo and Juliet," and *Wuthering Heights* not seem to bring such a dimension to our attention? Why do they focus, instead, on love's apparently *least* "rational" aspects: its *obsessive* quality, its disregard for death and other-worldly obstacles?

First of all, of course, these stories are meant to emphasize love's inspiration or intoxication, so as to distinguish it sharply from the sort of rationality that simply calculates how to achieve a predetermined goal. The heroes and heroines of these stories abandon, or sharply compromise, whatever predetermined goals they may have had, in order to immerse themselves in and celebrate the "kinship" that they've discovered. That is, our great love stories play the same role for us that the Dionysian cult played for the Greeks: they remind us of the shallowness of conventional "rationality," and they remind us of the value that we do attach to experiences of inspiration and intoxication.

But this doesn't by any means imply that they exclude the dimension of value, and thus implicitly of reason or intellect, that Plato finds in love. When these stories celebrate the "connection" that the lovers have discovered, which may lead them even into the jaws of death, they inevitably raise the question, What is it in her (or him) that fascinates him (or her)? And they answer that question. Tristan is the truest knight, Isolde is the fairest maiden, Romeo is the most dashing youth, Juliet is the most blooming maiden, Heathcliff is the most passionate and authentic, the least "conventional" young man, and Cathy is the most passionate and authentic young woman.

These specific qualities are presented as deserving of admiration and, if possible, emulation. They are, in effect, visions of what a life well lived must contain. In each case, the lovers *share* this vision—modulated, to varying degrees, for differing gender roles. It's what constitutes their connection, or bond, or "kinship." Without it, the connection would be unintelligible. With it, we can understand why the connection assumes such a paramount role in their lives. Each of them feels that a life lived in this connection and celebrating it is incomparably more valuable than a life lived outside it.

Plato's Aristophanes would say that the nature of the connection is simply ineffable, and can only be explained by resort to a mythical prehistory in which the two protagonists shared one body. Plato's Diotima says, on the contrary, the connection is a function of their shared *values*, in which they each seek to embody what's truly beautiful or "fine." Because they seek this, and because they succeed in it to a greater degree than the other people around them, they're "fated," we all feel, to connect.

Why is this connection so much more important for them than the value, say, of a long life full of creature comforts? And why do we, as onlookers, feel that their connection is of great importance for *us*? The lovers each feel that through their connection they achieve the "nearest thing to immortality" that they, as mortals, can achieve, because through it they break out of the limits of one finite human life, into a shared life that contains, in principle, all life.

It "contains all life" because we, the onlookers, feel the same thing: that through their relationship, the lovers break the bonds of finite human life *on our behalf*. Their relationship takes us all, to some degree, out of our finitude. It's not merely that they show us what might happen to *us*, as individuals; more importantly, they prove to us that the finitude of lives in general, including our own, is a superficial phenomenon. Their charisma is reflected on us; it shows that we aren't the humdrum birth-to-death plodders that we tend otherwise to think we are. This, I think, is why all of us, even those who are maximally indifferent to the propaganda machines of Hollywood and the fashion industry, find romantic love such a fascinating phenomenon.

How to nurture inspiration?

I hardly need to add that this fascination that we have leads us, in many if not most cases, to underestimate the sheer work that's required to make a relationship, or a marriage, "work." We imagine that because the result is transcendent, the means to the result are simply magical—even though hard experience continually shows us that this isn't the case. Given the now pretty long and often painful history of marriages based on visions of romance, it's natural to imagine that maybe the guiding idea of "passion" is hopelessly misleading if it's thought to provide a basis for marriage. Indeed, there's a tendency among love poets, such as those of the courtly love and "Tristan and Isolde" traditions, to conceive of romance in a way that makes it essentially incompatible with marriage.[22]

The tendency to conceive of eros "dualistically" as the *opposite* of everyday life, as the Tristan poets do, is probably the permanent danger to which the romantic love complex is exposed. In Plato's *Symposium*, the speech that corresponds to this Tristan dualism would be Aristophanes's, which ascribes the kinship between the lovers to their having originally shared a body, in a way that ordinary reason can't hope to understand. This kinship comes, as it were, from "outside" the world that we can understand, so that the only thing that can "explain" it is a myth. That being the case, there's no way for the people involved to nurture it, promote it, or deepen it. It's a gift from the gods; you either have it or you don't.

If that's what romantic love is, there's bound to be a lot of wishful thinking and a lot of painful disillusionment around it. If, however, Diotima is right in insisting, against Aristophanes, that eros has an inherent "intellectual" dimension, which is the lover's perception that his beloved has qualities that he too seeks to have and to promote, then the situation is different. Then there's room for shared work, within the relationship, that can tend to nurture, promote, and deepen the relationship, by nurturing and promoting the qualities that it's based on. "Inspiration" isn't simply a bolt from the blue; it can, in fact, be nurtured.

One modern writer who shows us how love involves a kind of reason that can be nurtured by interaction is Jane Austen. No doubt one reason why many of us find *Pride and Prejudice* and *Sense and Sensibility* inspiring is that Austen shows unusually well how constructive the relationship between erotic inspiration and reason can be: how they can constitute a single "education of love." While at the same time she convinces us that the eros that she's describing is genuine—that the parties are not being "rational" in the usual, boring sense of "calculating."

One wonders what the passionate Friedrich Nietzsche might have learned from Miss Austen's novels, if he had encountered them. To merely dismiss them, say because they end in marriage and "happily ever after" or because their main protagonists are female, would be a major intellectual error. When marriage is expected to reflect and embody intelligent eros, having a successful marriage is one of the major accomplishments that an adult of either sex can have.

"There if anywhere should a person live his life, beholding that Beauty"

Having explored some of what seem to me to be the most important implications of Diotima's speech, I now need to consider another aspect of her presentation, which dominates many interpretations. In contrast to the ascent from the Cave in *Republic* vii, in which the ascender eventually descends again into the Cave to share what he has learned, the *Symposium*'s "rising stairs" from 210a to 211d sound pretty much as though they are a one-way trip. The person who becomes a lover of all beautiful bodies is said to "despise . . . this wild gaping after just one body" (210b). The person who loves souls and activities and laws looks "mainly not at beauty in a single example, as a servant would who favored the beauty of a little boy or a man or a single custom (being a slave, of course, he's low and small-minded)" (210d). And when the climber finally "catches sight of something wonderfully beautiful in its nature," and "comes to know just what it is to be beautiful," Diotima concludes, "There if anywhere should a person live his life, beholding that Beauty" (211d).

These features of Diotima's speech have led some readers to suppose that the bliss of the climber who reaches this summit is such that he no longer has any interest in individual human beings as such and won't, for example, have a particular human lover. However, Diotima makes one further remark that makes one wonder:

> Only then will it become possible for him to give birth not to images of virtue (because he's in touch with no images), but to true virtue (because he is in touch with the true Beauty). The love of the gods belongs to anyone who has given birth to true virtue and nourished it, and if any human being could become immortal, it would be he (212a).

So here the theme of "giving birth" returns again, together with the theme of possible immortality. Why should the climber who has arrived at the summit, and can "live" in the sight of perfect Beauty, have any interest in giving birth to anything? And why should he have any interest in his own personal "immortality"? I'm going to return to this issue, and the general issue of "returning to the Cave," in the next chapter, where we'll also discuss the "demiurge" or craftsman in Plato's *Timaeus*. The demiurge is a divine figure who finds a reason to do more than just contemplate the Forms, and who thus models a kind of "descent" into dealings with individuals.

In the meantime, I simply suggest that the analysis that I've given of "birth in beauty," with the features that Diotima gives it, shows that it has a major relevance to our experience of loving other individuals. I'll use the remainder of this chapter to respond to issues that critics of the idea have raised, and thus develop its relevance in more detail.

Why Platonic love is not self-centered

Reading Socrates's and Diotima's account of love as seeking to satisfy a personal lack (*Symposium* 200–05), influential critics have wondered whether this "love" isn't purely egoistic, self-centered. In the 1930s, the Swedish scholar Anders Nygren contrasted this egoism, which he thought was characteristic of "pagan" culture, with the unconditional *agape* love that he said was ascribed to God in the Bible. More recently, Gregory Vlastos and Martha Nussbaum interpreted Diotima's account of "birth in beauty" and of the way in which legislators and poets have benefitted numerous generations as, likewise, egoistic, since Diotima describes this birth in beauty as producing the "nearest thing to immortality" for mortals. The lover that Diotima describes, they said, loves ultimately only himself and the Forms and what he can "create" in their image. There is no love here of the other person, for her own sake.[23]

To begin with, Plato doesn't speak of "creating" any part of one's beloved. Rather, the lover "gives birth," which is to say that an independent being comes into existence, who is influenced by the lover only in that the new being herself takes an interest in the Good.

The notion of the lover as wanting to "reproduce" himself in the beloved does, at first glance, look self-centered. But as I've explained, this "reproduction" is not of the lover's idiosyncratic characteristics, his height and weight and taste in ice cream. Rather, it's of the lover's universal characteristic: his love of what's truly Good, through which (as we know from *Republic* iv-vii) the lover is self-governing.[24] Because the new being likewise loves what's Good, the new being is likewise self-governing.

And it's *only* through this self-government that the lover can correctly see the new being as "reproducing" his own love of the Good. It's only by "giving birth to" a truly self-governing being that the lover can achieve what he's seeking to achieve. So the lover must love his beloved *as* a truly self-governing being, and not as a product of his efforts or of his personal preferences.

This is the paradox of teaching: that the teacher wants his student to become a genuine master, rather than someone who perfectly parrots the teacher's words. As Buddhists say, "If you meet the Buddha on the road, kill him!"—don't imitate him. The Buddha doesn't want imitations of himself, and neither does a true teacher or a Platonic lover.

To say that the lover wants the beloved to be self-governing is not to say that he's indifferent to what the beloved will choose. He wants her to choose the Good. But he wants this not because the Good is what he himself happens to choose, but because only the pursuit of the Good can make her self-governing and thus independent of her antecedents and environment, as he is (or tries to be).[25]

When we see how the pursuit of the Good makes a person self-governing, we see how the Platonic lover's self-"reproduction" is not egoistic. In the *Symposium*, Plato doesn't mention as he does in *Republic* book iv the way in which the pursuit of the Good makes a person self-governing ("concerned with what is truly himself and his own . . . he becomes entirely one" [443d]). But he must have it in mind, because without it, his account of interpersonal love would indeed not resemble anything that we can understand as interpersonal love.

When we bring this idea of self-government through pursuit of the Good over from the *Republic* to help us to understand the *Symposium*'s conception of love as soul-"reproduction," we are following the principle of interpretive charity. That principle advises us to prefer whatever interpretation makes the most sense of a writer's texts. Such charity in this case has two payoffs. First, it enables us to explain why Diotima regards "soul"-reproduction as preferable to bodily reproduction. She regards "soul"-reproduction as preferable because it reproduces one's choices, which, more than one's body, reflect oneself as "entirely one." And second, as I've just shown, it finds in Diotima's speech something that we can understand as love for the other person herself, as self-governing, as opposed to a concern that's really only for oneself.

So we make Plato's thought intelligible. And into the bargain we get the insight that I described, into our experience of love. Nobody wants his beloved to mimic himself, and at the same time nobody is indifferent to what his beloved seeks and chooses. In the people we love, we love and seek to encourage precisely the free pursuit of what is truly Good. How else could we say that we truly love them?

This, then, is my response to Vlastos's and Nussbaum's complaint that Diotima doesn't appear to describe love of particular persons for their own sake. Only a person who pursues the Good is self-governing and fully realized as a person. A person who seeks to "reproduce herself" will seek to reproduce her full reality, which is her self-government, and will thus seek to produce a person who pursues the Good. Because she seeks to produce the other as self-governing, she will love the other as one who is or can become self-governing, and not as a mere reproduction of herself. And loving another as self-governing is surely a way of loving the other for his own sake, rather than for the sake of something other than him.

Jonathan Lear thinks it's clear that in Diotima's account of love, "beautiful individuals have only instrumental value: they are to be used, stepped on, like rungs in a ladder which leads away from any concern for *them*" (Lear [1998], p. 163). I have explained that Diotima and Socrates are concerned about individuals in that they seek to give birth to self-government in them, by encouraging their pursuit of beauty or the Good. Thus the ladder leads not away from these individuals but to what they most deeply need. Like Vlastos and Nussbaum, Lear neglects Diotima's critique of Aristophanes's conception of love, by which Plato makes it clear how all love celebrates what it takes to be truly Good and thus how all love requires the ascent that Diotima and Socrates preach.

When we see how the pursuit of the Good makes a person self-governing, we see how the "reproductive" love that Diotima describes serves everyone's self-realization, rather than making (some of) us puppets of someone or something that's alien to us.[26] Thus we see how the love that Diotima analyzes is in fact the love of others for their own sake, which we all experience.

And we also see how the ascent to the "sea of beauty" (210d) and to true Beauty, which Diotima describes, serves self-government or individuality rather than (as is often supposed) eliminating it. That is, we see how Plato's "mysticism" (and, I would suggest, all true mysticism) goes beyond individuality by *perfecting* it, rather than by abolishing it. Which should be a salutary lesson to the wayward gurus and guru-followers who imagine that "enlightenment" can be achieved by ceasing to think for oneself, and instead accepting the absolute authority of someone who is ostensibly already enlightened. Rather than abdicating self-government, one should indeed "be a light unto oneself."

At the same time, Diotima's model makes it clear how the individualism of spiritual "ascent" doesn't lead to bleak or sterile isolation. It doesn't lead to what

Nietzsche, for example, depicts with his story of "Zarathustra," who is more at home with animals than with his fellow human beings. For true ascent is always seeking to give and receive aid toward (further or renewed) ascent: it's always seeking to reproduce "birth in beauty."

Uniqueness of the beloved

Gregory Vlastos's second objection to Diotima's account of love, besides the fact that it appears not to provide for loving a person for her own sake, is that it appears not to provide for loving a person as a unique whole. Rather, it identifies features of the person which one loves and suggests that one might love any number of people who have those features.

The issue here is that we tend to feel that the person we love is somehow not replaceable. Why do we feel this? Even if another person could have the same qualities and the same love of the Good in general, our beloved plays a unique role in our life because it was our encounter with him or her that opened up, for us, the dimension of complete caring which our great love stories celebrate. (And of which Diotima illuminates the essential aspect that a lover nurtures the other, facilitating their "birth in beauty.") The experience of discovering this dimension is unique in one's life, so that the person who first opened it up in one's life likewise seems unique. Even if another person in fact eventually occupies the same role (when one rediscovers ascent and complete caring, as quite a few people seem to do), it is such an intimate role that the flavor of "uniqueness" and irreplaceableness persists.[27] This is how a Platonic lover can come to feel that their partner is unique and irreplaceable, so that Plato in the *Phaedrus* (256a-d) in fact assumes that the best erotic relationships will involve lifelong fidelity.[28]

It's worth noting, in this connection, that our first experience of complete caring is likely to be from our mother. Not primarily as the one who physically gave birth to us, but as the one who gave us soul birth, by nurturing soul qualities. Though Diotima doesn't explore parenting explicitly, her metaphors of pregnancy and birth certainly invite such a comparison. She focuses on adolescence, rather than early childhood, because it's in adolescence that conscious reason begins to emerge, which early childhood in general lacks. (Elsewhere, in the *Republic* and *Laws*, Plato is very interested in the soul's formation in early childhood.)

In any case, it's a fact that the nurturing that lovers give each other reproduces the pattern of "for the other's sake" that is normally set, in one's life, by one's parents and especially one's mother. The felt irreplaceability of the mother/child relationship then recurs in the form of the felt irreplaceability of the relationship of lover and beloved. If the adolescent is "born" into adulthood, then that event is literally unique for him. So a relationship that facilitated that birth is, in that respect, likewise unique (though it may be a relationship that one had with a number of people). And if, as seems to be the rule in modern romance, both lover and beloved are "born" into new levels of maturity through their relationship, again the relationship is unique, in that respect.

From infancy to old age, relationships of this kind figure, fortunately, in most lives. Insofar as each such relationship figures at a unique moment in one's personal unfolding, the other party is a "unique whole," valued for their contribution at this unique moment in one's life.

To explain the sense of one's beloved's uniqueness in this way is not to reduce the beloved to what she contributes to one's life, because that contribution depends entirely, as I've explained, on one's perceiving her as self-governed. It's only by my appreciating my beloved as self-governed, that she is able to inspire the increase of self-government in me that Diotima calls "birth in beauty." Only a "whole person," herself involved in a process of birth, can inspire such a process in another. The uniqueness of this transaction, in both parties' lives, makes each of them unique for the other.

So again, the kind of relationship that Diotima discusses is not something that only schoolmasters or self-proclaimed philosophers might experience. Rather, it's a kind of love that probably most humans experience.

All-inclusive love

But as my remarks are beginning to suggest, Diotima's account applies not only to "romance" as we usually understand it but also to a much wider range of relationships. Vlastos is right to point out that Diotima herself says nothing about romantic exclusiveness or fidelity. I think this is because Plato does indeed intend to sketch a kind of love that can, in principle, be addressed to an unlimited number of others. Not because (as Vlastos supposes) it doesn't value these others for their own sake or treat them as unique, but because it does value every one of them for their own sake and treat them as unique.

Every individual comes into one's life at a unique point in one's personal evolution or "birth" and thus in a unique way, and every individual is likewise an opportunity (if the circumstances permit it) for one to contribute to some kind of "birth" in them. Certainly Socrates is always on the lookout for such opportunities, both in others and in himself.

So when Anders Nygren says that in contrast to eros, *agape* is "unselfish love, it 'seeketh not its own,'"[29] we could point out that eros as Plato interprets it need not be selfish either. It can promote, to the best of its ability, *everyone's* "own," everyone's self-government through pursuit of the Good, because these can all reproduce "its own."

Diotima doesn't say explicitly what I just said, but her examples of the poets and lawgivers give us an idea of the extent of the influence that an individual who seeks to be guided by the Good might exercise. To these we can add what Plato already knew about Socrates's influence on others, what we now know about Socrates's influence across millennia, and what we know of the influence of other spiritual teachers. In the next chapter I'll derive from the *Timaeus* a reason for thinking that Plato may indeed think, and be justified in thinking, that we rationally should seek to exercise effectively unlimited influence on behalf of "birth in beauty." If, as I said above, lovers break the bonds of finite human life on our behalf, so does Socrates when he makes it his personal business to inspire us all to "examine our lives" and be born in beauty.

If I'm right about this, then love as "birth in beauty" covers the whole range of human relationships, from the most intimate to the most inclusive. Together with the Forms, "birth in beauty" is another of the germinal ideas in Plato whose power to illuminate we are still discovering.[30]

I might add also something that's probably obvious already, which is that what Plato shows us in this account undermines gender stereotypes in a rather deep way. What he says about participating in "birth" obviously doesn't depend on one's possessing any particular physical equipment, and can apply to any gender whatever. So if Plato shows us, as I think he does, that "giving birth" is something in which everyone should and probably does want to engage, he shows us something of considerable interest about human nature as such.

Plato's reply to romantic anti-intellectualism

Returning to our initial issue, I've tried to make clear how Plato shows that interpersonal love and inspiration depend in an important way on reason or intellect. Love wants the object of its love to flourish, to be "born in beauty." But flourishing and beauty involve the possession of appropriate kinds of excellence, and thus they involve reason and intellect, which are necessarily invoked whenever judgments of excellence are made. Rather than being sheer feeling, love is a feeling that's deeply informed by reason.

This is just as much the case in the love of gods or of God as it is in the love of human beings. We can't make sense of the idea of loving a god whom we take to be characterized primarily by sheer "power." It's only insofar as a god has virtues, excellences, that we can speak of loving him or her.

This is also why Plato's notion that "philosophers" can become "like god" is not ridiculous. It's not ridiculous because to the extent that someone loves and thus tries to possess wisdom and other excellences, he or she resembles the gods, whom we love for possessing those excellences.

Of course, who the actual "philosophers" are who might do this is a wide open question. As we learn from the *Symposium*, they must be at least as invested in reproduction, in "*birth* in beauty," as they are in thought (that is, birth in *beauty*).

A "philosopher," as Plato understands the term, is a person who loves wisdom. Rather than being separate from the love of human beings, love of wisdom is an essential aspect of it, because loving human beings is seeking the good for them, and this requires clarity about what the good really is—that is, it requires wisdom.

The "intellectual" or wisdom aspects of love and of God have been badly neglected both by philosophy and by theology since the nineteenth century. Like Schleiermacher, Schopenhauer, Kierkegaard, and Nietzsche, most of us tend to assume that intellect is a dry, calculating, and constraining faculty, which has no relevance to exalted experiences like love, ecstasy, mysticism, or religion. As for "wisdom," we have stopped talking about it just about entirely. In contrast to knowledge, wisdom seems to be an obsolete concept. And we think of love and ecstasy purely as feelings, rather than as oriented by any conception of value. The result, as I've suggested, is that we have ceased to think of love and ecstasy as experiences that we can understand and cultivate in an intelligent way.

By the same token we tend to think of "God" in terms of sheer power or awesomeness, rather than in terms of excellence and freedom that we can to some degree understand and emulate. So depending on our personal preference we either affirm or deny the reality of that power or awesomeness and our "dependence" on it. Whereas with the help of Plato's account of love and excellence we could see how the divine excellence and divine freedom are present in our experience, and point beyond our experience to similar but higher levels which are not in principle inaccessible to us.

Awe and fear are still appropriate responses to the God whom we can to some degree understand and emulate, insofar as the freedom which this emulation involves requires us to abandon all of our familiar conceptions of ourselves: the "shadows" in the Cave. I mentioned in the previous chapter how Plato dramatizes the resistance that our "fear of freedom" can inspire. But this resistance is not the sole or primary way in which he describes us as responding to the ascent. Our ultimate response is joy in discovering our true self, the final resolution of our perennial "identity crisis." "There if anywhere should a person live his life, beholding that Beauty" (*Symposium* 211d).

Plato's straightforward explanation of how love is more than a feeling, how it requires and embodies intellect or wisdom, can help us to appreciate once again how to cultivate love, ecstasy, and awareness of the divine in our experience. For the divine as traditionally understood is precisely the unity of love with the good on which reason focuses. So when we are once again aware of this unity in our daily lives, we will have the opportunity to enhance this awareness, to take it to higher levels. Whereas as long as love, on the one hand, and reason's focus on truth, on the other, remain in separate compartments in our minds, this ascent won't even get started. Our experience will continue to be compartmentalized, conflicted (as in "head versus heart," science versus religion), and impoverished.[31]

Beauty, too, must not be ghettoized

An additional aspect of life which has been distorted by life's modern compartmentalization is the aesthetic aspect. When John Keats writes that "beauty is truth, truth beauty," we might initially interpret this as a declaration that art is the sole or the primary locus of truth—which is an ideology that leads to "l'art pour l'art," to conceptions of an individual life as ideally a purely aesthetic project, and so forth. Taking Keats's dictum in this way would make it another instance of romantic anti-intellectualism, as in Schleiermacher, Kierkegaard, and Nietzsche.

An alternative, more Platonic interpretation of Keats's dictum would put it in the context of the *Symposium*'s broader notion of "beauty" (*to kalon*) as including virtue or excellence of all kinds. So that beauty would include intellectual and moral as well as what we call aesthetic excellence. If we then remember the *Republic*'s demonstration of the role that excellence as the rational pursuit of the Good plays in accomplishing the unity of a person as such, we can understand aesthetic beauty as one aspect of an inclusive truth or reality that's also intellectual and moral. All of which for Plato—and in actual fact, I imagine, for Keats as well—can inspire the same passionate and intelligent love.

It will certainly still be the case that, as Plato says, "justice and self-control do not shine out through their images down here.... Beauty alone has this privilege, to be the most visible and the most loved" (*Phaedrus* 250b-d). That is, beauty is the way in which excellence makes itself "visible" in the world of images, of finite things and the senses, which is why we can more easily be inspired by it and come up with ideologies like aestheticism which segregate visible and audible beauty from other forms of excellence. But when we understand what it is that we're being inspired by, we will understand what unites the visible or audible and the invisible and inaudible aspects of excellence.

A more inclusive kind of truth, which is reason/love

When we see art and science in this way, art will neither be segregated from science, in splendid isolation as a sui generis "aesthetics," nor flatly be identified with science. Instead, we'll see both art and science as aspects of a more inclusive kind of truth, which they address in different ways. The same will hold, as I've described, for ethics and religion. Art, ethics, and religion, like science, are all ways in which we seek, and seek to promote, rational (intelligent) freedom. This seeking and seeking to promote are what we call love. And the more inclusive truth which all of these efforts seek and seek to promote is, in fact, the same rational freedom by which they seek it. This is the transcending and reconciling reality that surpasses all intra-cultural bickering.

In fact, of course, this unity of seeking and seeking to promote, of reason/love, is present in the practical experience of just about everyone. We *love* self-transcending nature, each other, justice, science, art, and God, and we have good *reasons* for loving them and wanting to promote them.[32] What we don't have is a vocabulary that reflects the unity of reason/love in this totality of Spirit. Instead, we have the compartmentalized pseudo-scientific vocabulary that flatly separates head from heart, "cognition" from "affect," "fact" from "value," and "science" from "love," "ethics," "art," "beauty," and "religion," and thus prevents us from describing and consciously appreciating the reason/love that all of these share. Whereas if we could describe and appreciate this reason/love, it seems likely that this would help us to practice it with greater synergy, and less conflict and confusion, than we currently experience.

We need an updated version of the "Philosophy of Spirit" portion of Hegel's *Encyclopedia of the Philosophical Sciences*—of the whole book, for that matter—to help us to get this whole uniquely satisfying picture into focus. Following, of course, Plato as well, whose analysis Hegel was elaborating. I hope that my suggestions here will encourage additional people to join in this work.[33]

How far does philosophy's love extend?

Understanding, as I hope we now do, how reason is an essential aspect of our love of (among other things) people, we can see how philosophy as the cultivation of reason and wisdom could help to cultivate the love of people as well. So that if philosophy were in fact interested in love of people, the two would make excellent partners.

In the spirit of compartmentalization, though, one might still wonder whether "philosophy" needs to be interested in love of anything besides "wisdom." Do Plato and his followers just happen to have a special interest in interpersonal love, which other "philosophers," other cultivators of reason or wisdom, needn't and in some cases apparently don't share? And how far does Platonic interpersonal love extend?

In the next chapter, I'll try to show how Plato shows that reason as such needs love that's in principle unlimited. This will take us further, as well, into Plato's theology, his account of the divine.

8 PLATO ON "BECOMING LIKE GOD"

Ch'io giunsi l'aspetto mio col valore infinito.
(I joined my vision with the Infinite Goodness.)
   DANTE, *DIVINE COMEDY, PARADISO*, XXXIII, 81

Why should "intellect" love human beings at all?

In the last chapter we explored the way in which love requires reason or intellect. Now we need to consider the converse question: How and whether reason or intellect requires love. Why should "intellect" love human beings at all? Why shouldn't it simply contemplate the Forms, indifferent to the antics of mere humans?

Diotima explains that *mortal* intellects, like ours, will want to be "immortal as far as is possible for something mortal" (207a), by reproducing themselves through others. This helps us to understand why we aren't satisfied by being completely self-contained—why we do love some others. But most of the *Symposium* invites us to read this account as addressing romantic love. Seen in that way, it gives us no reason to go beyond the love of one or a few others, whom we find particularly promising as continuers of our personal pursuit of the Good. And it doesn't show that apart from mortality, reason or intellect as such has any need of love. Do we, or does intellect as such, have any reason to love anyone beyond the small circle of our romantic interests?

In regard to this question, Plato gives us one exceptionally pregnant thought. It's in his description in the *Timaeus* of the demiurge, the "craftsman" who brings the world into existence.

> Why did he who framed this whole universe of becoming frame it? ... He was good, and one who is good can never become jealous of anything. And so, being free of jealousy [or "spite": *phthonos*], he wanted everything to become as much like himself as was possible. (29e)

Note the "everything," here. The demiurge seeks to extend his pursuit or embodiment of the Good not just into a few individuals, and not just into gods or humans, but (as far as possible) into *everything*.

If, as is clearly the case, the demiurge is divine, and if we remember Socrates's pronouncement in the *Theaetetus* that a philosopher will become "as much like God as possible" (176b), then this description of the demiurge gives philosophers a reason to try to promote the pursuit of the Good, or "birth in beauty," in everything. That's what God, as the demiurge, does, and to be like God, we must do the same.[1]

Plato's notion of "becoming like God" has recently come in for renewed examination by scholars, and its relevance to ethics has begun to be considered.[2] There are two major questions that need to be resolved here. First, why (in fact) should a human being want to become "as much like God as possible"? And second, why should we think that God as the demiurge "can never become jealous of anything," and therefore would "want everything to become as much like himself as was possible"?

Why become like God?

Socrates's stated reason in the *Theaetetus* for saying that we should "become like God" is that "evil" must "inevitably prowl about this earth," and we should therefore "make all haste to escape from earth to heaven" (176a-b). Since we can safely assume that he isn't advocating suicide, he must have something else in mind. We find out what this is when he goes on to say that the way to become "like God" is to become "just and pure, with understanding" (176b).

He has explained in the *Republic* that being "just" involves, at least, having one's rational part in charge of one's soul. So we can assume that one becomes like God by cultivating the soul harmony in which the rational part is in charge.

There is no emphasis, in the *Theaetetus* passage, on how becoming "just" affects our dealings with other people. On the contrary, much like the *Phaedo*'s notorious passage on escaping from imprisonment in the body, the *Theaetetus* emphasizes "escape from earth to heaven." So if we view this passage in the same way that we viewed the *Phaedo* passage earlier, its central message is not that we need to escape from evil, as such, but rather that we need to put our rational part in charge, because (as *Republic* iv tells us) we'll thereby be more fully ourselves.

What does being fully ourselves have to do with being "like God"? It's precisely God, Plato implies, who is fully "himself," by virtue of not being distracted by mortal or bodily concerns. So that to become like God is to become one's true self.

The *Timaeus* explains this in a second key passage:

> Now we ought to think of the most sovereign part of our soul as god's gift to us, given to be our guiding spirit.... So if a man has become absorbed in his appetites or his ambitions and takes great pains to further them, all his thoughts are bound to become merely mortal. And so far as it is at all possible for a man to become thoroughly mortal, he cannot help but fully succeed in this, seeing that he has cultivated his mortality all along. On the other hand, if a man has seriously devoted himself to the love of learning and to true wisdom, if he has exercised these aspects of himself above all, then there is absolutely no way that his thoughts can fail to be immortal and divine, should truth come within his grasp. And to the extent that human nature can partake of immortality, he can in no way fail to achieve this: constantly caring for his divine part as he does, keeping well-ordered the guiding spirit that lives within him, he must indeed be supremely happy. (90a-c)

That this is the activity of the "most sovereign [*kuriotaton*, most ruling] part of our soul" is a reminder that the "divine part," here, is the "reasoning part" that we learned about in *Republic* iv. When we rule ourselves and thus are fully ourselves, and find truth, our thoughts are "immortal and divine," and, so far as possible, so are we. To be fully oneself by ruling oneself is to be "like god."

It's important to notice how Plato's conception of "god," here, differs from conventional conceptions of God as supremely "powerful." As in Plato's successors like Hegel, God for Plato has the "power" not to move mountains and the like but to be completely himself, and thus (as I like to put it, following Hegel) to be fully real, as himself. And Plato here is saying that we have this same power, at least to some extent, and by exercising it we become as far as possible "immortal and divine."

So the philosopher seeks to become "like God" because God is fully real, as himself. But as we noted, the *Theaetetus*'s description of becoming like God says nothing about how someone who becomes like God will treat other people. It's the *Timaeus* that appears to tell us how God, and thus presumably also those who become "like God," will relate to others.

So this brings us to our second question.

Why can't God be "jealous"?

"One who is good can never become jealous of anything," so the demiurge made everything as much like himself as possible. Why can one who is good never become jealous of anything?

To answer this question, we can't simply assume that every god, as such, must be benevolent. Zeus was (traditionally) a guarantor of justice, but no one assumed that every god must play this role. A later Greek philosopher, Epicurus, described gods who took no interest whatever in what went on in the world. No one thought that his view could be dismissed simply on the grounds that obviously gods are benevolent. Zeus himself is described in a famous story as punishing the Titan, Prometheus, for giving fire to humans. (Much as the Book of Job, in the Hebrew Scriptures, presents a God who is far from being generous.) And to suppose, as Plato does, that a god must be (in some sense) "good" doesn't automatically entail that a god must provide benefits to mortals.[3]

In fact, common attitudes in ancient Greece endorsed human "jealousy," in the form of rivalry and caring for personal honors, as entirely natural and appropriate. This is why Achilles's "wrath," when he was denied his share of the spoils of war, in the *Iliad*, was a sympathetic theme for Homer's audience. Of course Greek social norms changed over the centuries down to Plato's time, but Achilles was always admired as a prototypical hero.

So Plato needs to provide an argument for Timaeus's principle that one who is good can't be "jealous." But all he provides here is a flat assertion that this is the case. We find similar negative comments about "jealousy" (*phthonos*) in other dialogues, including the *Protagoras*, *Symposium*, *Phaedrus*, *Republic*, and *Laws*. But none of these passages gives an explicit argument for this rather novel evaluative position that Plato is taking. Nor have I seen an argument presented on Plato's behalf.[4]

God as the One

I think we can find an argument for Plato's position on *phthonos* if we put the issue in the broadest context of what Plato was up to. In particular, we need to look at the way in which Plato associates Goodness with the "One." We've seen the central importance of his account in *Republic* books iv-vi of how a person "becomes entirely one" (443e), and how doing this involves a pursuit of the Good. We'll need to take account also of Plato's discussions of the One in his *Philebus* and *Parmenides* and of the reports of his oral teaching, in which he apparently associated the Good with the One.[5]

In the *Philebus*, Socrates describes the One as an independent principle, alongside the Many (16d). So the One is not, as we might suppose, just one number among others. Plato doesn't spell out, here, why the One should be special in this way.

The entire second part of the *Parmenides* is devoted to examining the "one" and the "others." Plato presents Parmenides, a famous Greek philosopher of the generation preceding Socrates's, who lived in Elea, a Greek city in Italy. Parmenides visits Athens and leads young Socrates through a series of arguments purporting to demonstrate all sorts of outlandish things: that the One "and the others both are and are not, and both appear and do not appear all things in all ways, both in relation to themselves and in relation to each other" (166c). We can assume that a concept that invites the detailed, even excruciating attention that Plato gives to it here, has central importance for him even if he doesn't always make that importance explicit elsewhere.[6]

It's important to notice something that Plato doesn't mention in the *Parmenides*, perhaps because he assumes that everyone will know it, which is that the "One" played a central role in Parmenides's own masterwork, his philosophical poem about "being." There, Parmenides maintained not only that "that which can be spoken and thought must needs *be*" (Fragment 6, Diels), so that we can't speak or think about what is not. He also maintained that what is, "was not in the past, nor shall it be, since it is now, all at once, *one*, continuous" (Fragment 8, emphasis added). That is, Parmenides was concerned not just to deny nonbeing but to insist on the *unity* of being.

Parmenides was the last of the great Greek thinkers of the century and a half preceding Socrates who sought a single unifying principle of everything. Thales with water, Anaximander with the "boundless," Anaximenes with air, and Heraclitus with his fire or *logos* are often described as "proto-scientific" by virtue of their desire to produce a unified "theory of everything." In each case, a kind of unity was the key desired outcome.

Parmenides followed suit in perhaps the most radical way possible, by nominating being itself as the unifying principle. However, Parmenides's proposal was so radical that its implications seem very difficult to accept. Since change apparently involves a transition from something's *not being* X to its *being* X (or vice versa), Parmenides's prohibition on speaking of *what is not* makes it hard to see how we can speak of anything as changing. As Parmenides says, there "is" no past or future in being as he understands it. And without a past, future, or change, it's hard to see how Parmenides's theory applies to the world that we seem to experience.

Many thinkers who succeeded Parmenides were very impressed by his conclusions. Democritus, the atomist, preserved something like Parmenides's unitary "being" in the form of his uncuttable "atoms." Other teachers turned increasingly away from grand theories of the cosmos, toward human affairs. If grand theory as in Parmenides was inapplicable to human experience, humans would have to go it alone. Protagoras taught that "man is the measure" of truth, and Gorgias taught that there was no truth at all. Socrates himself made a similar turning to "human affairs." While insisting that we should seek true virtue (*arete*, excellence), he gave no clear account of what truth would be. There are many parallels between this period in Greek thought and the more or less "humanistic" relativism that has become widespread in our own last couple of centuries, as theology and "metaphysics" have fallen into disrepute.

Plato was alarmed by these developments, seeing how arbitrary life could and did become when people followed the lead of figures like Protagoras, Gorgias, and (in the *Republic*) Thrasymachus. If the "measure" was merely "man," men could do anything they felt like doing. Plato embraced Socrates's doctrine of virtue as a necessary antidote to these views. And he set out to give it a foundation that would render it more than a slogan.

That foundation was, of course, the "Forms"—but not only the Forms. For as a plurality, the Forms lacked order and unity. They lacked "oneness." As Plato has Socrates explain in *Republic* book iv, the soul needs to become "entirely one" (443a). So the ascent of the soul's rational part, which Plato has Socrates describe in the Sun, Line, and Cave allegories in books vi and vii, leads to a single unifying goal, the "sun" or the Form of the Good. It's not surprising, then, that in his lecture on the Good, Plato apparently identified the Good with the One. He was identifying Socrates's pole star, the Good or Virtue, with Parmenides's pole star, being or the One.

But this combination of two apparently sharply contrasting views implied that both sides needed to be corrected. Socrates needed to be corrected by being given an "ontology," a doctrine of being and truth. And Parmenides needed to be corrected by being given an account of how being or the One can play a role in our apparently changing world. So in *Republic* book v, Plato's Socrates introduces a possible "intermediate" realm between "what *is* completely [and] is completely knowable" (namely, the Forms, or Parmenidean being) and "what is in no way [and] is in every way unknowable." This intermediate is what "is such as to be and also not to be" (477a), what "participates in both being and not being" (478d).

This, of course, is Plato's notion of "degrees of being," which we discussed in Chapter 5. The world of change, time, and human affairs has a degree of being—we can in fact usefully talk about it, though not "know" it—inasmuch as it "participates in" the eternal Forms, Goodness, being, and unity. Parmenides was right to insist that only the unchanging has full being, being as itself, but he was wrong to suggest that it is useless or impossible to talk about anything that has less than full being. Plato's whole account of the "soul," in *Republic* iv, is an account of something that *seeks to be* "entirely one" and thus to "be" in the full sense, to be as itself, but which often falls short of that goal. This seeking-to-be is the key thing that Parmenides had failed to get into focus, and to which Plato, by drawing on Socrates's teaching about "virtue," is directing our attention.

In this way, Plato shows us how "oneness" as being is our own constant pole star. We seek to be fully ourselves, to be as ourselves and not merely as the tools of our appetites and emotions. And we identify the divine as what is able consistently to be as itself, to be "one" and not many, rather than having to continually *seek* this, as we do.

"Jealousy" and the "One"

So what does all of this tell us about God's relation to *phthonos*, or "jealousy"? If I'm right in thinking that the person who "becomes entirely one," in *Republic* iv, does so in order to be self-governing rather than being governed by appetites and emotions that just happen to him, then the fullest unity is a function of self-government. Jealousy and spite, on the other hand, are clearly ways in which we're governed by our relations to others. So they are ways in which we're not "one," not self-governed, but instead we're multiple, governed by a multiplicity of beings. So for a being that aims, as Plato suggests we do, to be "one," self-governed, and thus fully itself, jealousy and spite are not the way to go.

So something that's *entirely* One can't be "jealous" of others, opposed to them (even by being "indifferent to" them) and thus governed by its relation to them. So if the demiurge is to be good and thereby One, he can't be "jealous." And this is why Plato tells us that the demiurge set out to make everything "as much like himself as possible"—to share his goodness as widely as possible. This is why, as the Greek/Roman Platonist Plotinus put it some centuries later, the One "overflows."[7]

This seems to be the reason why the demiurge as "intellect" is not indifferent to mere creatures like ourselves, but seeks to encourage us—all of us—to pursue the Good. In this way the demiurge is less "contained," less restricted by us than it would be if its relation to us were characterized by indifference or "jealousy." To the extent that the demiurge helps us to resemble it, we are like extensions of it, rather than separate containers around it, which would make it "many" (rather than one) by our relationships to it.[8]

As you'll notice, this is very much the idea of inner "freedom" that Hegel promoted. To the extent that a being excludes others from its sphere of concern, it is determined by this relationship (of exclusion) and it isn't self-determining or, in that sense, free. So the possessor of inner freedom doesn't exclude others from her sphere of concern.

This is Plato's and Hegel's answer to the traditional Greek theology of divine "jealousy," and likewise their answer to the capricious "God" of many stories in the Hebrew Scriptures and other religious traditions. It's not that God *happens to be* "love," but rather that God *must be* love in order to be fully free.

This seems to be what Plato is thinking about the demiurge, and therefore probably about "intellect" as such, in us as well as in gods. Insofar as we seek to be "one" by being guided (like the demiurge) by the Good, we too will avoid "jealousy" by taking a positive interest in everyone around us, lovingly promoting their self-government in the way that the *Timaeus* and Diotima in the *Symposium* both describe. This argument connecting the demiurge, the One, and humans' "becoming like God" shows us why "intellect" or reason as such will un-jealously "go down" as love of what we call "others," rather than merely contemplating the Forms.

Non-"jealousy" and the virtues

The next step is to explain how humans who love everything and promote everything's self-government, as the demiurge does, will develop the ordinary virtues.[9] I would suggest that humans who imitate the demiurge's desiring things to be as good as possible will provide what aid they can to others to become good, and this will constitute a large part of what we commonly call justice. For others can presumably best become good, or function well, when their efforts to interact productively with the world around them are respected and supported by those around them; and such respect and support are a large part of what we call justice.

As for dealings with one's own body, I take it that a human who tries to be like the demiurge will encourage her body to be as good (by contributing to self-government as pursuit of the Good) as possible, just as she encourages other people to do so. And this will be the basis of such virtues in her as courage and temperance. Courage and temperance both reflect a collaboration between one's rational part and one's body in which the rational part's broader conception of the Good makes appropriate allowance for the body's preservation and pleasure, without allowing them to dominate one's deliberations.[10]

As John M. Armstrong writes, Plato's idea in the *Laws* "is not that temperance and justice make us like god because god is temperate and just." (God can't be temperate and just, because God doesn't have to deal with a body, with its needs and appetites.) "Rather, we become like God by becoming measured. For souls such as ours, becoming temperate and just constitutes the appropriate measure."[11]

In this way it seems that "becoming like God" can be an effective ethical standard. Plato sketched it out more fully in his later works (*Philebus*, *Timaeus*, and *Laws*) and grounded it effectively on his argument for ascent in the *Republic* together with his systematic critique of "jealousy" in the *Republic*, *Philebus*, and *Timaeus* and his reported lecture on the Good. These show us how an "ascending" intellect needs to be loving toward all, in the way that the *Timaeus*'s demiurge is.

Divine "going down" in *Symposium* and *Republic*

I don't know whether Plato had in mind something like the *Timaeus*'s notion of divine "going down" when he wrote the *Symposium*. But it seems to illuminate the questions that we raised about the final portion of Diotima's speech, where the person who has seen Beauty is described as being able to give birth to true virtue, and thus to be immortalized. Why would he consider giving birth, rather than merely contemplating Beauty? Perhaps because he wants to be fully real and consequently self-governing and not "multiple" (again putting together *Republic*

443a and *Timaeus*), and therefore to "go down" in the manner of the demiurge and make things as good as possible. He doesn't aim to immortalize his mere particular self; rather, he aims to contribute, as the demiurge does, to the best possible world. But in this way he does in fact immortalize what's both best in himself and most fully himself. As we all can, to the extent that we approach knowledge of the Beautiful (or Good).

I suspect that this is also Plato's ultimate solution to the much-discussed problem in the *Republic* of why the Guardians, having seen the Good, would be willing to return to the Cave to share their knowledge with those who remained behind. Socrates's interlocutor asks, "Are we to do [the trainees] an injustice by making them live a worse life when they could live a better one?" Socrates's reply is that we'll tell them, "We've made you kings in our city . . . both for yourselves and for the rest of the city. You're better and more completely educated than the others. . . . Therefore each of you in turn must go down to live in the common dwelling place of the others and grow accustomed to seeing in the dark" (519d–520c). He makes a virtue of this, as he calls it, "compulsory" character of the going down, since it ensures that people won't be doing government service for glory or for money (521a).

These comments seem rather external. They have the unfortunate implication that people who, having seen the Good, are supposed to fully understand justice, will nevertheless receive the "just order" to go down as an unwelcome imposition ("something compulsory"). The demiurge in the *Timaeus* has a better attitude. He helps others to become good because he isn't "jealous" or spiteful—because, as I've suggested, he knows that dividing himself off from others would prevent him from being fully "one," fully self-governing (and divine). Philosophers who seek to "become like God" will apply the same thought to themselves.

As with the "noble lie," here again the *Republic*'s doctrine is rather external and controlling, while the *Symposium* and *Timaeus*, with their "birth in beauty" and their non-"jealousy," give us a more penetrating way of understanding the issue.

Philosophy's heart

The upshot of all of this is that the second half of Plato's double thesis seems to be confirmed: reason (in the form of rational self-government) requires and carries with it love of others, just as love requires and carries with it reason. As usual, we're talking here of ideal reason and ideal love, of which less fully developed versions of reason and love will, of course, fall short.[12]

This is also Plato's ultimate answer to the challenge that he posed for himself in the *Republic*, to show that a fully rational person has good reason to act justly toward others. The only way to be fully "one" is to love everything, and thus love everyone, as the demiurge does.[13]

To our world, in which we think of reason as by its nature cold and unfeeling and love as by its nature warm and unthinking, Plato's dual thesis that reason and love each require and involve the other must seem quite paradoxical. But I submit that we should take it very seriously, as Hegel, Emerson, Whitehead, and many modern poets, lovers, and scientists in practice do.

For if we can find the sweet and dynamic identity of love and intellect in everything that we do, we'll be less divided against ourselves and more at home in our world. We'll no longer be distracted by our current debilitating contrast between religious "love" and philosophical "reason." We'll rediscover both the heart's philosophy and philosophy's heart. And it will become evident that the Christian doctrine of love of one's neighbor and one's enemy is not the result of a randomly issued "commandment" or of a rationally optional "idealism" but rather a universal requirement of full individuality or self-government.

Is all of this just a wish-fulfilling fantasy of "sweetness and light"? It seems clear that the "masters of suspicion" including Hobbes, Marx, Nietzsche, and Freud, have all tried to give us access not just to truths but to truths that they hoped could make us more free, more in charge of our lives. In that way, they were all contributing to the "ascent" that Plato and his followers pursue, so we should welcome their contributions warmly (which of course need not mean uncritically).

What's more, in their rejection of dualisms and their preference for thinking of reality as one unified substance (which they usually refer to as "matter" or "nature"), Hobbes, Marx, Nietzsche, and Freud have an important point. Reality must indeed be unified, since otherwise it would have unexplained internal relationships, between its two or more "realms" or other ingredients, and we would have failed to find what is real as itself, and thus ultimately real. The materialists' or naturalists' mistake is not that they think of reality as unified but that they fail to see the role that's played, in reality's unification, by the vertical dimension of individuation through rational ascent or love. Rather than being given as a substance, reality is achieved through individuation. (So that as Hegel puts it, in a reality that's real as itself, "substance" must give way to "subject.")

The naturalist tradition throws out the baby of individuation, reason, and love along with the dualist bathwater. This baby, as we have now seen, is the key to Plato's account of a God who must love, as well as of humans who must emulate this God. These "two" realities are evidently one, while still being distinguished from each other on a vertical dimension of increasing success in individuation.

Is the Demiurge "immanent" or "transcendent"?

Returning to the *Timaeus*: the "demiurge" story is one of Plato's important passages relating to what we call "God." None of these passages is clearly intended to give a definitive account of what God is. The demiurge story is pivotal in the *Timaeus*, but it's brief and gives no specifics as to what the demiurge was or where he came from. Scholarly discussion of the passage has focused mainly on the question whether it should be taken at face value, as an account of the actions of a being at some point in the past, through which the physical world came into being. Or should it be taken figuratively as an account of a nontemporal, eternal relationship whereby the divine constantly produces and supports the world. The latter view has been attractive for interpreters who want the *Timaeus* to be consistent with the doctrine that Socrates laid down at *Phaedrus* 245e that souls exist eternally.

My discussion of what the passage implies regarding the functioning of a perfectly free intellect certainly hasn't taken it as an account of the contingent preferences and actions of one particular being, as the account of God's creative work in the book of Genesis often seems to be taken. But neither have I treated the demiurge as merely immanent in the physical world. If he is to be a model of unity (individuation) and self-government, he had better go beyond the lack of unity and lack of self-government that characterize much of the world. And this going beyond the world to greater self-government will make him more fully real, more real as himself, than the world.

In his *Plato on God as Nous*, Stephen Menn argues that rather than being "immanent" in souls and thus in the world, the demiurge, as nous ("intellect"), is "a single being . . . existing apart from the bodies and souls he creates."[14] Menn convincingly demonstrates that the demiurge can't simply exist "in" souls and the world, as though these were real independently of its being "in" them. But Menn's way of expressing this important fact, by describing nous as "a single being . . . existing apart from. . . ," suggests a "two-world" model, in which the world is one "being" (or collection of beings), and nous is another. Fortunately Menn goes on to say in proper Platonic fashion that "the *nous* that God *is* is just the *nous* that . . . souls *have* when they act according to reason" (p. 18). That is, the nous (intellect) is a "virtue" (p. 17) in which things in the world (such as souls) participate, as they participate in Forms. So we needn't suppose that tables and chairs and souls are "beings" in the same way that nous is a "being." Tables and chairs and souls get their being from their participation in Forms and nous. They don't exist separately, in the sense of not depending on Forms and nous for their being.

Nor, on the other hand, do Forms and nous exist separately from tables and chairs and souls. For nous "wants" everything, the world, to be as good as it can be; and it "wants" this precisely so as to be Good and One, itself. To be itself, it must do everything it can to promote goodness and oneness in the world. And thus it is not and cannot be itself without dealing with the world in this way.

So any talk of God's "existing apart from" the world, in Plato, must immediately be qualified by a reminder that what's supposedly "separate" is also intimately linked, in both directions. The divine is linked with the world by the divine's "wanting" and indeed needing to create the world, so as itself to be fully "One" and self-governing. (So as itself to be, as Hegel puts it, "truly infinite," not defined and thus governed by its difference from or exclusion of something other than it.) And the world is linked with the divine by the divine's giving the world whatever unity and thus full reality the world possesses.

This intimate linkage between the divine and the world is the fundamental principle by which Platonism distinguishes itself from the common notion of God as primarily a "separate being," and only secondarily "good," and so forth. By making Goodness primary, as what gives God the self-government and thus the kind of "separateness" that God does have, Platonism makes it clear how this "separateness" is not that of one simply "real" object alongside another simply "real" object. The world's reality depends forever on God's reality as what's fully Good and self-governing, and God's reality as fully Good and self-governing depends forever upon God's creating the world.[15]

In this way, the Platonic tradition avoids the dual alternatives of atheism and not-truly-infinite "God as a separate being" theism, the evil twins that dog so many of our discussions about "God." It avoids the incoherent conception of "transcendence" as separate existence.

Rather than "creationism," the central issue is value, purpose, and rational self-government

The primary division in ancient Greek cosmology is not between those who think the world had a beginning in time and those who think it did not. Rather, the primary division is between those who think of the world as ordered teleologically, toward goodness or benefit, and those who think of it as the product of chance. Plato the "creationist" and Aristotle the non-"creationist" both belong to the group who see the world as ordered toward goodness or benefit, while Leucippus, Democritus, Epicurus, and Lucretius are the leading ancient advocates of explaining the world in terms of chance.[16]

The role of this orientation toward goodness in making individual organisms truly "one," as in *Republic* iv (443e) and throughout Aristotle, is insufficiently appreciated in current discussions. This role explains why, as Plato suggests and Aristotle elaborates, all living things seek to emulate the divine.[17] We do so not because the divine is immortal and we don't want to die but because only the divine is fully itself, self-contained, "one" (and *therefore* immortal). We aren't seeking an immortality that from the usual modern point of view would seem entirely beyond our reach. Rather, we're seeking something that seems both desirable and quite possibly within our reach, namely, to be fully ourselves, by seeking what's truly good.

The Plato/Aristotle view that reality is oriented toward goodness can be plausible regardless of whether the physical sciences recognize this orientation. The sciences as we now practice them are deeply invested in the pursuit of "efficient" rather than "final" causes—of explanations in terms of "what started it" rather than in terms of "that for the sake of which it happened." They seek maximum predictive power, rather than to articulate our experience as a whole. So they can't realistically be expected to appreciate, in their normal activities, the way in which goodness functions in (full) reality. They can appreciate this only through a reflective self-awareness that goes beyond their normal activities and corresponds to what we traditionally call "metaphysics."

What this reflective self-awareness reveals is that our goal in scientific inquiry, as in other human activities, is to be rationally self-governing. Insofar as we're guided by an understanding of the real world, we're more rationally self-governing than if we're guided by our initial, untested ideas about the world. Because the sciences themselves aim to embody and facilitate rational self-government, the sciences' pervasive preoccupation with efficient causes for what they study cannot be cited as grounds for dismissing the reality of rational self-government.

The pursuit of what's truly real, through science, is evidence of our capacity to pursue something that may *or may not* be programmed into us by our genetic heritage or our environment. The pursuit of what's truly good is another instance of the same thing. There is no more reason to doubt the reality of the second than of the first. They both serve to make us ourselves, rather than mere puppets of what's other than us.

But to understand ourselves as seeking, in these ways, to be truly ourselves is to understand ourselves not in terms of efficient causes (what started the process) but in terms of a final cause (that for the sake of which the process happens)—the final cause in this case being our own rational self-government. And if it's reasonable for us to understand *ourselves* in this way—as scientists who examine their own activity as scientists surely must—then it must be reasonable to consider whether other phenomena in nature might be understood in similar ways. For example, it would be reasonable to consider whether plants and nonrational animals don't seek to be more self-governing than rocks, and thus to pursue more effectively oneness and what may be good for them. And similarly, it would be reasonable to consider whether all living things don't, in these ways, seek oneness and the "good," which rational living things have the additional feature of being able to clarify through thought, and thus to pursue more deeply.

From the point of view of our experience of seeking oneness and the good in sophisticated ways, through science and other means, we can see nature as a whole as engaged in less sophisticated versions of the same search. If we acknowledge the reality of teleology in ourselves, what reason could we have for refusing to consider its possible presence, in various forms, in the rest of nature? (Setting aside, of course, the practical usefulness of efficient causes as means of *controlling* what's other than us.)

I'm not proposing that we should think of the world projectively as composed of "people," "agents," or "consciousnesses" like ourselves. Rather, that we should consider ways in which things in the world approximate to the kind of rational self-government that we sometimes achieve. Plants approximate to it in that they preserve and reproduce a distinctive form. This is a simple kind of self-government. Nonrational animals approximate to it in that they make decisions about how to interact with their environments. This is clearly a more sophisticated kind of self-government. It's likely that in each of these cases, the organism's inner experience of what it does has important similarities to (as well as differences from) our own inner experience. But in every case there is an orientation and effort toward what the organism (as we could say by a kind of analogy) "conceives of" as good; and thus there is teleology.

Thus, understanding nature teleologically need not be a regression to pre-scientific animism or vitalism. It can instead be an elaboration of what's implied by the practice of science itself, insofar as that practice is an aspect of the pursuit of rational self-government.

So there is no need to regard Plato's and Aristotle's teleological cosmology as a quaint instance of premodern thinking. Instead, we can see it as an important way—possibly needing some restatement, but not unacceptable in principle—of articulating the consequences of the reality of rational self-government. Which is one of our own most central and undeniable features.

And thus, by the same token, while we might want to revise the conceptions of the divine that accompany Plato's and Aristotle's teleological cosmology, there is no reason to regard these conceptions as unacceptable in principle. For these conceptions are based, like the cosmology that goes with them, on an appreciation of the significance of rational self-government, for which Plato and Aristotle make a very good case.[18]

Since full reality is produced by cognition of value, cognition is not an add-on

We can now also see why with regard to the possibility of knowledge, Platonism doesn't encounter the issues in which non-teleological modern philosophy tends to become embroiled. If the fullest reality is achieved through knowledge of the Good, a certain kind of knowledge is already part of reality itself, and doesn't need to be added on to it. We know from our most familiar experience ("from inside," as I say) that some realities, which we sometimes achieve, are more fully real than others; and that we achieve these more real realities through knowledge. We can still ask, at any given moment, whether we are currently achieving that kind of reality and participating in the associated knowledge, but there is no question about their being possible.[19]

God and change

Alongside the *Republic*, *Symposium*, *Phaedrus*, and *Timaeus*, the other major text in which Plato addresses the divine is book x of his *Laws*, the lengthy dialogue on which he is said to have been working at the time of his death. Here he presents something like what has come to be called the "cosmological proof" of God. Distinguishing various ways in which motion can be brought about, the Athenian who is the main speaker suggests that motion that "moves both itself and other things" is "the most powerful and radically effective." He describes this kind of motion as equivalent to "life," which in turn is equivalent to "soul." So "soul," he says, "is the master, and matter its natural subject"; and soul is "a divinity" (894c–897b).

The Athenian's interlocutors find this argument convincing, but it's not difficult to identify the point at which many readers may not be convinced by it. This is where the Athenian attempts to establish that there must indeed be, in reality, a motion that "moves both itself and other things": a self-mover. His comment on this is,

> How could anything whose motion is transmitted to it from something else be the *first* thing to effect an alteration? It's impossible. In reality ... the entire sequence of their movements must surely spring from some initial principle, which can hardly be anything except the change effected by self-generated motion. (894e-895a)

And this self-generated motion is the "divine" whose reality he aims to establish.

The natural response to this sort of argument is, of course, to ask why there must be a "*first*" thing at all. Why must we assume that the sequence of motions that makes up the world ever had a beginning?

The Athenian provides no answer to this question. One has to say that the whole discussion, for this reason, is unsatisfying. Some explanation of the fact that Plato didn't try to make it more satisfying may be found in the fact that the purpose of the Athenian's discussion of the gods is explicitly to "persuade" (885e) the ordinary citizens of the city that he's describing, that the gods exist. That is, he aims to be persuasive rather than to present a proof.

God and "reality as oneself"

I think it's clear that Plato places far more weight, over all, on his account of transcendence in the *Phaedo*, *Republic*, *Symposium*, and *Timaeus*, than he places on the cosmological argument of the *Laws*. He develops his account of transcendence in much more detail, and it constitutes the appropriate background for his *Timaeus* story of the demiurge. The demiurge "was good" and sought to make the world "as much like himself as was possible." That is, the demiurge had the orientation to goodness and unity that Plato had analyzed in, especially, the *Republic*. This orientation makes it appropriate to describe the demiurge both as transcending the ordinary world by lacking worldly motivations of appetite and selfishness and as being more fully real than it, in the sense that he is more self-governing and thus more real as himself.

It's appropriate for Plato to place more weight on his account of transcendence in the *Phaedo, Republic, Symposium,* and *Timaeus,* because this is an account of what gives "God" *authority* for us, as opposed to the sheer power that one could see in the "first cause" as presented in the *Laws*. What's guided by the Good, and thus is fully one and maximally real, is an appropriate object of worship, in a way that a mere "cause" is not.

One could also suggest that the argument for divinity which Plato presents in the *Republic* provides resources with which the cosmological argument of the *Laws* could be restated and made much stronger. We could reformulate the Athenian's search for a "*first* thing to effect an alteration," as (instead) a search for something that's fully real, as itself.

The "first thing" was meant to explain all of the motions that succeeded it, and we wanted to know why there couldn't be an endless series of explanations, perhaps unknowable to us, but nevertheless each of them explaining the motion that followed it. The *Republic* suggests that a more important goal than a beginning point in time is what we might call a beginning point in reality—something that's fully real as itself, rather than deriving some of its character from its relationships to what's other than it.

It seems much more difficult to dismiss the *Republic*'s search for something that's fully real as itself than to dismiss the Athenian's search for a beginning point in time. The *Republic*'s search points to all of our most familiar forms of inquiry. What should I really believe? How should I really live? If we ask these questions, we are involved in the "transcending" process on which the *Republic* focuses. We are seeking a kind of "reality" that isn't present in whatever just happens to come into our heads. And we're seeking, like the demiurge, to *be* that kind of reality: to be more self-determining than we would be if we just believed, and did, whatever came into our heads. Furthermore, by seeking to find and to be that kind of reality, we actually *are* it, to some extent, and we know from this first-hand experience that rather than being an idle speculation, the notion of such a reality represents something real. This is how, as Hegel puts it, "substance is essentially subject" (*Phenomenology of Spirit*, Preface, §25): we turn out to be, in an important respect, the ultimate reality that we are searching for. Plato's argument in *Republic* iv-vii fully anticipates this shocking Hegelian conclusion.

Of course it's surprising to hear that our everyday experience of asking ourselves what we should really believe and what we should really do gives us access to the divine ultimate reality. But once one understands Plato's point, it's hard to dismiss it. For the outcome of asking what we should really believe and what we should really do is precisely something that's more self-governed, more (in that sense) transcendent, more real as itself, and more loving than what doesn't ask these questions. And what's more self-governed, more transcendent, more real as itself, and more loving has many of the attributes that we traditionally assign to God.[20]

Thus I hope I've made it clear how Plato's conception of the divine meets our needs. First, what is more self-governed, more transcendent, more real as itself, and more loving than anything else, deserves to be worshipped in a way that nothing else does. The presence of this divinity is the presence of love. And secondly, this divinity is something with which we are intimately familiar, through our own contributions to it. It's not a separate being from us, though it's certainly higher than much of what we are up to.

And thus once again, Plato combines metaphysics and epistemology, the doctrine of reality and the doctrine of knowledge, rather than separating them in the manner of skepticism and much modern philosophy. If the fullest reality is achieved through knowledge of the Good, a certain kind of knowledge is already part of reality itself, and doesn't need to be added on to it. Subject's access to substance is not a problem, because "substance *is essentially* subject." This is not because there is *nothing but* "subject," but because subject is more fully substance, more fully "itself," than anything else is. Or, as I've been putting it, since our primary experience is the identity crisis in which we fluctuate between having less reality as ourselves and having more, and having more reality as ourselves is an essential aspect of this fluctuation, we have direct knowledge of the higher reality that has more reality as itself.

"Mystical experience" in Plato

Finally I want to say a little more about the nature of Plato's "mysticism," the topic that I have been trying to reopen in these chapters. "Mysticism," as I've explained, is not about mystery or secrecy as such, but rather about direct knowledge of the divine. Such knowledge seems sufficiently mysterious from the point of view of the common ancient Greek conception of the divine as superhuman anthropomorphic beings, or from the point of view of the common present-day conception of the divine as "a being" that's separate from the world and has various superhuman qualities. Especially in the latter case, it's quite unclear how we could have knowledge of such a being.

I hope I've made it clear how this problem is solved by Plato's notion of the divine as extrapolating not human qualities like lust, anger, and jealousy but rather such comparatively "superhuman" qualities, which nevertheless are part of our experience, as self-government, justice, love, and "oneness." This notion of Plato's makes the divine a part of our experience while at the same time showing how it surpasses much of what we are. And in this way it shows how we can in fact have direct knowledge of something that at the same time deserves to be described as transcendent and "superhuman."

Now, the progress we've made in understanding this subject should help us to understand the status of the famous "mystical" images that we encounter in the *Republic*, *Symposium*, and *Phaedrus*. In the *Symposium*, Plato has Diotima say that "and there in life . . . there if anywhere should a person live his life, beholding that Beauty" (211d). In the *Republic*, Socrates says of the real lover of learning that "once getting near what really is and having intercourse with it and having begotten understanding (*nous*) and truth he knows, truly lives, is nourished, and . . . is relieved from the pains of giving birth" (490a-b). And later he says that those who've been educated to the highest point would "refuse to act, thinking that they had settled while still alive in the faraway Isles of the Blessed" (519c). And in the *Phaedrus*, "It would awaken a terribly powerful love (*deinous erotas*) if an image of wisdom (*phronesis*) came through our sight as clearly as beauty does." (250d). These can all be taken as allusions to (actual or possible) experiences of the extraordinary kind that we have come to call "mystical experiences."

Commentators on Plato often don't have much to say about these allusions, perhaps thinking that if one hasn't had the kind of experience that Plato seems to be alluding to, one can't say very much about them. Or perhaps fearing that if we acknowledge that Plato is interested in "mystical experiences," we and Plato may be dismissed as purveyors of what unfriendly critics call "New Age fluff." For my part, I've been suggesting since Chapter 1 that we don't need to have the extraordinary experiences that we call "mystical experiences" in order to have full access to the truth that these experiences announce. For we have such access frequently, in our everyday experiences of inner freedom, love, forgiveness, and so forth, which don't *announce themselves as* experiences of something transcendent or divine, but which nevertheless are that. And with the help of spiritual teachers like Plato, Rumi, Hegel, and Emerson, we can come to understand how these "everyday" experiences are in fact experiences of something that's transcendent and that deserves to be called divine.

I'll say some more in the next and final chapter about this issue of apparently different ways of experiencing the transcendent and divine. What I want to point out now is that like transcendence and divinity in general, what Plato says in these famous passages is in principle just as accessible to those of us who haven't had extraordinary "mystical experiences" as it is to those who have had them.

For we can understand Plato's remarks as commenting on the place at which we arrive when we have understood, perhaps with his help, what is the real significance and nature of our everyday experiences of inner freedom, love, and so forth; namely, that these are experiences of something that's transcendent and divine. When we understand this, we have indeed (as it seems to me) arrived at something like the "Isles of the Blessed," and we probably do feel a "terribly powerful love" for this place. For we have indeed (metaphorically speaking) "begotten understanding and truth," about ourselves and the ultimate reality. So that we do indeed "truly live," we are indeed "nourished," and we are indeed "relieved of the pains of giving birth"—for we now know that we know God.[21]

Plato doesn't say, in so many words, that we know God in everyday experience. But he does make it clear, in both the *Republic* and the *Symposium*, that the extraordinary experiences that he describes reveal the truth that was already present in everyday experiences, but which we didn't previously appreciate in them. When Plato tells us that the objects that we experience in the world "participate" in the Forms (*Phaedo* 100c, *Parmenides* 129a) he tells us that the world that we experience is not completely separate from the "higher world" of the Forms. We see this also in the fact that we (through our rational part) seek to be guided not just by appetites and emotions but by what's truly good. These are both ways in which the Forms are present in the "lower world," often without our being aware of their presence as such. Likewise, nous or intellect or the "demiurge" is present, in all of our endeavors, whether we are aware of it as such or not. In all of these ways, the divine is present in our everyday doings, though in general we're not aware of it as such. Thus we can say that when Plato describes us as gaining direct knowledge of the Form of the Good or the Beautiful, he is not describing us as encountering something that we had never encountered before in any way. Rather, he's describing us as encountering it "itself by itself," rather than (as we ordinarily encounter it) mixed with much that's other than it. This new awareness, the encountering it "itself by itself," is transformative enough; there's no need for it to be an awareness of a brand new object with which we had no previous acquaintance whatever. The extraordinary experiences that Plato evokes are experiences of discovering what was most real in what we've been experiencing all along.

Nor does this claim that we know God reflect any kind of hubris or grandiosity on our part. For what we're speaking of is precisely knowledge of the implications of our own ongoing "ignorance" or questioning, our open-minded inner freedom, which (to one degree or another) we share with everyone—and which constitutes the most real thing, the greatest fulfillment. As Plato says, "There if anywhere should a person live his life, beholding that Beauty."

Arriving at this place can certainly be a prolonged and arduous process, involving a considerable reorganization of one's inner life. It isn't always easy to "obey thyself" or to understand what that carries with it. But there is no reason why this process must involve an extraordinary "mystical experience," in the usual sense of that phrase. The "terribly powerful love" and the other features that Plato lists may be unfamiliar, and in that sense extraordinary, experiences, but they differ from the usual "mystical experiences" in that they can continue indefinitely.

I'll say more about this question in the next and final chapter.

9 ORDINARY AND EXTRAORDINARY EXPERIENCES OF GOD

This is the grass that grows wherever the land is and the water is,
This is the common air that bathes the globe.

This is the breath of laws and songs and behaviour,
This is the tasteless water of souls. . . . this is the true sustenance.
        WALT WHITMAN, *LEAVES OF GRASS*, "SONG OF MYSELF," SEC. 17

I've shown how Plato lays the foundation for the sort of philosophy that, in Hegel and other modern thinkers, resolves perennial issues about "inner" and "outer," mind and body, freedom and nature, ethics and rational self-government, value and fact, and religion and science. I hope I've made their invaluable work more accessible than it may have been previously.

In this final chapter, I want to say some more about how Plato and the others interpret, in particular, what we call "religious experience." And thus to contribute something to the discussion that William James set in motion with his rich lectures on *The Varieties of Religious Experience* (1902).

Our everyday experiences of God

I've been suggesting that our discoveries of inner freedom are experiences of God. For through freedom, love, and forgiveness, we and the world become more self-determining, more ourselves, and thus more fully real; and this fuller reality is God.

The dramatic experiences of liberation that we occasionally have can help us to recognize and appreciate the many smaller experiences of liberation that we have practically every day. And thus to realize that we experience God practically every day, though we may not realize that God is what we're experiencing. This is what the poets of love, from Rumi through Wordsworth, Whitman, and Mary Oliver, have been trying to help us to realize. When Whitman writes of the "common air that bathes the globe" and that provides "the true sustenance" for souls, he's evoking the experience, which we have practically every day, of God as freedom and love.

This is why, in my comments about "mysticism," I haven't focused on any of the supposedly definitive singular experiences that various mystical traditions describe or allude to. I have focused instead on the more familiar multiple experiences of inner freedom, free inquiry, forgiveness, and love. With the help of teachers like Plato, Hegel, and the mystical poets, experiences of this kind can lead to the kind of understanding of mysticism that I have been advocating in this book. What's more, however, they seem to me to be more definitive, more conclusive, than the extraordinary experiences that we hear about.

I've explained why I think it makes sense to call experiences of liberation and love experiences of God. They constitute something that's more self-determining and in that sense more fully real than our merely "mechanical" responses to the external world. But if inner freedom, forgiveness, open-minded thought, and love are what God *is*, we experience God whenever we experience them.[1] Some of us less often and some of us more often, we all have these experiences, which give us direct access to God.[2]

Extraordinary "mystical experiences" may well be absolutely conclusive for the people who experience them. But it's always open to bystanders to ask why they should be convinced by an experience that they themselves haven't had. Indeed, the person who has had the experience might still wonder, when she's no longer immediately "in its grip," what exactly she is justified in concluding on the basis of the experience.

By contrast, the common experiences of inner freedom, forgiveness, and so forth don't convince us by sheer power, and they don't go away and stay away for long periods, as extraordinary experiences tend to do. Instead, the common experiences convince us by presenting something that we can see is always available to us, whenever we open our minds and hearts. That's why I call these common experiences more definitive than the extraordinary ones.

It's certainly true that most of us don't realize that these common experiences give us access to God. Western cultures tend to dismiss the idea that ordinary people can experience God. We're told either that there is no God or that God is a separate being whom most people can know only through faith, and not through personal experience.

In fact, even most of what we read about "mysticism" has the (probably unintended) effect of reinforcing, through its emphasis on extraordinary experiences, the assumption that most people don't and won't experience God.

Teaching like that of Plato, Hegel, Rumi, or Walt Whitman, which might overcome these unfortunate influences by showing us the great significance of our everyday experiences, isn't available to everyone, everywhere.

Against the assumption that most people don't and won't experience God, Eckhart Tolle writes that "I don't call it finding God, because how can you find that which was never lost, *the very life that you are*? . . . There can be no subject-object relationship here, no duality, no you *and* God. God-realization is the most natural thing there is."[3] And he describes this God-realization as the result of "surrender to what *is*."[4]

I would add that this "very life that you are," or this "what *is*"—that is, what *really* is, in you—is your everyday dreams of and efforts toward inner freedom and love. These dreams and efforts are the presence within you of something that's higher, more self-determining, and thus more fully real than your everyday self-importance, desires, suffering, and so forth. Because you are already intimately familiar with these dreams and efforts, you are already intimately familiar with something that's higher, more self-determining, and more fully real—that is, you are already intimately familiar with God.

I associate this presence of God within us with the Buddhist doctrine that Buddha nature is always present in everything—that (as I gather that some say) "everything is a Buddha." (And likewise with the Vedanta doctrine that Atman is Brahman.) We have only to realize what we have always been. I do think it's helpful, for this purpose, to spell out in ordinary language *how* these things are true, as I have tried to do in this book.

What our extraordinary experiences do and don't accomplish

But even a person who has received the teaching of someone like Plato, Hegel, Rumi, or Whitman may be reluctant to abandon the comfort of assumptions that they've been used to all their lives. This is why the extraordinary experiences that "mystics" report often have a major impact on the people who have them. They break through the assumptions that most of us have lived with for most of our lives—that God can't be experienced directly, but is only an object of "faith" and may not even exist, so that a person who claims to have experienced God is not making sense and may be just plain crazy.

William James collected many reports of experiences that announced themselves as experiences of something divine in his *The Varieties of Religious Experience*. Here is one example:

> We were on our sixth day of tramping. . . . I felt neither fatigue, hunger, nor thirst, and my state of mind was equally healthy. I had had at Forlaz good news

from home. . . . I can best describe the condition in which I was by calling it a state of equilibrium. When all at once I experienced a feeling of being raised above myself, I felt the presence of God—I tell of the thing just as I was conscious of it—as if his goodness and power were penetrating me altogether. The throb of emotion was so violent that I could barely tell the boys to pass on and not wait for me. I then sat down on a stone, unable to stand any longer, and my eyes overflowed with tears. I thanked God that in the course of my life he had taught me to know him. . . . Then, slowly, the ecstasy left my heart; that is, I felt that God had withdrawn the communion which he had granted, and I was able to walk on, but very slowly, so strongly was I still possessed by the interior emotion. . . . The state of ecstasy may have lasted four or five minutes. . . . [In it,] God was present, though invisible; he fell under no one of my senses, yet my consciousness perceived him.[5]

This person obviously was profoundly moved by his experience. We are probably quite moved by reading it. It seems churlish to ask what (if anything) he really knew as a result of his experience, and what we can know as a result of reading his story. But these are reasonable questions, and there is a small library of cool, analytical books that address them.[6] I myself am inclined to think that all that this man could really know on the basis of this experience alone was that he had in fact had a profound emotional experience. Not that he had actually felt "God."

But I'm not interested in arguing for this conclusion. As you know from what I've been saying, I have a different approach to this whole issue. I'm convinced that as far as the knowledge of God is concerned, we don't need to decide whether experiences like the one that this man had are "veridical." We don't need to decide this because there are good reasons to think that we can and do know God directly; that is (in the first dictionary sense of the word) we can and do have "mystical" knowledge of God, *regardless of* "mystical experiences" like the one that this writer reported.

"Mystical experiences" are important not as the basis of our knowledge of God, but simply (and this is importance enough) because they often help us dramatically in getting beyond the groundless but powerful assumptions that I mentioned. That is, the assumptions that God can't be experienced directly, but is only an object of "faith" and may not even exist, so that a person who claims to have experienced God is not making sense and may be just plain crazy. Someone who has "felt the presence of God" or has been moved by the story of such an experience is likely to question these assumptions in a way that someone who hasn't felt that presence or been moved by such a story is less likely to question them. This is why many of us are fascinated by stories of mystical experiences. They encourage us to put our familiar assumptions in brackets and consider looking at the world in a different way.

"Ordinary" experiences are more definitive

What the writers in the Platonic tradition do, then, is to provide those of us who have this interest in looking at the world in a different way with a worked-out account of such a way, which shows how we do actually know God. They show us that we know God through our everyday experiences of inner freedom, love, forgiveness, and so forth, which don't announce themselves as experiences of something divine but which we nevertheless have good reasons to understand as being that.

These experiences are relevant because the only God that's truly infinite, and thus truly transcendent, is *composed of* experiences like these. It's truly transcendent because not being separate from us, this God isn't bounded by us and thus limited in the way that all separate and bounded things are. And it's "God" because it's self-determining, real as itself, and perfectly loving.

So these experiences of freedom, love, forgiveness, and so forth are the way in which God is present, in our lives. We know God directly through these experiences because what we have good grounds for regarding as aspects of God as such are immediately present in them. By contrast, in a "mystical experience" such as the one whose description I quoted, in which "God" is "felt" to be present, we have no grounds for regarding the presence as divine except the overwhelming conviction of the person who had the experience. Whereas in our experiences of freedom, love, and so forth, God (rather than being "felt" to be present) can be *known by us as identical with the experience itself.* God can be known by us in this way, in these experiences, because thinkers like Plato and Hegel have given us good reasons to believe that experiences like these are what God is composed of. So that God's presence in these cases isn't open to question in the way that a "feeling" of his presence which is conveyed to us by an otherwise unknown faculty is open to question.

Of course, one can also question Plato's and Hegel's interpretation of these everyday experiences of freedom, love, and forgiveness as being the immediate presence of God. There can be plenty of discussion about that. My point is that the way Plato and Hegel interpret these experiences doesn't involve inferring the existence of something that's supposed to be *separate from the experiences*, as interpreting a "feeling" as being caused by God evidently must.[7]

So if we understand how our everyday experiences of freedom, love, forgiveness, and so forth help to constitute God, we'll see that our having knowledge of God needn't involve extraordinary experiences such as the state of ecstasy whose description I quoted. Through our everyday experiences, we already know God, in the most direct and conclusive way possible.

And by "we," I mean all of us, including the many people who have no idea that they know God, and may indeed doubt or deny that there is any God. Whether we're aware of it or not, we know the true God.

Our everyday experiences contain a wealth that we don't ordinarily suspect. Whereas our extraordinary experiences, emotionally overpowering though they very likely are, are less cognitively rich than they may initially seem. Because it's doubtful whether, when we take them as "extraordinary," they give us direct knowledge of anything but themselves.[8]

We should line up extraordinary experiences with ordinary ones

It's only insofar as we see our extraordinary experiences as *ordinary*, and line them up alongside the innumerable other experiences that give us access to God because they are God, that they too give us this access. Insofar as, like our moments of freedom and open-minded thought, a "feeling of God's presence" manifests some kind of loving intelligence, perhaps in our unconscious mind, it too helps to constitute God. It helps to constitute God because it's yet another instance of love's presence in one's life. But then rather than being a *special* source of knowledge, it's on the same plane as one's many other "ordinary" sources of knowledge of God. It's only when we interpret the extraordinary experience as one of a large number of experiences, most of them comparatively "ordinary," that constitute God, that it does in fact help us to know God.

When we put this man's report of his ecstatic experience in this context, some interesting details emerge. What does he mean when he says that he "experienced a feeling of being raised above himself" and follows this with the statement that he "felt the presence of God"? We can safely assume that his "being raised above himself" was not a literal being lifted up in space. Rather, I imagine, it was a metaphorical raising "above" his ordinary self: the same kind of raising that we see in the Platonic allegories of exiting the Cave, and so forth. When he adds that it was "as if [God's] goodness and power were penetrating me altogether," we can associate this, similarly, with Platonism's doctrine that God is within us. Where what's "within" often seems to "penetrate" us from outside inasmuch as God transcends our ordinary selves and often comes upon us without our expecting it, because it isn't what our ordinary self had in mind at all.

So this man's overpowering experience contained much of the conceptual structure that we're familiar with from our exploration of the Platonic literature. And which we can readily connect with our "everyday" experiences of our own "rising above" our prior self in the sense of our prior appetites, opinions, and so forth, and consequently acquiring a new or renewed sense of who or what we really are. The only difference being that the entire syndrome came upon this man all at once, as it were, and apart from any apparent specific prior issue. Perhaps his life had simply made him ready, at this point in time, to learn in an explicit way what it had for a long time implicitly been about. As he says, God "*in the course of my life . . .* had taught me to know him."

If what I've just said is correct, then this man's powerful "feeling of God's presence" was similar in important respects to the (mostly) more everyday experiences that Platonism identifies as aspects of God. And in that way it does in fact confirm, as far as a single experience can, the general Platonic understanding of our knowledge of God. While once again undermining the idea that this knowledge depends in essential ways on extraordinary experiences that we don't encounter in our everyday lives. For what this man "discovered" seems likely to have already been present for a long time in his life, in less explicit and less overwhelming forms.

What mysticism and religion are actually about

Whatever the truth may be about this particular case, it turns out, if what I've been suggesting over all is correct, that the direct experience of God needn't be primarily a matter of the extraordinary experiences that we usually call "mystical experiences." Rather, it can be a matter of the everyday experiences of freedom, love, forgiveness, and so forth, which we can come to appreciate as constituting God.

And indeed this is true of religion in general, of which mysticism in this sense turns out to be an indispensable part. If Platonic philosophy has contributed something vital and indispensable to religion, it's the understanding of the way freedom, love, forgiveness, and open-minded thought constitute God. For this shows us that religion is about what's transcendent *in everyone's experience*, rather than being about a being that's outside the experience of most of us. So that religion is transcendent by being rational (rather than by being mysterious), and it's rational by transcending (rather than by merely "calculating"). From the fact that transcendence goes beyond "calculation," we got the idea that it's not rational at all, which gave rise to our ongoing disputes between science and religion. But rational mysticism explains how this was all unnecessary, since true transcendence itself is rational in the sense that it reflects thought, and thus can be and is part of our everyday experience.

My suggestion, then, is that our relationship to God, which is celebrated by mysticism and by religion, doesn't primarily have to do either with mystery or with extraordinary "mystical experiences." Nor does it primarily have to do with the extraordinary experiences that have been had by "prophets" and teachers. Rather, it has to do with the endless, everyday experience of inner freedom, love, forgiveness, and open-minded thought, in which every one of us participates to some degree and in some way. These are mysterious enough from the point of view of calculating, self-centered "reason." But we all understand them, nevertheless, from our everyday experience of them.

In fact, it's only this everyday experience of inner freedom, love, forgiveness, and so forth that enables us to understand and find relevant the extraordinary experiences that we hear about and the teachings that we receive from mystics, prophets, and other religious teachers. We find what we receive from them intelligible and relevant only insofar as we ourselves have had a taste of inner freedom, love, forgiveness, and so forth. What this means is that we judge the experiences and teachings of these extraordinary figures, and we ought to judge them, by the same standards by which we judge ourselves and our own experiences, namely, by the "higher" authority that we find in some of our own experiences, and not in others.

We, the "ordinary" people, who distinguish between our own "ordinary" experiences in the course of our own everyday "identity crises," are in charge here, whether we realize this or not. Since the issue is how *we* should live *our* lives, we had better be in charge.

And of course the really great teachers recognize this state of affairs. Homer shows that even Achilles can go beyond his self-centeredness and his enmity. Plato says that "the power to learn is in everyone's soul" (*Republic* 518c; see Chapter 6). The Buddha tells us to "be a lamp unto ourselves." Jesus says that "the last shall be first" (Mt. 20:16), that is, that the highest is the highest only insofar as the lowliest freely acknowledge it, because they embody it.

So the highest authority can't be in someone else's experience. It must be in everyone's experience. As in William Blake's grains of sand and wild flowers, and Walt Whitman's leaves of grass:

> This is the grass that grows wherever the land is and the water is,
> This is the common air that bathes the globe.
> This is the breath of laws and songs and behaviour,
> This is the tasteless water of souls. . . . this is the true sustenance.[9]

To be inspired by this air or breath, and fed by this water or true sustenance, we need only become aware of ourselves, of what we constantly do. Of our freedom and the resulting love, or love and the resulting freedom. This is the highest, the most central and most real; this is what we are when we really are.

APPENDIX: COMPARISONS BETWEEN THE PLATO/ HEGEL ARGUMENT FOR A GOD WITHIN US, AND SEVERAL WELL-KNOWN ARGUMENTS FOR GOD

The well-known arguments for God's existence that we find in authors like St. Anselm, St. Thomas Aquinas, and C. S. Lewis can be understood as attempting to achieve the level of generality that the less well-known Plato/Hegel argument achieves. It's the failure of these well-known arguments to achieve the generality that Plato and Hegel achieve, that prevents the well-known arguments from being fully convincing.

C. S. Lewis's argument from the Moral Law

Consider C. S. Lewis's argument from our consciousness of the Moral Law, which he presented in his book, *Mere Christianity*, first published in 1952 and still selling briskly. Lewis thinks it's clear that the Moral Law cannot have been instilled in us by nature, but must have been inserted into us by something "like a mind" which is "outside the universe."[1] And this thing that's like a mind, outside the universe, he suggests, is what God is. So from our consciousness of the Moral Law, we can conclude that God exists.

You might ask why our sense of a "moral law" couldn't have been produced in us by a process of evolution by natural selection. It would reflect the survival advantages that our species presumably derives from its members' not murdering each other, not stealing from each other, and so forth. To this, Lewis replies that the

Moral Law that he's talking about isn't just whatever constraints we may feel that could serve that particular evolutionary purpose. Rather, it's the ultimate standard by which we *judge between* whatever feelings we have about what we should do. It's well known that such feelings often conflict with each other. We need only think of the difficulties that we get into in connection with issues like abortion or war, where strong moral feelings pull us in opposing directions. The Moral Law itself, Lewis says, is the standard by which we decide which of our competing feelings should actually govern our decision.[2]

So the Moral Law has a kind of "authority" that no particular feeling has; and we can't simultaneously respect that authority, as Lewis assumes that we do, and assert that it's merely the result of a process of evolution. Imagine a writer who tells us that morality can be explained as a product of evolution, and also claims to think that it's *only* the survival advantage to her species that explains why she herself thinks that it would be wrong for her to kill her parents. So if it turned out that her species would actually benefit from her killing her parents, then she would decide that it would be perfectly alright for her to kill them, after all. We might wonder whether her feelings on this subject really amount to what we think of as "morality." Does she recognize nothing about her relationship to her parents, entirely apart from any consequences it may have for her species, that makes murdering them unacceptable?

I agree with Lewis's argument completely, up to this point. It's another version of the thought that I expressed in Chapters 1 and 3—that we seek to be guided by something that has more authority than our initial feelings and opinions. "God," Lewis is saying, is that higher authority. But, investigating what this "God" is, why should we suppose that the authority that the Moral Law has, results from its having been inserted into us by something that's "outside the universe"? It's not immediately clear why something that's outside the universe should have more authority over us than something that's inside it. If Lewis says that the authority comes from the fact that the mind-like thing that's outside the universe *created* us, we still need to know why we should think that that fact gives it authority over us.

Clearly, Lewis needs to say more about where this mind-like thing's authority comes from. Plato and Hegel do say more. They explain the divine Law's authority by understanding the divine not as separate from and opposed to (flatly "outside") the universe, but as the universe's own going beyond itself through our search for a higher authority than our initial, externally generated desires and opinions. The divine Law deserves our respect and obedience because it results from or responds to our trying to be guided by something that has more authority than our initial, externally generated desires and opinions. What results from or responds to this must possess this authority.

The Plato/Hegel argument for God resembles Lewis's argument in taking as its point of departure the way moral thinking points beyond the merely natural world. (In Plato's and Hegel's case, the point of departure isn't just our moral thinking but our thinking about what we should be guided by, in general.) But as we've just seen, the Plato/Hegel argument does a better job than Lewis does of explaining where God's authority and morality's authority come from—what it is that makes this "mind-like thing" *higher*.

St Thomas Aquinas's argument for a "first mover"

A second example is St Thomas Aquinas's famous argument, in his *Summa theologica* (1265–74), for a "first mover." Aquinas argues that "whatever is in motion must be put in motion by another," but "this cannot go on to infinity, because then there would be no first mover, and consequently no other mover; ... as the staff moves only because it is put in motion by the hand." The "first mover" that must therefore exist, he says is "what everyone understands to be God."[3]

This argument strongly resembles Plato's argument in *Laws* x, which I summarized in Chapter 8. The historical link between the two is Aristotle's notion of a "prime mover," in his *On the heavens*, which St. Thomas studied.

Bertrand Russell and other critics object to arguments like these that they see no reason why there shouldn't be an infinite series of "movers," receding endlessly into the past. Why should we suppose that there's any similarity between the case of a "staff," and the case of the universe? Apart from Plato and Hegel, I haven't found a persuasive suggestion as to how Aquinas could effectively answer these objections.

What Plato's and Hegel's discussions of God suggest is that Aquinas probably assumes that reality must ultimately be more *self-determining* than the members of Russell's infinite series of "movers" can be. Reality must ultimately be what it is by virtue of itself, and not always by virtue of its relation to something other than itself; and it's hard to see how the infinite series, as a collection, could achieve a self-determination that none of its members, taken individually, can achieve. This is what gives relevance to Aquinas's analogy of the staff that "moves only because it is put in motion by the hand": We imagine that the owner of the hand is self-determining in a way that the staff is not. The universe can't depend on something other than itself for its basic character, as the staff depends on the person who uses it for *its* basic character. Or if the universe does depend on something else for its basic character, there had better not be an infinite regress of dependings, because that can't produce self-determination.

Aquinas isn't assuming a supernatural "mind," as such; he's merely assuming that the ultimate reality shouldn't rely on something else to make it what it is. This is precisely Hegel's explicit primary assumption, in his account of what constitutes full "reality." Hegel spells out what Aquinas doesn't, and thus he presents an argument that while resembling Aquinas's, is more complete and thus more plausible than Aquinas's.

As I suggested in Chapter 8, the gist of Hegel's argument appears to have been laid out much earlier in Plato's arguments in the *Republic*, *Timaeus*, and *Philebus* regarding transcendence, unity, and the Good. And neither Plato's argument nor Hegel's depends upon the specific, Aristotelian cosmology that Aquinas adopts. So the demise of Aristotle's cosmology, in modern times, doesn't affect the Plato/Hegel argument.

St Anselm's ontological argument

A final traditional argument for God's existence is known as the "Ontological Argument." St Anselm proposed it in his *Proslogion* (1077–78), and Rene Descartes and other modern thinkers presented versions of it. This argument appeals to the common definition of God as "the sum of all perfections." It then points out that something that exists is surely more perfect than something that doesn't exist; so that God, who is the sum of *all* perfections, must exist.

Immanuel Kant criticized this argument by distinguishing existence from other predicates like goodness, blueness, and so forth. He argued that we have to be able to think of a thing's qualities apart from the question of whether the thing exists or not. So that we can say that a good blue dog is the same thing, a good blue dog, regardless of whether it exists or not. But if it's the same thing, it must have the same qualities. So its existence can't be one of its qualities, in the way that goodness and blueness are.

Because of Kant's critique, the "ontological argument" hasn't been widely accepted in the last couple of centuries. It seems too outrageously paradoxical to suggest that simply by inspecting something's definition, as "the sum of all perfections," you can conclude that it must exist.

However, the argument for God that I've given you from Plato and Hegel captures something that seems to be genuinely valid, in the ontological argument. The Plato/Hegel argument focuses on what I've called full reality, or reality as oneself, and suggests that the way to achieve such reality is through freedom and love. Secondly, it argues that if such reality is achieved, then there is a highest reality composed of freedom and love, which lends nature whatever full reality it possesses, and fulfills individuals in a way that nothing else can. (This is what we call "God.") And thirdly it argues that anyone who discusses these matters with an open mind, acts in a way that embodies the freedom and love that constitute the highest reality; so the highest reality *is*, to some extent at least, achieved.

This argument resembles the ontological argument in that its starting point is the concept of a highest, or full, reality, and it proceeds by arguing, as the ontological argument does, that there's something about the concept of a highest reality that makes it very difficult to deny that such a reality exists. According to Plato and Hegel, what makes it difficult to deny that the highest reality exists is that when we engage in argument, we seem to presuppose the presence of freedom and love, which (however) constitute the highest reality. So simply engaging in argument, presupposes God; much as, according to Anselm's argument, simply thinking about God, presupposes God's existence. Plato and Hegel bring out a "practical" side to Anselm's argument, which Anselm didn't bring out: that the *activity* of argument, or searching for the truth, has a divine quality.

And this seems like the right direction to move in, to reformulate Anselm's argument, since surely it's our activity of questioning our initial ideas and trying to find more adequate ones that gives plausibility to the idea of a "higher" and more perfect being, in the first place. So it's because of the phenomenon of free and loving "ascent," which Plato and Hegel bring to our attention, that people have taken seriously the possibility of the most perfect being that is the topic of Anselm's argument. And, indeed, our experience of free and loving "ascent" is the best evidence we could have of the reality of this being.

NOTES

Introduction, pp. 1–8

1. When I say that we have "direct" knowledge of a higher reality or God, I don't mean that this knowledge is simple and requires no interpretation or thought. What I mean is that we know this higher reality or God by (in part) *being* it, rather than through some channel that leads from it to us.

2. Aristotle, *Nicomachean Ethics* X.7, 1177a14–15. In the *Metaphysics*, Aristotle tells us that "since there is someone who is even above the student of nature (for nature [*phusis*] is one particular genus of what there is), the investigation of these things must also belong to him whose inquiry is universal and deals with primary substance. The study of nature is also a kind of wisdom but it is not the primary kind" (*Metaphysics* IV.3, 1005a32–35). So what is higher or "divine" is not only "in us," it is a feature of being as being. For a detailed account of how Aristotle is, in an important sense, a "Platonist," see Lloyd Gerson (2005). On the *Metaphysics* passage, see Irad Kimhi (2018), p. 27.

3. G. W. F. Hegel, HSL p. 149; SuW 5:164; GW 21:136. "The real," here, is *das Reale*. The infinite is "real" because, unlike the finite, it's self-determining. It makes itself what it is.

4. A. N. Whitehead (1933), p. 25.

5. Wittgenstein, *Notebooks 1914-1916* (1961), October 8, 1916. The "ladder" image is in *Tractatus Logico-Philosophicus* (1921), 6.54.

6. Wittgenstein, *Notebooks 1914-1916* (1961), October 7, 1916.

7. J. N. Findlay (1967), p. 197. More details on this in Chapter 2.

8. Thomas Nagel (2012), p. 17.

9. John McDowell (1994) and (2009), Michael Thompson (2008), Sebastian Rödl (2007), (2012), and (2018), Andrea Kern (2017), Wolfram Gobsch (2013) and (2017), and Irad Kimhi (2018). I discuss McDowell and Rödl in Chapter 2, below. Regarding Kimhi, see my next note.

10. Irad Kimhi endorses Aristotle's view that (as Kimhi puts it) "nature *is* a whole . . . but a *limited* one, since 'there is someone still further above the student of nature': the philosopher," who (in Kimhi's view, which he clearly imputes to Aristotle as well) studies "the logical 'I'" ([2018], p. 27 and p. 2). (I quoted in note 2 of this chapter, the passage from Aristotle's *Metaphysics* to which Kimhi is alluding.) Accordingly, Kimhi gives an extensive critique, in his Chapters 1 and 2, of Gottlob Frege (1848–1925),

one of the founding figures of "analytic philosophy," for whom an association of logic with the "I" or with "self-consciousness" would amount to an unacceptable "psychologism." Sebastian Rödl presents a parallel critique of Frege in his (2012), Chapter 1, and (2018), Chapter 2. When we reinstall the "I" in its place of authority in logic and metaphysics we reestablish the traditional hierarchy of the rational self vis-à-vis nonrational beings, not, however, as a separate being or domain, but as a mode of functioning in which the nonrational goes beyond or surpasses its nonrationality. This nondualistic hierarchy is the primary subject of this book.

Chapter 1: "A Worm! A God!", pp. 9–28

1 Lloyd Gerson says that from Plato's *Republic* "we learn that an embodied person is an ongoing identity crisis" ([2003], pp. 123–24). I have the impression that my presentation, inspired by Plato, of this "crisis" largely agrees with what Gerson finds in Plato.

2 By "inner freedom" I mean the inner process by which we make decisions, as opposed to the outer circumstances such as coercion by other people which may reduce what we might call our "outer freedom" (the options that are available for us to choose between). We can have what I call "inner freedom" regardless of what our outer circumstances may be if, as I say, we make up our own minds what to do. And when I speak of making up our own minds, I mean a process that involves some kind of thought, as opposed to simply doing whatever pops into one's head. I think we are often aware of not really making up our minds but simply reacting to desires or urges and postponing or choosing not to engage in the sort of thought that's involved in making up our minds. When we do this, we lack what I'm calling inner freedom. From this I hope it's clear that I'm not addressing the question of whether we have what many people call "free will," by which they mean the ability to act in a way that we're not "caused" to act. I think that what most of us primarily care about is not what "causes" what we do (which is perhaps a rather abstruse question), but whether we can really make up our minds what to do. (Certainly the two questions might be related, through some sort of high-level discussion.) It seems that we could hardly care about what we believe and what we do, if we truly believed that we don't ever really make up our minds what to believe or do. I'll discuss these issues in Chapter 3 and especially Chapter 7.

3 Socrates praises the "examined life" in Plato, *Apology of Socrates* 38a. Plato suggests his explanation of Socrates's praise in *Republic* books iv-vii, which I'll discuss in Chapters 5 and 6. The pursuit of truth and inner freedom (the "examined life") needn't prevent one from pursuing "lower" goals as well; it simply requires that the lower goals must be consistent with truth and inner freedom. The "usual assumption" that the self is equally present in any project, whether the project is "higher" or "lower," was advocated in ancient times by Protagoras and Epicurus, among others, and in modern times by thinkers like Thomas Hobbes, David Hume, Bertrand Russell, and Bernard Williams (1986). Versions of the "contrasting view," that the pursuit of truth and inner freedom makes us real as ourselves in a way that other pursuits don't, are advocated by Plato, Aristotle, the Stoics, the "Neoplatonists," Immanuel Kant, Hegel, Emerson, and in our time by writers including Gary Watson (1975), Charles Taylor (Introduction and papers 1-5 in [1985], volume 1), Susan Wolf (1990), and Sebastian Rödl (2007, 2012, 2018).

4 I'm less interested in the question of who influenced whom, historically, than in the question of what's true. But it does seem likely that Indian thought influenced early Greek thinkers, through contacts via well-documented trade routes. The influence may have run in the opposite direction, later on. See Thomas McEvilley (2002). The "modern" global dialogue is by no means the first one.

5 Karl Rahner (1978), p. 63. Fiona Ellis (2014) drew this passage in Rahner to my attention. Hegel articulated the same objection to conceptions of God as a separate being, in his critique of what he called the "spurious infinity" (*schlechte Unendlichkeit*), in his *Science of Logic* (1812–14) and elsewhere. I explain Hegel's critique in several chapters below and in chapter 3 of Wallace (2005).

6 Or, if you prefer, God could be the "outside" of the world, meaning that as the source of all that's real in the world, God surpasses it in all ways. (Is this the thought that inspires what people call "panentheism"?) Neither of these metaphors, that "God is inside the world" and that "the world is inside God," is meant to be taken literally as a statement about the spatial arrangement of two separate beings, so we don't have to interpret them as contradicting each other. I'll explain in Chapter 8 how Plato's comments about the divine can be understood as making it more "inner" than the world (and equally more "outer," in the sense of transcendent).

7 St Paul, Acts 17:28, "In him [that is, God] we live and move and have our being"; Augustine, *Confessions*, III.vi (11), "You [that is, God] were more inward [to me] than my most inward part." Paul's and Augustine's God is certainly "higher" than Paul or Augustine, but evidently not entirely separate from them. Many "Fathers of the Church" refer to the possibility of humans' *theosis* or "becoming God," which would hardly be possible if God were simply a separate being from us. "The Word of God became man, that thou mayest learn from man how man can become God" (Clement of Alexandria, *Exhortation to the Heathen*, ch. 1, par. 871). (See the Wikipedia article, "Divinization [Christian]," citing among many other sources the *Catechism of the Catholic Church*; and for commentary see Michael J. Christensen and Jeffery A. Wittung, eds. [2007].) Thus when Sam Harris (2014), p. 21, describes the Abrahamic religions as "incorrigibly dualistic . . . the human soul is conceived of as genuinely separate from the reality of God," he overlooks a considerable quantity of more or less "canonical" Christian writings. In recent times, A. N. Whitehead spoke of "the inclusion of God in every creature": "The world lives by its incarnation of God in itself" ([1926/1996], pp. 94, 156). Karl Rahner wrote, "*That* God really does not exist who operates and functions as an individual existent alongside other existents, and who would thus as it were be a member of the larger household of all reality" ([1978], p. 63). According to Paul Tillich, "To call God transcendent . . . does not mean that one must establish a 'superworld' of divine objects. It does mean that, within itself, the finite world points beyond itself. In other words, it is self-transcendent" ([1957], vol. 2, pp. 6–7). Though Tillich didn't credit Hegel, what Tillich is driving at here is made much clearer by Hegel in the accounts (in his *Science of Logic* and elsewhere) on which I draw in this book. It's certainly true that numerous writers have assumed that "God" would be "a being," and thus apparently quite separate from us. (A few random recent examples are Timothy A. Robinson [2002], p. xv, Owen Flanagan [2007], p. 259 note 11, and Ronald Dworkin [2013], p. 17.) And the same writer may slip from one way of describing God to another. But I think I've said enough to show that the conception of God as a separate being is not the only "traditional" religious conception in the west.

8   The common theme of "negative theology" that we can't know God because God is unlike anything that we are familiar with reflects the important truth that unlike the things around us, God is not "a being." So we can't know God in the way that we know the things around us. But Platonism points out that in the same way, and for the same reason, we can't know *ourselves*. For, because of our ongoing "identity crisis," we too are not simply "beings," in the way that (say) rocks might be. But it seems clear that once we give up the notion that we are "beings," we *can* know ourselves, namely through our awareness of our efforts to be free, and so forth. And in that way, Platonism says, we know God as well.

9   As a description of our fundamental challenge, the term "nihilism" was introduced by F. H. Jacobi and made famous by Friedrich Nietzsche. In his *Nihilism* (1969), Stanley Rosen refers frequently to Plato and to Hegel, but he doesn't focus on Plato's account of the soul's self-government or Hegel's corresponding account of inner freedom, which make it clear why a human being can't ultimately be satisfied by nihilism.

10 A particularly illuminating psychological account of aspects of nihilism is Donald Kalsched (2013).

11 In addition to Plato, Hegel, Emerson, Whitehead, Wittgenstein, J. N. Findlay, and Iris Murdoch, western philosopher mystics who left more or less systematic writings include Empedocles, Heraclitus, Parmenides, Plotinus, Iamblichus, Proclus, Pseudo-Dionysius, John Scotus Eriugena, Meister Eckhart, Shahab al-Din Suhrawardi, Muhyiddin Ibn Arabi, Nicolas Cusanus, Marsilio Ficino, Henry More, Ralph Cudworth, Nicolas Malebranche, Samuel Taylor Coleridge, F. W. J. Schelling, F. H. Bradley, J. M. E. McTaggart, and Henri Bergson.

12 Regarding the notion of mysticism as "other-worldly," it may be that Irwin and Adamson were led to this interpretation by the work of J. N. Findlay, who speaks of mysticism's "other-worldly geography" and the like. I criticize Findlay's account in Chapter 2. When Irwin and Adamson use Findlay's term as though it captures a defining characteristic of "mysticism," they neglect the more central traditional notion of a direct knowledge of God or the ultimate reality.

13 One could object that Plato and Hegel often seem to speak of "God" in the common way, not as "in" the world but as a separate being. With regard to Plato, as I'll explain in Chapters 5 and 8, this objection underestimates the implications of (a) his doctrine of higher degrees of reality in which the lower degrees "participate," (b) his description of the rational part of the soul as "divine" (*Timaeus* 90a), and (c) his evident view (*Timaeus* 29e-30a) that because God cannot be "jealous," God (the demiurge) *has to* create a world. These doctrines mean that God is clearly not "separate" from the world in the way that we often suppose. As far as I can see, the "mystical" interpretation is the only one that takes proper account of these features of Plato's writings. As for Hegel, my Hegel book (Wallace [2005]) shows in detail how he presents the divine as present in the world and directly knowable by us. Hegel didn't explicitly describe himself as a "mystic," but he came very close to doing so. In §82A of his *Encyclopedia Logic* (which is an extract from a lecture) he is reported as saying that "the meaning of the speculative [that is, of his own preferred kind of philosophy] is to be understood as being the same as what used in earlier times to be called 'mystical'. . . . When we speak of 'the mystical' nowadays, it is taken as a rule to be synonymous with what is mysterious and incomprehensible. . . . [However,] 'the mystical' is certainly something mysterious, but only for the understanding" (i.e., for *Verstand*, as opposed to Reason or *Vernunft*, on which "speculative" philosophy

is based). In his LPR, Hegel makes the same identification of mysticism with "speculative philosophy" (LPR 3:280, VPR 3:206) and describes the "*unio mystica*" as supposing that "God alone is true actuality, [so that] insofar as I have actuality I have it only in God" (LPR 1:444-445, VPR 1:332-333), which is a doctrine that we encounter repeatedly in his own works. Plus, he showed enthusiasm for such acknowledged mystics as Proclus, Meister Eckhart, Jelaluddin Rumi, and Jakob Boehme. For more on Hegel's rational mysticism, see Wallace (2005), pp. 104–9, 256 and (2010–2011), pp. 123–35.

14 If we had no trace of freedom, truth, love, or beauty in ourselves, we wouldn't be able to imagine what they could be, or dream of having them. So one might say that "philo-sophia," the "love of wisdom," already *is* wisdom, to a significant degree. (This of course does not require that this "wisdom" takes the form of "propositions" for whose truth one has evidence.)

15 Heinrich Heine (1981), p. 47, (1860), vol. 5, p. 99. Stanley Rosen makes the same mistake as Heine when he writes that "one may say that Hegel makes the suppression of nihilism dependent upon hybris, or the sanctioning of man's desire to be a god" ([1969], p. 234). Since hybris has everything to do with self-importance, someone who has become "divine" by transcending ordinary human self-importance is hardly engaged in hybris. See also the references in note 7 in this chapter to Christian teachings on *theiosis* or "becoming God."

16 Eckhart Tolle (1999), p. 187.

17 Insofar as it celebrates science, freedom, goodness, and so forth, humanism is beyond reproach. But insofar as it fails to identify the way in which these constitute what transcendence, infinity, and religion are about, it is limited and unfree. I discuss Ludwig Feuerbach's doctrine that humans, as such, are God in Chapter 3.

18 A. N. Whitehead (1925/1996), pp. 155–56.

19 "Auguries of Innocence," in William Blake (2005), p. 295.

20 On millenarian and apocalyptic hopes and terrorism, see Norman Cohn (1957/1970), and F. Dostoevsky, *Crime and Punishment* and *The Possessed*. It's possible to see some of this impatience in Plato's writings as well, but there it's combined (as I'll explain in Chapter 5) with the reconciliation that I describe here.

21 I will say some more about the issue of forgiving imperfection in Chapter 6.

22 The integrative efforts of Huston Smith (1976), Bernard McGinn (1991–), and Ken Wilber (2000) draw on Plato and, in some cases, on Hegel. Specialists in Plato and/or Hegel who defend rational mysticism (though not always under that name) are A. J. Festugiere (1935/1975), J. N. Findlay (1967) and (1974), Werner Beierwaltes (1972/2004), Jens Halfwassen (1992) and (1999/2005), Lloyd Gerson (2003) and (2013), and David J. Yount (2014) and (2017). I discuss Findlay in Chapter 2.

23 Insofar as beauty and the arts go beyond our daily efforts to stay alive, they illustrate very well the dimension of "higher" as opposed to "lower" kinds of functioning with which the Platonic tradition is concerned. As a powerful form of freedom and intelligent love, beauty and the arts show how rather than being flatly opposed to the physical world, freedom and love emerge from within it. And at the same time they constitute a kind of "thought" and they contribute to the higher reality and "truth." Our natural response to the outstanding achievements of every art form and to the beauty of nature is reverence. ("Beauty alone has this privilege, to be the most clearly

visible and the most loved"; Plato, *Phaedrus,* 250e.) I offer some thoughts about beauty's relation to freedom and thought in Chapter 2 (comments on Iris Murdoch) and in Chapter 7 and its footnotes.

24 "Pragmatism," as in C. S. Peirce, William James, and John Dewey, might be taken as implying that we should pursue truth not as such but only insofar as it can make a "practical difference." Traditional metaphysics suggests that the only way to determine whether any particular "difference" ought to be taken into account is through thought, and thus through the pursuit of truth as such, so that if the criterion of "making a practical difference" is supposed to be different from traditional metaphysics, it's either vacuous (because it doesn't tell us what a "practical" difference is) or dogmatic.

25 The articles on "Idealism," for example, in the online *Stanford Encyclopedia of Philosophy* (article by Paul Guyer and Rolf-Peter Horstmann, accessed in December 2015) and in the *Routledge Encyclopedia of Philosophy* (article by T. L. S. Sprigge) (1998) both describe the two basic forms of "idealism" in a way that makes them correspond to Berkeley's and Kant's versions, respectively.

26 See, for example, E. B. Holt et al. (1912), and Maurizio Ferraris (2015).

27 I give a general introduction to Hegel in Chapter 3. For a systematic outline of his unification of science, art, religion, and philosophy, see my "How Plato and Hegel Integrate the Sciences, the Arts, Religion, and Philosophy" (forthcoming).

28 Quotes from Emerson, *Nature* (first published 1836), Chapter VIII, and "The Method of Nature" (first published 1841), as reprinted in Emerson (2001), pp. 54 and 92.

29 R. G. Collingwood (1924), p. 36.

30 A. N. Whitehead (1929), p. 23.

31 Jonathan Lear (1990), pp. 219–21.

32 Robert M. Wallace (2005). On "true infinity," see especially Chapter 3. In Chapter 2 of the present book (footnote 5), I give references to some of the scholars who interpret Hegel as rejecting "transcendence" in favor of "immanence" and I explain how he is in fact formulating what I call a "true transcendence."

33 See note 7 to this chapter for citations.

34 Besides *Symposium* 210d, I mean *Republic* 490b ("Once getting near what really is and having intercourse with it and having begotten understanding and truth, he knows, truly lives, is nourished. . ."), 519c ("thinking that they had settled while still alive in the faraway Isles of the Blessed"), 585d ("a more true pleasure"), *Symposium* 211d ("And there in life . . . there if anywhere should a person live his life beholding that Beauty"), 212a-b ("The love of the gods belongs to anyone who has given birth to true virtue and nourished it, and if any human being could become immortal, it would be he"), and *Timaeus* 90c ("To the extent that human nature can partake of immortality, he can in no way fail to achieve this"). Recent scholarship and reference works generally seem to shy away from these passages.

35 To name only some of the other prominent writers who have been fed by Plato's thinking: Moses Maimonides, Jelaluddin Rumi, St Thomas Aquinas, Meister Eckhart, Benedict Spinoza, George Herbert, Thomas Traherne, Gottfried Wilhelm Leibniz, F. W. J. Schelling, William Blake, Percy Shelley, John Keats, Emerson, Walt Whitman, Virginia Woolf, T. S. Eliot, C. G. Jung, Paul Tillich, Karl Rahner . . . . More comprehensive historical narratives of Platonism in philosophy can be found

in John Findlay (1974), chapter 9; in the three volumes of Terence Irwin (2011); in Christoph Horn et al., eds. (2009), "Wichtige Stationen der Wirkungsgeschichte," pp. 387-522; and in Hans Blumenberg (1996). Important parts of the story are examined by Terence Irwin (1989), Stephen R. L. Clark (2013), Peter Adamson (2014), Algis Uzdavinys (2008), Lloyd P. Gerson (2005) and (2013), Lloyd P. Gerson, ed. (2011), Stephen Menn (1998), Carlos Fraenkel (2013), Arbogast Schmitt (2012), Douglas Hedley and Sarah Hutton, eds. (2008), Iris Murdoch (1993) (on Plato, Schopenhauer, Wittgenstein), Frederick Beiser (2009) (on aesthetic Platonism in Germany), Andrew Cole (2014) (on Neoplatonism and Hegel), A. J. Festugiere (1935/1975), Werner Beierwaltes (1972/2004), Jens Halfwassen (1992, 1999/2005), Arthur Versluis (2014) (on the Platonism of Bronson Alcott and Ralph Waldo Emerson), Stuart Gerry Brown (1945), and Jay Bregman (1990). For commentary on important parts of Platonism's deep and pretty much uninterrupted influence in literature, see Anna Baldwin and Sarah Hutton, eds. (1994), and Martha Nussbaum (2003), Part III.

Chapter 2: "That which shows God in me, fortifies me", pp. 29–66

1 Emerson, "An Address" (1838); in Emerson (2001), p. 74.

2 St Paul: Acts 17:28. For St Athanasius and others, see the Wikipedia article, "Divinization [Christian]," citing among many other sources the *Catechism of the Catholic Church*; and see Michael J. Christensen and Jeffery A. Wittung, eds. (2007). This theme in Christian thought is ignored by many writers, including Stanley Rosen. Citing the intimate connection that Hegel claims to establish between God and humans, Rosen writes that "it seems evident that [Hegel] cannot be an orthodox Christian" ([2014], p. 452). But in view of the authoritative Christian literature that I just mentioned, the evidence that Rosen cites does not establish this.

3 *The Essential Rumi* (2004), p. 13.

4 Karl Rahner (1978), p. 63.

5 Scholars who think that Hegel rejects transcendence in favor of immanence include J. N. Findlay (1967), p. 17 ("a conception of radically immanent teleology that is largely a borrowing from Hegel"); Karl Ameriks, "The Legacy of Idealism in the Philosophy of Feuerbach, Marx, and Kierkegaard" (2000), pp. 259–60, and *Kant and the Fate of Autonomy* (2000), pp. 186 ("traditional transcendent notions of . . . divinity") and 336 ("a separate deity"); Terry Pinkard (2002), p. 303; William Desmond (2003), p. 2; Frederick Beiser (2005), pp. 44, 143; Stephen Houlgate (2006), p. 435; A. W. Moore (2012), p. 178; and Ludwig Siep in N. Mooren and M. Quante, eds. (2018), p. 770 ("immanentistisch") and p. 772. Of course if by "transcendent" you simply mean "separate from the world," then it's true that Hegel's God isn't "transcendent." But then you've abandoned the word's etymology ("going beyond," that is, essentially surpassing the world) in favor of a notion, separateness, that has no place in sophisticated theology.

6 See Wallace (2005), chapter 3, for more on this argument in Hegel.

7 Hegel's God is more "personal" than we are because it's "supremely free" (HSL p. 841, SuW 6:570, GW 12:251). This ultimate, non-anthropomorphic God loves us,

Hegel shows, as "its own self." ("The universal . . . could also be called *free love* and *boundless blessedness,* for it bears itself towards what is different from it as towards its own self" [HSL, p. 603, SuW 6:277, GW 12:35].) In this teaching, Hegel is elaborating on Plato's doctrine that the demiurge, the creator, wanted the world "to become as much like himself as was possible" (*Timaeus* 29e).

8   A recent author who identifies God with the true Good is Robert M. Adams (1999). As Adams notes, his book is very Platonic. In Chapters 5–8 I will show how this identification of God with the true Good works in Plato's texts.

9   On the famous line in Luke, see Ilaria Ramelli (2009), available online (March 2013).

10 Plotinus, *Enneads*, V.I.11 (emphasis added). Elsewhere, unfortunately, Plotinus often contrasts "here," our present life, with "there," our life when we return to the One, thus seeming to suggest that the One is not "here" within us, but somewhere else. Confusing metaphors!

11 On the continuity between Plato and the so-called "Neoplatonists," see Lloyd Gerson (2013) and David J. Yount (2014). Gerson traces a similar continuity between Plato and Aristotle in his (2005).

12 Augustine, *Confessions*, III.vi.11, p. 43.

13 We "worship" Spinoza's "God or Nature" by loving it as the sole complete precondition of our existence and flourishing, and this worship raises us above our less intelligent affects such as fear and greed. In this way, Spinoza's God is "higher." We make a vertical "ascent" from (as Spinoza says) bondage to freedom, and this vertical dimension is analogous to the dimension by which God, for traditional Jews and Christians, surpasses what's merely human. This analogy between Spinoza's thinking and traditional theism wasn't recognized by his critics, or by such surveyors of philosophical theology as Hume in his *Dialogues Concerning Natural Religion*, Rousseau in his *Emile*, and Kant in his Critiques and his other writings. Kant describes Spinozism and other forms of what he calls "enthusiasm" (*Schwärmerei*) as "a concept in which the understanding is simultaneously exhausted and all thinking itself has an end" ("The End of All Things," Ak. 8:336)—a description that hardly does justice to Spinoza's "intellectual love of God." However, Spinoza's thinking differs from most of the Platonic tradition in reducing valuing to appetitive desiring, and in failing to give an account of our love of other people. Spinoza privileges theory over practice and knowledge over action, and he thinks he knows nature (which is to say, reality as a whole) as egoistic and mechanistic. So, like Thomas Hobbes, Spinoza preaches what we might call enlightened self-interest, rather than the kind of honesty or justice that expresses one's recognition of the inherent value of other people. Indeed, since as I've suggested an egoist is governed by his boundaries vis-à-vis others and thus isn't fully self-governed or free, the egoism that Spinoza claims to know to be true undermines his claim to be presenting a doctrine of liberation. So Kant and others were right to fear that Spinoza had not identified a basis in reality for the kind of value or the kind of value-directed human functioning that they cared about. Since I share Kant's concern about these issues, I favor Plato's (and Hegel's) conception of ascent, in which we explore value and reality (practice and theory, action and knowledge) inseparably, over Spinoza's in which what value there is, is an aftereffect of an apparently value-free reality. And I likewise favor Plato's and Hegel's "God" over Spinoza's "God." But a balanced assessment of Spinoza must acknowledge that unlike, say, Hobbes, he was in fact trying to present a form of ascent or inner freedom, and thus a kind of transcendence.

14 The best studies of Kant's theology that I know of are Christopher J. Insole (2013) and (2016), though Insole doesn't seem to appreciate the full cogency of non-Christian Platonic theology.

15 My most detailed and comprehensive account of Hegel is Wallace (2005). For more concentrated and better focused accounts, see Wallace, "How G. W. F. Hegel's Broadly Platonic Idealism Explains Knowledge, Value, and Freedom," forthcoming in B. Göcke and J. R. Farris, eds., *Rethinking Idealism and Immaterialism*, and also Wallace (2018).

16 Emerson (1979), "The Over-Soul," p. 160. On Emerson's Platonism, see Stuart Gerry Brown (1945), Jay Bregman (1990), and chapter 4 of Arthur Versluis (2014).

17 Emerson (1979), pp. 40 and 37.

18 Emerson (1979), p. 161.

19 Robert D. Richardson Jr. (1995), pp. 472–75.

20 William James's failure to connect with Emerson's notion of the "self-existing Supreme Cause" can be seen in *The Varieties of Religious Experience* (1902/1987), p. 36 (in Lecture 2), where he alludes to Emerson's "worship of mere abstract laws," p. 58 (in Lecture 3) ("abstract divineness of things"), and p. 461 n. 82 (in Lecture 20) ("only a medium of communion").

21 William James, *A Pluralistic Universe* (1909/1987), pp. 770–81. It seems that James's friend and colleague, Josiah Royce, who espoused a variety of "idealism," hadn't been able to explain this for him either.

22 Heidegger spoke occasionally, in a mythic/prophetic manner, of "a god," but left it entirely unclear what this "god" might be or how we might relate to it.

23 A.N. Whitehead (1933), p. 25.

24 A.N. Whitehead (1926/1996), p. 155.

25 Whitehead (1926/1996), pp. 155–60.

26 One not insignificant index of the limitedness of Whitehead's influence today is the fact that A. W. Moore's quite broadly conceived *The Evolution of Modern Metaphysics* (2012) contains no discussion of Whitehead. (Nor, unfortunately, of Murdoch or Polanyi, either.)

27 Whitehead's admirer Charles Hartshorne doesn't clarify the role of freedom in transcendence any more than Whitehead did. Hartshorne describes "process theism" or "panentheism" as the doctrine of an "eternal-temporal consciousness, knowing and including the world" ([1953/2000], p. 17). I applaud the non-separateness of God and world which the view aims to achieve, but I doubt that the best final account of their relationship is that God "includes" the world (or, as Hartshorne says elsewhere, that the world is a "constituent" [p. 19] of God). A "constituent" must apparently be real in the same sense in which that which it helps to constitute is real. In which case, that which it helps to constitute (namely, God) is limited by its relation to this equally real thing (the world), and thus is not infinite and not fully self-governing. Hartshorne accepts the consequence that God is not infinite (p. 436), but regards it as the only way to secure freedom for humans. But what he secures for us as "freedom" is only alternative possibilities, not rational self-government. Neither God nor humans, as Hartshorne describes them, are (fully) rationally self-governing. They are both finite, each limited by the other. It is not clear that there is anything here that deserves to be called "transcendence." Hartshorne doesn't consider the possibility (which I find in

Plato, Plotinus, Hegel, and Emerson) that our freedom or self-government might be identical to God's freedom or self-government. This view is not "pantheism," because it finds the divine freedom or self-government "in" what is *not* divine, namely, us. And neither is it "panentheism," as defined by Hartshorne, because it denies that we and God are equally real, one helping to "constitute" the other (and thus also limiting the other). Hartshorne's co-editor, William L. Reese, says that he and Hartshorne found Hegel too ambiguous to grasp in their categories (p. xi). My chapters 2–4 aim to explain the fairly straightforward proposal that I think Hartshorne and Reese failed to appreciate in Hegel, and my chapters 5 and 8 aim to identify the makings of this proposal in Plato.

28 Whitehead's vindication of religion vis-à-vis science in Whitehead (1926) boils down to the fact that religion "insists" (p. 143) on the value dimension of reality. Unlike Plato and Hegel, Whitehead doesn't point out the rational freedom that value-discussion has in common with science, or the way in which the pursuit both of science and of value brings into being a self-governing reality, and thus a reality "as itself." Once again, the Platonic notion of a higher degree of reality and the drama of ascent to it do not come into play.

29 Connecting the Good with reality amounts to wishful thinking: Bertrand Russell (1918/2004), pp. 5 and 24. And the same view in 1945: Bertrand Russell (1945), p. 126.

30 Bertrand Russell (1918/2004), p. 22.

31 G. E. Moore, "The Refutation of Idealism," *Mind* 12 (1903), pp. 433–53: "The trivial proposition which I propose to dispute is this: *esse* is *percipi*" [to be is to be perceived] (par. 5); Bertrand Russell (1912/1959), p. 14: "Very many philosophers, perhaps a majority, have held that there is nothing real except minds and their ideas. Such philosophers are called 'idealists.'" These are their descriptions of the "idealism," represented in their day by Bradley and Bosanquet, which they seek to unseat. You will note (see especially the Introduction and Chapter 3) that nothing that I say about rational mysticism in this book depends upon accepting this kind of "idealism."

32 The numbers indicate Wittgenstein's numbered paragraphs. The translations are my own, starting primarily from the Pears/McGuinness translation (1961) but favoring a somewhat more literal approach.

33 Wittgenstein (1961), October 7, 1916.

34 Wittgenstein (1961), October 8, 1916 (translation slightly revised).

35 A. W. Moore heroically takes Wittgenstein's doctrine of "nonsense" at face value, allowing that in a useful sense ethics, aesthetics, and Wittgenstein's own presentation of "value," "God," and "the mystical" may be "nonsense"—and explaining in detail why this needn't prevent them from containing "inexpressible" but genuine "knowledge" ([1997], pp. 216–18). What seems missing here, as in Wittgenstein himself, is an appreciation of the straightforward kind of knowledge that results when we see how science, art, and other ways of rising above natural stimulus-and-response bring a new kind of reality into the world. Namely, the reality of what governs itself, through (various kinds of) "reason."

36 In fact Wittgenstein seems to dismiss inner experience as of interest only to "psychology" (6.423, "the will as a phenomenon is only of interest to psychology"). Presumably he thinks that inner experience is merely an additional set of "facts," included in the "world" and not transcending it. But this simply presupposes that our

fundamental experience is the registering (describing) of "facts" or "phenomena," rather than the drama that Plato and Hegel describe, in which what we're aware of is the effort of what we would like to be, to emerge. So that the activity of describing is fully intelligible to us only as one aspect of this drama that we are.

37 A. W. Moore interprets Wittgenstein's gnomic remarks about "good or bad willing" changing the world only through the world's "waxing or waning as a whole" (6.43) as alluding to an issue of "wholeness, autonomy, integrity, being at one with the world" (Moore [2001], p. 194; compare Moore [2012], p. 252). This may be a correct interpretation, but Wittgenstein is hardly helpful on the subject of wholeness, autonomy, or integrity. On a topic on which others whom he doesn't name (Plato, Kant, Hegel) have written many analytical pages, Wittgenstein offers us only a single uninterpreted metaphor.

38 Later, Wittgenstein also read Tolstoy, William James, Kierkegaard, and Angelus Silesius. See B. F. McGuinness (1966). On Schopenhauer's influence on Wittgenstein, see Iris Murdoch (1992), chapters 1–3, Bryan Magee (1997), chapter 14, and A.W. Moore (2001), p. 226. Wittgenstein gives no sign of having read Plato, Kant, or Hegel with the degree of interest with which he had initially read Schopenhauer.

39 "Statements of value . . . are simply expressions of emotion": Ayer (1946, n.d.), p. 103. Ayer stated in his Preface (p. 31) that his "views . . . derive from the doctrines of Bertrand Russell and Wittgenstein."

40 Ayer's discussion of "mystical intuition" on pp. 118–19 of Ayer (1946) makes no reference to Wittgenstein's account of "the mystical" in the *Tractatus*.

41 Martin Heidegger "demonized" science quite literally: the spiritual "enfeeblement" ([1953/1961], p. 37) produced by "the onslaught of what we call the demonic" (p. 38) is exemplified by science (pp. 39–40). And he was systematically anti-Platonic: In Plato, "the vision makes the thing. Now this vision becomes decisive, instead of the thing itself" (p. 153). Heidegger didn't notice how the thing's own "vision" (the *idea*) enables it to *be* "itself," by pursuing the Good rather than being determined by its heritage and environment; nor did he notice how the activity of modern science does the same thing, insofar as it enables us to be guided by truth rather than by mere opinion.

42 Findlay describes the first volume and a half of his two volumes as articulating "a conception of radically immanent teleology that is largely a borrowing from Hegel" ([1967], p.17). See also Findlay (1967), p. 197: "Whereas for Hegel the alienation in question is exclusively a this-world affair, on our view it covers another world or worlds as much as our own"; and the title of Findlay (1967) Chapter 6: "Other-worldly Geography."

43 HSL p. 145 (translation revised); GW 21:133; SuW 5:160.

44 As Plato says, "The lover is turned toward the great sea of beauty" (*Symposium* 210d). Regarding the role of art in unification through love, Plato is famously critical of the arts in *Republic* books ii, iii, and x. But he is also well aware that he himself is an artist (Socrates at *Republic* 488a: "How greedy for images I am"). Plato is critical of the arts and of popular religion because he wants to purify them, and he wants to purify them because he sees that they contain an important germ of truth, or of the unification that Murdoch speaks of here. Hegel, for his part, brings art and divinity together (via religion and philosophy) in a similar way under the rubric of "Absolute Spirit" in his *Encyclopedia of the Philosophical Sciences*. I explain this Hegelian unification in Wallace (2018).

45 Wilfrid Sellars, "Philosophy and the Scientific Image of Man," in his (1963), p. 4.

46 Wilfrid Sellars, op. cit., p. 40.

47 Wilfrid Sellars (1997), p. 45. With the mock-French title, *Meditations Hegeliennes*, Sellars is alluding to Edmund Husserl's *Cartesian Meditations*, in which Husserl explored themes that he took to be Cartesian. So Sellars is suggesting that his own essay has an important affinity with Hegel.

48 This is Kant's problem, which he addresses in the "Schematism" section of the *Critique of Pure Reason*, of how pure concepts or categories, such as causality and substance, can apply to the material that we're "given" by sensation. On how Salomon Maimon brought out this problem for Kant, in a way that suggests the inadequacy of mere "schematism" as a solution, see Frederick C. Beiser (1987), pp. 285–99.

49 For an explanation of Hegel's contrast between what's "concrete" and what's "abstract," together with his notion of the "concrete universal," see Wallace (2005) pp. 228–30.

50 McDowell argues in this essay that rather than "arguing that there can be self-conscious individuals only in mutually recognitive communities," Hegel "makes the attempt to disavow dependence on what is in fact one's own life vivid with the image of trying to end the life of the other that confronts one" ([2009], pp. 154, 162). In Wallace (2005), I came to a similar conclusion that "Hegel's argument for mutual recognition does not make anything a 'social construct'" (p. 289). Robert Brandom had asserted (and in this he has been followed by Robert Pippin and Terry Pinkard) that "to be a self . . . is to be taken or treated as one by those one takes or treats as one; to be recognized by those one recognizes" ([2002], pp. 216–17). I replied that "what freedom requires, according to the 'recognition' argument in [Hegel's *Encyclopedia*'s] *Philosophy of Spirit*, is not membership in a mutual-recognition club, but willingness to accept objectively-qualified others into the club that one wants to belong to, objectively, oneself" (Wallace [2005], p. 289). An interpretation of Hegel that resembles mine has now been argued with much greater textual detail by Jens Rometsch (2017). To Brandom's social constructivism, McDowell replied that "if self-legislation of rational norms is not to be a random leap in the dark, it must be seen as an acknowledgement of an authority that the norms have anyway. . . . What controls one's life is still in oneself, in whatever it is about one that enables one to recognize that the norms are authoritative. But their authority is not a creature of one's recognition" ([2009] p. 105; see his more detailed responses to Pippin's social constructivism, pp. 166–184 and 185–203). I obviously agree with McDowell in objecting to random leaps in the dark. See also Sebastian Rödl (2007), pp. 114–20.

51 HSL pp. 145–146 (emphasis added by Miller; translation revised by myself, because Miller didn't catch the reflexive aspect of "*Hinausgehen über sich*"); GW 21:133; SuW 5:160.

52 Wolfram Gobsch gives a detailed and illuminating account of the difference between John McDowell and Hegel in his (2017).

53 For more on this ascent to infinity or "reality" in Hegel see Wallace (2005), Chapter 3; Wallace (2018); and Wallace (forthcoming). For extensive discussions of the "transformation" of animal nature into rational nature, see Andrea Kern and Christian Kietzmann, eds. (2017).

54 Deriving thought's categories from its dealings with time, Rödl's CT overcomes the divorce between forms of intuition and forms of thought, by which Kant unintentionally allowed room for metaphysical skepticism (CT p. 42). In this solution, Rödl in effect follows Salomon Maimon (Beiser [1987], pp. 300–1) and Hegel (*Encyclopedia*, part 2, on space and time).

55 According to Irad Kimhi, who is opposing the main twentieth-century tradition in philosophical logic (Frege, Russell, Quine), "The various capacities which philosophical logic finds itself called upon to elucidate—capacities for *judgment*, for *language*, for the deployment of *logical words*... and for *self-consciousness*...—are all one and the same capacity" ([2018], p. 16, emphasis added). *Self-consciousness* is this capacity because "the impossibility of *thinking* contradictory judgments together is a matter of the self-consciousness of the *together*" (p. 53.) (There is no "I" in something that "thinks" contradictory judgments "together.") As for *logical words*, "Conjunction is essential to the act of bringing several judgments together in one consciousness. This act cannot be expressed by a mere *list* of assertions one after another—for each item on the list might belong to a different state of consciousness" (p. 58). And "negation is essential to the act of identifying ourselves as disagreeing with a judgment" (p. 58). Finally, *language* is essential to logic insofar as language expresses the self-conscious commitments and disagreements that are the business of logical words. Frege's "linguistic turn" is "partial and incomplete," insofar as he allows for intellects that could be engaged with content without "thinking *thinking*" (p. 64), that is, without self-consciousness. Whereas Kant correctly, in Kimhi's view, finds this "notion of activity... incoherent: a form of intellectual activity separate from self-consciousness of the activity" (p. 64). But if logic, language, and self-consciousness are all the same capacity, then the Frege-Russell-Quine effort to expel the self and so-called "psychologism" from logic and science is futile, and we must consider the possibility that the self is as real as or more real than anything else. Kimhi refers to this result as "the unity of thinking and being" (Kimhi [2018], p. 28).

56 Another very helpful essay that Rödl published in 2017 on the identity of rational spontaneity and material substance (or on what I call the material world's transcending itself) is his "Selbsterkenntnis des Selbstbewegers" (2017).

57 As Hegel confirms with his comment at HSL 138; GW 21:125; SuW 5:150 on infinity as the advent of "freedom."

58 Walt Whitman, *Leaves of Grass* (1855/1976), sections 48–50.

Chapter 3: Freedom and full reality, pp. 67–86

1 Stephen Theron draws attention to John Henry Newman's *Essay on the Development of Christian Doctrine* (1845), as showing that doctrine and "orthodoxy" need not be viewed as beyond development. See Theron (2014), pp. 10, 292, 337. He acknowledges that because "development" itself is developing, Newman's view isn't yet widely recognized as "orthodox."

2 Immanuel Kant, *Metaphysik L1* (Akad. 28:268), as quoted by Christopher J. Insole (2013), p. 75.

3 Beiser (1987) gives a vivid account of the intellectual and cultural situation in Germany at the end of the eighteenth century, to which Hegel responded.

4 *The Marx-Engels Reader*, p. 302.

5 HSL p. 603, SuW 6:277, GW 12: 35.

6   Ludwig Feuerbach (1957, originally published 1854), p. 78.

7   Ludwig Feuerbach (1957), p. 86 (emphasis added).

8   Ludwig Feuerbach, "Preliminary Theses for the Reform of Philosophy" (1842), in Feuerbach, *The Fiery Brook* (1972), p. 166; emphasis added.

9   *The Fiery Brook* (1972), p. 168.

10 Feuerbach, Preface to the second edition of *The Essence of Christianity* (1843), in *The Fiery Brook* (1972), p. 252; emphasis in the original.

11 John Edward Toews (1980), pp. 175–99, describes the biographical and historical context of Feuerbach's proclivity for dualism.

12 On Hegel's account of "contradiction" and how it relates to his ethics and theology, see Wallace (2005), chapter 4 on "contradiction" and chapters 3–6 on ethics and theology.

13 *The Marx-Engels Reader*, p. 301.

14 It's true, of course, that some people who have been described as "mystics" show little interest in reason. But the primary meaning of mysticism is not a rejection of reason, but the direct or immediate knowing of God.

15 On this recurring pattern see Cohn (1957/1970).

16 Hegel, LPWH (1975), pp. 198–206.

17 Hegel, LPWH (1975), p. 197.

18 Hegel, LPWH (1975), p. 67.

19 For a detailed account of Absolute Spirit, see my "How Plato and Hegel Integrate the Sciences, the Arts, Religion, and Philosophy" (forthcoming). When Hegel wrote in his *Philosophy of Right*, §258R, that "the state consists in the march of God in the world," he immediately went on to explain that "in considering the Idea of the state, we must not have any particular states or particular institutions in mind; instead, we should consider the Idea, this actual God, in its own right." And this "Idea," as I have said, is only explained in his *Science of Logic*.

20 From what I've said it should be clear that contrary to Francis Fukuyama's widely read essay, "The End of History?" (1989), Hegel has no truck with any idea of an "end of history" that could take place within time. In ascribing this idea to Hegel, Fukuyama didn't and couldn't cite Hegel's texts. An illuminating discussion of the whole Fukuyama episode is provided by Philip T. Grier in Jon Stewart, ed. (1996), pp. 183–98.

21 The best-known promoter of a "non-metaphysical Hegel" was Klaus Hartmann (1972).

22 Terry Pinkard (2012), p. 18.

23 Lloyd Gerson (2013), p. 10.

24 Pippin (2018), p. 9. William F. Bristow draws a similar contrast between Platonism and "subjectivity" in his (2007), pp. 113–14.

25 Plato in fact presents in book x of his *Laws* an influential "cosmological argument" for God as a self-moving first mover. "The motion which can generate itself is infinitely superior" (894d). This discussion makes no direct reference to humans. But I will suggest in Chapter 8 that Plato's strongest argument for the reality of a self-mover is in fact his account of human rational freedom in the *Republic* and elsewhere.

26 Bertrand Russell (1912), chapter 1: "Very many philosophers, perhaps a majority, have held that there is nothing real except minds and their ideas. Such philosophers are called 'idealists.'" More recently, Miles Burnyeat ("Idealism and Greek Philosophy" [1982]) assumed that "idealism" is essentially Berkeley's view.

27 Actually, setting "God" on one side, doctrines that resemble Berkeley's were proposed by John Stuart Mill and Ernst Mach in the nineteenth century and by Bertrand Russell himself and A. J. Ayer in the twentieth century ("phenomenalism"). The relation between ideas and physical reality is a difficult issue, and Berkeley's solution to it is as plausible as some of the other leading proposals.

28 Kant doesn't say in so many words that the mind "imposes" key features on the world, but an alternative formulation is hard to find, and Kant's letter to Markus Herz of February 2, 1772 (cited by Robert Pippin [2018], p. 12 n. 17), invites such an interpretation.

29 Socrates says in his defense speech at his trial, as reported by Plato, that "the unexamined life is not worth living for men" (*Apology* 38a). Plato elaborates this thought into a theory of our inner freedom or self-government ("becoming entirely one," *Republic* 443d), which is evidently central to what he elsewhere calls "becoming like God" (*Theaetetus* 176b). That this is the world's fullest reality we can see from the *Timaeus*, in which the divine craftsman sought to make the world "as much like himself as was possible" (*Timaeus* 29e), and the design of human beings, in particular, is the main theme of the remainder of the dialogue. I develop this account of Plato in Chapters 5–8. Hegel's parallel thought is developed throughout his *Encyclopedia of the Philosophical Sciences*, as I explain in Wallace (2005).

30 George Santayana (1967), p. 63. Similar complaints have been registered by many "new realists," from 1912 (E.B. Holt et al., *The New Realism*) to 2015 (Maurizio Ferraris, *Introduction to the New Realism*).

31 Thomas Nagel writes that "a religious solution gives us a borrowed centrality through the concern of a supreme being" ([1986], p. 210). Nagel doesn't envisage the possibility that Plato and Hegel propose, that we are "central" insofar as we *participate in* the supreme being.

32 F. H. Bradley maintained in his *Appearance and Reality* (1893) that "our experience, where relational, is not true" (p. 29). (Compare p. 322: "To be defined from without is, in principle, to be distracted within.") His thesis appears to depend on the Hegelian notion that I'm presenting, that what succeeds in being itself is more real "as itself," and in that sense is more real, period, and more "true." Unfortunately, Bradley didn't explore the way we *experience* being real as ourselves, by thinking rather than being merely reactive about what to do and what to believe. Consequently, he didn't link his thesis about "relations" to the Platonic process of "ascent" or its Hegelian equivalent. The widespread failure to make this linkage clear was a major factor in the confusions that have prevailed about "idealism" in the twentieth century and down to the present.

33 *On the Genealogy of Morality*, third treatise, section 25.

34 *The Essential Rumi* (2004), p. 123.

35 This is the gist of Hegel's refutation of "rational egoism" in his HSL (1812/1814) and his *Encyclopedia* (1817ff.) (see Wallace [2005], pp. 126–40, 260–65, and 319–20). For Plato's version of the same argument, see Chapters 7 and 8.

36 One problem with much discussion of causation is that people often assume that genuine causes must be "physical." This would imply that when we say that we believe something because we have good reasons for believing it, this is not a "causal" explanation. But this seems arbitrary. See S. Goetz and C. Taliaferro (2011), chs. 6 and 7, and Rödl (2007), passim.

37 Interesting questions about our capacity for rational self-guidance have been raised by Benjamin Libet's well-known experiments about the relationship in time between electrical "readiness potential" in the brain and subjects' awareness of making a decision. There seems to be no good reason to think that Libet's experiments demonstrate that we aren't capable at all of rational self-guidance. They do suggest, which should be no surprise, that much of our mental processing is unconscious. But it doesn't follow from this that our actual decisions aren't conscious. For a detailed critique of Libet's interpretation of his experiments, see Alfred Mele (2009), Chapters 3 and 4. It would be quite unfortunate if Libet's experiments did demonstrate what he thinks they do, since this would imply that we aren't capable of conscious reasoning about whether they do this.

Chapter 4: Full reality is God, pp. 87–104

1 Plato suggests this (as I'll explain in Chapters 5–8) through his account of the "soul" and "intellect" in his *Republic*, *Phaedrus*, and *Timaeus*, and his account of immortality in his *Symposium*.

2 Plotinus, *Enneads*, V.I.11. It is certainly the case that Plato normally speaks of the "demiurge" or "intellect" or "the Good" as though it were a separate being from the world. This is because he is telling only a "likely story" (as he says in the *Timaeus* [29d]) or giving us a preliminary sketch (as he says in the *Republic* [435d]). But I will show in Chapter 8 that the connection between humans and God which Plato envisages (the philosopher "becomes like God" [*Theaetetus* 176b] by caring for his "divine part" [*Timaeus* 90a], and God in his turn cannot be "jealous" but must create a world [*Timaeus* 29e-30a]) can reasonably be summed up in an image like Plotinus's.

3 *The Essential Rumi* (2004), p. 13.

4 The response to "doubt"—suggesting that doubt itself helps to constitute God—that I've given in this section is articulated by Hegel in his *Science of Logic*, as I explain in Wallace (2005), pp. 109–16. Plato seems to suggest the same response when he describes Socrates as lacking knowledge of the Good, but continuing to seek it (*Republic* 506c), and goes on to describe the (seeking) philosopher as becoming like God (*Theaetetus* 176a, *Symposium* 212b).

5 In remarks like this one in his *Opus postumum* (which is a manuscript that he left at his death), Kant appears to abandon the unstable solution to the problem of divine creation and human freedom which he had presented in his major published works of the 1780s and 1790s. For a detailed account of the unfolding of Kant's thought on these issues, see Insole (2013), and for an overview see Insole (2016).

6 Richard Dawkins (2006), p. 31.

7 C. S. Lewis (2001), p. 37.

8   Hegel's whole system is concerned with the issue of being self-governing by being guided by something higher; and this higher guide plays the same role, in Hegel's thinking, that the Good plays in Plato. Indeed, it appears under the name of the "Good" in the final section of Hegel's *Science of Logic*, on the "Absolute Idea." For a detailed account of how "ascent" to higher standards structures Hegel's metaphysics and theology, from "true infinity" to "absolute Spirit," see Wallace (2005), Chapters 3–6. Bertrand Russell misread Hegel in the same way that Lewis did: "In Hegel . . . not only evil, but good also, is regarded as illusory" ([2004], p. 8). Russell and Lewis were probably misled by the ostensibly Hegelian F. H. Bradley, who wrote that "goodness is a subordinate and, therefore, a self-contradictory aspect of the universe" ([1893], p. 371; on his relation to Hegel see p. 318 n.1). Bradley didn't notice how, in Hegel as in Plato, the finite becomes more "real" precisely by being guided by a higher standard, or how that standard finally appears in Hegel's *Logic* as the "Good," itself.

9   Lewis (2001), pp. 26–27.

10 Fritjof Capra (1977); Fred Alan Wolf (1996); Deepak Chopra (1996); "What the 'Bleep' Do We Know?" (film, 2004).

11 Chapter 25 of *The Daodejing* (2001), p. 175. I've altered the translation of the final word, following the translators' "Important Terms," p. 394.

12 In his classic study, *Natural Supernaturalism. Tradition and Revolution in Romantic Literature* (1971), M. H. Abrams takes it that the Romantic poets' "natural supernaturalism" (p. 68) breaks with the outright supernaturalism and outright transcendence that were postulated by premodern theology ("displacement from a supernatural to a natural frame of reference" [p. 13]). My thesis in this book is that sophisticated premodern religious thinkers like Plato, Plotinus, and Augustine located God "within us" and thus within nature as well as "beyond us" and beyond nature, so that the Romantics' "natural supernaturalism" in fact *continued*, rather than breaking with, the most sophisticated premodern tradition (the one that understood what true transcendence must be like).

13 I should add that some institutions such as the Roman Catholic Church impart a sophisticated Augustinian philosophical theology, and thus a conception of transcendence that doesn't make it in principle "separate," to their more intellectually inclined members.

14 My disagreement with Charles Taylor about God, "belief," and "transcendence" or "immanence" begins with his stimulating book, *Hegel* (1975), in which I think he failed to understand Hegel's critique, in his *Science of Logic*, of the conventional conception of transcendence (which Hegel calls the "spurious infinity"). I explain Hegel's critique of the conventional conception of transcendence, and I discuss Taylor's interpretation of Hegel, in Chapter 3 of Wallace (2005).

15 As in Thomas Nagel's *Secular Philosophy and the Religious Temperament* (2009) and Michael B. Gill's *The British Moralists on Human Nature and the Birth of Secular Ethics* (2011).

16 This discussion began with Aldous Huxley (1945) and (1954), and includes R. C. Zaehner (1957) (much of which is a critique of Huxley), Steven T. Katz, ed. (1978), Robert K. C. Forman, ed. (1990), Robert K. C. Forman (1999), Jerome Gellman (2001), and Jerome Gellmann, "Mysticism," Stanford Encyclopedia of Philosophy, online 2010.

17 Unfortunately, Huxley set himself up for the critique that Zaehner and Katz directed at him because he placed great weight on the extraordinary experiences of a relatively small number of people who have subjected themselves to extreme mental and moral discipline. So Zaehner and Katz could reasonably ask, Why has this discipline apparently produced quite different results in different cultures? Huxley wasn't aware of the argument for a mystical higher reality which Plato and Hegel based on more "ordinary" experiences.

18 Zaehner (1957) stresses this issue of the difference between monistic and theistic mystical experiences.

Chapter 5: Plato's progress, pp. 105–134

1 There is ongoing scholarly disagreement about the respective roles of politics and religious issues in Socrates's trial and conviction. (See Thomas C. Brickhouse and Nicholas D. Smith [2002].) The accusers' allegations were religious, not political. But it seems safe to say that many of the jurors must have been aware, from long observation and gossip, that a significant number of Socrates's associates were not supporters of Athens's democracy. And it's all but certain that a large majority of the jury in the trial identified with the democratic side.

2 F. Nietzsche (1967), p. 519. "*Ressentiment*," French for "resentment," connotes a seeking for revenge.

3 In his *Treatise* (1978), David Hume objects to the doctrine that "every rational creature is obliged . . . to regulate his actions by reason" (p. 413), maintaining on the contrary that "reason is, and ought only to be the slave of the passions, and can never pretend to any other office than to serve and obey them" (p. 415). Hume doesn't explain where the authority of this "*ought* only to be" comes from. Friedrich Nietzsche, in his *Zarathustra* (1883–85), probably has both Christianity and Platonism in mind in his highly critical sections "On the Afterworldly" and "On the Despisers of the Body." We can see from these sections that Nietzsche assumes that "pure spirit and the good as such" (whose invention by Plato he laments in his *Beyond Good and Evil* [1966], p. 2) will "despise" the body and its desires. A similar view of Plato is promoted by Russell (1945); by Martha Nussbaum (1986), Chapters 5 and 6 on Plato; and by Simon Blackburn (2007). A different view is represented by Terence Irwin (1989), pp. 114–15; Richard Kraut, in his Introduction to Kraut, ed. (1992), pp. 9–10; and Lloyd Gerson (2003). Irwin and Kraut suggest that the mature Plato is not "other-worldly." Gerson defends the *Phaedo*, together with the dialogues that follow it, as presenting not an antagonistic dualism but a radical argument to the effect that the human body is less real than the soul. "The fundamental contrast for Plato is between the ideal disembodied person or self we strive to become and its embodied image" (p. 9), where an "image," for Plato, is less real than what it's an image of. I will develop a thought similar to Gerson's.

4 It has long been common to describe Plato's metaphysics as a "two-world" view, in which one world is that of the Forms and the other is that of bodies and sensation. I find this traditional label quite unfortunate, because it suggests that these "two worlds" are in some important way equal. They are both described as "worlds." Whereas the gist of what I think Plato wants to say about them is precisely that

they're not equal, because only the world of the Forms is fully "real." The "body" or the senses may present distractions, but they don't constitute a separate "world," and we don't need to go to another place to find the truth.

5 Gerson (2003), p. 57, underscores the positive nature of this passage.

6 I'm using the phrase "parts of the soul" loosely here, because it's widely used to refer to what Plato discusses in *Republic* book iv. In fact I sympathize with Jennifer Whiting's argument that Plato doesn't intend here to present a doctrine about the make-up of "the soul" as such, but only to describe the condition into which a soul can fall if it doesn't operate in an ideal way ("Psychic Contingency in the *Republic*" [2012]).

7 David Hume (1978), p. 415.

8 Skinner wrote that "the disputing of values is not only possible, it is interminable. To escape from it we must get outside the system. . . . When we can design small social interactions and, possibly, whole cultures with the confidence we bring to physical technology, the question of value will not be raised" (*Daedalus* [1961], pp. 535–36, 545). To which one can only reply that while Skinner himself might not raise it, others may have more inquiring minds than his. In contrast to Socrates (Plato, *Apology of Socrates*, 38a), Skinner in this essay was, in effect, an apostle of the "unexamined life."

9 See previous note.

10 A. J. Ayer ([1935/1946], p. 103) dramatically asserted that "in so far as statements of value . . . are not scientific, they are not in the literal sense significant, but are simply expressions of emotion which can be neither true nor false." Platonists, in response, point out that we appear to be able to think in a disciplined way about what's really good. I'll discuss Plato's account of this process in a bit more detail in the next chapter. For a nuanced defense of the idea that what's good could be a fact like other facts, see Thomas M. Scanlon (2016).

11 *Republic* 515d: "things that *are* more" (*mallon onta*); *Republic* 585c: "this *is* more" (*mallon einai*); *Timaeus* 28a: "It . . . never *really is*" (*ontos de oudepote on*); *Republic* 478d: "what purely is (*tou eilikrinos ontos*)." Further references can be found in Gregory Vlastos (1973 and 1981), pp. 43–44.

12 Plato doesn't explicitly describe the soul's "being itself" as making the soul more "real." But in the *Phaedo* he describes the soul and the Forms as "kin" (79d) and "like" one another (80b). In the original passage that we looked at, he associates the soul's being "by itself" (65d) with the Forms' becoming clear to it (65–66). And the conclusion of the *Phaedo* as a whole is, of course, that the soul is probably immortal, just as the Forms are. Thus we can probably safely suppose that one way in which the soul ideally approaches the Forms and fulfills its kinship with them is by becoming, like the Forms, more real than soulless bodies are.

13 You might ask whether the reality of this "Form" needs to be "separate" from the reality of the human being that's seeking to be guided by it. This issue has led to a great spilling of ink between Platonists, Aristotelians, and others. My suggestion would be that the Form needs to be "separate" in the sense that it needs to have a rational authority that we can't find in what we receive through our sense organs or our heredity. For the purposes of the present book, it's enough to say that we all accept this authority in practice, insofar as we engage in discussion of questions of truth and value. As Plato says, "Everyone wants the things that really *are* good"

(*Republic* 505d). Whatever despair we may sometimes express about determining what these really good things are, it's highly unlikely that B. F. Skinner or anyone else has been able to refrain from having such discussions with himself and his intimates when they were faced with major life decisions.

14 Lloyd Gerson points out that Plato's account of persons describes personhood as an accomplishment, rather than just a given (Gerson [2003], pp. 3, 113). Plato's student, Aristotle captures something like this in his account of "actuality" or "actualization" (*energeia*) as the fullest reality.

15 Influential recent commentators have criticized what they call Vlastos's "two worlds" interpretation of Plato in these papers (see G. Fine, "Knowledge and Belief in Republic V" [1978] and "Knowledge and Belief in Republic V-VII" [1990/1999], and P. Adamson (2014), ch. 22; and compare Irwin (1995), pp. 266–69). Gail Fine defines a "Two Worlds" interpretation of Plato as one according to which "knowledge" (*episteme*) can only be of Forms, and "belief" (*doxa*) can only be of objects of sensation. She suggests that a more plausible account of the key passage about knowledge and belief in Republic v (473c-480a) would take Plato to be distinguishing knowledge and belief as different ways of relating to *propositions*, rather than as ways of relating to different *objects* in the world. My suggestion that Plato is thinking of how the soul both is and is not (inasmuch as it sometimes pursues the Good and sometimes doesn't) explains why Plato would be particularly concerned about the category of *objects* that both are and are not. This category includes us, as we usually conceive of ourselves. F. J. Gonzalez, "Propositions or Objects?" (1996), argues that Fine's interpretation can't make sense of Plato's text because it leaves belief with no distinctive domain "over" which it is "set" (pp. 264–68, referring to 477a9). On Fine's interpretation, belief applies to propositions just as knowledge applies to (some of the same) propositions. (On Fine's interpretation, see also Lloyd Gerson [2003], pp. 161–66.) Fine is right to prefer the thought that the objects of sense are in some way identical to the objects of intellect. But she is mistaken if she thinks that this means we can ignore Plato's suggestion that the objects of intellect are "more real" than the objects of sense. They are more real insofar as we (and along with us, the rest of the world of the senses) only sometimes live up to them and thus achieve full reality or identity as ourselves. This is the complexity of "being identical to."

16 Thus rather than being "other-worldly," in the sense of postulating a separate "world" from this one, Plato postulates a scale of increasing reality in this "world." So when Plato has Socrates say that "a man should make all haste to escape from earth to heaven" (*Theaetetus* 176a-b), we should understand this as hyperbole—as indeed what follows makes pretty clear: "And escape means becoming as like God as possible; and a man becomes like God when he becomes just and pure, with understanding."

17 Plato's *Sophist* suggests that he was reconsidering the sharp line that he had drawn in the *Republic* between what fully "is" and what has "change, life, soul, and intelligence" (248e). Stephen Menn ([1995], p. 70 n. 2) suggests that Plato, here, wants to get his earlier self "to admit that the human realities are also realities alongside the divine ones." One wonders whether Menn thinks that the later Plato assigns no more "reality" to Forms than to their images. It seems to me that in order to retain what drives both his notion of Forms and his recognition in the *Sophist* that there can be no sharp dividing line between the divine and the human, Plato needs to think of the relation between the universal and the particular in the way that Hegel does, as a

unity in difference, or a "concrete universal" (on which see Wallace [2005], p. 229). In this conception, the universal or Form is different from its particular instantiations, but not separable from them. Plotinus has a conception similar to this when he locates intellect and God "within us" but still beyond our "momentary acts" (*Enneads* VI.I.11). These conceptions preserve the higher authority and in that sense the fuller reality of the divine, without separating it entirely from the "change, life, soul, and intelligence" that concern the speaker in the *Sophist*.

18   J. N. Findlay (1974), pp. 3, 412.
19   Lloyd Gerson (2003), p. 281.
20   Bertrand Russell (2004), p. 15.
21   Martha Nussbaum (1986/2001), p. 161. Nussbaum goes on to say that Nietzsche's "insight" doesn't do justice to the "complexity" of Plato's arguments. She doesn't make it clear whether those arguments would succeed without the alleged *ressentiment*.
22   Martha Nussbaum (2003), p. 494, n. 16.
23   On Hegel's doctrine that "substance is essentially subject" (*Phenomenology of Spirit*, Miller trans., §25; SuW 3:28), see Wallace (2005), pp. 88–90 and 224–28.
24   Eric Perl (2007), p. 8.
25   Chapter 2 of Schindler (2008) surveys numerous attempts to explain the relation that Plato is driving at between goodness and truth. Unlike Schindler and the other commentators he surveys, I rely on Plato's account in *Republic* books iv-vii of how the pursuit of goodness produces unity (443e), and thus (one might say) full reality or "truth," in the soul.
26   "Sense-data" theories: Bertrand Russell (1912/1997); A.J. Ayer (1956). Criticisms: W. V. O. Quine, "Two Dogmas of Empiricism" (1953), Wilfrid Sellars (1956/1997), John McDowell (1994), and Sebastian Rödl (2012). Hegel had given a similar critique, in the first chapter of his *Phenomenology of Spirit* (1807/1977), in response to Immanuel Kant's dualism of "intuition" and "concept" in his CPuR (1781/1787).The critique of empiricism that Hegel, Quine, Sellars, McDowell, and Rödl carry out makes Plato's emphasis on intellect as opposed to sensation as our access to the one real world seem quite reasonable. Everything that we can speak of is intelligible, so our access to it is through intellect; and its intelligibility (the Forms) is in it, in some fashion.
27   For further illumination of Plato's distinctive account of knowledge, see Lloyd Gerson (2003) and (2013). I suspect that the notion of a faculty of *anamnesis*, or "recollection," which Plato introduces (*Meno* 81-86, *Phaedo* 72-76) as a means by which we could gain access to the Forms (which we might have known directly before we were born), is also, in effect, directed at who or what we ourselves really are when we're distinguished from what our embodied experience has made us.
28   Hans Blumenberg, "An Anthropological Approach to the Contemporary Significance of Rhetoric" (1987), p. 431/"Anthropologische Annäherung an die Aktualität der Rhetorik," in his (1981), p. 107.
29   Blumenberg, "Anthropological Approach," p. 429/"Anthropologische Annäherung," 104.
30   Blumenberg, "Anthropological Approach," pp. 432, 455/"Anthropologische Annäherung," pp. 107, 133.
31   "Ur-Platonism," again, is Lloyd Gerson's coinage in his (2013), p. 10.

32 This Parmenides fragment, which has been translated in very different ways, is listed as Fragment 3 in G. S. Kirk and J. E. Raven, eds. (1969), p. 269.

33 The separation of "ought" from "is" is a characteristic feature both of empiricism (see David Hume [1978], pp. 468–69) and of Kantian thinking. I will say some more about the contrasting "teleological" view of life and reality, for which "ought" and "is" are intimately entwined, in Chapter 8. I discuss Hegel's version of this entwinement, which is most evident in his account of the "ought" and the infinite, in chapter 3 of Wallace (2005), and in "How G. W. F. Hegel's Broadly Platonic Idealism Explains Knowledge, Value, and Freedom" (forthcoming).

34 Such comprehensive accounts of education in Plato as Robert E. Cushman (1958), and Rashana Kamtekar, "Plato on Education and Art" (in Gail Fine, ed. [2011]), unfortunately don't consider "birth in beauty" and midwifery as suggesting an alternative account of how the necessary "turning" can take place.

35 I'll discuss Plato's quite inegalitarian political suggestions in the next chapter. The process of facilitating the emergence of free selfhood clearly needn't take place exclusively or even primarily in schools. Besides Socrates, Plato, Rousseau, and John Dewey, some recent advocates of education as facilitating the emergence of free selfhood are A. S. Neill, Paulo Freire, John Holt, and Ivan Illich.

Chapter 6: Plato, freedom, and us, pp. 135–156

1 The Cave allegory actually has four phases, which are further illuminated by the parallel stages of the Line and the Sun, which precede the Cave. I don't have space to go into these important details.

2 On the continuity between Plato's and Aristotle's ethics, see Terence Irwin (1989), chapter 7, and Lloyd Gerson (2005), chapter 8.

3 Carlos Fraenkel (2013), p. 295.

4 For the "voluntarist" theory of freedom which I mention here, see Thomas Reid (1788) and Immanuel Kant, CPuR (1781). For the "empiricist" theory of freedom (also known as the "compatibilist" theory) see Thomas Hobbes (1651), chapter 21, paragraphs 1–4, and David Hume (1978), Part III, sections 1 and 2, and (1902), pp. 80–103. Versions of these theories that have been developed by twentieth-century philosophers can be found in Gary Watson, ed. (1982). I discuss these theories in more detail in Wallace (2005), pp. 22–27 and 82. Twentieth-century philosophers whose thinking about freedom resembles Plato's and Hegel's "rationalism" or "idealism," rather than either voluntarism or empiricist compatibilism, include Gary Watson and Charles Taylor (whose central papers are reprinted in Watson's [1982]) and Susan Wolf (1990).

5 I mentioned in the previous note that in recent decades, several important Anglo-American philosophers (Watson, Taylor, Wolf) have advocated conceptions of individual freedom and responsibility that resemble Plato's conception. However, the implications of their work don't seem to have received much attention from (for example) psychologists or other social scientists, who are some of the people to whose work it should be especially relevant.

6 Karl Popper (1945); Isaiah Berlin, "Two Concepts of Liberty" (1958), in his (1969).
7 I explain Hegel's conception of freedom in detail in Wallace (2005). For an explanation of Hegel's conception of the "state"—which has been misinterpreted by Popper and others as having a "totalitarian" character—see Allen Wood's "Editor's Introduction" to G. W. F. Hegel, *Elements of the Philosophy of Right* (1991), and Robert M. Wallace (1999).
8 John Bussanich (1999) gives a good discussion of these insufficiently discussed features of Socrates's behavior.
9 Though in the same passage in *Republic* book x where Plato's Socrates speaks of the "ancient quarrel between [poetry] and philosophy," he also says that "if the poetry that aims at pleasure and imitation has any argument to bring forward that proves it ought to have a place in a well-governed city, we at least would be glad to admit it" (607c). Earlier on, in book vi, Socrates humorously and quite accurately describes himself as "greedy for images" (488a). And Socrates's argument at the very end of the *Symposium* that authors should be able to write both comedy and tragedy surely has to be intended as a comment on Plato's own writing, in the *Symposium*. Plato is well aware that he himself is, among other things, a poet, and he is quite consciously leaving us with the task of figuring out how to reconcile his critique of poetry with his unapologizing practice of it. Hegel responds to Plato's challenge with his account of "absolute Spirit," in which Art is surpassed by Religion and both are then surpassed by Philosophy. His point is that when conceptual thinking, as in Philosophy, is possible, it's superior to the imagistic thinking of Religion and to the sheer imagery of Art. But this is not to say that conceptual thinking can or should be carried on in complete independence from imagery. On the contrary, Hegel's basic principle that the infinite *is* only as the self-transcending of the finite (HSL pp. 145–46, SuW 5:160, GW 21:133) tells us that conceptual thinking will appreciate and seek to embody what's true in all of the preceding phases of Nature and Spirit, including Art (and thus poetry) and Religion. That is why Hegel lectured at length on the philosophy of art and the philosophy of religion (not to mention politics, psychology, biology, etc.). In these elaborations, Hegel is simply filling in some of the empty spaces in the vision that Plato outlined for us in the *Republic*, *Symposium*, *Phaedrus*, and *Timaeus*.
10 Soren Kierkegaard (1843/1941).
11 Plato acknowledges this in the "God-given madness" section of the *Phaedrus* (244–45). Hegel acknowledges it in his discussion of the preconscious "feeling soul," in G. W. F. Hegel (1971), pp. 94–139, pars. 405–8.

Chapter 7: Plato on reason, love, and inspiration, pp. 157–184

1 An important thread of seventeenth- and eighteenth-century philosophy in England and Germany (the Cambridge Platonists and Shaftesbury, and Leibniz through Mendelssohn) did give a central role to love and was largely inspired by Plato. (See Douglas Hedley and Sarah Hutton, eds. [2008], and Frederick Beiser [2009].) I quoted Hegel's single most important statement on love in Chapter 2: "The universal

is therefore *free power*; . . . it could also be called *free love*" (HSL, p. 603, SuW 6:277, GW 12: 35). For an explanation of the significance of love in Hegel's system, see Wallace (2005), chapters 3–6 and especially p. 216.

2   Needless to say, Roman Catholic higher education and writing represent an exception to my generalizations here and elsewhere in this book.

3   Interpretations of Plato on love which I have found helpful are A. J. Festugiere (1935/1975); Suzanne Lilar (1965), chapter on "The Pagan Moment"; L. A. Kosman (1976); R. E. Allen (1991); James M. Rhodes (2003); Rosemary Desjardins (2004), chapter 5; Frisbee Sheffield (2006); and Jill Gordon (2012). Rhodes gives the most coherent account that I've seen of the entire *Symposium*, together with its historical context, while Kosman comes closest to what I want to say about "birth in beauty" in the *Symposium*.

4   This was the theme of Nietzsche's first book, *The Birth of Tragedy* (in Nietzsche [1968]; first published 1871). It enabled this highly trained classical philologist to assert with a straight face that "Socrates might be called the typical *non-mystic*, in whom, by a hypertrophy, the logical nature is developed as excessively as instinctive wisdom is in the mystic. . . . It is only in the spirit of music that we can understand the joy involved in the annihilation of the individual" (Nietzsche [1968], pp. 88, 104). A recent version of this canard that classical philosophy suffocates inspiration is Hubert Dreyfus and Sean D. Kelly (2011), which I reviewed in the London *Times Literary Supplement*, July 8, 2011 (review available online, September 2013). Effective ripostes to the assumptions about Socrates that Nietzsche articulates here can be found in Jonathan Shear (1990), chapters 1–3 (which compare Plato's account of Socrates to accounts of Zen, Yoga, and Vedanta), and John Bussanich (1999).

5   E. R. Dodds (1951), pp. 218–19.

6   A useful survey of Athens's romantic practices can be found in C. D. C. Reeve's Introduction to his (2006). Suzanne Lilar gave a rich and balanced account of the effect of ancient Greek gender roles on Plato's thinking about love in the chapter, "The Pagan Moment," of her (1965).

7   James M. Rhodes (2003), p. 184.

8   Agathon's speech and Socrates's dialogue with Agathon, which I'm skipping over here, are well analyzed by James Rhodes in chapter 5 of his (2003).

9   F. Sheffield writes that Plato provides "a description of the philosophical character in action from the outset," or he speaks to those who are "intellectually inclined from the outset" (Sheffield [2006], pp. 117–19 and p. 119 n. 7). For a similar view see G. R. F. Ferrari, "Platonic Love," in R. Kraut, ed. (1992), p. 261.

10 Ken Wilber usefully identified the assumption that we must either embrace individuality as such or reject it and regress to a previous stage, as the "pre-/trans-fallacy": the assumption that any state that's "beyond" or "trans-" individuality is equivalent to what is developmentally "pre-" (prior) to it (Wilber [2000], pp. 210–13). One prominent writer who makes this assumption is Sigmund Freud in his discussion of Romain Rolland's "oceanic feeling," in Freud (1989), chapter 1.

11 The *Symposium* speaks here of beauty, whereas the *Republic* speaks of the Good. Plato explains the intimate connection between beauty and goodness in an important passage in the *Phaedrus*, where he has Socrates say that "justice and self-control do not shine out through their images down here. . . . Beauty alone has this privilege, to

be the most visible and the most loved" (250b-d). That is, of the Forms, beauty is the most visible, it "shines out," and thus (we may take it) it serves often as the visible or sensible representative of the ultimate Form, which is the Good.

12 Commentators on the *Symposium* and the *Phaedo* generally seem to accept the claim that souls can exhibit beauty more clearly than bodies do as a Platonic axiom that doesn't need defense. But it seems that what underlies it is, as I suggest here, that because one's soul expresses one's choices, it expresses *oneself* more than one's body (as such) does.

13 This issue about Diotima's argument was particularly stressed by Gregory Vlastos, in his influential paper, "The Individual as Object of Love in Plato," in Vlastos (1973).

14 Here is the answer to Martha Nussbaum's complaint ([2003], p. 498) that "the Platonic lover, . . . viewing the object of her love as a seat of valuable properties, and therefore as a suitable vehicle for creation, neglects in the process the other person's own agency and choice." On the contrary, since the Platonic lover cares about her beloved's soul, she cares about her beloved's activities and ideas, and thus precisely about her beloved's agency and choice.

15 Martha Nussbaum paints a more appealing picture of Alcibiades in chapter 6 of her (1986/2001). But in doing so she downplays the most salient features of Alcibiades's reputation: that he was ultimately a traitor to Athens and that he was suspected of having desecrated religious statues and mysteries. Surely Plato expects his audience to have these features in the forefront of their minds and to draw the obvious contrast with Socrates.

16 F. Sheffield ([2006], p. 204) appropriately describes Alcibiades's attachment to Socrates as "idolatrous."

17 This is my response to Martha Nussbaum's question, "Where . . . do all these 'must's come from?" in Diotima's description of the "ascent" ([1986/2001], p. 179). They come not from a "prudent" (p. 179) decision to come up with "intersubstitutable" beauties (p. 180) in case one loses the first beauty but rather from the lover's desire that he and his beloved should enjoy, as much as possible, what's truly good or beautiful and not just whatever currently seems to them to be good. Attention to the parallels between ascent in the *Symposium* and ascent in the *Republic*, and to the context of the latter, makes this clear.

18 Freud [1989], pp. 29–30, 32–34. If the "drives" were merely mechanical, as Freud's metaphors often seem to suggest, then it's hard to imagine how this "sublimation" could take place. Freud's persisting attachment to mechanical metaphors such as "displacement" (Freud [1989], p. 29) prevents him from spelling out, as Plato and his successors including Hegel do, how the primitive mental forces collaborate with reason by recognizing that it's only through reason's guidance that they can participate in higher forms of organization. More specifically, it's only in this way that they can participate in self-determination, freedom, and the fullest reality. C. G. Jung's interpretation of sublimation as "ascent" ([1974], pp. 129–31), rather than as "displacement," is more in line with Platonism, though Jung's indications of what this "ascent" might amount to for people who are imbued with modern science need the kind of supplementation that I have tried to provide in this book.

19 "Resistances to Psychoanalysis," *Standard Edition* 19:218.

20 Arthur Schopenhauer, *The World as Will and Representation* (1958), vol. 2, ch. 44.

21 The evocative stories that Hubert Dreyfus and Sean Kelly recount, in Dreyfus and Kelly (2011), of ecstasies that "whoosh up" in a group of people, all lend themselves readily to Plato's account. They are all cases in which the group shares a perception that they have witnessed something truly excellent, whether the excellence is ethical, artistic, or athletic. And thus the philosophers of intellect and value, from Plato through Kant and Hegel, can illuminate these shared experiences in a way that anti-"intellectual" writers cannot. The claim is not, of course, that intellect can produce these valuable phenomena single-handedly, but that it's a necessary ingredient in our love of them, insofar as we judge and (when appropriate) will try to defend our judgment that they are truly excellent.

22 Denis de Rougemont (1983) gives an extended and provocative discussion of the incompatibility of love and marriage according to *Tristan* and the "courtly love" poets. Like Richard Wagner and Hollywood, de Rougemont doesn't focus on or take seriously Plato's suggestion that there's an important connection between eros and true rationality.

23 Anders Nygren contrasted the "acquisitive" and "egocentric" character of Platonic eros with the "sacrificial" and "unselfish" character of what he called *agape* (Nygren [1932/1982], p. 210). Gregory Vlastos described Diotima's view in similar terms: "It is not said or implied or so much as hinted at that 'birth in beauty' should be motivated by love of persons—that the ultimate purpose of the creative act should be to enrich the lives of persons who are themselves worthy of love for their own sake" (Vlastos [1973, 1981], p. 31). In her (2001), Martha Nussbaum picked up Vlastos's notion that Platonic love is "creative," and wrote of "Diotima: Love as Creation in the Fine and the Good" (pp. 486–500). "The Platonic lover, . . . viewing the object of her love as a seat of valuable properties, and therefore as a suitable vehicle for creation, neglects in the process the other person's own agency and choice. . . . The idea that each person has her own distinct life to live simply plays no role in the analysis" (Nussbaum [2001], pp. 498–99).

24 When Jonathan Lear says that "it is this particular subjectivity with which we are pregnant" (Lear [1998], p. 166), he neglects the role of the Good and the beautiful in unifying (*Republic* 443e) the soul and thus making it self-governing. This role is entirely compatible with Lear's claim that "the body, its drives, and the bodily expression of mind all lend vitality to 'higher' mental functions" (same page).

25 "The love which . . . calls the other to be his true self, is a love which at once recognizes and bids the other to his true virtue and beauty," and "this is the meaning of Diotima's definition of love as ['birth *in beauty*']" (Louis Kosman, "Platonic Love," in Soble, ed. [1989], p. 159 and note 29; emphasis added). From what Kosman says and from what I've said about the pursuit of the Good leading to self-government, it's clear that (contrary to Nussbaum [2001], p. 499) Plato definitely does speak to the fact "that each person has her own distinct life to live."

26 Terence Irwin maintains that what he describes as Diotima's notion of propagating oneself through others ("A is concerned for B as a way of propagating A") does not involve an "objectionably domineering attitude" to others (Irwin [1995], p. 311). Plato "can claim to justify non-instrumental concern for another, for the other's sake. . . . For if we actually propagate *ourselves* in other people, then we have the same sort of reason to care about the other people as we have to care about ourselves" (p. 313; emphasis added). Though I agree that what Irwin describes isn't literally "instrumental," since it doesn't make an instrument of something other than "oneself,"

it's not clear how propagating "my" self in another person is not domineering. For the description ("propagating A in B") leaves one wondering what is the significance of what B was prior to the propagation. A. W. Price wonders, "What confirms that the [beloved's] better self, as conceived by the lover, is the true self? The only test remaining would seem to be the future, and that can be made to measure" (Price [1989], p. 101). Jennifer Whiting raised a similar issue of apparent "colonization" of the other, in connection with Irwin's similar account of Aristotle on friendship (Whiting [1991], p. 9). If, on the other hand, I'm right that what is "propagated" by love as Diotima understands it is, in fact, *self-government*, then it's impossible in the nature of the case for the propagator to dominate the propagatee's functioning. As Louis Kosman says (in Soble, ed.[1989], p. 159), the lover "calls the other to be his true self, . . . bids the other to his true virtue and beauty." The relevance of what the other already was, prior to the "propagation," is that the other and those who knew him can undoubtedly feel or see in him the potential for the virtue and beauty that are actualized ("called," as Kosman puts it) through the "propagation."

27 Regarding uniqueness, Richard Kraut offers these comments: "It is obviously true of each lover that there is only one person with whom he has had *these* fine discussions and produced *these* fine children" (in G. Fine, ed. [2011], pp. 301–2). Troy Jollimore (2011) develops a similar thought about what he calls "love's blindness."

28 As Richard Kraut points out in G. Fine, ed. (2011), p. 302.

29 Nygren (1932/1982), p. 210.

30 "Birth in beauty" describes us as emerging into self-government through a quasi-natural process of "birth." Something similar seems to reappear in (a) Aristotle's conception of "matter" as having within it a principle of (i.e., the potentiality for) a certain kind of actualization or form, (b) Plotinus's description of the world as "turning back" toward the One, and (c) Hegel's account of the infinite emerging from the finite, and Spirit from Nature. In contrast to the usual materialist assumption that matter is something that merely happens, in the course of time, to take on certain living and intelligent forms, (a)–(c) all identify a fundamental process "in" the physical world that tends toward a kind of self-government. They all see what I've been calling "transcendence" as quasi-natural.

31 The recent turning by Elizabeth Anscombe, Alasdair MacIntyre, and others toward a neo-Aristotelian "virtue ethics" is a salutary development in that it reopens the questions of "wisdom" and the relation between head and heart. Its weakness is that it tends not to appreciate how Kant's and Hegel's interest in autonomy or freedom is in principle continuous with Plato's and Aristotle's interest in reason, so that German Idealism is in principle aligned with, rather than opposed to, "virtue ethics."

32 I say we love *self-transcending* nature because I don't think one can be inspired by, and thus love, sheer mechanism as such. Whereas a "*world* in a grain of sand," and "*heaven* in a wild flower"—those we can love. We see in the flower something analogous to what we see in a beautifully souled human being. It's an inner freedom made outwardly visible. To take some other examples of natural beauty: in a beautiful (or "sublime") landscape, sunset, or galaxy, we see the spectacle of a world that cares little for us, but yet in some way has given birth to us. It is free of our anxieties and troubles, and its grandeur, creativity, and fecundity are qualities that we admire and would like (if we were able) to emulate. And indeed we may be able to emulate them, insofar as our understanding of who we are goes beyond our finite, human boundaries. This is how nature can inspire us despite being prima facie "inhuman."

This is also how I would interpret Hegel's description of the beauty of nature as "an imperfect incomplete mode [of beauty], a mode which in its substance is contained in the spirit itself" (*Aesthetics*, vol. 1, p. 2). Since the infinite *is* only as the self-transcending of the finite (HSL pp. 145–46, SuW 5:160, GW 21:133), nature is an essential aspect of Spirit or freedom, and we find nature beautiful insofar as we experience it as transcending itself (or insofar as we experience it, as Hegel says, as "contained in its substance" in spirit). The second and third volumes of Hegel's *Encyclopedia of the Philosophical Sciences* explain how nature does this (and see Wallace [2005], chs. 3 and 6).

33 Pieces of this work have been done and are being done by many people. As I've mentioned, comprehensive outlines are provided by Plato, Aristotle, Hegel, and R. G. Collingwood (1924); and see Wallace, "How Plato and Hegel Integrate the Sciences, the Arts, Religion, and Philosophy" (forthcoming).

Chapter 8: Plato on "becoming like God", pp. 185–204

1 Terence Irwin ([1995], p. 309) discusses the *Timaeus*'s passage about the demiurge's lack of jealousy so as to provide what he calls a "full picture of the motives that Plato takes to support interpersonal propagation." But his discussion of the demiurge forms, in effect, a parenthesis, from which he returns on p. 310 to Diotima's focus on self-preservation. His discussion of the philosopher's relation to his community and to humankind in general, in the remainder of the chapter, makes no reference to the demiurge model and appears not to rely on it. But certainly at least by the time one comes to the philosopher's dealings with humankind as a whole (p. 316), the demiurge model would be a more promising basis than Diotima's model, by itself. For it's difficult to imagine how humankind as a whole could be needed in order to ensure the continuation of the qualities that the philosopher values in herself.

2 David Sedley (1999) and Julia Annas (2000), Chapter 3, discuss Plato's theme of "becoming like God" without viewing it as having the potential to be an effective foundation for ethics. John M. Armstrong (2004) shows how Plato's *Laws* spells out ways in which we can become like God through leadership and membership in a just community.

3 E. R. Dodds surveyed Greek depictions of divine "jealousy" (*phthonos*) in chapter 2 of his (1951).

4 F. G. Herrmann ("*Phthonos* in the world of Plato's *Timaeus*," in D. Konstan and N. K. Rutter, eds. [2003], pp. 58–59) lists *Protagoras* 320c1 and 2, *Symposium* 210d6, *Phaedrus* 247a7 and 253b7–c2, *Republic* 499d10–501b8, and *Laws* 679c. But after reviewing the *Timaeus* passage and this background in some detail, Herrmann concludes that "it is still not clear . . . why goodness excludes any withholding and hindering and debarring," which are actions that he has found in the semantic field of *phthonos* (p. 75).

5 The one fully explicit linking of an identification of the Good and the One with Plato himself is in fact in a fragment of a music theorist and student of Aristotle, Aristoxenus, who reported that Plato's public lecture *On the Good* "turned out to be

about mathematics—numbers, geometry, astronomy—and to crown all about the thesis that the good is [the] one, [which] seemed to [the listeners] something quite paradoxical" (J. Barnes, ed. [1984], vol. 2, p. 2397). I insert "[the]" before "good," here, in line with the argument of C. C. W. Taylor (in G. Fine, ed. [2011], p. 181, n. 19) that there would have been nothing especially "paradoxical" in asserting merely that "the good is one." Taylor explains that the definite article, "the," is often elided after *einai*, "to be," in Greek. Aristotle himself links the doctrine that the good is the one with those (meaning, presumably, Plato) "who maintain the existence of unchangeable substances" (*Metaphysics* 14.4.1091b13–15; cf. *Eudemian Ethics* 1218a19ff). It's possible, of course, that Aristotle didn't fully understand what Plato was driving at in the lectures that he reports, but it seems very unlikely that he invented anything substantial in them or that he ascribed to Plato ideas that really belonged to other people, for there were presumably plenty of people alive when Aristotle was writing who could have corrected him on points like these. One can find these "unwritten doctrines" potentially important and illuminating with regard to the dialogues, without believing that Plato reserved them for insiders or that he ultimately rejected writing (on the grounds that he mentions in the *Phaedrus* or in the *Seventh Letter*). For accounts of the oral teachings and their relation to the dialogues, see H. J. Krämer (1959) and (1990), J. N. Findlay (1974), Kenneth Sayre (1983), and Lloyd Gerson (2013), pp. 91–129. An expert who minimizes the significance of Aristotle's testimony is Harold Cherniss (1944) and (1945), to whom all of the above authors respond.

6 A stimulating account of Plato's overall relation to Parmenides is given by H. J. Krämer (1959), pp. 487–551.

7 *Enneads* V.2.1. This "overflowing" is one of the two great themes of Plotinus's metaphysics, the other being the "turning back" (*epistrophe*) in which beings in the world realize that their unity depends upon the One. The same pattern of outflow and turning back structures Hegel's *Encyclopedia of the Philosophical Sciences*, the outflow occurring in the course of the Logic section and the turning back occupying the sections on Nature and Spirit.

8 Michael Hanby suggests (following D. C. Schindler) that in dealing with the difference between Forms and their images, "Plato seems to be on the horns of a dilemma. To admit that the principle of unity—beauty or the good—is also the principle of difference appears to introduce division into the simple unity of the transcendent source. To admit a second positive principle to account for this difference seems tantamount to affirming the Gnostic ultimacy of two principles, which is unintelligible and thus irrational" ([2017], p. 56). I am suggesting that Plato sees that since "jealousy" determines one by one's relation to the other that one is jealous of, the Good can be fully "one," fully self-contained, only if it's "generous" (as Hanby puts it, p. 74) rather than "jealous." So no second principle is required; properly understood, oneness alone does the trick.

9 Julia Annas ([2000], p. 64) comments that the demiurge "certainly has a mind and intelligence, and desires things to be as good as possible, but this does not seem like much of a basis for acquiring virtues."

10 It's true, as Julia Annas points out ([2000], p. 65), that Socrates in the *Theaetetus* passage makes the philosopher who seeks to "become like God" appear to be completely unaware of the world and his body. I take this as either (a) comic hyperbole or (b) the tendency that I noted in Plato's talk about "flight from the world," to have contempt for lower things. Possibility (b) seems to directly contradict the attitude of the demiurge in the *Timaeus*, who rather than having contempt for the world, does everything he can to make the world as good as it can be. I don't think Plato can have it both ways, both fly from the world and imitate the demiurge. I would say the same about Plotinus's apparent dismissal of "civic" virtue, which Annas discusses (pp. 66–70). If we human beings are to imitate the demiurge, I don't see how we can dismiss conventional virtues. In order to be self-governing, God must be benevolent, so those who seek to be "like God" must likewise be benevolent. And I don't think benevolence is compatible with contempt.

11 John M. Armstrong (2004), p. 181.

12 Anders Nygren (1932/1982) argued that in contrast to the "agape" love that Christianity finds in its God, Platonism's "eros" is inherently self-centered. Nygren didn't consider how nominally "egoistic" self-propagation must propagate true self-government, and thus promote the independent functioning of others, nor did he consider how someone who seeks to "become like God" must be benevolent in the same way as the demiurge who tries to make the world as much like himself (i.e., as self-governing) as possible. So that self-propagation and becoming like God both entail unselfish benevolence.

13 In chapter 18 of Irwin (1995), Terence Irwin concludes that Plato's argument in the *Republic* can't "justify all the legitimate demands of morality. For we might insist that the moral claims of other people on us do not depend on their being our friends or on their belonging to some community that we care about" (p. 316). I have suggested that in the *Republic* together with the *Timaeus* and *Philebus*, Plato presents good reasons for believing that a fully rational person will try to "become like God" by doing everything she can to make the world as a whole as good as it can be. In this way she will care about and foster all humans and (indeed) everything.

14 Menn (1995), p. 12, agreeing with R. Hackforth, "Plato's Theism," in R. E. Allen, ed. (1965). F. M. Cornford and Harold Cherniss in different ways took the demiurge to be immanent in souls and thus in the world (F. M. Cornford [1937], Harold Cherniss [1944]). Menn's view is supported by Thomas K. Johansen (2004) and David Sedley (2007).

15 Like Plato's theology as I have described it, Plotinus's account of the One and the world as related to each other through "proceeding outward" (*proodos*) and "turning back" (*epistrophe*) seems likewise to be based on our experience of turning toward Oneness in pursuit of our own self-government. "Turning back" is our pursuit of Oneness in ourselves (which is why Plotinus says that the One is "in us" [*Enneads* V.I.11]), and "proceeding outward" is the character of what has truly "turned back" and become One. It cannot be One if it limits itself by excluding others from its concern, so it doesn't do that.

16 In chapter 6 of Sedley (2007), David Sedley makes clear the fundamental agreement between Plato and Aristotle as supporters of teleology. This makes one wonder why he chose to focus his book on the ancient world's apparently less fundamental disagreements about "creationism" (the issue on which Plato and Aristotle appear to disagree) rather than on its apparently more fundamental disagreements about teleology versus chance. The present-day disputes between "creationists" and mainline scientists (where the former have in mind "a being" of great power) have this same feature, that they distract us from the more fundamental issue of whether *goodness*, as such, plays an essential role in reality. If the divine is truly infinite, it can't be characterized merely by power, but must have the authority that goes with (the

pursuit of) goodness. This is the simple message of Platonism which is lost in the din of popular disputes about supreme "beings."

17 Aristotle, *Eudemian Ethics* 1249b13–15: "For it is not by giving commands that god is ruler, but as the good towards which practical wisdom gives commands."

18 The best-known modern treatment of the issue of teleology is Immanuel Kant's *Critique of Judgment* (1790). Because Kant did not see how rational self-government can be understood as an intensification of the more rudimentary forms of self-government that I've just mentioned, his treatment left an unclarified residue of dualism between "nature" and what is other than nature (Ak 5:184), or between "constitutive" principles such as efficient causation and merely "regulative" ones such as teleology (Ak 5:361). This is where Plato, Aristotle, and Hegel provide a more satisfying conception. On Hegel's treatment of teleology, see chapter 5 of Wallace (2005) and p. 249 in particular.

19 As I've mentioned, Lloyd Gerson gives lucid accounts of Plato's treatment of knowledge in his (2003) and his (2013). Andrea Kern (2017) is an important contemporary account, based on Aristotle, of knowledge.

20 In his useful analytical survey of interpretations of Plato's "theology," Michael Bordt categorizes them as "religious," "metaphysical," or "cosmological" (C. Horn et al., eds. [2009], pp. 200–10). "Religious" interpretations are most influenced by Plato's critique of conventional religion in book ii of the *Republic*; "metaphysical" interpretations are most influenced by Plato's account of the Forms and the Form of the Good, in *Republic* books vi-vii; and "cosmological" interpretations are most influenced by Plato's creation story of the "demiurge" in the *Timaeus* and his argument for the existence of gods in *Laws* x. Bordt plausibly suggests (p. 210) that an interpretation that follows *Laws* x 897b1 in identifying "God" with "nous" (intellect or reason) can combine the strong points of all three approaches. I would simply add that the "metaphysical" aspect is nevertheless more fundamental than the other two, because only Plato's metaphysics (together with his account of the soul in *Republic* iv) explains why a "theology" is rationally necessary at all. The cosmological argument set forth in *Laws* x is, as I've suggested, inadequate as it stands, and it has to be supplemented by the account of the soul's "transcendence" or upward motion in the *Phaedo* and especially in *Republic* iv-vii in order to constitute a convincing argument for a transcendent dimension of reality as a whole, and thus establish the need for a "theology." Besides which, only the "metaphysical" argument in *Phaedo* and *Republic* explains why theology's God possesses authority, as opposed to mere power.

21 In his valuable (1935/1975), which is the most comprehensive account of Plato's rational "mysticism" that I have found, Andre Jean Festugiere understands Plato's notion of mystical "vision" or *theoria* as referring to episodes in a person's life which begin and end and are thus directly comparable to what we call "mystical experiences." I'm sure that Festugiere's interpretation captures part of what Plato had in mind in the passages that we're discussing, but I strongly suspect that Plato was open to the broader interpretation that I'm proposing, as well. For it seems to capture the meaning of Plato's key descriptors as well as Festugiere's more conventional interpretation does. When Plato speaks of "vision" in these contexts he doesn't, of course, mean vision through our physical eyes. So there is no need to assume that this "vision" is always episodic, beginning and (most importantly) ending in time, in the way that physical vision does. And the *Symposium* passage

seems to speak against such assumptions when it says that "there if anywhere should a person *live his life*, beholding that Beauty" (211d, emphasis added). David J. Yount describes the vision of the Good as an "everlasting and self-sustaining experience" ([2017], p. 23), though he also says that "one does not lose the *fruits of*" that experience (same page, my emphasis), thus somewhat obscuring the clarity of his previous claim.

Chapter 9: Ordinary and extraordinary experiences of God, pp. 205–212

1. No doubt people also experience God in contemplative prayer, as David Bentley Hart maintains in chapter 6 of his (2013). But I think it's a mistake to suppose that prayer that we intend as such is the only or even the primary way in which we experience God.

2. When I speak of us as having "direct access to God," as our own inner freedom, forgiveness, and so forth, readers who are familiar with Hegel may wonder: Doesn't Hegel say that "there is nothing in heaven or in nature or mind or anywhere else which does not equally contain both immediacy and mediation" (HSL p. 68, SuW 5:66, GW 21:54), so that the notion of "direct" (i.e., presumably, immediate) "access" is perhaps questioned by Hegel? The "direct" access that I describe is certainly also indirect, inasmuch as to understand *what* we have access to, through it, we need a good deal of additional information and thought. What these experiences are experiences of (whether it's "freedom," "forgiveness," "God," or anything else) isn't written on their foreheads; like everything important, these concepts are sophisticated, as well as simple. But the access that we have to God through these experiences is nevertheless direct in a way that the access that we might have to some object that's "outside" our world is not. It's direct inasmuch as freedom, forgiveness and God (according to Hegel's account) are *in us* in a way that external objects aren't.

3. Eckhart Tolle (1999), p. 187; first emphasis added.

4. Eckhart Tolle (1999), p. 191.

5. William James, *The Varieties of Religious Experience* (1997), p. 70 (in Lecture 3).

6. See W. T. Stace (1960), William J. Wainwright (1981), Jerome Gellmann (2001), Jerome Gellmann, "Mysticism," Stanford Encyclopedia of Philosophy online 2010, and Richard H. Jones (2017).

7. Finding meaning in experiences of cosmic unity or of "pure consciousness" (Forman [1990], Shear [1990]) will likewise require going beyond their immediate content. What is the importance of unity or of pure consciousness? What do they tell us about ourselves and our lives? These experiences can answer these questions only by being interpreted. By contrast, our everyday experiences of inner freedom, love, forgiveness, and so forth carry their meaning on their face, as it were. If "God" has the significance that inner freedom, love, and forgiveness have, then we understand immediately how "God" is significant for our lives.

8. To mention another kind of "extraordinary experience," many people from antiquity through Aldous Huxley down to the present have thought that experiences generated

by substances like soma/haoma, mescaline, LSD, ayahuasca, ibogaine, or alcohol give us access to something divine. I doubt whether many of these experiences give us access to anything divine, though they certainly often give us a vacation from our normal experience of an apparently very undivine reality. What seems to be absent from most, though perhaps not all of these experiences is a process of inner integration that generates genuine inner freedom and (thereby) genuine experience of the divine. Here again, as with the more widely acknowledged kinds of "mystical experience," apparently extraordinary experiences need to be set alongside more ordinary experiences of liberation and understood and evaluated in the same way that we understand and evaluate these "ordinary" experiences.

9 Walt Whitman (1976), p. 41.

Appendix: Comparisons between the Plato/Hegel argument for a God within us, and several well-known arguments for God, pp. 213–217

1 C. S. Lewis (2001), pp. 22, 24.
2 C. S. Lewis (2001), p. 10.
3 *Summa Theologica*, Question 2, Article 3, "On the contrary," first way.

BIBLIOGRAPHY

Abrams, M. H., *Natural Supernaturalism: Tradition and Revolution in Romantic Literature*. New York, NY: Norton, 1971.
Adams, Robert M., *Finite and Infinite Goods: A Framework for Ethics*. New York, NY: Oxford University Press, 1999.
Adamson, Peter, *Classical Philosophy: A History of Philosophy Without Any Gaps*, vol. 1. Oxford: Oxford University Press, 2014.
Alighieri, Dante, *Divina Commedia:* Texts from *The Divine Comedy of* Dante Alighieri, trans. Allen Mandelbaum. New York: Bantam, 1982–1984. Translations by the present author.
Allen, R. E., *The Dialogues of Plato. Vol. 2: The Symposium*. New Haven, CT: Yale University Press, 1991.
Allen, R. E., ed., *Studies in Plato's Metaphysics*. London: Routledge and Kegan Paul, 1965.
Ameriks, Karl, ed., *The Cambridge Companion to German Idealism*. Cambridge: Cambridge University Press, 2000.
Ameriks, Karl, "The Legacy of Idealism in Feuerbach, Marx, and Kierkegaard." In Ameriks, 2000.
Annas, Julia, *Platonic Ethics, Old and New*. Ithaca, NY: Cornell University Press, 2000.
Anscombe, G. E. M., "Modern Moral Philosophy." *Philosophy* 33:124 (January 1958), pp. 1–16.
Armstrong, John M., "After the Ascent: Plato on Becoming Like God." *Oxford Studies in Ancient Philosophy* 26 (2004), pp. 171–83.
St. Augustine, *Confessions*, trans. Henry Chadwick. Oxford: Oxford University Press, 1992.
Ayer, A. J., *Language, Truth and Logic*. London: Gollancz, 1946; reprinted New York, NY: Dover, n.d.
Ayer, A. J., *The Problem of Knowledge*. London: Macmillan, 1956.
Baldwin, Anna, and Sarah Hutton, eds., *Platonism and the English Imagination*. Cambridge: Cambridge University Press, 1994.
Barnes, Jonathan, ed., *The Complete Works of Aristotle*. Oxford: Oxford University Press, 1984.
Baynes, Kenneth, James Bohman, and Thomas McCarthy, eds., *After Philosophy: End or Transformation?* Cambridge, MA: MIT Press, 1987.
Beierwaltes, Werner, *Platonismus und Idealismus*. Frankfurt: Klostermann, 1972 and 2004.
Beiser, Frederick C., *Diotima's Children: German Aesthetic Rationalism from Leibniz to Lessing*. Oxford: Oxford University Press, 2009.
Beiser, Frederick C., *The Fate of Reason: German Philosophy from Kant to Fichte*. Cambridge, MA: Harvard University Press, 1987.

Beiser, Frederick C., *Hegel*. New York, NY: Routledge, 2005.
Bergson, Henri, *The Two Sources of Morality and Religion*. Henry Holt, 1935; reprinted Garden City, NY: Doubleday Anchor, no date.
Berlin, Isaiah, "Two Concepts of Liberty" (1958), in his *Four Essays on Liberty*. Oxford: Oxford University Press, 1969.
Blackburn, Simon, *Plato's Republic: A Biography*. New York, NY: Atlantic Monthly, 2007.
Blake, William, *Selected Poems*, ed. G. E. Bentley, Jr. New York, NY: Penguin, 2005.
Blumenberg, Hans, "An Anthropological Approach to the Contemporary Significance of Rhetoric." In Baynes, Bohman, and McCarthy, eds. 1987.
Blumenberg, Hans, *Höhlenausgänge*. Frankfurt am Main: Suhrkamp, 1996.
Blumenberg, Hans, *Wirklichkeiten in denen wir leben*. Stuttgart: Reclam, 1981.
Bosanquet, Bernard, *What Religion Is*. London: Macmillan, 1920.
Bradley, Francis Herbert, *Appearance and Reality: A Metaphysical Essay*. Oxford: Clarendon Press, 1893.
Bradley, Francis Herbert, *Ethical Studies*. Oxford: Oxford University Press, 1927/1962.
Brandom, Robert, *Tales of the Mighty Dead: Historical Essays in the Metaphysics of Intentionality*. Cambridge, MA: Harvard University Press, 2002.
Bregman, Jay, "The Neoplatonic Revival in North America." *Hermathena* 149 (Winter, 1990), pp. 99–119.
Brickhouse, Thomas C., and Nicholas D. Smith, *The Trial and Execution of Socrates. Sources and Controversies*. Oxford: Oxford University Press, 2002.
Bristow, William F., *Hegel and the Transformation of Philosophical Critique*. New York, NY: Oxford University Press, 2007.
Bröcker, Walter, "Platons Ontologischer Komparativ." *Hermes* 87:4 (December 1959), pp. 415–25.
Brown, Stuart Gerry, "Emerson's Platonism." *New England Quarterly* 18:3 (September 1945), pp. 325–45.
Burnyeat, Miles, "Idealism and Greek Philosophy: What Descartes Saw and Berkeley Missed." *Philosophical Review* 91 (1982), pp. 3–40.
Bussanich, John, "Socrates the Mystic." In Cleary, ed., 1999.
Campbell, Joseph, *The Hero with a Thousand Faces*. New York, NY: Pantheon, 1949.
Capra, Fritjof, *The Tao of Physics*. New York, NY: Bantam, 1977.
Cherniss, Harold, *Aristotle's Criticism of Plato and the Academy*. Baltimore, MD: Johns Hopkins University Press, 1944.
Cherniss, Harold, *The Riddle of the Early Academy*. Berkeley, CA: University of California Press, 1945.
Chopra, Deepak, *Quantum Healing*. New York, NY: Bantam, 1996.
Christensen, Michael J., and Jeffery A. Wittung, eds., *Partakers of the Divine Nature: The History and Development of Divinization in the Christian Traditions*. Cranbury, NJ: Associated University Presses, 2007.
Christman, John, "Autonomy in Moral and Political Philosophy." Stanford Encyclopedia of Philosophy online, 2009.
Clark, Stephen R. L., *Ancient Mediterranean Philosophy*. London: Bloomsbury, 2013.
Cleary, John J., ed., *Traditions of Platonism: Essays in Honor of John Dillon*. Aldershot: Ashgate, 1999.
Cohn, Norman, *The Pursuit of the Millenium*. Oxford: Oxford University Press, 1957/1970.
Cole, Andrew, *The Birth of Theory*. Chicago, IL: University of Chicago Press, 2014.
Collingwood, R. G., *Speculum Mentis or The Map of Knowledge*. Oxford: Oxford University Press, 1924.

Conze, Edward, *Buddhism: Its Essence and Development*. New York, NY: Harper, 1959.
Cornford, F. M., *Plato's Cosmology*. London: Routledge and Kegan Paul, 1937.
Cushman, Robert E., *Therapeia: Plato's Conception of Philosophy*. Chapel Hill, NC: University of North Carolina Press, 1958.
The Daodejing, in *Readings in Classical Chinese Philosophy*, eds. Philip J. Ivanhoe and Bryan W. Van Norden. Indianapolis, IN: Hackett, 2001.
Dawkins, Richard, *The God Delusion*. New York, NY: Houghton Mifflin, 2006.
Desjardins, Rosemary, *Plato and the Good: Illuminating the Darkling Vision*. Leiden and Boston, MA: Brill, 2004.
Desmond, William, *Hegel's God: A Counterfeit Double?* Aldershot: Ashgate, 2003.
Dodds, E. R., *The Greeks and the Irrational*. Berkeley, CA: University of California Press, 1951.
Dreyfus, Hubert, and Sean D. Kelly, *All Things Shining. Reading the Western Classics to Find Meaning in a Secular Age*. Detroit, MI: Free Press, 2011.
Dworkin, Ronald, *Religion Without God*. Cambridge, MA: Harvard University Press, 2013.
Eckhart, Meister, *Selected Writings*, trans. Oliver Davies. London: Penguin, 1994.
Ellis, Fiona, *God, Value, and Nature*. Oxford: Oxford University Press, 2014.
Emerson, Ralph Waldo, *Emerson's Prose and Poetry*, eds. Joel Porte and Saundra Morris. New York, NY: Norton, 2001.
Emerson, Ralph Waldo, *The Essays of Ralph Waldo Emerson*. Cambridge, MA: Harvard University Press, 1979.
Ferraris, Maurizio, *Introduction to New Realism*. London: Bloomsbury, 2015.
Festugiere, A. J., *Contemplation et vie contemplative selon Platon*. Paris: Vrin, 1935/1975.
Feuerbach, Ludwig, *The Essence of Christianity*, trans. G. Eliot. New York, NY: Harper, 1957.
Feuerbach, Ludwig, *The Fiery Brook: Selected Writings of Ludwig Feuerbach*, trans. Z. Hanfi. Garden City, NY: Doubleday Anchor, 1972.
Findlay, John Niemeyer, *The Discipline of the Cave* and *The Transcendence of the Cave*. London: Allen and Unwin, 1966-1967.
Findlay, John Niemeyer, *Hegel: A Re-Examination*. London: George Allen and Unwin, 1958.
Findlay, John Niemeyer, *Plato: The Written and Unwritten Doctrines*. New York, NY: Humanities Press, 1974.
Fine, Gail, "Knowledge and Belief in *Republic* V." *Archiv für Geschichte der Philosophie* 60 (1978), pp. 121–39.
Fine, Gail, "Knowledge and Belief in *Republic* 5-7." In S. Everson, ed., *Cambridge Companions to Ancient Thought*, vol. 1. New York, NY: Cambridge University Press, 1990, pp. 85–115, and in Fine, ed., *Plato 1*, pp. 215–46.
Fine, Gail, ed., *The Oxford Handbook of Plato*. New York, NY: Oxford University Press, 2011.
Fine, Gail, ed., *Plato 1*. Oxford: Oxford University Press, 1999.
Fine, Gail, ed., *Plato 2*. Oxford: Oxford University Press, 1999.
Flanagan, Owen, *The Really Hard Problem: Meaning in a Material World*, Cambridge, MA: MIT Press, 2009.
Forman, Robert K. C., *Mysticism, Mind, Consciousness*. Albany, NY: SUNY Press, 1999.
Forman, Robert K. C., ed., *The Problem of Pure Consciousness: Mysticism and Philosophy*. New York, NY: Oxford University Press, 1990.
Fraenkel, Carlos, *Philosophical Religions from Plato to Spinoza: Reason, Religion, and Autonomy*. New York, NY: Cambridge University Press, 2013.

Freud, Sigmund, *Civilization and Its Discontents*. New York, NY: Norton, 1989.
Freud, Sigmund, *Standard Edition of the Complete Psychological Works of Sigmund Freud*. London: Hogarth, 1981.
Fukuyama, Francis, "The End of History?" *The National Interest* 16 (1989), pp. 3–18.
Gellman, Jerome, *Mystical Experience of God, A Philosophical Enquiry*. Aldershot: Ashgate, 2001.
Gellmann, Jerome, "Mysticism." Stanford Encyclopedia of Philosophy 2010, http://plato.stanford.edu/entries/mysticism/
Gerson, Lloyd P., *Ancient Epistemology*. New York, NY: Cambridge University Press, 2009.
Gerson, Lloyd P., *Aristotle and Other Platonists*. Ithaca, NY: Cornell University Press, 2005.
Gerson, Lloyd P., ed., *The Cambridge History of Philosophy in Late Antiquity*. 2 volumes. New York, NY: Cambridge University Press, 2011.
Gerson, Lloyd P., *From Plato to Platonism*. Ithaca, NY: Cornell University Press, 2013.
Gerson, Lloyd P., *God and Greek Philosophy: Studies in the Early History of Natural Theology*. London: Routledge, 1990.
Gerson, Lloyd P., *Knowing Persons: A Study in Plato*. Oxford: Oxford University Press, 2003.
Gill, Michael B., *The British Moralists on Human Nature and the Birth of Secular Ethics*. Cambridge: Cambridge University Press, 2011.
Gobsch, Wolfram, *Bedingungen des Unbedingten: Warum nur Tiere denken können*. Dissertation, Basel, 2013.
Gobsch, Wolfram, "Der Mensch als Widerspruch und absolutes Wissen: Eine hegelianische Kritik der transformativen Theorie des Geistes." In Kern and Kietzmann, eds. 2017.
Göcke, Benedikt and Christian Tapp, eds., *The Infinity of God*. Notre Dame, IN: University of Notre Dame Press, 2017.
Goetz, Stewart and Charles Taliaferro, *A Brief History of the Soul*. Chichester: Wiley-Blackwell, 2011.
Gonzalez, Francisco J., *Dialectic and Dialogue: Plato's Practice of Philosophical Inquiry*. Evanston, IL: Northwestern University Press, 1998.
Gonzalez, Francisco J., "Nonpropositional Knowledge in Plato." *Apeiron* 31 (1998), pp. 235–84.
Gonzalez, Francisco J., "Propositions or Objects? A Critique of Gail Fine on Knowledge and Belief in Republic V." *Phronesis* 41 (1996), pp. 245–75.
Gordon, Jill, *Plato's Erotic World: From Cosmic Origins to Human Death*. New York, NY: Cambridge University Press, 2012.
Grier, Philip T., "The End of History and the Return of History." In Jon Stewart, ed., *The Hegel Myths and Legends*. Evanston, IL: Northwestern, 1996, pp. 183–98.
Guyer, Paul, and Rolf-Peter Horstmann, "Idealism." Stanford Encyclopedia of Philosophy online, accessed 2015.
Habermas, Jürgen, *Moral Consciousness and Communicative Action*, trans. C. Lenhardt and S. W. Nicholsen. Cambridge, MA: MIT Press, 1992.
Halfwassen, Jens, *Der Aufstieg zum Einen: Untersuchungen zu Platon und Plotin*. Stuttgart: Teubner, 1992.
Halfwassen, Jens, *Hegel und der spätantike Neuplatonismus. Untersuchungen zur Metaphysik des Einen und des Nous in Hegels spekulativer und geschichtlicher Deutung*. Bonn: Bouvier 1999; Hamburg: Meiner, 2005.
Hanby, Michael, *No God, No Science?* Chichester: Wiley-Blackwell, 2017.
Harris, Sam, *Waking Up: A Guide to Spirituality Without Religion*. New York, NY: Simon and Schuster, 2014.

Hart, David Bentley, *The Experience of God: Being, Consciousness, Bliss*. New Haven, CT: Yale University Press, 2013.
Hartmann, Klaus, "Hegel: A Non-Metaphysical View." In A. MacIntyre, ed., *Hegel: A Collection of Critical Essays*. New York, NY: Anchor, 1972, pp. 101–24.
Hartshorne, Charles, and William L. Reese, eds., *Philosophers Speak of God*. Amherst, NY: Humanity Books, 2000 (originally Chicago, IL: University of Chicago Press, 1953).
Hasker, William, *The Emergent Self*. Ithaca, NY: Cornell University Press, 1999.
Hedley, Douglas, and Sarah Hutton, eds., *Platonism at the Origins of Modernity: Studies on Platonism and Early Modern Philosophy*. Dordrecht: Springer, 2008.
Hegel, G. W. F., *Aesthetics: Lectures on Fine Art*, trans. T. M. Knox. 2 volumes. Oxford: Oxford University Press, 1975.
Hegel, G. W. F., *Elements of the Philosophy of Right*, ed. A. W. Wood, trans. H. B. Nisbet. Cambridge: Cambridge University Press, 1991.
Hegel, G. W. F., *The Encyclopedia Logic*, trans. T. F. Geraets, W. A. Suchting, and H. S. Harris. Indianapolis, IN: Hackett, 1991.
Hegel, G. W. F., *Gesammelte Werke. Kritische Ausgabe*. Hamburg: Meiner, 1968-. Cited as "GW."
Hegel, G. W. F., *Hegel's Philosophy of Mind*, trans. William Wallace. Oxford: Oxford University Press, 1971.
Hegel, G. W. F., *Hegel's Science of Logic*, trans. A. V. Miller. Atlantic Highlands, NJ: Humanities Press, 1989. Cited as "HSL."
Hegel, G. W. F., *Lectures on the Philosophy of Religion*, trans. Peter C. Hodgson. 3 volumes. Berkeley, CA: University of California Press, 1984–1987. Cited as "LPR."
Hegel, G. W. F., *Lectures on the Philosophy of World History: Introduction*, trans. H. Nisbet. Cambridge: Cambridge University Press, 1975. Cited as "LPWH."
Hegel, G. W. F., *Phenomenology of Spirit*, trans. A. V. Miller. Oxford: Oxford University Press, 1977.
Hegel, G. W. F., *Vorlesungen über die Philosophie der Religion*, ed. W. Jaeschke. 3 volumes. Hamburg: Meiner, 1983–1985. Cited as "VPR."
Hegel, G. W. F., *Werke*, eds. E. Moldenhauer and K. M. Michel. Frankfurt am Main: Suhrkamp Verlag, 1970-. Cited as "SuW."
Heidegger, Martin, *Identity and Difference*. Chicago, IL: University of Chicago Press, 2002.
Heidegger, Martin, *An Introduction to Metaphysics*, trans. R. Manheim. Garden City, NY: Doubleday, 1961.
Heine, Heinrich, *Confessions*, trans. P. Heinegg. No place given: Joseph Simon, 1981.
Heine, Heinrich, *Heinrich Heine's Sämmtliche Werke*. Philadelphia, PA: John Weit, 1860.
Hobbes, Thomas, *Leviathan*. 1651.
Holt, Edwin B., Walter T. Marvin, William P. Montague, Ralph B. Perry, Walter B. Pitkin, and Edward G. Spaulding, *The New Realism: Cooperative Studies in Philosophy*. New York, NY: Macmillan, 1912.
Horn, Christoph, Jörn Müller, and Joachim Söder, eds., *Platon-Handbuch: Leben—Werk—Wirkung*. Stuttgart: J.B. Metzler, 2009.
Houlgate, Stephen. *The Opening of Hegel's Logic: From Being to Infinity*. West Lafayette, IN: Purdue University Press, 2006.
Hume, David, *Enquiries Concerning Human Understanding and Concerning the Principles of Morals*, ed. L. A. Selby-Bigge. Oxford: Oxford University Press, 1902.
Hume, David, *A Treatise of Human Nature*, ed. L. A. Selby-Bigge. Oxford: Oxford University Press, 1978.
Huxley, Aldous, *The Doors of Perception*. New York, NY: Harper, 1954.

Huxley, Aldous, *The Perennial Philosophy*. New York, NY: Harper, 1945.
Insole, Christopher J., *The Intolerable God: Kant's Theological Journey*. New York, NY: Oxford University Press, 2016.
Insole, Christopher J., *Kant and the Creation of Freedom: A Theological Problem*. New York, NY: Oxford University Press, 2013.
Irwin, Terence H., *Classical Thought*. New York, NY: Oxford University Press, 1989.
Irwin, Terence H., *The Development of Ethics: A Historical and Critical Study*. 3 volumes. New York, NY: Oxford University Press, 2011.
Irwin, Terence H., *Plato's Ethics*. New York, NY: Oxford University Press, 1995.
Jaeschke, Walter, *Hegel Handbuch. Leben-Werk-Schule*. Stuttgart: Metzler, 2003.
James, William, *A Pluralistic Universe*, 1909; reprinted in William James (1987).
James, William, *The Varieties of Religious Experience:. A Study in Human Nature*. 1902; reprinted in William James (1987).
James, William, *Writings 1902–1910*. New York, NY: Literary Classics of the United States, 1987.
Johansen, Thomas K., *Plato's Natural Philosophy*. Cambridge: Cambridge University Press, 2004.
Jollimore, Troy, *Love's Vision*. Princeton, NJ: Princeton University Press, 2011.
Jones, Richard H., *The Philosophy of Mysticism*. Albany, NY: SUNY Press, 2017.
Jung, Carl Gustav, *Dreams*. Princeton, NJ: Princeton University Press, 1974.
Jung, Carl Gustav, *Modern Man in Search of a Soul*. New York, NY: Harcourt, 1933.
Kalsched, Donald, *Trauma and the Soul: A Psycho-Spiritual Approach to Human Development and Its Interruption*. New York, NY: Routledge, 2013.
Kant, Immanuel, *Critique of Pure Reason*. 1781/1787. Cited as "CPuR."
Kant, Immanuel, *Kants gesammelte Schriften*. Berlin Akademie der Wissenschaften, 1900-. Cited by "Ak." volume and page number.
Katz, Steven T., ed., *Mysticism and Philosophical Analysis*. New York, NY: Oxford University Press, 1978.
Keats, John, *Keats's Poetry and Prose*, ed. Jeffrey N. Cox. New York, NY: W.W. Norton Co., 2008.
Kern, Andrea, *Sources of Knowledge: On the Concept of a Rational Capacity for Knowledge*. Cambridge, MA: Harvard University Press, 2017.
Kern, Andrea, and Christian Kietzmann, eds., *Selbstbewusstes Leben: Texte zu einer transformativen Theorie der menschlichen Subjektivität*. Frankfurt am Main: Suhrkamp, 2017.
Kierkegaard, Soren, *Fear and Trembling*, trans. Walter Lowrie. Princeton, NJ: Princeton University Press, 1941.
Kimhi, Irad, *Thinking and Being*. Cambridge, MA: Harvard University Press, 2018.
Kirk, G. S., and J. E. Raven, eds., *The Presocratic Philosophers*. Cambridge: Cambridge University Press, 1969.
Konstan, David, and N. Keith Rutter, eds., *Envy, Spite and Jealousy: The Rivalrous Emotions in Ancient Greece*. Edinburgh: Edinburgh University Press, 2003.
Korsgaard, Christine, *The Sources of Normativity*. Cambridge: Cambridge University Press, 1996.
Kosman, L. A., "Platonic Love." In W. H. Werkmeister, ed., *Facets of Plato's Philosophy*. Assen: Van Gorcum, 1976. Corrected version in Soble (1989).
Kouzmanoff, Kathleen, *Lifewheel: Your Choices at Life's Every Turn*. Self-published, 2005.
Krämer, Hans Joachim, *Arete bei Platon und Aristoteles. Zum Wesen und zur Geschichte der platonischen Ontologie*. Heidelberg: Universitätsverlag Heidelberg (Abhandlungen

der Heidelberger Akademie der Wissenschaften, Philosophisch-historische Klasse: Jahrgang 1959, 6th Abhandlung), 1959.
Krämer, Hans Joachim, *Plato and the Foundations of Metaphysics*, trans. J. R. Catan. Albany, NY: SUNY Press, 1990.
Kraut, Richard, ed., *The Cambridge Companion to Plato*. New York, NY: Cambridge University Press, 1992.
Lane, Melissa, *Plato's Progeny: How Socrates and Plato Still Captivate the Modern Mind*. London: Duckworth, 2001.
Lear, Jonathan, *Love and Its Place in Nature: A Philosophical Interpretation of Freudian Psychoanalysis*. New York, NY: Farrar, Straus & Giroux, 1990.
Lear, Jonathan, *Open Minded: Working Out the Logic of the Soul*. Cambridge, MA: Harvard University Press, 1998.
Lewis, C. S., *Mere Christianity*. New York, NY: HarperCollins, 2001.
Lilar, Suzanne, *Aspects of Love in Western Society*. New York, NY: McGraw-Hill, 1965.
Löwith, Karl, *From Hegel to Nietzsche: The Revolution in Nineteenth-Century Thought*. Garden City, NY: Doubleday Anchor, 1967.
Löwith, Karl, *Meaning in History*. Chicago, IL: University of Chicago Press, 1949.
MacIntyre, Alasdair, *After Virtue: A Study in Moral Theory*. Third edition. Notre Dame, IN: University of Notre Dame Press, 2007.
Magee, Bryan, *The Philosophy of Schopenhauer*. Oxford: Oxford University Press, 1997.
Marx, Karl, and Friedrich Engels, *The Marx-Engels Reader*, ed. Robert C. Tucker. New York, NY: Norton, 1978.
McDowell, John, "The Apperceptive I and the Empirical Self: Towards a Heterodox Reading of 'Lordship and Bondage' in Hegel's *Phenomenology*." *Bulletin of the Hegel Society of Great Britain* 47/48 (2003), pp. 1–16; reprinted in McDowell (2009).
McDowell, John, *Having the World in View: Essays on Kant, Hegel, and Sellars*. Cambridge, MA: Harvard University Press, 2009.
McDowell, John, *Mind and World*. Cambridge, MA: Harvard University Press, 1994.
McDowell, John, *Mind, Value, and Reality*. Cambridge, MA: Harvard University Press, 1998.
McEvilley, Thomas, *The Shape of Ancient Thought: Comparative Studies in Greek and Indian Philosophies*. New York, NY: Allworth, 2002.
McGinn, Bernard, *The Presence of God: A History of Western Christian Mysticism*. New York, NY: Crossroad, 1991–.
McGuinness, B. F., "The Mysticism of the *Tractatus*." *Philosophical Review* 75:3 (1966), pp. 305–28.
Mele, Alfred, *Effective Intentions: The Power of Conscious Will*. Oxford: Oxford University Press, 2009.
Menn, Stephen, *Descartes and Augustine*. Cambridge: Cambridge University Press, 1998.
Menn, Stephen, *Plato on God as Nous*. Carbondale, IL: Southern Illinois University Press, 1995.
Millar, Alan, Review of Ralph Wedgwood, "The Nature of Normativity." *Mind* 119 (January 2010), pp. 262–66.
Moore, Adrian W., *The Evolution of Modern Metaphysics: Making Sense of Things*. Cambridge: Cambridge University Press, 2012.
Moore, Adrian W., *The Infinite*. Second edition. New York, NY: Routledge, 2001.
Moore, Adrian W., *Points of View*. Oxford: Oxford University Press, 1997.
Moore, George Edward, "The Refutation of Idealism." *Mind* 12 (1903), pp. 433–53.

Moore, George Edward, "The Value of Religion." *International Journal of Ethics* 12 (1901), pp. 81–98.
Mooren, Nadine, and Michael Quante, eds., *Kommentar zu Hegels Wissenschaft der Logik*. Hamburg: Meiner, 2018.
Murdoch, Iris, *Metaphysics as a Guide to Morals*. New York, NY: Penguin, 1993.
Nagel, Thomas, *Mind and Cosmos: Why the Materialist Neo-Darwinian Conception of Nature Is Almost Certainly False*. New York, NY: Oxford University Press, 2012.
Nagel, Thomas, *Secular Philosophy and the Religious Temperament*. New York, NY: Oxford University Press, 2009.
Nagel, Thomas, *The View From Nowhere*. New York, NY: Oxford University Press, 1986.
Neumann, Erich, *Amor and Psyche: The Psychic Development of the Feminine. A Commentary on the Tale by Apuleius*. New York, NY: Bollingen, Princeton University Press, 1956.
Neumann, Erich, *The Origins and History of Consciousness*. Princeton, NJ: Princeton University Press, 1954.
Nietzsche, Friedrich, *Basic Writings of Nietzsche*, trans. W. Kaufmann. New York, NY: Random House, 1968.
Nietzsche, Friedrich, *Beyond Good and Evil* (1886), trans. W. Kaufmann. New York, NY: Random House, 1966.
Nietzsche, Friedrich, *Thus Spake Zarathustra*, 1883–1885.
Nietzsche, Friedrich, *The Will to Power*, trans. W. Kaufmann and R. J. Hollingdale. New York, NY: Harper, 1967.
Nussbaum, Martha, *The Fragility of Goodness*. New York, NY: Cambridge University Press, 1986; updated edition, 2001.
Nussbaum, Martha, *Love's Knowledge*. New York, NY: Oxford University Press, 1992.
Nussbaum, Martha, *Upheavals of Thought: The Intelligence of Emotions*. New York, NY: Cambridge University Press, 2003.
Nygren, Anders, *Agape and Eros*. Chicago, IL: University of Chicago Press, 1982.
Perl, Eric, *Theophany: The Neoplatonic Philosophy of Dionysius the Areopagite*. Albany, NY: SUNY Press, 2007.
Pinkard, Terry, *German Philosophy 1760–1860: The Legacy of Idealism*. Cambridge: Cambridge University Press, 2002.
Pinkard, Terry, *Hegel's Naturalism: Mind, Nature, and the Final Ends of Life*. Oxford: Oxford University Press, 2012.
Pippin, Robert, *Hegel's Realm of Shadows: Logic as Metaphysics in the Science of Logic*. Chicago, IL: University of Chcago Press, 2018.
Plato. *Complete Works*, ed. John M. Cooper. Indianapolis, IN: Hackett, 1997.
Plato on Love, ed. C. D. C. Reeve. Indianapolis, IN: Hackett, 2006.
Plevrakis, Ermylos, *Das Absolute und der Begriff. Zur Frage philosophischer Theologie in Hegels Wissenschaft der Logik*. Tübingen: Mohr Siebeck, 2017.
Polanyi, Michael, *Personal Knowledge: Towards a Post-Critical Philosophy*. Chicago, IL: University of Chicago Press, 1958, corrected edition 1962.
Popper, Karl, *The Open Society and Its Enemies*. London: Routledge, 1945.
Price, A. W., *Love and Friendship in Plato and Aristotle*. Oxford: Oxford University Press, 1989.
Quine, W. V. O., "Two Dogmas of Empiricism," in his *From a Logical Point of View*. Cambridge, MA: Harvard University Press, 1953.
Rahner, Karl Karl, *Foundations of Christian Faith: An Introduction to the Idea of Christianity*, trans. William V. Dych. London: Darton, Longman and Todd, 1978.

Ramelli, Ilaria, "Luke 17:21: 'The kingdom of God is inside you.' The Ancient Syriac Versions in Support of the Correct Translation." *Hugoye: Journal of Syriac Studies* 12:2 (2009), pp. 259–86. (Available online, March 2013).
Rawls, John, *A Theory of Justice*. Cambridge, MA: Harvard University Press, 1971.
Reid, Thomas, *Essays on the Active Powers of Man*. 1788.
Rhodes, James M., *Eros, Wisdom, and Silence*: *Plato's Erotic Dialogues*. Columbia, MO: University of Missouri Press, 2003.
Richardson, Robert D. Jr., *Emerson. The Mind on Fire*. Berkeley, CA: University of California Press, 1995.
Robinson, Timothy A., ed., *God*. Second edition. Indianapolis, IN: Hackett, 2002.
Rödl, Sebastian, *Categories of the Temporal: An Inquiry Into the Forms of the Finite Intellect*. Cambridge, MA: Harvard University Press, 2012.
Rödl, Sebastian, "The Science of Logic as the Self-Constitution of the Power of Knowledge." In Markus Gabriel and Anders Moe Rasmussen, eds., *German Idealism Today*. Berlin: DeGruyter, 2017.
Rödl, Sebastian, "Selbsterkenntnis des Selbstbewegers." In Kern and Kietzmann, eds., 2017, pp. 209–25.
Rödl, Sebastian, *Self-Consciousness*. Cambridge, MA: Harvard University Press, 2007.
Rödl, Sebastian, *Self-Consciousness and Objectivity: An Introduction to Absolute Idealism*. Cambridge, MA: Harvard University Press, 2018.
Rometsch, Jens, "Why There Is No 'Recognition-Theory' in Hegel's 'Struggle of Recognition': Towards an Epistemological Reading of the Lord-Servant Relationship." In Markus Gabriel and Anders Moe Rasmussen, eds., *German Idealism Today*. Berlin: De Gruyter, 2017, pp. 159–85.
Rorty, Richard, *Contingency, Irony, and Solidarity*. Cambridge: Cambridge University Press, 1989.
Rosen, Stanley, *The Idea of Hegel's Science of Logic*. Chicago, IL: University of Chicago Press, 2014.
Rosen, Stanley, *Nihilism: A Philosophical Essay*. New Haven, CT and London: Yale University Press, 1969.
de Rougemont, Denis, *Love in the Western World*. Princeton, NJ: Princeton University Press, 1983.
Rumi, Jelaluddin, *The Essential Rumi*, trans. Coleman Barks. New York, NY: Harper, 2004.
Russell, Bertrand, *A History of Western Philosophy*. New York, NY: Simon and Schuster, 1945.
Russell, Bertrand, *Mysticism and Logic*. London: Longmans, Green, 1918; reprinted Mineola, NY: Dover, 2004.
Russell, Bertrand, *The Problems of Philosophy*. 1912; reprinted New York, NY: Oxford University Press, 1997.
Santayana, George, *The Genteel Tradition: Nine Essays by George Santayana*, ed. Douglas L. Wilson. Cambridge, MA: Harvard University Press, 1967.
Sartre, Jean-Paul, *Notebooks for an Ethics*. Chicago, IL: University of Chicago Press, 1992.
Sayre, Kenneth, *Plato's Late Ontology: A Riddle Resolved*. Princeton, NJ: Princeton University Press, 1983.
Scanlon, Thomas M., *Being Realistic About Reasons*. New York, NY: Oxford University Press, 2016.
Schindler, D. C., *Plato's Critique of Impure Reason: On Goodness and Truth in the Republic*. Washington, DC: Catholic University of America Press, 2008.
Schmitt, Arbogast, *Modernity and Plato: Two Paradigms of Rationality*. Rochester, NY: Camden House, 2012.

Schneewind, Jerome B., *The Invention of Autonomy: A History of Modern Moral Philosophy*. Cambridge: Cambridge University Press, 1997.
Schopenhauer, Arthur, *The World as Will and Representation*, trans. E. J. F. Payne. Indian Hills, CO: The Falcon's Wing, 1958.
Sedley, David, *Creationism and Its Critics in Antiquity*. Berkeley, CA: University of California Press, 2007.
Sedley, David, "The Ideal of Godlikeness." In Fine, ed., *Plato 2*. 1999.
Sellars, Wilfrid, *Empiricism and the Philosophy of Mind*. Cambridge, MA: Harvard University Press, 1997.
Sellars, Wilfrid, *Science and Metaphysics: Variations on Kantian Themes*. New York, NY: Humanities Press, 1968.
Sellars, Wilfrid, *Science, Perception, and Reality*. New York, NY: Humanities Press, 1963.
Shear, Jonathan, *The Inner Dimension. Philosophy and the Experience of Consciousness*. New York, NY: Peter Lang, 1990.
Sheffield, Frisbee C. C., *Plato's Symposium: The Ethics of Desire*. Oxford: Oxford University Press, 2006.
Skinner, B. F., "The Design of Cultures." *Daedalus* 90:3 (1961), pp. 534–46.
Smith, Huston, *Forgotten Truth: The Common Vision of the World's Religions*. New York, NY: Harper, 1976.
Soble, Alan, ed., *Eros, Agape, and Philia: Readings in the Philosophy of Love*. New York, NY: Paragon, 1989.
Spinoza, Baruch, *The Ethics and Selected Letters*, trans. Samuel Shirley. Indianapolis, IN: Hackett, 1982.
Sprigge, T. L. S., "Idealism." In Edward Craig, ed., *Routledge Encyclopedia of Philosophy*. New York, NY: Routledge online, 1998.
Stace, Walter T., *Mysticism and Philosophy*. New York, NY: Lippincott, 1960.
Stewart, Jon, ed., *The Hegel Myths and Legends*. Evanston, IL: Northwestern University Press, 1996.
Strauss, Leo. *Natural Right and History*. Chicago: University of Chicago Press, 1953.
Taylor, Charles, *Hegel*. Cambridge: Cambridge University Press, 1977.
Taylor, Charles, *Philosophical Papers*, vols. 1 and 2. Cambridge: Cambridge University Press, 1985.
Taylor, Charles, *A Secular Age*. Cambridge, MA: Harvard University Press, 2007.
Taylor, Charles. *Sources of the Self: The Making of the Modern Identity*. Cambridge, MA: Harvard University Press, 1989.
Theron, Stephen, *The Apotheosis of Logic*. Newcastle upon Tyne: Cambridge Scholars Publishing, 2017.
Theron, Stephen, *The Orthodox Hegel: Development Further Developed*. Newcastle upon Tyne: Cambridge Scholars Publishing, 2014.
Thompson, Michael, *Life and Action: Elementary Structures of Practice and Practical Thought*. Cambridge, MA: Harvard University Press, 2008.
Tillich, Paul, *Systematic Theology*. Chicago, IL: University of Chicago Press, 1951–1963.
Toews, John Edward, *Hegelianism: The Path Toward Dialectical Humanism*. Cambridge: Cambridge University Press, 1980.
Tolle, Eckhart, *The Power of Now: A Guide to Spiritual Enlightenment*. Novato, CA: New World Library, 1999.
Underhill, Evelyn, *Mysticism: A Study of the Nature and Development of Man's Spiritual Consciousness*. London: Methuen, 1911.

Uzdavinys, Algis, *Philosophy as a Rite of Rebirth: From Ancient Egypt to Neoplatonism*. Dilton Marsh: Prometheus Trust, 2008.
Versluis, Arthur, *American Gurus: From Transcendentalism to New Age Religion*. New York, NY: Oxford University Press, 2014.
Vlastos, Gregory, *Platonic Studies*. Princeton, NJ: Princeton University Press, 1973 and 1981.
Wainwright, William J., *Mysticism: A Study of Its Cognitive Value and Moral Implications*. Brighton: Harvester, 1981.
Wallace, Robert M., *Hegel's Philosophy of Reality, Freedom, and God*. New York, NY: Cambridge University Press, 2005.
Wallace, Robert M., "How G. W. F. Hegel's Broadly Platonic Idealism Explains Knowledge, Value, and Freedom." Forthcoming in B. Göcke and J. R. Farris, eds., *Rethinking Idealism and Immaterialism*. Routledge.
Wallace, Robert M., "How Hegel Reconciles Private Freedom and Citizenship." *Journal of Political Philosophy* 7 (1999), pp. 419–33.
Wallace, Robert M., "How Plato and Hegel Integrate the Sciences, the Arts, Religion, and Philosophy." Forthcoming in *Hegel-Jahrbuch*.
Wallace, Robert M., review of Hubert Dreyfus and Sean D. Kelly, *All Things Shining: Times Literary Supplement*, July 8, 2011.
Wallace, Robert M., "Infinity and Spirit: How Hegel Integrates Science and Religion, and Nature and the Supernatural." In Göcke and Tapp, eds., *The Infinity of God*. 2018.
Wallace, Robert M., "True Infinity and Hegel's Rational Mysticism: A Reply to Professor Williams." *The Owl of Minerva* 42:1–2 (2010–2011), pp. 123–35.
Watson, Gary, "Free Agency." *Journal of Philosophy* lxxii (1975), pp. 205–20.
Watson, Gary, ed., *Free Will*. Oxford: Oxford University Press, 1982.
Wedgwood, Ralph, *The Nature of Normativity*. Oxford: Oxford University Press, 2007.
"What the 'Bleep' Do We Know?" Film, 2004.
Whitehead, Alfred North, *Adventures of Ideas*. New York, NY: Macmillan, 1933.
Whitehead, Alfred North, *Process and Reality*. New York, NY: Macmillan, 1929.
Whitehead, Alfred North, *Religion in the Making*. New York, NY: Macmillan, 1926; reprinted New York, NY: Fordham University Press, 1996.
Whitehead, Alfred North, *Science and the Modern World*. New York, Macmillan, 1926.
Whiting, Jennifer, "Impersonal Friends." *The Monist* 74 (1991), pp. 3–29.
Whiting, Jennifer, "Psychic Contingency in the *Republic*." In Rachel Barney, Tad Brennan, and Charles Brittain, eds., *Plato and the Divided Self*. Cambridge: Cambridge University Press, 2012.
Whitman, Walt, *Leaves of Grass: The First (1855) Edition*, ed. Malcolm Cowley. New York, NY: Penguin, 1976.
Wikipedia article, "Divinization (Christian)." Accessed July 9, 2014.
Wilber, Ken, *Sex, Ecology, Spirituality*. Collected Works of Ken Wilber, vol. 6. Boston, MA and London: Shambala, 2000.
Williams, Bernard, *Ethics and the Limits of Philosophy*. Cambridge, MA: Harvard University Press, 1986.
Wittgenstein, Ludwig, *Notebooks 1914–1916*, eds. E. Anscombe and G. H. Von Wright, trans. E. Anscombe. New York, NY: Harper, 1961.
Wittgenstein, Ludwig, *Tractatus Logico-Philosophicus*, trans. David Pears and Brian McGuinness. London: Routledge, 1961 (first published 1921).
Wolf, Fred Alan, *The Spiritual Universe: How Quantum Physics Proves the Existence of the Soul*. New York, NY: Simon and Schuster, 1996.

Wolf, Susan, *Freedom Within Reason*. Oxford: Oxford University Press, 1990.
Young, Edward, *Night Thoughts*, ed. Stephen Cornford. Cambridge: Cambridge University Press, 1989.
Yount, David J., *Plotinus the Platonist: A Comparative Account of Plato and Plotinus' Metaphysics*. London: Bloomsbury, 2014.
Yount, David J., *Plato and Plotinus on Mysticism, Epistemology, and Ethics*. London: Bloomsbury, 2017.
Zaehner, R. C., *Mysticism, Sacred and Profane: An Inquiry Into Some Varieties of Praeternatural Experience*. Oxford: Oxford University Press, 1957.

INDEX

Abrams, M. H.
  Natural Supernaturalism 234
Adamson, Peter 16
Alcibiades 30, 35
Anaxagoras 126
Anaximander 189
Anaximenes 189
Annas, Julia 246–7
Anscombe, G. E. M. 140
anthropotheism 71
Aristotle 4, 25, 28, 108, 140
  not a naturalist 77–8, 218
  reality and goodness 196, 198
  second nature 55
ascent, *see also* transcendence
  in Hegel 59–60, 78
  rational or Platonic 4, 7, 37, 89, 217
Austen, Jane 158, 175
authenticity 30
Ayer, Alfred Jules 6, 48–9, 123
  Language, Truth, and Logic 48
  value as emotion 48

beauty
  in everything 19
  natural 244
    reason in 21, 222–3
Beghards 103
being oneself 29, 64
Bergson, Henri 5, 13, 98
Berkeley, George 8, 81–2
Berlin, Isaiah 146–7
Blake, William 19
Blumenberg, Hans 4
  critique of Plato 124–5
body
  mind and 3, 24

Bordt, Michael 248
Bosanquet, Bernard 39, 40, 70
Bradley, Francis Herbert 5, 39–40, 44, 232, 234
Brahman 10
Brandom, Robert 229
Bröcker, Walter 4, 118
Buddha nature 10

Caird, Edward 39
Callicles, in Plato's Gorgias 151
Cambridge Platonists 173
Campbell, Joseph 30
Capra, Fritjof 98
Carnap, Rudolph 49
charisma 83
Charmides, Plato's cousin 151
choice 1
Chopra, Deepak 98
Christman, John 140
Collingwood, Robin George 25
common sense 4, 81
creationism 247
Critias, Plato's uncle 151

Dante Alighieri 28, 158
Darwinism 119
Dawkins, Richard 96
deism 98–9
Democritus 196
Descartes, Rene 92, 108
Dewey, John 130
Dickinson, Emily 28
Dionysus 160
disenchantment of the world 55, 157
Dodds, E. R. 159
Dreyfus, Hubert 243

dualism   6, 7, 37, 45, 48, 49, 71, 76
   Hegel's critique of   105
   Plato and   105
   rational ascent and   4
Dubois, W. E. B.   139

Eckhart, Meister   103, 108
Emerson, Ralph Waldo   5, 25, 26
   "The Over-Soul"   38–9
   Plato and Plotinus and   38–9
   "Self-reliance"   38–9
empiricism   28
   critics of   238
Epicurus   112, 196
Erasmus   108
eternity
   in an hour   19
ethics   2, 69, 244
Euthyphro, in Plato   35
examined life   10
existentialism   28, 121
externality
   to each other   2–3

fact
   value and   2, 23, 24
   value reconciled with   23
faith   14, 37
Fechner, Gustav   40
Festugiere, Andre Jean   248
Feuerbach, Ludwig   71–2, 89
   Essence of Christianity   71–3
Ficino, Marsilio   173
Findlay, John Niemeyer   5, 6, 21, 120
   his "other-worldly geography"   51
first-person view
   vs. third-person view   7
Foot, Philippa   49
forgiveness   19, 20
Forman, Robert K. C.   249
freedom   29–30
   causation and   85
   depends on freedom of all   19
   empiricist theory of   144–6
   God and   67
   inner   10, 29, 31, 219
      reason in   21
   love and ethics and   17

   mechanism and   24
   mutual influence and   86
   Plato and   140–2
   truth and   121
   voluntarist theory of   144
Freud, Sigmund   30, 104, 241
   sublimation   171, 242
Fukuyama, Francis   231

Gautama, Siddhartha   35
Gauthier, David   49
Gentile, Giovanni   70
Gerson, Lloyd   78, 120, 219
Gibbard, Allan   49
Gnostics   106, 108
Gobsch, Wolfram   6, 7, 21
God   1
   arguments for existence of   213
   authority of   11, 31
   conventional
      doesn't transcend   32
      isn't orthodox   96
   direct knowledge of   218, 249
   as distinct but not separate   12
   as doubt   92
   experience of   204–12
      everyday   205–12, 210
      extraordinary   207, 249
   freedom and   67, 91
   human responsibility and   68, 93
   love and   67
   orthodox vs. Pelagian   94
   Plato/Hegel   69
   science as a part of   22
   separate
      not self-governing   32, 94
      orthodox Christian thinking and   221
   as separate being   11, 87–8
   truly infinite
      can't exclude   18
   in us   14, 17, 31, 88–9, 90, 100–1
      gives beatitude/salvation   33
      gives world full reality   33
      grandiosity?   17
      loves everything   33
      not impersonal   34
      prayer and   91

whom we can know   12–14
who we are   17
   but we often don't know this   18
   Is this grandiosity?   17
worthy of worship   12, 31
Gorgias   140, 189
Greek cosmology
   goodness *vs*.chance   196
guidance, higher source of   5

Hare, Richard   49
Hart, David Bentley   248–9
Hartshorne, Charles   226
Hegel, G. W. F.   4, 12, 37
   arts and   240
   critique of the finite   50
   Encyclopedia of the Philosophical Sciences   20
   ethics   69
   fascism and   76
   God in us   70–1
   grandiosity?   17
   his God
      Christian teachings and   26
      deism and   98
      grandiosity?   222
      Heidegger's requirements and   99
      pantheism and   97
      truly transcendent   26, 32
   history   74–6
   idealism   8, 24, 62, 73, 81–2
   infinity
      critique of the spurious   51
      as finite's self-transcending   57
      true   26
   love and intellect   72
   Marx and   70, 73, 148
   a mystic?   16, 221
   naturalism and   4, 76
   Nazis and   148
   Phenomenology of Spirit   20
   Plato and   37, 78–9
   Plotinus and   246
   reality   60, 80–2
      as oneself   60
   reason and nature   57–61
   religion and   69, 70–1

   Science of Logic   20, 73, 76
   secularism and   75
   separate God not self-governing   32
   Spirit   25
      contrasted to Nature   77
   state and Idea   231
   transcendence
      critique of ordinary conceptions of   51
   the True and the Good   64–5, 234
Heidegger, Martin   4, 41, 49, 99
   on philosophers' God   99
   on Plato's idealism   127, 228
   on science   228
Heine, Heinrich   17
Heraclitus   189
Herbert, George   173
hero's journey   29
Hitler, Adolf   149–50
Hobbes, Thomas   112, 151
Homer   34
hopes
   millennarian and apocalyptic   20
humanism   18, 101, 222
humans
   as humans, are not God   18
   as inner freedom and love, are God   18
Hume, David   4, 37, 109, 112
Huxley, Aldous   102, 235
   The Perennial Philosophy   102

idealism
   existence of what's not self-determining and   25
   George Berkeley   24, 81
   Immanuel Kant   24, 81
   Plato/Hegel   8, 24, 62, 80–2
      anthropocentric?   82
      self-transcendence and   25
   point of   120–1, 127
ideals   1
identity, higher and lower   10
identity crisis   9, 14, 18, 47, 125
   traditional inner drama   47
Ilyin, Ivan   70
infinity   54
   true   18, 26, 50, 58, 89, 96

intellect
    love or emotions and   3
Irwin, Terence   16, 243, 245, 247

Jaeschke, Walter   76
James, William   5, 41, 42, 205, 207
    British Idealists and   39–40
Jefferson, Thomas   139
Jesus   35–6
    overriding value is inner   36
Jung, Carl Gustav   30, 104, 152–3
    sublimation   242

Kalsched, Donald   221
Kant, Immanuel   8, 28, 37, 69, 139
    dualism   108, 248
Katz, Steven   102
Keats, John   183
Kelly, Sean   243
Kern, Andrea   7
Kierkegaard, Soren   40, 41, 154–5, 159
Kimhi, Irad   7, 218, 230
knower
    world and   3, 24
knowledge
    modern problem of   3
Korsgaard, Christine   49
Kosman, Louis   243–4

Lear, Jonathan   25, 178
Leibniz, G. W.   173
Leucippus   196
Lewis, Clive Staples   97
    argument from moral law   213
        Plato/Hegel version of   214–15
Libet, Benjamin   233
Locke, John   139–40
love   2
    reason in   21
    romantic   174
    stories   173–4
Löwith, Karl   74–6
    dualism in   73
Lucretius   196
Luther, Martin   108

McDowell, John   5, 7, 49, 55
    "The Apperceptive I..."   57
    Mind and World   55–61, 56–7

our identity crisis and   56
reason and nature   55
Robert Brandom and   229
MacIntyre, Alasdair   140
Marx, Karl   39, 40
    on dialectic   73
    Hegel and   70
Mass
    Roman Catholic   31
materialism   28
me
    you reconciled with   23, 54
mechanism
    freedom and   24
Mele, Alfred   233
Menn, Stephen   195–6
Millar, Alan   150
mind
    body and   3, 24
    freedom and   3
modernity
    immanence and   26
Moore, A. W.   227
Moore, George Edward (G.E.)   44, 81
    "The Value of Religion"   44
Murdoch, Iris   5, 6, 13, 21
    art-object and person-object   52–3
    on God   52
    love has power   52
mysticism   1, 5, 15
    how it is perennial   102
    individuality and   166
    monistic vs. theistic   103–4
    philosophy explains   20
    primary meaning of   15
    as rational   1, 16, 73
    as salvation or awakening   16
    what I don't mean by   15
mystics
    Christian   36
    Islamic   36
    western philosopher   221

Nagel, Thomas   7, 232
naturalism   23, 49
    Hegel and   4, 76
Neumann, Erich   30
Nicolas Cusanus   172
Nietzsche, Friedrich   4, 41, 83, 108–9, 109, 151, 159

nihilism   14, 49, 221
Nussbaum, Martha   4, 27, 121, 176
   Plato answers   242, 243
Nygren, Anders   176, 180, 247

object
   reality and   24
   subject and   23, 24
      reconciled   23
objectification   23
objectivity
   beyond   23

panentheism   226
pantheism   97
Parmenides   127, 188–90
philosophy
   love and   157
Pinkard, Terry   76–8
Pippin, Robert   71, 78–9
Plato   10
   Alcibiades, picture of   131
   anamnesis   238
   apparent dualism in   108, 148
   arts and   228, 240
   ascent from the Cave   30, 35, 137
      allegory of freedom   138
   beauty and the Good   241
   becoming like God   185
      virtues and   192
   continuity with later Platonists   36
   critics of   4, 106
   critique of naturalism   111, 126, 194
   education   129–30
   Euthyphro, picture of   130–1
   fact and value reconciled   127, 238, 239
   forgiving and   149
   Form of the Good   123, 135–6
   Forms   115, 117, 120, 123
      separateness of   236–7, 238
   freedom and   140
   God (*see also* Plato, Timaeus dialogue)
      cosmological proof   199
      immanent or transcendent?   194
      jealousy and   28, 187, 191
      One and   188, 245–6
      reality as oneself and   156
      transcendence proof   199–201
      true Good   35

   god-given madness   153
      contra Kierkegaard   154–5
      kinds of   153–4
   going down   192–3
   homosexual romance in   160
   humankind's dark side and   150–2
   idealism   24–5
   Jung and   153
   knowledge and   123
   Laws
      cosmological proof of God   199
   love (*see also* Plato, Symposium)
      critics of Plato on   243
      of individuals   27, 175, 178
      reason and   27, 35, 158
   mathematics and   110, 136
   Meno dialogue   110
   modern philosophy and   139
   a mystic?   16, 221
   mystical images in   202–3
   nondual rationalism in   109
   not, on the whole, denigrating bodies   27, 109–10
   Parmenides dialogue   188
   personalities studied by   129–30
   Phaedo dialogue   23, 126
   Phaedrus dialogue   153
   Philebus dialogue   188
   philosopher can become like God   156
   rational mysticism of   28
   reality
      degrees of   27, 115, 128, 237
      as oneself   116, 120, 122, 135, 139
   reason
      love and   27, 35, 158, 193–4
   Republic   25, 30, 116, 165
   ressentiment   120–1
   seeking-to-be   190
   soul
      beauty and   242
      by itself   110
      journeys of   126
      kinship to Forms   236
      parts of   30, 111, 130
      subsumes body   125
      turning the whole   127
   Symposium   25, 30, 130, 131 (*see also* Plato, love)
      Alcibiades's speech   169

androgynous love   171
Aristophanes's speech   162, 174
birth in beauty   244
Diotima's speech   162
homosexual romance in   160
ladder of love   167
learning about the good   163
love as reproduction   164–70
love of individuals   175–8
reason in inspiration   170, 181
reproduction of the good   166–7
self-government and   176–8, 180
sophists in   161
soul-children more immortal   165
tragedy and comedy   131
uniqueness of the beloved   179
Theaetetus dialogue   130, 186
    becoming like God   186
Thrasymachus, picture of   131
Timaeus dialogue   185
    God not jealous   187, 245
traumas experienced by   106–8, 142
true good   111–15, 135
    knowledge   135
    pleasure   135
two-world view?   235, 237
why be moral?   28
Plato/Aristotle
    cognition built into reality   198
    reality and goodness   196–8
Platonism   4
    early modern   240
    histories of   223
Plotinus   28, 36, 108, 130, 246, 247
    Hegel and   248
Polanyi, Michael   6, 7, 21, 50, 108
Popper, Karl   146
postmodernism   28
pragmatism   223
Protagoras   140, 189

quantum theology   97
Quine, W. V. O.   6, 49, 123

Rahner, Karl   11, 12, 32, 33
reality   1
    degrees of   3, 6, 24, 115–20
    higher   1, 5, 9, 10, 11, 22
        as the divine   11
        science as a part of   22

most real   7
object and   24
as oneself   3, 8, 10, 57, 81, 116, 219
subject and   24
ultimate   2
reason
    love and   158–84, 184, 185, 193–4
    nature and   53
reconciliation, cultural   25
religion   2, 69
    everyday experience and   209–12
    extraordinary experiences
        and   211–12
    in the making   2
    traditional   2
        contains core of truth   34, 87, 92
Rhodes, James   161
Rödl, Sebastian   5, 6, 7, 21, 61–5, 108,
        123
    action and normativity   62
    Categories of the Temporal   61
    idealist and materialist   63
    self-consciousness   61
    on self-constitution   63
Rorty, Richard   4
Rosen, Stanley   221, 222, 224
Rougemont, Denis de   243
Rousseau, Jean-Jacques   37, 129–30,
        139
Rumi, Jelaluddin   36, 84, 90, 108
Russell, Bertrand   4, 6, 42–4, 109, 121,
        123, 215
    "Mysticism and Logic"   44
Ruysbroeck, Jan van   103

St Anselm
    ontological argument   216
        Plato/Hegel version   216
St Athanasius   12, 31, 33
St Augustine   12, 28, 33, 36, 90
St John of the Cross   103
St Paul   12, 31, 33
St Teresa of Avila   103
St Thomas Aquinas
    argument for first mover   215
        Plato/Hegel version   215
Santayana, George   82, 121
Sartre, Jean-Paul   41, 139
scala naturae   117
Scanlon, Thomas   49

Schleiermacher, Friedrich   40, 159
Schneewind, J. B.   140
Schopenhauer, Arthur   5, 48, 108, 172
   The World as Will and
      Representation   48
science   1–2
   ideologies that claim to speak for   21
   as a part of God   22
   rational ascent and   2, 6, 23, 100
   relation to religion   2, 23
scientism   28, 47, 48
secular
   equals non-transcendent?   26, 99
Sedley, David   247
self-government   1, 2, 29, 85
   failure in   132
   not self-centered   31
   separation and   3
selfishness
   going beyond   2
self-preservation
   going beyond   22
self-reliance   30
Sellars, Wilfrid   5, 53, 123
   compared to Plato and Hegel   54
   normativity and natural laws   53–5
   why be moral   53–4
   why truth and science   54
separation   23, 32
   self-government and   3
   Socrates goes beyond   35
Shakespeare, William   157
Shaw, George Bernard   98
Shear, Jonathan   249
Sheffield, Frisbee   163
Skinner, B. F.   112–14, 236
Socrates   35
   death of   106–7
   mysticism of   241
Spinoza, Benedict   37, 108
   partial Platonism of   225
spiritual groundedness   83
stoicism   30
Strauss, Leo   140
subject
   object and   23–4
      reconciled   23, 127
   reality and   24, 122
substance
   vs. sense perception   123

Taoism   10, 98
Taylor, Charles   101, 140
   Hegel   234
   A Secular Age   101
Thales   189
theology
   negative   221
   Platonic philosophical   1
Theron, Stephen   230
Thompson, Michael   7
Thrasymachus   30, 140, 151
Thucydides   150
Tillich, Paul   12, 33
Tolle, Eckhart   18, 207
transcendence   1, 4, 11, *see also* ascent
   in humanism and philosophy   101–2
   immanence united with   4
   rational   1, 79
   through innerness   11
   true   11, 13, 25, 26, 32–3, 50

unity
   as ourselves   1
   through rational activity   3
   with God   23

value   2
   fact and   2, 23, 24, 64
   fact reconciled with   23
Vedanta   103
   Advaita   103
   Dvaita   103
Vlastos, Gregory   4, 27, 118, 176
Voltaire   37

Weber, Max   23, 55, 157
Wedgwood, Ralph   150
Whitehead, Alfred North   5, 7, 12, 19, 20,
      25, 26, 28, 41–5, 108
   Adventures of Ideas   41
   our identity crisis and   42
   religion in the making   41, 44
   Science and the Modern World   42
Whiting, Jennifer   236
Whitman, Walt   39, 66, 206, 212
Wilber, Ken
   pre/trans fallacy   241
Wittgenstein, Ludwig   5, 20, 26, 28
   dualism in   45
   identity crisis and   47

influenced by Schopenhauer   48
  notebooks 1914–1916   6, 46
    good life   6
    true world among shadows   46
  Tractatus Logico-Philosophicus   45–8, 108
Wolf, Fred Alan   98
Wollstonecraft, Mary   139
Women in classical Athens   160
Woolf, Virginia   139

Wordsworth, William   28
world
  knower and   3, 24
worship
  God as deserving   12

you
  me reconciled with   23

Zaehner, R. C.   102